Spaces of Disappearance

The Architecture of Extraordinary Rendition

Jordan H. Carver

01.05.2005
30.04.2005
02.05.2005
29.04.2005
29.04.2005
30.04.2005
02.05.2005
29.04.2005
03.05.2005
29.04.2005
30.04.2005

29.04.2005
30.04.2005
03.05.2005
29.04.2005
30.04.2005
30.04.2005
30.04.2005
30.04.2005
06.05.2005
30.04.2005
29.04.2005
29.04.2005
03.05.2005

04.05.2005
30.04.2005
01.05.2005
05.05.2005
03.05.2005
28.04.2005
28.04.2005
02.05.2005
06.05.2005
06.05.2005
06.05.2005
02.05.2005
12.05.2005
28.04.2005
30.05.2005

06.05.2005
02.05.2005
30.04.2005
01.05.2005
05.05.2005
28.04.2005
28.04.2005
28.04.2005
30.04.2005
30.04.2005

UR

Urban Research (UR), the imprint of Terreform, is a series of books examining the world's cities. Understanding that no single approach is adequate to the promise and problem of the urban, we publish a wide range of design and analysis, and welcome proposals for future books.

UR11:
Spaces of Disappearance:
The Architecture of Extraordinary Rendition

Published by Terreform, Inc.

First Printing, 2018

By Jordan H. Carver
Copy Editor: Stephen Hoban
Proofreader: Caitlin Blanchfield
Design: Isaac Gertman, The Independent Group
Drawings: Lindsey Wikstrom-Lee

ISBN 978-1-947198-01-2
Printed by Taylor Specialty Books in the United States.

Cover: Aerial image of the "salt pit," a former brick factory turned CIA-run black site in Afghanistan. Image: Google, DigitalGlobe.

UR Books may be purchased at urpub.org.

For quantity and/or special sales, please contact the publisher:

terreform
center for advanced urban research
180 Varick Street, Suite 1514
New York City, New York
+ 1 212 762 9121
www.terreform.info

Spaces

[redacted]

The Architecture of Extraordinary Rendition

of

[redacted]

Disapp-

[redacted]

earance

[redacted]

Jordan H. Carver

UR

NEITHER CONFIRMED NOR DENIED

Felicity D. Scott

Introducing his 1964 manual, *Counterinsurgency Warfare: Theory and Practice,* French military strategist David Galula invoked a gaming metaphor to speak of unknowable outcomes born of situational complexities in war. "No chess player has ever found, nor is any likely to find, a sure way of wining from the first move," he argued. For regardless of a player's strategies and tactics, and even armed with the "electronic computer," chess games remained too complex to compute a course towards checkmate. Their dynamics remained fluid and their endpoints indeterminate. Uncertainty prevailed, that is, even when the rules of a game and its playing field were known in advance (like chess), when actors on both sides shared symmetrical spatio-temporal logics and had access to similar matériel. War, Galula went on, with evident understatement given its attendant violence, "is not a chess game but a vast social phenomenon with an infinitely greater and ever-expanding number of variables, some of which can elude analysis."[1] Given the shifting and elusive nature of war, and given its importance to the security of nations and states, warfare had long been a subject of analysis, a type of analysis which, Galula claimed, operated at the nexus of "philosophical" study and experience, of thinking and acting, of theory *and* practice. Galula's focus, as indicated in his title, was not conventional or interstate wars but so-called "modern" or "revolutionary" wars, particularly insurgencies affiliated with anti-colonial struggles, wherein the rules and playing fields or terrain had become even more elusive, uncertain, or unknowable to European powers. Indeed, Galula spoke of two "distinct warfares"—the revolutionary and the counterrevolutionary—noting that the protagonists (the insurgent and the counterinsurgent), along with their weapons, strategies, and tactics were radically "asymmetrical," albeit remaining mutually intertwined within the environments or "theaters" of war.

Addressed to "the problem in general," *Counterinsurgency Warfare* was commissioned by Harvard University's Center for International Affairs, a research unit established in 1958 by Henry Kissinger and Robert R. Bowie, its first director. Among the center's founding claims was the need for new notions of sovereignty that might better account for the increasingly interconnected condition of the New World Order that emerged in the wake of World War II, and with the decline of European colonialism, a reconfiguration of economic and military power for which the United States played a leading role and was a major beneficiary. "Since insurgency seems likely to be a frequent occurrence in unstable new nations," Bowie posited, referring not just to anti-colonial struggles but to Communist "subversive" wars, "there should be many opportunities to test

1. David Galula, *Counterinsurgency Warfare: Theory and Practice* (New York: Frederick A. Praeger, 1964), ix.

2. Robert R. Bowie, "Foreward," in Galula, *Counterinsurgency Warfare*, v.

3. Bruce Hoffman, "Foreword to the New Edition," in David Galula, *Pacification in Algeria, 1956–1958* (Santa Monica, CA: RAND Corporation, 2006), vi, vii.

[Galula's] models and principles under various conditions."[2] There would indeed be many opportunities to put Galula's theories to work, and *Counterinsurgency Warfare* is widely cited as informing the central tenets of US counterinsurgency strategies for decades to come, beginning with violent manifestations in Vietnam. More recently, it was foundational to, and is repeatedly cited in, the US Army's 2006 field manual 3-24, Counterinsurgency. Galula had extended first-hand experience (or "practice") in war—as a French Army officer during World War II, with anti-colonial struggles in Algeria, where he was stationed from 1956-58, and with civil war in Greece and China. On account of this expertise, he was earlier commissioned by the RAND Corporation to write an account of his experience in Algeria. Funded by the US Department of Defense's Advanced Research Projects Agency (DARPA), this treatise was published in 1963 as *Pacification in Algeria, 1956–1958,* and was also recovered in 2006. Recalling Bowie's speculations on putting theory into practice, the new edition's preface suggested nothing less than that Galula's "words, written over forty years ago, have a continuing, undeniable relevance, given the challenges that today confront the United States in Iraq—as well as with insurgencies elsewhere that we will likely face in the future." Reiterating the sense of *Pacification*'s "almost timeless resonance nearly half a century later," the preface concluded, "The parallels with America's own recent experiences in Iraq are striking."[3]

The 2003 US-led intervention into Iraq was, on the one hand, in many regards related to the extended militarization and shifting geopolitical landscape that emerged after World War II, a period we still often refer to, somewhat inexplicably, as the "post-war" period. Yet, on the other hand, the continuities implied by deriving strategic and tactical lessons from, and even reprinting Galula's landmark texts for instrumental purposes, can mask fundamental discontinuities at play. Jordan Carver's *Spaces of Disappearance: The Architecture of Extraordinary Rendition* offers us a complex map and timely reading of such discontinuities and of the convoluted spatial and legal topologies through which they were engineered during the regime of self-proclaimed "wartime president" George W. Bush. Reflecting back on this recent history of violence through a critical, architectural lens, Carver articulates a compelling conceptual and evidentiary terrain and an ethico-political framework through which to return not just to the war in Iraq but also to that in Afghanistan and the even more nebulous War on Terror. He identifies an apparatus of warfare that also, in different ways, tends to "elude analysis," to recall Galula's words, and details not two, but a proliferating matrix of "distinct warfares," with their "infinitely greater and ever-expanding number of variables." Yet the epistemic uncertainty, ambiguities, and unknowability, along with the convoluted spatio-temporal logics Galula attempted to theorize from his experience of war, enter Carver's picture not as problems to be solved by military strategy but as political instruments that should be revealed in all their cynicism and contested. Wars in Galula's time were already characterized by strategic blurring of political, military, and civil agents and goals; they did not only take place between soldiers on a military battlefield. But with the added withdrawal of limits to temporal duration, spatial extension, and adversaries in the wars launched by the Bush administration—they spoke of "perpetual war" and the "*global* war on *terror*"—the ambiguities Galula faced appear distinctly historical, even classical, not that understanding war was ever simple. Terms like "post-war," to reiterate, seem outdated, and it is at times not self-evident what a war zone looks like, where and how it manifests, although the violence and destruction wrought on bodies, populations, environments, and states is more than visible in many parts of the world. As Carver reminds us, people have died, and continue to die in large numbers, they have been tortured, their forms of life have been dismantled.

What follows is a remarkable (if haunting) reading of the multiple "architectures" of this US-led perpetual and global war, a reading that details the elaborate spatio-legal topology of the dispersed sites and variegated techniques set up to render invisible but also to manage a series of illegalities, ostensibly in the name of national security. Carver traces the intricate connections between the extraterritorial logics of Guantánamo Bay, the eruption of so-called black sites and other spaces of detention and torture specifically designed for the program of "extraordinary rendition" and "enhanced interrogation", and the legal acrobatics of the Bush administration that put these elements in place and to work in the wake of 9/11. It is a story ranging in scale from the global reach of a prison complex, as it seeks to operate outside the conventions of national and international law, to an individual prison cell, a story identifying techniques through which this apparatus touches down in particular places and upon particular bodies and psyches in the most violent of ways. Architecture enters this picture as a form of disciplinary expertise and analysis, but also in the somewhat more conventional sense of reading the prison cells and detention complexes, as they assume a strategic role in new forms of global governance. Indeed, we find modern architecture's one-time dream of universalized, modular, industrially mass-produced dwellings unmoored from its destination as providing low-cost shelter for working or mobile communities. Minimal, mass-produced units emerge into this picture not just on account of an economic calculus and ability to be rapidly deployed, but as spaces engineered for maintaining life without physical comfort or access to a political community, spaces whose lack of visual distinction and potential environmental confusion form part of a program of psychological violence. Importantly, Carver situates this architecture within the larger complex of other architectures in which such a cell is deployed, rendering their interconnected logics visible. To this end, the book has three parts: First, "A Bureaucratic Sovereignty" details the convoluted or unsettled sovereignties claimed and created by the US administration, along with the "lawfare" deployed to dehumanize so-called "enemy combatants" and to justify their "enhanced" interrogation as it morphed into torture. Second, "Technologies of Dislocation" follows the incarceration units manufactured by SteelCell in Atlanta, Georgia, as they are put to work in Eastern Europe and the Middle East as key parts of a global system of detention and torture geared towards "ghost detainees" and "forever prisoners," and operating under the rubric of extracting information. Third and finally, "Accountability and Abstraction" elucidates the complex topology of knowledge and its intentional obfuscation at work in this story, focusing on the 2014 *Committee Study of the Central Intelligence Agency's Detention and Interrogation Program* (aka the "Torture Report").

Spaces of Disappearance enters the complex terrain of twenty-first century warfare recognizing that "realities" have, quite literally, changed. Arguments based on liberal ideologies and institutions—on national or international law, on calls to transparency, on providing uncontested proof, on human rights claims—might fail to grasp the new regimes of power/knowledge and new forms of sovereignty and hatred engineered during the Bush presidency, along with failing to render visible their ongoing impact—politically, psychologically, and physically, as well as nationally and globally—over a decade and a half later. This potential failure does not, however, mean that we should not seek to understand how these systems were created and operated. Indeed, given their legacy it seems particularly important to do so. The situation is, however, complicated: for the architects of these wars were also, as Carver explicates, engineers of a structural obfuscation of facts, of the disappearance not only of bodies and places but of evidence as such. Beyond the classified status of military and intelligence documents, we find a more intensive production of conditions of unknowability and invisibility leading to what Carver calls, following Peter Galison, an "antiepistemology." In response, the essays that follow draw knowingly upon multiple, dispersed forms of evidence from investigative journalism, witness accounts, bureaucratic memos, and other government documents, which are brought together to render visible the contours of the "architectures" of these wars without assuming any totalizing picture.

The events and actors addressed in this book hover in a fascinating zone, being no longer "news" and not-quite-history, yet their effects and vocabulary are hauntingly present. As we struggle to develop forms of critique during our current "post-truth" moment, in the era of so-called fake news and alternative facts, and amidst a still-rising tide of nationalism, xenophobia, racism, and anti-Islamic sentiment, we find here a prehistory of this waning of reality and, in this sense too, it is a particularly important story to tell, now. *Spaces of Disappearance* opens with a reflection on Donald Rumsfeld's notorious exegesis of "known unknowns"—the first of many reminders of the proliferation of terms and sayings and the revalencing of a more familiar lexicon of politics and war during the Bush years. In concluding, I want to recall another much-cited passage from this era, which seems newly relevant in the wake of this research. On October 17, 2004, Ron Suskind recounted a recent conversation with an aide to President Bush, widely attributed to Karl Rove.

> *The aide said that guys like me were "in what we call the reality-based community," which he defined as people who "believe that solutions emerge from your judicious study of discernible reality." I nodded and murmured something about enlightenment principles and empiricism. He cut me off. "That's not the way the world really works anymore," he continued. "We're an empire now, and when we act, we create our own reality. And while you're studying that reality—judiciously, as you will—we'll act again, creating other new realities, which you can study too, and that's how things will sort out. We're history's actors...and you, all of you, will be let to just study what we do."*[4]

4. Ron Suskind, "Faith, Certainty and the Presidency of George W. Bush," *The New York Times Magazine*, October 17, 2004.

Looking back, from the perspective of our post-truth media-political culture, we might say that the Bush administration succeeded in creating futures untethered from the epistemology of the "reality-based community." But looking forward, we might also recognize that faced with such obfuscation and the expanding empire it serves, we can find a mandate to respond. For, to return to where I began, Galula reminds us, perhaps inadvertently, that such "games" are risky, their endpoints elusive and indeterminate, their courses might be redirected. Theoretical and scholarly work might, in response and as a response, seek to identify instabilities at play within and on account of the "ever-expanding number of variables," and put them to work to other ends. We might recognize in these fluidities the potential for re-revalencing or redeploying words and images in the media-political landscape, even from a radically asymmetrical position. One way to respond, then, as set out in this book, is to develop techniques that help us to identify traces of evidence and read the logics and dynamics launched during these wars, to look at their many interrelated architectures and their effects. Faced with spaces of disappearance, that is, *Spaces of Disappearance* seeks to render them legible and less obscure, even while recognizing that the specific techniques might well have already changed.

PART I

POLITICS, SOVEREIGNTY, AND SECRECY

Fig. 1.1
Donald Rumsfeld at a Department of Defense press conference.
February 12, 2002.

INTRODUCTION: SOME THINGS THAT ARE KNOWN AND MANY MORE THAT ARE NOT

"In the weeks after 9/11, lawyers at State, Defense, the White House, and Justice formed an inter-agency task force to study the issues relating to detention and trial of members of al Qaeda. The one thing we all agreed on was that any detention facility should be located outside the United States. Civilian criminal courts might not even be able to handle the number of captured terrorists—overwhelming an already heavily burdened system. We researched whether the courts would have jurisdiction over the facility, and concluded that if federal courts took jurisdiction over POW camps, they might start to run them by their own lights, substituting familiar peacetime prison standards for military needs and standards."[1]

John Yoo, former Deputy Assistant U.S. Attorney General in the Office of Legal Counsel, Department of Justice, 2006

"Known unknowns are gaps in our knowledge, but they are gaps that we know exist," Donald Rumsfeld says in the first line of his memoir. "If we ask the right questions" he goes on, "we can potentially fill this gap in our knowledge, eventually making it a known known."[2] That the former secretary of defense opens his memoirs in this way underscores the lasting quality of this most enigmatic of statements, uttered in a February 12, 2002, Department of Defense press conference. In it, Jim Miklaszewski, an NBC News Pentagon correspondent, asked Rumsfeld a question about reports stating, contrary to Bush administration claims, that there were no "weapons of mass destruction" in Iraq. "Reports that say that something hasn't happened are always interesting to me," he responded, "because as we know, there are known knowns; there are things we know we know. We also know there are known unknowns; that is to say we know there are some things we do not know. But there are also unknown unknowns—the ones we don't know we don't know."[3]

Since he was forced out of the Department of Defense at the end of 2006, Rumsfeld has taken ownership of his much-quoted aphorism as a type of personal branding, and, as he mentions in his memoir, his name has become associated with the majority of online search results for "known unknown." In an essay on the etymological history of "known unknown," filmmaker Errol Morris describes the unknown as historically linked to savagery and barbarism and the known to civilization, scientific discovery, and evidence. The "known unknown" ushers in the "era of investigation and discovery."[4] This multipart essay on the secretary served as an addendum to his 2013 documentary on the topic, in which Morris encourages Rumsfeld to complete the missing piece of his semantic matrix: the "unknown known."

1. John Yoo, *War By Other Means: An Insiders Account of the War on Terror* (New York: Atlantic Monthly Press, 2006), 142.

2. Donald Rumsfeld, *Known and Unknown: A Memoir* (New York: Sentinel, 2011), xiv.

3. US Department of Defense, "DoD News Briefing—Secretary Rumsfeld and Gen. Myers," February 12, 2002, archive.defense.gov/Transcripts/Transcript.aspx?TranscriptID=2636.

4. Errol Morris, "The Certainty of Donald Rumsfeld (Part 2)," *New York Times,* March 26, 2014, opinionator.blogs.nytimes.com/2014/03/26/the-certainty-of-donald-rumsfeld-part-2.

Rumsfeld offers this definition: "Things that you think you know, that it turns out, you did not."[5]

In reflecting on his time with Rumsfeld and the making of his film, Morris concluded that after thirty-three hours of interviews he knew less about the Iraq War than when he started. "How could that be? How could I know *less* rather than more?"[6] To answer in pure Rumsfeldian logic, the Iraq War and everything else that happened in the shadow of September 11 were unknown unknowns that became known unknowns and, finally, unknown knowns. Known knowns were never part of the plan.

In his own peculiar way, Rumsfeld elegantly outlined the cognitive gray area lying just beyond knowledge. And in so doing, he described not only his attitudes toward truth and transparency, but also a method for understanding and relating to information generally, and to government power specifically. Rumsfeld is content with a gap between what we know and what we don't, and he is even more comfortable implying that the government always knows more than the public—whether or not such knowledge is supported by fact.

In the intervening years, Rumsfeld's quote has become a pop culture reference. It was the first "poem" in a humorous collection of Rumsfeld's "structurally challenging" musings.[7] The Known Unknowns is the name of several bands, and the phrase forms part of an album title for the Three 6 Mafia, a Memphis-based hip-hop group not known for political messaging. The quote has its own Wikipedia page and even its own Urban Dictionary entry.[8]

Rumsfeld's logic encapsulates the cognitive dissonance of not just the Iraq War, but also the larger so-called War on Terror and the associated flurry of government policies quickly implemented after September 11. From the beginning, the War on Terror was a fraught construction, christened with a name so vague it grew to encompass any military or diplomatic action demanded by the partisans of American politics. As named, the new war allowed the fight against terrorism to stand in for American justice and self-preservation.[9] And yet, after nearly eight years of George W. Bush's presidency, eight more under President Barack Obama, a drawdown of U.S. troops in Iraq and Afghanistan, and the execution of Osama bin Laden, a war initiated as one against terror continues today in full force, under different names and increasingly expansive forms of violence.[10] The administrative rationale for the war's pervasiveness continues to be governed by the logic of the unknown.[11]

If the Rumsfeldian construction of knowing and unknowing can be understood as an epistemology, it is one predicated on the acceptance of unknowing. Moreover, it is a knowledge system subservient to power structures that decide what is known and what is not, what can be seen and what remains hidden. That a Secretary of Defense privy to knowledge inaccessible to the broader public is in a position to outline the relationship between the known and the unknown underscores the fundamental tension between knowledge and power.

5. *The Unknown Known*, directed by Errol Morris (Beverly Hills, CA: Anchor Bay Entertainment, 2013).

6. Errol Morris, "The Certainty of Donald Rumsfeld (Part 1)," *New York Times*, March 25, 2014, opinionator.blogs.nytimes.com/2014/03/25/the-certainty-of-donald-rumsfeld-*part-1*.

7. Donald H. Rumsfeld, *Pieces of Intelligence: The Existential Poetry of Donald H. Rumsfeld*, ed. Hart Seely (New York: Free Press, 2003), viii.

8. See en.wikipedia.org/wiki/There_are_known_knowns and http://www.urbandictionary.com/define.php?term=known+unknown.

9. One of the first utterances of the "War on Terror" was during remarks given by President Bush at Camp David on September 16, 2001, when he said, "This crusade, this war on terrorism, is going to take a while." Addressing a joint session of congress on September 20, 2001 Bush warned, "Our war on terror begins with Al Qaeda, but it does not end there." See US White House, "Remarks by the President Upon Arrival," September 16, 2001, georgewbush-whitehouse.archives.gov/news/releases/2001/09/20010916-2.html and US White House, "Address to a Joint Session of Congress and the American People," September 20, 2001, georgewbush-whitehouse.archives.gov/news/releases/2001/09/20010920-8.html.

10. See *The Drone Memos*, a book similar in methods to this one. Jameel Jaffer, ed., *The Drone Memos: Targeted Killing, Secrecy, and the Law* (New York: New Press, 2016).

11. How the myriad conflicts birthed from the semantic instigation of the War on Terror and the policies legitimizing it will proceed during Donald J. Trump's presidency is a question for future studies. However, the intellectual elegance of the "known knowns" has already been replaced with ham-fisted phrase "alternative facts," and the purposefully unstable rhetoric used during the Bush and Obama administrations has been replaced with unapologetic lies.

According to Jacques Rancière, Rumsfeld's logic is inherently aesthetic, since the power to make knowledge known is the same power that can make things—objects and subjects—visible (or keep them invisible).[12] For Rancière the link between aesthetics and politics is visibility, and it is the various asymmetric power structures embedded within politics that decide what is visible—that is, what is known and what is not. The role of aesthetic representation takes on a deeper meaning as it traverses redacted documents, secret government programs, and the material conditions of secret prisons and torture. Aesthetic representations of the War on Terror sit uncomfortably between regimes of knowledge and regimes of material production, between what we know, what we see, and what we can't see but think we know.

One of the most highly classified and still unknown aspects of the War on Terror is the Enhanced Interrogation Techniques (EIT) program. The EIT program is a blanket term used to describe the Central Intelligence Agency's detention and interrogation program. EIT had two basic components, the secret CIA-operated "black sites" located in Afghanistan and other third-party countries, and the development of harsh interrogation techniques to be used on prisoners suspected of terrorism held in the secret prisons. The program was designed and implemented around the world soon after the September 11 attacks. Prisons were quickly cobbled together in Thailand and Afghanistan, with purpose-built facilities later constructed in Poland, Lithuania, Romania, and Guantánamo Bay, Cuba. The interrogation techniques carried out within the black sites were taken from American military training programs known to leave lasting physical and psychological effects on prisoners. Information about the existence of the prisons and the torture carried out within the black sites began to appear in media reports and through leaked government documents. As a result, on September 6, 2006, President Bush gave a press conference in which he both acknowledged the existence of the interrogation program and effectively announced its end.[13]

The secret CIA prisons *did* exist, and yet they have been rendered unrepresentable by being kept invisible. As such, the known unknown can be understood not just as an epistemology of knowledge but of a knowledge-to-secrecy relationship or, as Peter Galison claims, an "antiepistemology," a system of knowledge predicated on classification and obfuscation.[14] How this relationship is mediated by aesthetic representation is a foundational question for this study.

In the years since the attacks in New York, Washington, D.C., and Pennsylvania, the United States has undergone profound changes in its self-image, its media, and its political environment. Part of this evolution during the Obama years was a sense of "Bush fatigue"—that there could be little added by once again diving into the administration's mishandling of the post-9/11 information wars. With the election of Donald J. Trump, an American president is questioning

12. Jacques Rancière, *The Politics of Aesthetics*, trans. Gabriel Rockhill (London: Continuum, 2014), 1.

13. Alluding to the existence of the EIT program, Bush stated, "In addition to the terrorists held at Guantánamo, a small number of suspected terrorist leaders and operatives captured during the war have been held and questioned outside the United States, in a separate program operated by the Central Intelligence Agency." US White House, "President Discusses Creation of Military Commissions to Try Suspected Terrorists," September 6, 2006, georgewbush-whitehouse.archives.gov/news/releases/2006/09/20060906-3.html.

14. "Epistemology asks how knowledge can be uncovered and secured. Antiepistemology asks how knowledge can be covered and obscured. Classification, the antiepistemology par excellence, is the art of nontransmission." Peter Galison, "Removing Knowledge," *Critical Inquiry* 31, no. 1 (Autumn 2004): 237.

America's position at the top of the global, liberal order for the first time since the end of World War II.[15] What remains constant are the presence of American troops in Iraq and Afghanistan and—even as political upheaval, "Arab Spring" revolutions, and the complex Syrian civil war has challenged American dominance—the influence of American power throughout the region.

As the wars in Afghanistan and Iraq continue late into their second decade, and as US military action has expanded into sweeping surveillance techniques and a classified drone program, many of the Bush administration's claims of sovereign authority and exceptional power remain official US policy. Likewise, Guantánamo Bay's prison facilities, the most prominent international symbol of the war and the legal contortions used to justify it, remains in operation. The prison's continued use is material proof that the legal arguments presented within the upper echelons of the Bush administration remain in place, even if the war's strategic goals and presence within the public imagination have shifted. The detention facilities on the southern shores of Cuba haunted the Obama administration even as members of the Republican Party celebrated them. It remains to be seen what their role will be in American foreign and domestic policy during the Trump presidency.

Many of the figures investigated in this book—presidents and vice presidents, CIA directors and operatives, lawyers, and key Bush administration officials—have left office and published their own, mostly self-congratulatory chronicles of what happened during the early years of the War on Terror.

In his memoir, George W. Bush invoked the "ticking time bomb" rationale for torture, claiming, "I would have preferred that we get the information another way. But the choice between security and values was real."[16] He goes on to repeat the discredited claims that torturing prisoners yielded actionable intelligence and was therefore justified in the end. Vice President Dick Cheney says the EIT program was "safe, legal, and effective," and ridicules Obama for limiting interrogation techniques to those outlined in the Army Field Manuals and for reading suspected terrorists caught in the United States their Miranda rights.[17] George Tenet, Director of the CIA during the EIT program, glosses over the politics of interrogation, claiming the program was run under the president's unilateral powers and little objections about it were ever raised.[18] John Rizzo, a lawyer for the CIA and leading architect of the EIT program, has said that his biggest regret about the role he played was that he simply didn't notify enough members of congress about the CIA's activities.[19] And John Yoo, one of the leading figures behind the legal rationale for "enhanced interrogation" offers a spirited defense of the administration's policies. Written in the language of a meticulous law professor, Yoo criticizes the international community, the media, and the Democrats, among others, and shifts the blame for any of the problem his memos created to other people who didn't quite understand the nuance of his careful legal thinking.[20]

15. Warnings about the death of liberalism will likely prove hyperbolic, but the language Trump used throughout the presidential campaign in 2016 marked a significant shift in the political discourse that had long held sacrosanct America's dominant position within transnational relations. Lisa Lowe writes that while liberalism is a project that promises, "rights, emancipation, wage labor, and free trade," such rewards are "reserved for some and wholly denied to others." Lisa Lowe, *The Intimacies of Four Continents* (Durham, NC: Duke University Press, 2015), 3. And Domenico Losurdo warns that "it should not be forgotten that not only did the classics of the liberal tradition refer to democracy with coldness, hostility and sometimes frank contempt, but regarded its advent as an unlawful, intolerable rupture of the social contract and hence as a legitimate cause for the 'appeal to Heaven' (in Locke's words) or to arms." Domenico Losurdo, *Liberalism: A Counter History* (New York: Verso, 2011), 341.

16. George W. Bush, *Decision Points* (New York: Crown Publishers, 2010), 169.

17. Dick Cheney, *In My Time: A Personal and Political Memoir* (New York: Threshold Editions, 2011), 362.

18. George Tenet, *At the Center of the Storm: My Years at the CIA* (New York: Harper Collins Publishers, 2007), 242.

19. John Rizzo, *Company Man: Thirty Years of Controversy and Crisis in the CIA* (New York: Scribner, 2014), 201.

20. John Yoo, *War By Other Means: An Insiders Account of the War on Terror* (New York: Atlantic Monthly Press, 2006). See especially "Interrogation," 165–203.

Adding to the list of books by former Bush administration officials and intelligence officers is a growing number written by academics, historians, and journalists offering alternative accounts of the multiple wars on terror—the conflicts in Iraq and Afghanistan, the internal wars of surveillance and information gathering, terrorist attacks within American borders and around the world, the expansive drone program and the secret policies that justify it, the problem of ISIS, and the possibility of homegrown terrorist attacks. There have been books on the politics that sold the wars and on the wars' political fallout. Books on Guantánamo Bay, the CIA detention program, and about the torture of prisoners in both. There is even a small collection of books written by prisoners and former prisoners held and abused by US forces.

Alongside the memoirs, histories, and academic studies—all of which explain the War on Terror from some vantage—are projects that attempt to show what the War on Terror *looks* like. Trevor Paglen and John Emerson have mapped CIA rendition flights showing the global scale of prisoner transfer.[21] In addition, Paglen traveled to Afghanistan in an attempt to document black site facilities and he has taken what might be the only publicly available photograph of the Salt Pit, one of the more notorious US-operated black sites.[22] Terrorism investigator Crofton Black and photographer Edmund Clark have worked together to create a multimedia doisser including images of rendition facilities, black site prisons, and supporting documents.[23] The result is a complex and incomplete collection of spotty evidence provided by Black and images photographed by Clark. They depict banal spaces exploited by the US government during the rendition program. Office parks, industrial facilities, military offices, and small airports are each represented as nodes in an expansive network of power and secrecy. Clark punctuates the project with photographs of domestic spaces, the homes of prisoners once held in black sites and who are now free. By collapsing his images with an archive of bureaucratic paperwork and government documents, Clark binds the intimacy of the home together with the institutional violence of interrogation.

Artists such as Jenny Holzer, Laura Poitras, Taryn Simon, and David Taylor have responded to the problems of representation with their own aesthetic practices, making films, using documents and "evidence" to create works of art, and deploying the mediums of creative expression to question the representations of state power, secrecy, and violence.[24] Curator Claire C. Carter, who organized an exhibition featuring many of these artists, explains, "these artists have each undertaken a weighty responsibility: to make the invisible visible for the rest of us."[25] The multimedia researchers and designers Metahaven go a step further and claim that the methods of making visible can themselves be "instrument[s] of genuine political change."[26] Transparency and political accountability, they argue, cannot be measured simply as a quantity of publicly available documents, but in *how* such documents are leaked, published, and broadly distributed.[27] As such, design, architecture, and cultural production play an

21. Trevor Paglen and John Emerson, "Rendition Flights 2001–2006," in *An Atlas of Radical Cartography*, ed. Lize Mogel and Alexis Bhagat (Los Angeles: Journal of Aesthetics and Protest Press, 2008).

22. Trevor Paglen, "The Black Sites," 2006, www.paglen.com/?l=work&s=blacksites.

23. Crofton Black and Edmund Clark, *Negative Publicity: Artefacts of Extraordinary Rendition* (New York: Aperture Foundation, 2015).

24. Claire C. Carter, *Covert Operations: Investigating the Known Unknowns* (Santa Fe, NM: Radius Books, 2014); Laura Poitras, *Astro Noise: A Survival Guide for Living Under Total Surveillance* (New York: Whitney Museum of American Art, 2016).

25. Carter, *Covert Operations*, 23.

26. Metahaven, *Black Transparency: The Right to Know in the Age of Mass Surveillance* (Berlin: Sternberg Press, 2015), 1.

27. Ibid., 1–7.

important role in information distribution and democratic communication, serving not merely as simple aestheticizations of power.

This book builds on the aforementioned works and links them together by questioning the role of aesthetics in the War on Terror. Specifically, this is an investigation into the war's spatial manifestations, realized at a variety of scales, from broad conceptions of sovereign power to individual prisons cells used in top-secret black site facilities. Here, aesthetics is registered in two valences: the experience of secrecy and in the role of representation in the service of illuminating complex subjects. This book is situated firmly within the conceptual and anti-epistemological gray area Rumsfeld describes, between the known and the unknown. Facts, figures, maps, drawings, and ideas are presented as things we now know about how the war was spatially administered, but with the caveat that there are still many more things we do not.[28]

While it directly addresses torture and the War on Terror, the particular emphasis of this book is on how the attacks of September 11 led to a highly designed, meticulously planned, and globally realized regime of detention and interrogation. By narrowly focusing on the black sites and the political machinations behind them, these essays aim to illuminate the deeply considered design methodologies that exploited legal and territorial claims made by the US Government to build secret prisons around the world and torture prisoners within them. Yet the essays reach beyond the architectural details of individual prisons to address the sovereign decisions that supposedly justified their existence in the first place. In other words, by reading government documents architecturally, it becomes possible to uncover a specific design intent. The logics of national sovereignty connect to the architecture of solitary prison cells.

What is known about the black sites consists of hundreds of dispersed newspaper articles, redacted documents, NGO publications, satellite images, court records, first-person accounts, investigative books, government reports, and a single Senate investigation released in 2014. This book takes the disparate collection of publicly available documents as its research archive. Limiting the scope of evidence to available publications was done in order to present a more comprehensive accounting of the scattered knowledge about the many spaces involved in the EIT and black site programs.

The Senate's report was intended to fully investigate the CIA interrogation program and act as an official record of government accountability. In contrast to its intended goals, the publicly available version of the report was incomplete, and crucial details about the prisons' locations, design, use, and prisoner occupation remain cloaked under marks of black redaction.

Much like the prisons themselves, this book's analytic methods are networked and diffuse. It delves into what the Bush administration meant by sovereignty while at the same time questioning the material existence of the secret prisons and rationales used to fill them. This

28. The most comprehensive account of the EIT program, including prison names, locations, and prisoner manifests, remains the Senate Intelligence Committee report on the CIA's Detention and Interrogation Program. Only ten percent of the full report has been made public, and it is rife with redactions. Until the entire report is released, many of the details behind the individual prisons and the program at large will remain secret. For more on the report, see chapter three.

examination into a highly nebulous topic accounts for the arguments made by multiple government agencies that constructed new classifications of enemy subjects. Coinciding with the sovereign claims of the Bush administration, executive branch lawyers positioned the prisoner subjects not within the discourse of human rights and international treaty obligations, but as objects of information warfare and intelligence extraction. The government understood prisoners held in black sites not as human beings, but as vessels for actionable intelligence. Thus, the spaces of their confinement were designed and mobilized within the logics of interrogation and information extraction, not the international norms governing detention and armed conflict.

Finally, this work questions the politics and spectacle surrounding the Senate investigation as a performance of accountability. That is, the investigation had the appearance of accountability without any of its actual substance or effect. Millions of dollars and years of Senate committee work were dedicated to answering the most pressing questions about the EIT program. The final document created headlines and cable news segments, and members of opposing political parties made respective statements damning the CIA or the committee process. And yet the torture report, as it is known, made visible very little. It contributed little new knowledge while illuminating just how much remains hidden and unknown.

At the center of this book is the classified incarceration network itself. Analysis of its creation expands into an investigation about the spatial politics of state power and human rights. A study of architectural edifices, created in secret for the explicit purpose of torturing those deemed enemies of the state, requires an expansive understanding of architectural context.

The title of this book is a reversal of Hannah Arendt's conception of "the space of appearance." For Arendt, the space of appearance was a space where people would interact, a space of "speech and action," and a space where people would appear together and perform civic duties. The space of appearance, in short, is a space where politics can be enacted, where "the public realm can be organized."[29] The ease with which Arendt moves between and joins together the public realm and political action has long animated architects and urbanists (along with many others— including critics and detractors) who have read her description of the political realm in spatial and architectural terms, at scales both intimate and urban.[30] Arendt's phrase conjures literal, even romantic, spaces where politics can be performed—spaces of action and speech, disagreement and dialogue, and above all else representation, openness, and transparency. But, Arendt warns, a life without speech and action—that is, a life beyond the space of appearance—"is literally dead to the world; it has ceased to be human life."[31]

In reversing Arendt's formulation of political space, the black sites are revealed as spaces beyond politics, beyond civic life, and beyond humanity. If the space of appearance can be architecturally manifest

29. Hannah Arendt, *The Human Condition* (Chicago: University of Chicago Press, 1958), 198–99.

30. Ken Frampton cites the space of appearance in his classic essay on "Critical Regionalism" and his book of collected essays, *Labor, Work and Architecture,* is dedicated to Hannah Arendt. Kenneth Frampton, "Towards a Critical Regionalism: Six Points for an Architecture of Resistance," in *The Anti-Aesthetic: Essays on Postmodern Culture* ed. Hal Foster (New York: The New Press, 2002) and Kenneth Frampton, *Labor, Work and Architecture: Critical Essays 1968-1982* (Cambridge, MA: MIT Press, 1985). George Baird borrows the phrase for the title of a book that critiques postmodernism and its seeming lack of political engagement. George Baird, *The Space of Appearance* (Cambridge, MA: MIT Press, 2003). More recently, Reinhold Martin puts Arendt's idea in dialogue with Hardt and Negri's "commons" to call into question the status of the "public" and the infrastructures and institutions that create so-called public space. Reinhold Martin, "Public and Common(s)," *Places Journal*, January 2013, doi.org/10.22269/130124.

31. Arendt, *The Human Condition,* 198–99.

as public space, the spaces of disappearance might then have a similar material, tectonic, and territorial reality. The secret prisons proved to be spaces designed to contain subjects without speech, restrained in action, and stripped of humanity. They were cast outside their own politics and hidden from ours. This book is an attempt to trace the boundaries delineating the secret prisons as particular spaces of disappearance, integral to the early War on Terror, and administered through claims to sovereign power, architectural logistics, and political spectacle.

January 11, 2017, marked the fifteenth anniversary of the first prisoners arriving at Guantánamo Bay. They were first held in open-air, chain-link pens. Fifteen years later there are at least six detention facilities, most of which are minimally populated or completely empty. Yet despite the steady, if sporadic, release and transfer of prisoners, forty-one remain, including ten who have been recommended for transfer and thirty-one who are being held indefinitely, without charges.[32] Among those thirty-one are Abu Zubaydah, Khalid Sheikh Mohammed, and Abd al-Rahim al-Nashiri.[33] All three were held in and renditioned between multiple black site locations. They were subject to the harshest interrogation techniques, including waterboarding. All are being held without trial, as any evidence against them was collected through torture and is thus inadmissible in American courts. Several of the other remaining prisoners were similarly detained in CIA black sites and tortured under the auspices of enhanced interrogation.

Guantánamo Bay, as a US military outpost, is over one hundred years old. As a detention facility, it has bested the tenures of both Bush and Obama. Obama campaigned in 2007 with the explicit promise of transferring the remaining prisoners and closing the base's prison facilities. During one of the primary debates he said, "Our legitimacy is reduced when we've got a Guantánamo that is open, when we suspend habeas corpus."[34] In direct contrast, Obama's successor, Donald J. Trump, has vowed to keep Guantánamo open and "load it up with some bad dudes."[35] On torture, Trump asked an audience at a campaign event, "What do you think about waterboarding?" As the crowd cheered, he answered, "I like it a lot. I don't think it's tough enough."[36]

While Obama's promise to close the Guantánamo Bay prisons was never realized, an informal plan outlining how to accomplish his goals was submitted to Congress by the Department of Defense in early 2016. In it, the Department said the prison's "continued operation weakens our national security by furthering the recruiting propaganda of violent extremists, hindering relations with key allies and partners, and draining Department of Defense resources."[37] The plan concludes with a plea to close the detention facilities stating, "it is time to bring this chapter of American history to a close."[38]

32. Prisoner count as of January 20, 2017, the day President Trump took office. For an up-to-date accounting of the prisoner population, see "The Guantánamo Docket," *New York Times*, projects.nytimes.com/Guantanamo/detainees.

33. Many of the prisoner's names have alternative spellings. Names throughout this book are based on spellings from human rights reports, the prisoner's lawyers, and common English language usage.

34. "Democratic Debate Transcript, New Hampshire," Council on Foreign Relations, June 3, 2007, www.cfr.org/elections/democratic-debate-transcript-new-hampshire/p13520.

35. David Welna, "Trump Has Vowed to Fill Guantanamo with 'Some Bad Dudes' — But Who?" National Public Radio, November 14, 2016, www.npr.org/sections/parallels/2016/11/14/502007304/trump-has-vowed-to-fill-Guantanamo-with-some-bad-dudes-but-who.

36. Ben Jacobs, "Donald Trump Renews Support for Waterboarding at Ohio Rally: 'I Like It a Lot,'" *Guardian*, June 28, 2016, www.theguardian.com/us-news/2016/jun/28/donald-trump-ohio-rally-isis-torture-tpp-rape.

37. US Department of Defense, "Plan for Closing the Guantanamo Bay Detention Facility," February 23, 2016, www.defense.gov/Portals/1/Documents/pubs/GTMO_Closure_Plan_0216.pdf.

38. Ibid., 8

A BUREAUCRATIC SOVEREIGNTY

For all its outsize importance in twenty-first-century politics, Guantánamo Bay is a relatively small piece of land and sea sitting on the southern coast of Cuba. The area is known almost entirely as the home of Naval Station Guantanamo Bay, a US Navy outpost in operation for over one hundred years. The forty-five square miles of land contains various naval, marine, and coast guard facilities. Along the southern edge of the American-held territory facing the Caribbean Sea is Joint Task Force Guantanamo (JTF-GTMO), a collection of prisons and detention facilities that collectively forms Camp Delta.[1] The forty-one remaining prisoners held in Camp Delta are the last remaining detainees from the US government's War on Terror imprisonment strategy and the Central Intelligence Agency's Enhanced Interrogation Techniques (EIT) program.

For the prisoners coming out of the EIT program, Guantánamo Bay was the last stop in a network of prisons located throughout the world and operated by the CIA for the first five years of the War on Terror. Known as "black sites," these prisons' existence was only acknowledged by President Bush in 2006. At a press conference in the East Room of the White House, Bush stated, "In addition to the terrorists held at Guantánamo, a small number of suspected terrorist leaders and operatives captured during the war have been held and questioned outside the United States, in a separate program operated by the Central Intelligence Agency."[2] It was the first time the administration admitted what had been widely reported in the news media: the CIA had transferred, held, and interrogated prisoners in undisclosed locations around the world. While acknowledging the existence of the previously secret program, the President's statement also marked its conclusion, noting that the program had ceased and all prisoners held by the CIA had been released or transferred to Guantánamo Bay.

An investigation about how the black sites came into existence, where they were located, and how they operated begins in Guantánamo Bay—not the Guantanamo Bay Naval Base, or even Camp Delta, but the territory of Guantánamo Bay as it was leased to the US Navy in 1903. The US government gained control over the small piece of Cuban land through an American-backed Cuban independence movement in the late nineteenth century. Spain had exerted colonial rule over Cuba for centuries, and the US Government, knowing Cuba's strategic geographic importance as an access point to the Caribbean region and South America, saw an opportunity to claim support for the Cuban people while securing its own military and economic interests. Backed by the US military, the independence movement within Cuba was one theater of the Spanish-American War fought in many

1. Camp Delta consists of at least seven individual prison and detention facilities: Camp One, Camp Three, Camp Four, Camp Five, Camp Five Echo, Camp Six, and Camp Seven. Prior to January 2002, prisoners were brought to Camp X-Ray, constructed from open air, chain-link holding cells that have since been retired.

2. For a full transcript of President Bush's press conference, see US White House, "President Discusses Creation of Military Commissions to Try Suspected Terrorists" (statement of President George W. Bush), September 6, 2006, georgewbush-whitehouse.archives.gov/news/releases/2006/09/20060906-3.html. For reporting on the statement, see "Bush Admits to CIA Secret Prisons," BBC News, September 7, 2006, news.bbc.co.uk/2/hi/americas/5321606.stm.

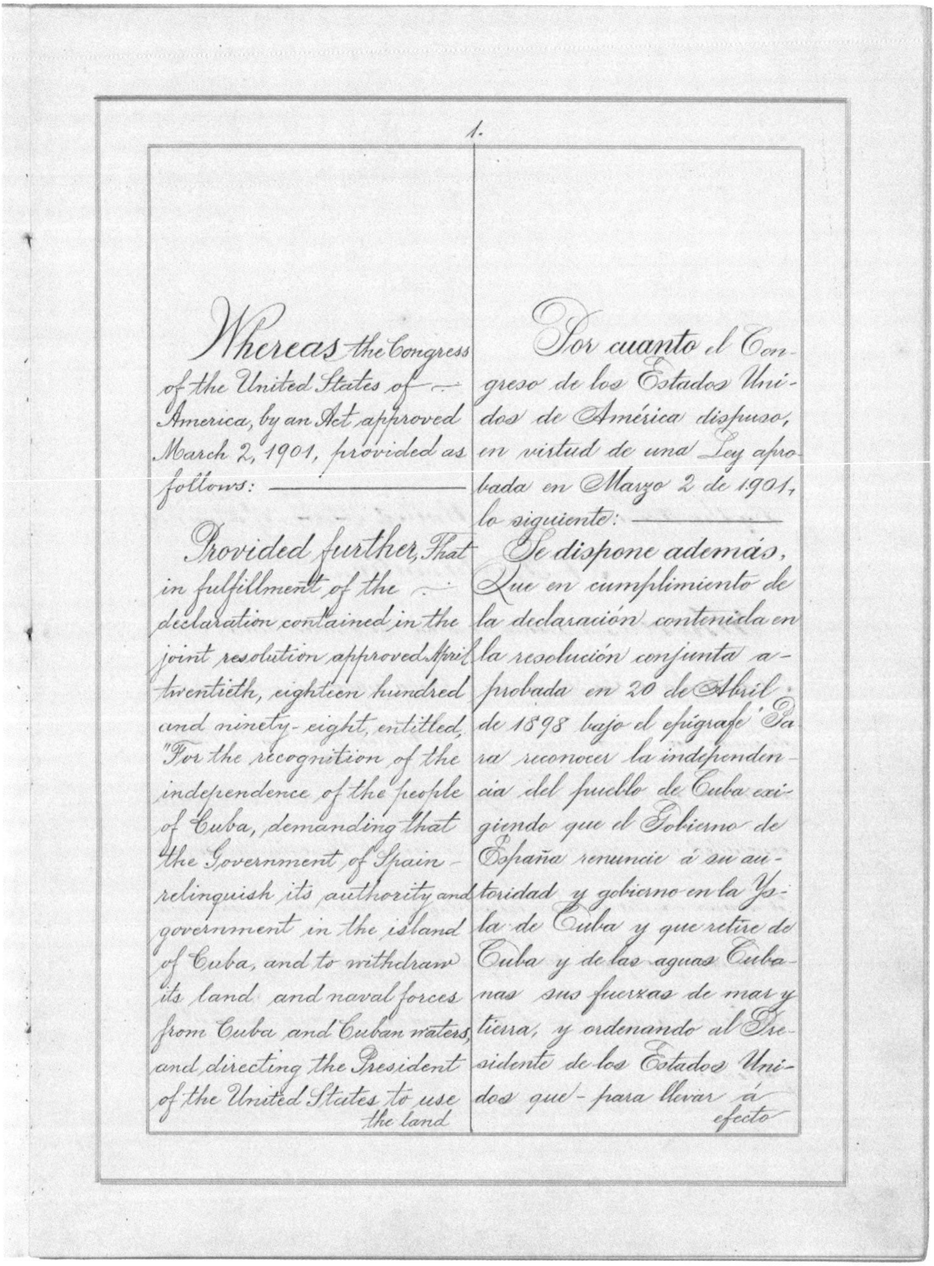

1.

Whereas the Congress of the United States of America, by an Act approved March 2, 1901, provided as follows: ——

Provided further, That in fulfillment of the declaration contained in the joint resolution approved April twentieth, eighteen hundred and ninety-eight, entitled, "For the recognition of the independence of the people of Cuba, demanding that the Government of Spain relinquish its authority and government in the island of Cuba, and to withdraw its land and naval forces from Cuba and Cuban waters, and directing the President of the United States to use the land

Por cuanto el Congreso de los Estados Unidos de América dispuso, en virtud de una Ley aprobada en Marzo 2 de 1901, lo siguiente: ——

Se dispone además, Que en cumplimiento de la declaración contenida en la resolución conjunta aprobada en 20 de Abril de 1898 bajo el epígrafe "Para reconocer la independencia del pueblo de Cuba exigiendo que el Gobierno de España renuncie á su autoridad y gobierno en la Ysla de Cuba y que retire de Cuba y de las aguas Cubanas sus fuerzas de mar y tierra, y ordenando al Presidente de los Estados Unidos que - para llevar á efecto

Fig. 1.2
Platt Amendment Approved March 2, 1901, signed May, 22 1903.

Spanish colonies at the turn of the twentieth century. The defeat of the Spanish colonial forces in 1898 eventually led to an independent Cuban state in 1902. Between the defeat of Spain and the founding of Cuba, the Cuban constitution was conceived and drafted with explicit deference to American territorial and political interests. That is to say, from the very birth of an independent Cuban nation, Guantánamo Bay, and its strategic location in terms of defense and commerce, has played a crucial role in American-Cuban relations. Those interests were enshrined in Cuba's founding constitution as the formal means by which the US has maintained a continuous military presence within the Caribbean region.

Before the international agreements establishing Cuba's independence from Spain and the leasing of Guantánamo Bay to US forces, the American government passed and enacted the Platt Amendment to the 1901 Army appropriations bill. The amendment stipulated both the terms of withdrawal for American troops at the end of the Spanish-American War and the establishment of Guantánamo Bay as their permanent military outpost. Section VII of the Amendment states:

> *That to enable the United States to maintain the independence of Cuba, and to protect the people thereof, as well as for its own defense, the government of Cuba will sell or lease to the United States lands necessary for coaling or naval stations at Certain specified points to be agreed upon with the President of the United States.*[3]

This clause—predicated on maintaining both Cuba's freedom and security—acted as the catalyst for the bilateral agreements leasing Guantánamo Bay to the United States. To a certain extent, this passage continues to legitimate the existence of the US military on Cuban territory to the present day even as many of the other Platt Amendment provisions were renegotiated as part of the Cuban-American Treaty of Relations in 1934. On the condition of America's intervention in removing direct Spanish rule, the US government inserted the Platt Amendment into the Cuban constitution in exchange for military assistance, and in doing so established its own colonial outpost on the island. The amendment gave the US broad authority to intervene in Cuban national affairs "for the preservation of Cuban independence." The amendment also allowed the US to claim control over specifically designated parcels of Cuban territory, for an indefinite amount of time, to exert military power over the island and Caribbean region. Such a claim was formally realized on February 23, 1903, when President Theodore Roosevelt signed the Agreement Between the United States and Cuba for the Lease of Lands for Coaling and Naval Stations (often referred to as the Cuban-American Treaty or the US-Cuba lease agreement). This agreement leased a small selection of Cuban territory to the US government, one

3. "Transcript of Platt Amendment (1903)," Our Documents (Washington: The National Archives and Records Administration, 2011), www.ourdocuments.gov/doc.php?flash=true&doc=55&page=transcript.

part of which was Guantánamo Bay. Article I of the agreement clearly defined the territorial extent of the lease:

> *In Guantanamo (see Hydrographic Office Chart 1857). From a point on the south coast, 4.37 nautical miles to the eastward of Windward Point Light House, a line running north (true) a distance of 4.25 nautical miles; From the northern extremity of this line, a line running west (true), a distance of 5.87 nautical miles; From the western extremity of this last line, a line running southwest (true) 3.31 nautical miles; From the southwestern extremity of this last line, a line running south (true) to the seacoast.*[4]

In addition to the physical boundaries of the ceded territory, the agreement outlines the legal rights and juridical designation each nation shall extend over it. Such territorial control was described in Article III:

> *While on the one hand the United States recognizes the continuance of the ultimate sovereignty of the Republic of Cuba over the above described areas of land and water, on the other hand the Republic of Cuba consents that during the period of the occupation by the United States of said areas under the terms of this agreement the United States shall exercise complete jurisdiction and control over and within said areas with the right to acquire (under conditions to be hereafter agreed upon by the two Governments) for the public purposes of the United States any land or other property therein by purchase or by exercise of eminent domain with full compensation to the owners thereof.*[5]

The second part of the agreement states that these lands were to be leased for the "annual sum of two thousand dollars, in gold coin of the United States, as long as the former shall occupy and use said areas of land by virtue of said agreement."[6] For two thousand dollars (later amended, once after the US left the gold standard and then again to take into account currency adjustments), the US took formal control over Guantánamo Bay while Cuba retained formal sovereignty. The fact that a difference between sovereignty and control was elaborated at all made the forty-five square miles of Guantánamo Bay a spatial anomaly set between two forms of state power. The distinction between sovereignty and control is one that American courts have sporadically debated, and the legal difference between the terms remains a cornerstone of the contentious relationship not only between the US and Cuba but also between opposing schools of American legal scholarship.

4. "Agreement Between the United States and Cuba for the Lease of Lands for Coaling and Naval stations; February 23, 1903," Avalon Project, Yale Law School (accessed October 30, 2011), avalon.law.yale.edu/20th_century/dip_cuba002.asp.

5. Ibid.

6. Michael J. Strauss, *The Leasing of Guantánamo Bay* (Westport, CT: Praeger Security International, 2009), 233.

TRANSFER OF GUANTANAMO.

United States Acquires a Coaling Station in Cuba.

WASHINGTON, Nov. 11.—Without any formality the United States has come into actual possession of the coaling station at Guantanamo.

Although the flag raising has not taken place, it was learned at the Navy Department to-day that the transfer was effected in a quiet manner several days ago.

A Board of Inspection consisting of Major Gen. Chaffee, Assistant Chief of Staff; Gen. Gillespie, Chief of Engineers, and Capt. Dayton of the navy, left to-day for Norfolk, where they will board the cruiser Buffalo, now fitting there, for a visit to Guantanamo and Bahia Honda, the other coaling station granted to the United States under agreement with Cuba.

Fig. 1.3
New York Times article documenting the transfer of Guantánamo Bay to US control. Official date of transfer unknown.

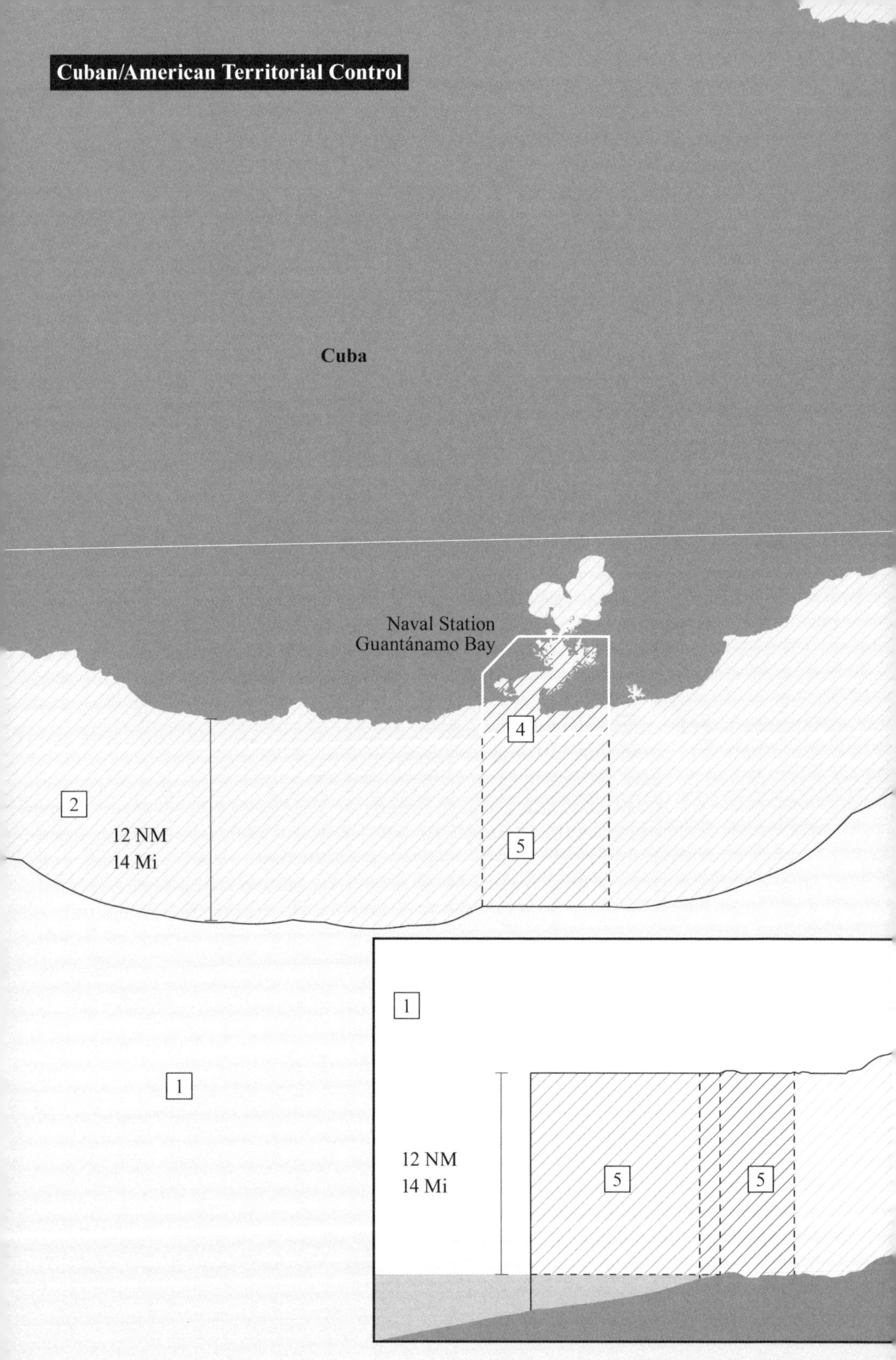
Cuban/American Territorial Control
Cuba
Naval Station
Guantánamo Bay
4
2
12 NM
14 Mi
5
1
1
12 NM
14 Mi
5
5

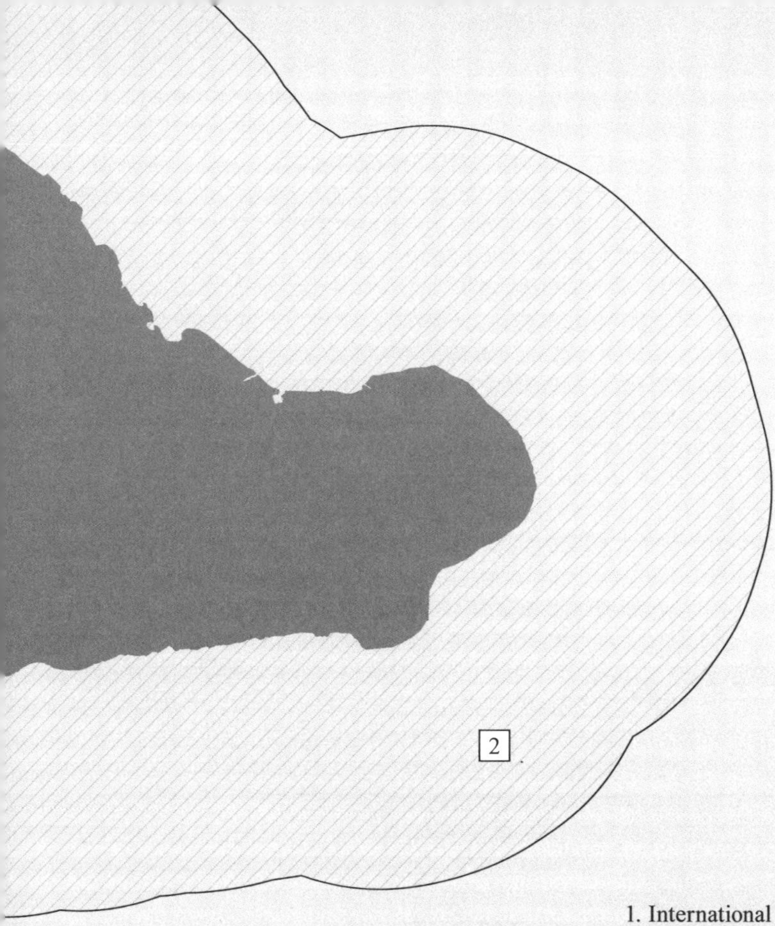

1. International Waters/Air Space
2. Cuban Territorial Waters
3. Cuban Air Space
4. US Controlled Waters
5. Unknown Waters/Airspace

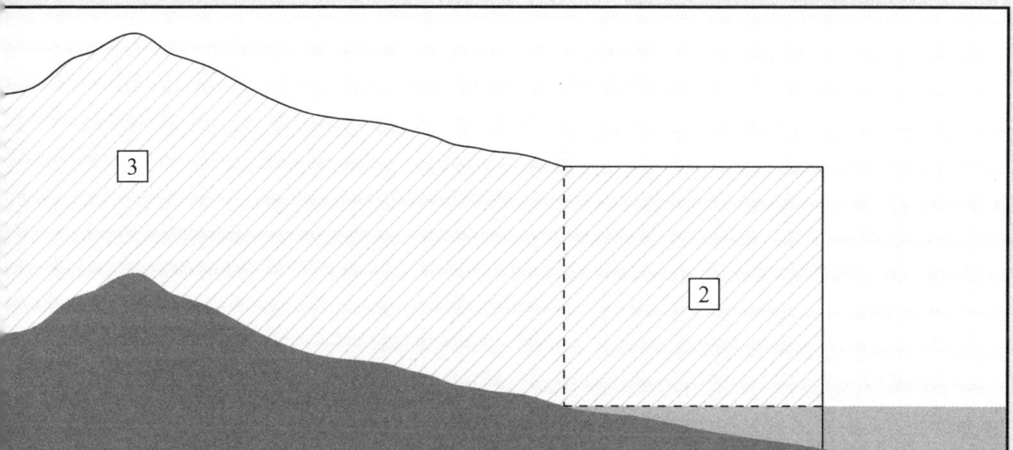

7. For more on the intricate legal history of Guantánamo Bay, see Strauss, "Jurisdiction at Guantánamo Bay," in *The Leasing of Guantánamo Bay,* 78–103.

The courts have yet to establish any conclusive legal precedent for this complicated distinction that can be broadly applied to federal legislation. Whether executive and legislative policies have *sought* legal precedence or have been enacted to *establish* it is an ongoing legal question. Over the years there have been several court cases where the issue of American sovereignty has been argued, but a ruling has never conclusively established working definitions as to where US law begins and ends with regards to Cuba.[7] In lieu of definitive legal frameworks, the policy for operations in Guantánamo has been defined by action. Legal arguments are often made ex post facto, leaving administration officials and government agencies fighting to substantiate them in court. This policy is what allowed for the expansion from the initial use of Guantánamo Bay as a "coaling and naval station" into a fully functional naval base, a temporary refugee camp for Haitian immigrants, and an offshore prison enclave. With the United States exerting complete jurisdiction—by building a military outpost—Cuba cannot exercise ultimate sovereignty. Or, to put it another way, Cuba does in fact have ultimate sovereignty over Guantánamo Bay, but only enough to cede it.

The space claimed by the US government between sovereignty and control allows for broad interpretations of law, rights, and military legitimacy. The irregular, and often secretive, negotiation between American juridical and administrative factions reveals a rich assemblage of politics, logistics, technology, globalization, and warfare, with many transnational and regional factors and interests creating a diverse terrain for policy making and military action. But there is a distinct spatial analogue tying many of these competing dynamics together. Policies informed by the political and security necessities dictated by the War on Terror, secret memos, hundred-year-old treaties, and ideologically infused policies are all revealed in their most contemporary manifestations "on the ground" in clandestine prisons, logistics networks, and contemporary theaters of war.

Ever since the United States inserted the Platt Amendment into the Cuban constitution, the territory of Guantánamo Bay has been a space of contention, first as a type of territorial recompense for American military aid and later as an image deployed by both countries when politically advantageous. The tension created by a foreign military presence within Cuba was exacerbated after the 1959 revolution when the US-backed Batista government was overthrown by Fidel Castro and the 26th of July Movement. It is a historical anomaly that the 1903 constitution, and the later agreements ceding territory to the US, was never renegotiated or dismissed outright by the post-revolutionary government. The Cuban leaders never formally appealed to any international institution to request that the treaties be revoked during the ascension of the Castro government, and since then their authority to do so has waned. Every year the US Treasury sends a check to the Cuban government, and until his death Castro dutifully deposited

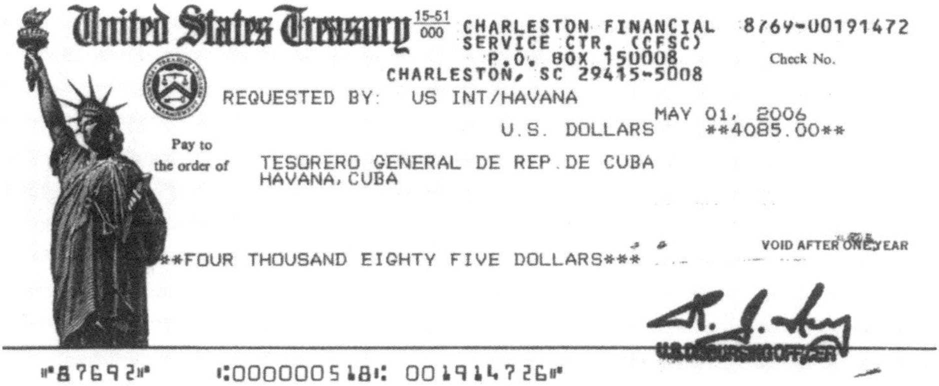

Fig. 1.4
Guantánamo Bay Lease Payment, 2006.
Payments are mediated by the Swiss embassy in Havana.

them not into a bank, but a cigar box on his desk.

Guantánamo Bay was, until the reestablishment of diplomatic relations in 2016, the only US military or extraterritorial holding within a hostile nation or one with which the US had no diplomatic ties. Prior to September 11, the role of the leased territory often functioned as a bargaining chip held out to the Cuban government during times of political turmoil, such as the 1962 Cuban Missile Crisis, and as an incentive to adopt more America-friendly reforms. It remains to be seen what may or may not happen with the base as the two countries begin normalizing relations, but the status of the naval base as an American outpost does not appear to be among the many points of negotiation between the two countries. For American political purposes, however, Camp Delta remains a contested image of either folly or strength. The persistent use of the Guantánamo Bay prisons continues to serve political purposes across the ideological spectrum. Right-leaning politicians regularly cite Guantánamo as an easy answer to more complex questions related to international terrorism and national security. For politicians on the left it remains a symbol of human-rights violations, jihadist recruitment, and America's claim to power outside of international norms.

The status of Guantánamo Bay throughout the War on Terror—and beyond—has reinforced its political and spatial importance as a territory that cannot be easily defined with historical models of state sovereignty. Using a definition set out by political scientist Robert Jackson as a starting point, state sovereignty can be seen as "a defined and delimited territory, with a permanent population, under the authority of a government."[8] As such, the presiding government power "holds supreme authority domestically and independent authority internationally, at one and the same time."[9] This notion of sovereignty, often referred to as Westphalian, was first established in the seventeenth century and has persisted, generally intact, ever since.[10] It is understood as a shift in sovereign authority from the ecclesiastical order to the nation state, which is recognized as a sovereign governing body with jurisdiction defined and limited by territorial boundaries. This evolution of sovereignty is intimately linked to the emergence of the modern nation state and the territorial delimiting of authority through borders and defensible space.

While still relatively intact in a geopolitical and practical legal sense, Westphalian sovereignty has evolved greatly over the twentieth century.[11] The creation of the United Nations in 1945, the advent of the European Union in 1958, and the expansion of neoliberal capitalism after World War II have unsettled the definition of state boundaries assumed within Westphalian sovereignty. With the spread of expansionist economic policy, global trade, and the creation of worldwide transportation and communication infrastructures in the twenty-first century, sovereign space expands to the horizon and is unsettled by networks of capital relations, material production, national security, and many other features of what can be called "national interests."

8. Robert Jackson, "Introduction: Sovereignty at the Millennium" in *Sovereignty at the Millennium*, ed. Robert Jackson (Oxford: Blackwell Publishers, 1999), 5–6. Jackson's definition can be read as a distillation of the major historical concepts in sovereignty scholarship including foundational texts by Jean Bodin, Thomas Hobbes, and Jean-Jacques Rousseau.

9. Jackson, "Introduction: Sovereignty at the Millennium."

10. Named after the Peace of Westphalia signed in 1648 and normatively understood as the beginning of the sovereign nation state.

11. Hent Kalmo and Quentin Skinner have go so far as to say sovereignty, as a concept, is in "fragments," and that there is not, nor should there be, "a single agreed-upon concept of sovereignty for which one could offer a clear definition." See Hent Kalmo and Quentin Skinner, "Introduction: A Concept in Fragments," in Sovereignty in fragments: the past, present and future of a contested concept, ed. Hent Kalmo and Quentin Skinner (Cambridge: Cambridge University Press, 2013), 5.

These developments have brought forth new theories and conceptions of sovereignty, troubling the status of territory as a de facto requirement for sovereign power. Guantánamo Bay, black sites, and other extraterritorial spaces can be understood within this evolution as a spatial and material permutation of logistical movement, military strategy, and information systems.

The black sites' connection to the early land lease of Guantánamo Bay opens several lines of inquiry for understanding how sovereignty has been interpreted, reconceived, and spatialized to deal with the very real threats laid bare by the September 11 attacks. In his essay "Problematic Sovereignty," political scientist Stephen Krasner argues that current notions of sovereignty are no longer applicable to modern conflict and nation-state relations. As a multifaceted concept, sovereignty for Krasner relies on several components, including administrative control, border administration, international recognition, and the ability to enter into international negotiations.[12] By adding criteria to his definition of sovereignty, Krasner lessens the importance of defined state boundaries. Importantly, he notes that not all of these factors need to be present to exercise sovereignty. This leads to a more abstract understanding of sovereignty, where sovereign claims are accordingly problematic in the realm of international law. In Krasner's framework, the black sites undermine, stretch, and test all of these notions.

Based on the conceptualization of sovereignty set out by the US government, one that oscillates between strictly defined national borders and more broadly understood military control, Guantánamo Bay functions as a pivot point in claiming and ceding different forms of sovereign authority. The administrative logic of Guantánamo Bay allows the American state to claim the right to both exercise its own sovereign power and to negate that of others. The Camp Delta prison complex at Guantánamo Bay served as both a spatial and legal challenge to contemporary nation-state sovereignty while acting as the center of the global black site network, an incarceration regime outside US and international jurisdiction yet within the control of American military power. America's shifting conception of sovereignty is linked both in spirit and juridical construction to negotiations in the early twentieth century surrounding the original Cuban-American lease agreement *and* to the attacks of September 11.

Through investigating the black sites, the problematic conceptions of contemporary sovereignty raised by Krasner and others are presented in extreme relief. By creating the black site prison network, the Bush administration exploited the unsettled legal history of Guantánamo Bay in a specific way that left the question of American nation-state legal authority and jurisdiction equally unsettled. As Guantánamo historian Michael Strauss notes, "With both sides of jurisdictional questions being readily supportable by sound arguments based on well-established rules and opinions, legal decisions about jurisdiction at Guantánamo Bay have remained inconsistent to this day."[13] Any traditional conception of sovereignty, even

12. Stephen D. Krasner, ed., *Problematic Sovereignty: Contested Rules and Political Possibilities* (New York: Columbia University Press, 2001), 2.

as definitions have expanded beyond the nation state, fall short of explaining the physical and operative qualities of Guantánamo Bay and the larger network of black site prisons.

The black sites appear as a disparate network of prisons hastily created for the purpose of interrogating Al Qaeda operatives and other suspected terrorists following the September 11 attacks. They were, in part, reactionary constructions, pieced together from spare parts, under secret authorizations. Yet behind their somewhat haphazard materiality was the political momentum of fear, exploited by Bush administration officials to alter long-held juridical processes.

The territorial dispersal of black sites resists any attempt to conceptualize them within a normative understanding of sovereignty. While the black sites *could* be described with similar discursive language—they exist within nation states, they have physical locations, they contain human life (regardless of definition), and their existence has been internationally recognized—they have been designed to skirt and stretch these rigid characteristics. Like the evolution of what constitutes a nation state, the limits of national borders, notions of physical location, and the definition of "human" have also become contested.

Shortly after the events of September 11, the US government quickly moved to reorganize the political, social, and spatial structure of the American state. Crucial to this reorganization was the assemblage of incarceration sites to process the influx of prisoners captured on the new and highly expansive battlefield of the War on Terror.[14] An assemblage, in this sense, is understood as a composition of legal, spatial, human-rights, and national-security dimensions.[15] Guantánamo Bay as a territorial and legal exception is just one dimension that helps constitute a newly conceived sovereignty in response to the political and military needs of the War on Terror. Together with language preserved in memos and legal arguments, the assemblage methodologically and descriptively creates an ontological landscape in which to understand the emergence of the black sites.

The sovereign-assemblage, as defined here, can be understood as a set of spaces and spatial relationships. Such spaces, while manifest in material forms in the battlefield and prison cells, are not strictly confined to clearly delineated boundaries. The spaces claimed as sovereign through the black sites are plastic and adaptable, molded and formed based on the claims of American power and presidential prerogative. The dimensions constructing such an assemblage layer onto one another, like a palimpsest, forming new possibilities—legal, logistical, political, spatial—and new formations of movement and organization. Like a palimpsest, the various layers that build sovereign claims never quite disappear. They can be continually recast, chameleon-like, to new conditions both on the ground and within the political-juridical spectrum. The result of defining sovereignty as a shifting assemblage results in a complex, multidimensional, and politically malleable territory.

At first, the black sites seem to operate like other so-called

13. Strauss, *The Leasing of Guantánamo Bay*, 81.

14. Here, the term assemblage is influenced by Gilles Deleuze and Félix Guattari's description of an assemblage as an "increase in the dimensions of a multiplicity," which itself has no object or subject, only "determinations, magnitudes, and dimensions"—that is, attributes and boundaries without objects, or "known unknowns," to quote Donald Rumsfeld. In this study, an assemblage is understood as a set of rules and their material expressions. See Gilles Deleuze and Félix Guattari, *A Thousand Plateaus: Capitalism and Schizophrenia* (Minneapolis: University of Minnesota Press, 1987), 8.

15. Ibid., 21.

neoliberal landscapes, and to a certain extent, they share with them a structural similarity. Tax haven expert Ronen Palan describes these places as something that comes about "as states divided their sovereign domains into two juridical realms: 'onshore,' where they apply fully their regulations and taxation, and myriad offshore enclaves, where they relax or withdraw some of those regulations."[17] It would also fit into the description of a zone, defined by theorist Keller Easterling as something that exists "in legal lacunae and political quarantine."[18] Saskia Sassen might qualify these sites as a new "legal regime" and locate them within the broader context of globalization.[19] The absence of a more specific term to label these types of territorial arrangements is not for lack of effort. Definitional ambiguity is central to their very existence; to name them properly would mean locating them properly, and therefore defining them within a recognizable juridical authority, whether international, national, or local. It would give them legal accountability—even nominally—under a sovereign power.

Although a specific term or particular word may not be able to perfectly describe these types of spaces, evidence of their existence can be traced through document trails, trade agreements, and tax loopholes. They are implicit sites, not clearly defined but clearly operational. Their presence can be pieced together through a forensic patchwork of spreadsheets, invoices, and multimedia communications along with legal analysis, treaties, and, of course, material evidence in the form of built environments.

In her book *Enduring Innocence,* Easterling examines the spatial product—golf courses, ports, technology campuses, enclaves, and other spaces that, through marketing and logistics, avoid the "political inconveniences of location."[19] Spatial products are manufactured specifically to serve globalized economic forces. The black sites might similarly be thought of as a type of "sovereign product"—that is, sovereignty as an illegal bootleg rather than an official release, a mixture of space and international law, where both are conceived specifically to be negated. Black sites were created by the US government as a reformulation of sovereign power in spaces designed to negate sovereign claims. But due to the constantly shifting characteristics of these sovereign products, this definition too seems inadequate for understanding the black sites network. The shape-shifting, protean characteristics of these spaces can be better understood as active productions rather than identifiable and static products.

Guantánamo Bay provides an unstable foundation for expansive American legal and territorial claims after September 11. Through memos, Bush administration officials made evidentiary claims for new forms of American sovereign power following the attacks. These memos consisted of legal theory, government policy, and historical records, forming an ideological patchwork aimed at asserting power under the president that would traditionally be beyond the remit

16. Ronen Palan, *The Offshore World: Sovereign Markets, Virtual Places, and Nomad Millionaires* (Ithaca, NY: Cornell University Press, 2003), 2.

17. Keller Easterling, "The Zone," in *Visionary Power: Producing the Contemporary City,* ed. Christine de Baan, et al. (Rotterdam: NAi Publishers, 2007), 75. See also Keller Easterling, "Zone: The Spatial Softwares of Extrastatecraft," *Places* (June 2012), placesjournal.org/article/zone-the-spatial-softwares-of-extrastatecraft/.

18. Saskia Sassen, *Losing Control? Sovereignty in an Age of Globalization* (New York: Columbia University Press, 1996), 25.

19. Keller Easterling, *Enduring Innocence: Global Architecture and Its Political Masquerades* (Cambridge, MA: MIT Press, 2005), 1.

of executive authority. Originally designated "top secret" or "classified," the memos entered the public domain during the latter years of the Bush presidency through leaks, Freedom of Information Act requests, and official administration releases. Some of these documents still retain levels of redaction—moments of black-mark editing— while others were released in their entirety. Many have been declassified and made publicly accessible while many more circulate through unofficial channels.

Referencing such diverse subjects as the American Revolution, the *Federalist Papers,* the Cuban-American Treaty, and several court cases on the treatment of prisoners from the Civil War to World War II to the Vietnam War, the memos present protocols for the War on Terror as the latest installment of constantly evolving juridical precedent. As modern warfare has adapted to new technologies, it would seem reasonable—the memos argue—for the laws governing it to adapt in kind. Legal and administrative memos were the vehicles by which laws were formulated and interpreted. They created new policies for a war that was itself said to be new.[20]

The memos reveal both the logic for creating new types of sovereign power and the administration's aspirations for its permanence. Administration officials used the memos to propose new legal rationales for offshore prisons, new prisoner designations and prisoner treatment, and to give actions that were already happening legal cover. These opinions were quickly adapted and administered as law. Only later, after the memos were leaked or released, were they interpreted as unsound legal opinions that led to torture. The memos themselves do not provide explicit evidence of torture. They do however unveil the systematic thinking and justifications behind it, and as a point of entry, they also conceptualize the space where the acts of torture eventually occurred. In this sense, the memos act as an interpretive blueprint, designating where prisoners should be held, under what conditions, and what sorts of interrogation techniques could be enacted upon them.

The memos are thus generative, they constitute and reformulate sovereign power toward political ends. Secondarily, they serve to keep the newly constituted sovereign power flexible, continually creating and occupying voids within the expansive spatio-legal landscape of the War on Terror and beyond. The first instantiation of this generative process was the declaration of a state of emergency by President Bush. The state of exception, understood as a sovereign claim, is a bureaucratic mechanism generating an infinite space of potential—a legal designation without the governing weight of precedence or legislation. The memos, legal opinions, and other classified documents took advantage of this potential to reformulate the laws of war toward very specific political and security agendas.

The memo is a commonplace bureaucratic tool. Some are simple directives to be widely disseminated; others carry sensitive information or significant legal weight. Some of the Bush administration

20. The memos used for this analysis were retrieved from online sources, primarily the Torturing Democracy website maintained by the National Security Archive and Washington Media Associates. See "Read the Key Documents," Torturing Democracy (accessed November 7, 2016), nsarchive.gwu.edu/torturingdemocracy/documents/.

memos pertaining to the early years of the War on Terror, the treatment of prisoners, and sites of offshore interrogation are highly complex. Others are more straightforward, drafted to undermine existing laws and international treaty obligations. As used to plan the early years of the War on Terror, the memos have a functional similarity to an inside joke—they were written for a very select group of people and had the effect of creating an alternate reality that stood in contrast to prevailing legal norms. The language of the memos is sometimes dense and often repetitive; similar phrasing across multiple memos reinforces the administration's message to disregard legal standings and basic human rights. In doing so, the exceptional and contested claims begin to read as consensus opinion and conventional thinking.

Opening his famous 1922 essay *Political Theology,* German jurist and political philosopher Carl Schmitt states, "Sovereign is he who decides on the exception."[21] He goes on, "What characterizes an exception is principally unlimited authority, which means the suspension of the entire existing order. In such a situation it is clear that the state remains, whereas law recedes."[22] If the state is understood as both a territory and its governing structure, what are its defining characteristics when the relationship between territory and law has been severed? Territory under this condition would not be "extralegal" since it is purposefully created by the law, even though it sits outside normative national or international juridical order. As Laleh Khalili describes such spaces are created by an "excess of law, rules, procedures, legal performances made by the government to legitimate control."[23] The exception, in this sense, is generative, where the state, rather than being "left behind," extends past the traditional understanding of of legal jurisdiction. The Schmittian terms of sovereignty—focusing on the sovereign ruler—are not one and the same as state sovereignty, but in the case of the black sites and the administration of power during the early years of Bush's War on Terror, they slip into one another.

Eighty-four years after the publication of *Political Theology,* during a White House press conference responding to criticisms of how then Secretary of Defense Donald Rumsfeld was conducting the Iraq War, President Bush made his infamous declaration, "I'm the decider."[24] Bush's declaration was indeed decisive, and it rested on a theory of the unitary executive, where the sovereign declarations of the commander-in-chief cannot be challenged, either by domestic law or international treaty.[25] Under the unitary executive theory, the president is a sovereign individual, the embodiment of the law itself. And since he, as president, has been constitutionally vested with sovereign power, his actions become law as they are exercised through the production of memos, legal opinion, and executive action. Chris Edelson has written, "The unitary executive theory, as implemented by the Bush administration, was claimed to justify effectively unchecked presidential power over the use of military force, the detention and

21. Carl Schmitt, *Political Theology: Four Chapters on the Concept of Sovereignty* (Chicago: University of Chicago Press, 2005), 5.

22. Ibid., 12.

23. Wring about Guantánamo Bay Khalili says, "The whole complex, and the worldwide network of lawyers, legal scholars, advocates, military judges and prosecutors, human rights activists, and news reporters, attests to something else again: a space of legal dispute. Not of lawlessness, as it is claimed again and again, but of excess of law, rules, procedures, legal performances made by the government to legitimate control, and contested by those who seek to subject the detainees there to an alternate regime of legality. At Guantánamo Bay, there is no 'deficit of lawyers or legal analysis' but a kind of palimpsest of what may prove expedient for the government." See Laleh Khalili, *Time in the Shadows: Confinement in Counterinsurgencies* (Stanford: Stanford University Press, 2013), 74.

24. "Quotation of the Day," *New York Times,* August 19, 2006, query.nytimes.com/gst/fullpage.html?res=9905E7DE143FF93AA25757C0A9609C8B63.

25. The unitary executive theory was strongly supported by Vice President Dick Cheney and Office of Legal Counsel attorney John Yoo. Summarizing unitary executive theory as applied during the Bush administration, Chris Edelson writes, "According to the unitary executive theory, since the Constitution assigns the president *all* of 'the executive power', he can set aside laws that attempt to limit his power over national security." See Chris Edelson, "Exploring the Limits of Presidential Power," American Constitution Society Blog, December 2, 2013, www.acslaw.org/acsblog/exploring-the-limits-of-presidential-power.

interrogation of prisoners, extraordinary rendition and intelligence gathering."[26]

That Bush's claim of being "the decider" occurred in reference to the supervision of the Iraq War, itself supposedly one piece of the larger War on Terror, is no coincidence. Within the shifting conceptualization of sovereignty remains the exercise of power over space and the inherent tension that arises in defining which spaces fall within and without the theater of war. The War on Terror has not so much challenged this aspect of sovereignty, but has complicated the methods by which power can be exercised and jurisdictions defined.

The War on Terror was, and continues to be (even if the term itself has fallen out of favor), enacted through a broad array of methods, from the deployment of troops to the passing of sweeping new legislation, each with a distinct spatial register.[27] The War on Terror was never intended to be located strictly outside US borders. The same state of emergency that launched the war abroad brought new domestic laws and security policies, which in turn, brought the war into everyday American life. More importantly, it has profoundly shaped how America declares and fights wars and the legal terrain governing the sovereign power of the state and its elected officials.

On September 14, 2001, President Bush exercised his executive authority and declared an official state of emergency. That day he released a statement that said, "A national emergency exists by reason of the terrorist attacks at the World Trade Center, New York, New York, and the Pentagon, and the continuing and immediate threat of further attacks on the United States."[28] Bush then mobilized the legal offices of his administration to draft documents strengthening the war powers of the executive branch and to begin establishing protocols that would soon entail a global scope for the upcoming conflict.[29]

On the same day that President Bush proclaimed a national emergency, CIA stations were notified to start "seeking input on appropriate locations for potential CIA detention facilities."[30] As Jane Mayer and other reporters have noted, this signaled a stark shift in the scope of CIA operations. Traditionally the CIA is concerned with foreign intelligence and information gathering. Housing and interrogating of suspected terrorists—or anyone else—is a task that has traditionally been the sole domain of the FBI or other military divisions more versed in interrogation and incarceration methodologies.[31]
On September 17, three days after President Bush signed a covert Memorandum of Notification (MON) authorizing the Director of Central Intelligence, George Tenet, to "undertake operations designed to capture and detain persons who pose a continuing, serious threat of violence or death to U.S. persons and interests or who are planning terrorist activities."[32]

The MON formally authorized the CIA to locate, capture, detain, and interrogate unknown persons suspected of terrorism or planning terrorist attacks against the United States. Again, due to the

26. Ibid. It should also be noted that President Obama did little to reign in the expansive executive authority established by President Bush.

27. President Obama may have stopped using the phrase "War on Terror," but this was more of a semantic shift than a legal one. Many of the policies enacted during the Bush administration are still being pursued, the wars in Iraq and Afghanistan continue, the prisons of Guantánamo Bay are still in operation, and drone programs have been greatly expanded.

28. President George W. Bush, Proclamation No. 7463, 66 Fed. Reg. 48199 (September 18, 2001). See memo from September 18, 2001, Selection 1.

29. Article II, Section 8 of the US Constitution grants Congress the authority to declare war.

30. The Memorandum of Notification was quoted in the Senate Select Committee on Intelligence study on the CIAs detention and rendition program. See US Senate, *Committee Study of the Central Intelligence Agency's Detention and Interrogation Program, Senate Select Committee on Intelligence,* December 9, 2014, 11. http://purl.fdlp.gov/GPO/gpo53907.

31. Although, as Tim Weiner writes, the CIA has a history of running interrogation sites dating back to at least the 1950s including instances in Germany, Japan, Panama, Vietnam, and Egypt. See Tim Weiner, *Legacy of Ashes: The History of the CIA* (New York: Anchor Books, 2008), 556.

32. US Senate, *Committee Study of the Central Intelligence Agency's Detention and Interrogation Program,* 11.

traditional division of powers, detention and interrogation had been conducted by the FBI or the military, whereas the CIA had previously focused on espionage and intelligence gathering abroad. Vesting the CIA with the power to detain and interrogate prisoners gave them the formal authority to establish and operate the black site prisons.[33] Yet the MON did not outline procedures or practices for interrogations and was not specific about the types of interrogation methods that could—or could not—be used on the prisoners.

The Memorandum of Notification was followed the next day by the Authorization for Use of Military Force (AUMF). On September 18, the president signed the authorization stating,

> *That the President is authorized to use all necessary and appropriate force against those nations, organizations, or persons he determines planned, authorized, committed, or aided the terrorist attacks that occurred on September 11, 2001, or harbored such organizations or persons, in order to prevent any future acts of international terrorism against the United States by such nations, organizations or persons.*[34]

With the signing of the AUMF, the War on Terror officially began. The authorization ceded a large number of war powers from Congress to the executive branch, giving the president broad authority to conduct the war as he deemed necessary. The expansive and open-ended nature of the 2001 authorization can be registered by the fact it was retained and persistently invoked by President Obama. Obama continued operations in Iraq and Afghanistan, launched drone strikes around the world, and deployed military actions against the Islamic State of Iraq and Syria (ISIS) under the authority of the AUMF signed by Bush.

By the end of September 2001, the CIA had taken control of planning and construction for the detention facilities in which prisoners captured in the newly declared war were to be housed and interrogated. At the time, they were considering at least four countries and at least seven separate and still unknown locations.[35] In a heavily redacted email, the CIA acknowledged its lack of experience running detention facilities but noted they would be operated "in a manner consistent with, but not pursuant to, the formal provision of appropriately comparable Federal instructions for the operation of prison facilities and the incarceration of inmates held under maximum lawful security mechanisms."[36] They would also meet "U.S. POW Standards."[37] The standards for prisoner of war (POW) detention would later be rewritten—and largely discarded—by Bush administration lawyers.

These declarations are the first examples of the post-September 11 American juridical landscape. The attacks themselves remade passenger aircraft into projectile weaponry and focused the global aims of al-Qaeda onto several distinct points on the East Coast—a means

33. David Johnston, "At a Secret Interrogation, Dispute Flared Over Tactics," *New York Times*, September 10, 2006.

34. The authorization was passed by congress on September 14, 2001. See "Joint Resolution to Authorize the Use of United States Armed Forces against Those Responsible for the Recent Attacks Launched against the United States" (PL 107–40, September 18, 2001).

35. US Senate, *Committee Study of the Central Intelligence Agency's Detention and Interrogation Program*, 11.

36. Quote from an email between the Counterterrorism Center and the CIA. See US Senate, *Committee Study of the Central Intelligence Agency's Detention and Interrogation Program*, 12.

37. Ibid.

permitting habeas jurisdiction within the sovereign territory of the United States, which does not include GBC. Second, no federal statutes include GBC within the territorial jurisdiction of any federal district court. The fact that the United States can exercise some "jurisdiction" and "control" over the base is not the relevant factor for purposes of the analysis in *Eisentrager*. Presumably the United States similarly exercised considerable "jurisdiction" and "control" over the Landsberg Prison, which was under the command of an American Army general at the time, where the applicants in *Eisentrager* were held. That, however, was not deemed relevant to the Court's analysis.

Third, the *McNary* and *Sale* cases cited above are not persuasive authority for extending habeas jurisdiction to GBC. To begin with, the cases did not address habeas jurisdiction at all and thus never squarely confronted the analysis in *Eisentrager*. Instead, *McNary*, for example, addressed whether the United States, in interdicting Haitian refugees and detaining them at GBC, had violated international treaties and agreements, statutes, and executive orders. In fact, we have not found any case directly addressing habeas jurisdiction over an alien held at GBC. In addition, both *McNary* and *Sale* have been vacated. *McNary* was vacated as moot by the Supreme Court, *see* 509 U.S. 918 (1993), and *Sale* was subsequently vacated by Stipulated Order, *see Cuban American Bar Ass'n*, 43 F.3d at 1424. More importantly, the analysis in *Sale* has also been expressly rejected by the Eleventh Circuit. *See id.* at 1425 ("The district court here erred in [relying on *Sale* and] concluding that Guantanamo Bay was a 'United States territory.' We disagree that 'control and jurisdiction' is equivalent to 'sovereignty.'") (citation omitted). Finally, to the extent the Second Circuit in *McNary* relied on the theory that GBC was within the "special maritime and territorial jurisdiction" of the United States under 18 U.S.C. § 7, it is particularly weak authority for habeas jurisdiction here. Section 7 of title 18 defines places or circumstances where certain criminal laws of the United States shall apply to proscribe conduct. 18 U.S.C. § 7 (1994). The mere fact that U.S. criminal law applies, however, does not bring a place within the territorial jurisdiction of a federal district court. As the Supreme Court explained in *Vermilya-Brown*, a nation may extend its statutes to regulate conduct "on areas under the control, though not within the territorial jurisdiction or sovereignty, of the nation enacting the legislation." 335 U.S. at 381. Laws are frequently applied extraterritorially to conduct occurring *outside* a nation's territorial jurisdiction, but the mere application of law in such a case does not alter the territorial jurisdiction of the courts or their power to grant the writ of habeas corpus. Indeed, the venue provision for cases arising under the special maritime and territorial jurisdiction of the United States expressly acknowledges this distinction. It sets out the venue for crimes that occur "out of the jurisdiction of any particular State or district." 18 U.S.C. § 3238 (1994).

In addition, the Second Circuit has subsequently repudiated the cursory analysis in *McNary*, which essentially assumed that 18 U.S.C. § 7 applied to GBC. Instead, the Second Circuit has held that the statute has no extraterritorial application. *See United States v. Gatlin*, 216 F.3d 207, 214 (2nd Cir. 2000). After holding that § 7 had no territorial application for the case before it, the *Gatlin* Court noted that "the United States base at Guantanamo Bay is technically outside the territorial boundaries of the United States" and declined to express a view on "whether our *dictum* in *McNary* was correct." *Id.* at 214 n.8.[6] *McNary*'s reliance on 18

[6] Although the Second Circuit has held that 18 U.S.C. § 7 does not apply extraterritorially, we caution against relying too heavily on that rationale. This office has opined that GBC is within the special maritime and territorial . .

7

Fig. 1.5
Page 7 of the memo, *Re: Possible Habeas Jurisdiction over Aliens in Guantánamo Bay, Cuba* by Patrick F. Philbin, John C. Yoo written on December 28, 2001. The memo notes Guantánamo Bay (GBC) is outside the "territorial jurisdiction of "any federal district court" and that "control and jurisdiction" is not equivalent to sovereignty.

and method of terrorist attack that had escaped the imaginations of government officials in both the Bush and Clinton administrations. The attacks opened a void that was quickly occupied by new forms of political maneuvering and claims for authority. The executive declarations of a national emergency and the authorizations of force that followed transformed a day of terrorist attacks into a state of protracted war. The exception enacted shortly after the attacks destabilized the nation state both territorially and legally, forming a legal and administrative blank space. Within this space various juridical formations materialized, many of which were created specifically to enhance the power of the executive branch and fight against the bureaucracy of the state.

As defined by Giorgio Agamben, the state of exception exists in a "no-man's-land between public law and political fact."[38] This no-man's-land, while a useful metaphor, spatializes the distinctly administrative character inherent in suspending the rule of law. The legal no-man's-land becomes the spatial tabula rasa, a space of infinite possibilities, the effect of which is a type of legal and administrative cascade. Once begun, new forms of power become increasingly hard to resist. To put it another way, once an action has been taken within the state of exception, all consequent actions are both exceptional, justified, *and* legal. The Bush administration predicated its authority to create a far-reaching state of emergency as innate executive privileges under the duties of the president as commander in chief of the armed forces operating within the theater of war.[39] With the theater of war broadly defined in vague and abstract terms that encompassed the entire globe, the exceptional power claimed for the executive branch had newfound reach.

A tabula rasa, of course, cannot last long. The state of emergency quickly slid into the War on Terror—Congressionally declared or not—and the president became constitutionally obligated to take charge of the conflict in his role as commander in chief.[40] Although a declaration of war had not been officially declared, a memo from November 6, 2001, stated, "The terrorists' actions in this case are sufficient to create a state of war de facto that allows application of the laws of war."[41] By stating the need to apply the laws of war, the administration was acknowledging existing legal precedence. But at the same time, they were actively working to rewrite the preexisting legal framework governing war and armed conflict. Declaring a de facto state of war from the moment of the initial attack backdates any government action with the imprimatur of the newly minted legal opinions. More importantly, it serves to remove power from Congress, which is vested with the authority to declare war, and place it not with the president but as a type of ontological fact. Once war is declared, congressionally or de facto, the president is legally obligated to act as commander in chief to defend the country and, without the oversight of Congress, President Bush was free from a key check on executive power.

On November 16, 2001, after determining that "an extraordinary emergency exists,"[42] Bush, in his role as commander in chief, began

38. Giorgio Agamben, *State of Exception*, trans. Kevin Attell (Chicago: The University of Chicago Press, 2005), 1.

39. Article II, Section 1 of the US Constitution states, "The executive Power shall be vested in a President of the United States of America." Article II, Section 2 states "The President shall be Commander in Chief of the Army and Navy of the United States."

40. US Department of Justice, *Legality of the Use of Military Commissions to Try Terrorists*, Memorandum for the Counsel to the President, from Patrick F. Philbin, Deputy Assistant Attorney General, November 6, 2001, 1. See memo from November 6, 2001, Selection 1.

41. Ibid., 1. See memo from November 6, 2001, Selection 2.

42. Military Order of November 13, 2001, *Detention, Treatment, and Trial of Certain Non-Citizens in the War Against Terrorism*, 66 Fed. Reg. 57833 (November 16, 2001). See memo from November 16, 2001, Selection 1.

43. Agamben, *State of Exception*, 23.

44. US Department of Justice, *RE: Treaties and Laws Applicable to the Conflict in Afghanistan and to the Treatment of Persons Captured by U.S. Armed Forces in That Conflict,* Memorandum for Alberto R. Gonzales, Counsel to the President, from John C. Yoo, Deputy Assistant Attorney General, November 30, 2001, 1. See memo from November 30, 2001, Selection 1.

45. Ibid., 2. See memo from November 30, 2001, Selection 2.

outlining how non-American citizens engaged in hostilities with the United States or US troops were to be treated. The president again took advantage of legal memos to establish policy. Under the guidelines described in the memos, "terrorists" are subject to the president's orders and can be detained and tried as he sees fit.

If Bush's declaration of a state of emergency was the exceptional act that initiated the War on Terror, it is hard to trace the origins of the second, third, or any other moments of exception that followed. The lines of administrative and military action no longer flowed from one to another in a direct lineage. The evolution of an exception embodies the exception itself and creates a type of threshold or liminal state—a "zone of indifference"[43]—able to quickly adapt to political and logistical adversity. This is to say that the bureaucratic methodology of the exception—the writing of memos and the use of executive power—mimics the use of constitutionally defined power, yet remains undefined by it. To be seen as legitimate, even if that legitimacy is eventually challenged and denied, the exception must be declared from within an existing form of juridical precedence. It cannot be wantonly implemented without the substantiation of legal authority. In other words, the state of emergency that allows for extraordinary powers requires the mechanics of constitutionally defined governance.

As noted earlier, the memos released just after the September 11 attacks form the conceptual and ideological scaffolding for the state of emergency. In quick succession, the memos that followed worked to consolidate presidential power and to blur any fixed definition of how the newly declared conflict would be enacted. In a memo from November 30, 2001, titled *"RE: Treaties and Laws Applicable to the Conflict in Afghanistan and to the Treatment of Persons Captured by U.S. Armed Forces in that Conflict,"* John Yoo, then an official in the Department of Justice, placed the terms of prisoner engagement within a distinctly spatial register.

> *We conclude that these treaties do not protect the al Qaeda organization, which as a non-State actor cannot be a party to the international agreements governing war. We further conclude that the President has reasonable grounds to find that these treaties to not apply to Taliban militia.*[44]
>
> *Because al Qaeda is merely a violent political movement or organization, it is not a Nation State, and hence is ineligible to be a signatory to any treaty. Because of the novel nature of this conflict, moreover, we do not believe that al Qaeda would be included in non-international forms of armed conflict to which some provisions of the Geneva Conventions might apply. Therefore, the Hague Convention IV, the Geneva Conventions, and the WCA [War Crimes Act] do not apply to the conflict with al Qaeda.*[45]

> *In regard to the treatment of Taliban prisoners, we believe that the Geneva Conventions do not apply here because the Taliban is and was not a government and Afghanistan is not—and even prior to the beginning of the present conflict was not—a functioning State.*[46]

This strategy of legal reasoning exemplifies what Deputy Judge Advocate General Charles Dunlap refers to as "lawfare," where "law is used as a means of realizing a military objective."[47] By using such methods, the law becomes a tool to expand the theater of war and its rationale for existence. The theater of lawfare is that of research and argument, nuance and footnotes. It is, in essence, a preemptive act intended to remove constraints to military and intelligence operations, and in the context of the War on Terror, to actively place them outside the constraints of domestic and international law.

The Bush administration claimed the actions of the American state were justified under a rationale of lawfare, a justification understood as a reaction to dealing with groups and nations that lack easily identifiable and internationally recognized sovereign status. Al-Qaeda is a nonstate organization. While al-Qaeda behaves like a sovereign state in some regards—it controls territory and administers its own form of law—it nevertheless is not a sovereign nation as recognized by the United Nations or other global governing bodies. Likewise, Afghanistan, as host to al-Qaeda, is recognized as a nonfunctioning state, meaning it has lost its legitimacy as a sovereign nation by losing control of its national territorial (that is, by giving al-Qaeda safe refuge). As a nation in a state of failure, Afghanistan provided an environment for al-Qaeda to operate—two nonsovereign entities operating within the same territory.

Beyond similar political and methodological sympathies between the Taliban regime, which had nominal control of the country, and al-Qaeda, as a self-described jihadist organization, the claim that Afghanistan was a failed state played a major role in the rise and diminution of these two governing institutions. On the notion of a failed states, Kenneth Menkhaus writes, "Terrorist networks, like mafias, appear to flourish where states are governed badly rather than not at all."[48] Afghanistan was a failing state, whose unstable political, social, and economic environment enabled competing—and sometimes complimentary—notions of sovereignty to coexist. Importantly, Afghanistan was not a completely failed state, but operated in a state of failure. Had it completely failed, international action would have been called upon before September 11. Complete failure would elicit stronger action from the international community—and individual state intervention—on humanitarian grounds, whereas failing could be seen as an internal problem, to be treated with sanctions and other carrot/stick proposals.[49] The attacks of September 11, therefore, were the moment when Afghanistan reached the status of total failure, allowing the US to intervene with the backing—limited

46. Ibid., 2. See memo from November 30, 2001. Selection 3.

47. Charles J. Dunlap, "Lawfare: A Decisive Element of 21st-Century Conflicts?" *Joint Force Quarterly* 54, no. 3 (2009): 35.

48. Kenneth Menkhaus, quoted in Stuart Elden, *Terror and Territory: The Spatial Extent of Sovereignty* (Minneapolis: University of Minnesota Press, 2009), 103.

49. The line between failing and failure is purposefully obscure. Law professor Daniel Thürer claims the charters of the United Nations and existing human rights treaties, such as the Geneva Conventions, provide a framework for UN intervention in "failed state" scenarios. See Daniel Thürer, "The 'Failed State' and International Law," International Committee of the Red Cross, December 31, 1999, www.icrc.org/eng/resources/documents/article/other/57jq6u.htm.

and contentious as it may have been—of the world's governing institutions.

As a vehicle of bureaucratic authority, the memos served a fairly straightforward operational mandate: to establish certain functions of military operations above any jurisdiction of control, thereby placing the newly created enemy above any jurisdiction of protection. The declaration of December 28, 2001, captures this twin ambition, claiming that "different rules apply to enemy aliens held outside the United States."[50] The term "enemy aliens" was itself a fabricated category, created specifically to obfuscate previously recognized citizen or combatant designations such as prisoner of war.[51] The Bush administration claimed that by denying detainees prisoner-of-war status and reclassifying them as enemy aliens (and later "enemy combatants") they could create a new subject status, subverting any national or international legislation governing enemy status and placing the "enemy aliens" beyond the authority of any international governing institution. With similar reasoning, the Bush administration denied US legal jurisdiction over Naval Station Guantanamo Bay "because it is outside the sovereign territory of the United States."[52] This decision leaves the captured bodies within a designed yet undefined legal *and* territorial space—a double removal, and a spatio-legal hedge against national and international law.

In order to edify their legal rationale for holding prisoners in Guantánamo, the Bush administration mobilized the full organizational strength of the executive bureaucracy. Crucial to this effort was the White House legal counsel and the Office of Legal Counsel in the Department of Justice. Lawyers within these offices, including John Yoo and Jay Bybee, among others, quickly drafted detention and interrogation policy starting in late 2001. The memos had a self-referential quality, citing passages from previous memos. This self-citation and internal referentiality worked to reinforce dubious legal opinions through the power of repetition. Slowly, the opinions concretized into what appeared as valid policy and well-reasoned legal directives. The memos read as a unified networked document, referencing each other to build their cases regardless of whether the initial referent stood on unstable constitutional grounds or was contrary to national and international legal norms. A similar method was used to great effect by Dick Cheney in the lead-up to the Iraq War, when he leaked false information to news sources describing Saddam Hussein's nuclear capabilities. He then appeared on television and referenced his own (unattributed) false information as proof that Hussein was noncompliant with nuclear regulations and therefore that war was necessary to depose him of nuclear capabilities.[53]

The self-referential nature of the memos can be seen in the remarkable consistency of their writing. While composed by several authors, the content is strikingly similar, and the conclusions are nearly exact.

50. US Department of Justice, *RE: Possible Habeas Jurisdiction of Aliens Held in Guantanamo Bay, Cuba,* Memorandum for William J. Haynes II, General Counsel, Department of Defense, from Patrick F. Filbin, Deputy Assistant Attorney General and John C. Yoo, Deputy Assistant Attorney General, December 28, 2001, 2. See memo from December 28, 2001, Selection 2.

51. The term "prisoner of war" has a longer history and was used against Japanese, Italian, and German citizens during World War II. Franklin D. Roosevelt, Presidential Proclamation 2525, December 7, 1941. Proclamations 2526, 2527, December 8, 1941.

52. US Department of Justice, *RE: Possible Habeas Jurisdiction,* 3. See memo from December 28, 2001, Selection 3.

53. On the September 8, 2002, episode of *Meet the Press*, Vice President Dick Cheney quoted an article in the *New York Times* claiming Saddam Hussein was looking to acquire nuclear weapons material. The article, written by Judith Miller and Michael R. Gordon, used unnamed administration officials believed to have close ties with Cheney. The article, and much of Miller's reporting from the time, was later discredited by the *Times.* For a history of Miller's reporting and the run-up to the Iraq War, see Franklin Foer, "The Source of the Trouble," N*ew York Magazine,* June 7, 2004, nymag.com/nymetro/news/media/features/9226.

On November 30, 2001, John Yoo writes, "[W]e conclude that, based on appropriate presidential determinations, the [sic] neither the federal War Crimes Act, the Hague Convention IV, nor the Geneva Conventions would apply to the operations of the U.S. Armed Forces against the al Qaeda terrorist organization or the Taliban militia."[54] Twenty days later, Donald Rumsfeld reaches the same conclusion, stating, "The United States has determined that al-Qaeda and Taliban individuals under the control of the Department of Defense are not entitled to prisoner of war status for the purposes of the Geneva Conventions of 1949."[55] On January 22, 2002, Jay Bybee, then serving as Assistant Attorney General for the Office of Legal Counsel in the Department of Justice, writes, "[W]e conclude that neither the federal War Crimes Act nor the Geneva Conventions would apply to the detention conditions of al Qaeda prisoners. We also conclude that the President has the plenary constitutional power to suspend our treaty obligations toward Afghanistan during the period of the conflict."[56] And just over a week later, Alberto Gonzales, then Counsel to the President, concurred with the previous opinions, "In my judgment, this new paradigm renders obsolete Geneva's strict limitations on questioning of enemy prisoners and renders quaint some of its provisions."[57]

Writing with similar tone and legal reasoning, many of the figures within the highest ranks of the Bush administration worked to establish a uniform policy suspending the Geneva Conventions and to set new regulations for detaining and interrogating prisoners. All that remained to be done was securing the official approval of the president. On February 7, 2002, Bush announced:

> *I accept the legal conclusion of the Department of Justice and determine that none of the provisions of Geneva apply to our conflict with al Qaeda in Afghanistan or elsewhere throughout the world because, among other reasons, al Qaeda is not a High Contracting Party to Geneva. . . .*
>
> *I also accept the legal conclusion of the Department of Justice and determine that common Article 3 of Geneva does not apply to either al Qaeda or Taliban detainees, because, among other reasons, the relevant conflicts are international in scope and common article 3 applies only to "armed conflict not of an international character."*
>
> *Based on the facts supplied by the Department of Defense and the recommendation of the Department of Justice, I determine that the Taliban detainees are unlawful combatants and, therefore do not qualify as prisoners of war under Article 4 of Geneva. I note that, because Geneva does not apply to our conflict with al Qaeda, al Qaeda detainees also do not qualify as prisoners of war.*[58]

54. US Department of Justice, *RE: Treaties and Laws*, 44. See memo from November 30, 2001, Selection 27.

55. US Department of Defense, *Status of Taliban and Al Qaida,* Memorandum for Richard B. Myers, Chairman of the Joint Chiefs of Staff, from Donald R. Rumsfeld, Secretary of Defense, January 19, 2002, 1. See memo from January 19, 2002, Selection 1.

56. US Department of Justice, *Re: Application of Treaties and Laws to al Qaeda and Taliban Detainees,* Memorandum for Alberto R. Gonzales, Counsel to the President and William J. Haynes II, General Counsel to the Department of Defense, from Jay S. Bybee, Assistant Attorney General, January 22, 2002, 37. See memo from January 22, 2002, Selection 6.

57. US White House, Decision *Re Application of the Geneva Convention of Prisoners of War to the Conflict with Al Qaeda and the Taliban,* Memorandum for President George W. Bush, from Alberto R. Gonzales, Counsel to the President, January 25, 2002, 2. See memo from January 25, 2002, Selection 2.

58. US White House, *Humane Treatment of al Qaeda and Taliban Detainees,* Memorandum to Richard B. Cheney, Vice President et al. from President George W. Bush, February 7, 2002, 2. See memo from February 7, 2002 (A), Selection 2.

With this declaration President Bush effectively solidified what had up until that point been an amorphous legal argument, transubstantiating it from legal opinion to actionable mandate, with the imprimatur of the commander in chief and the authority of sovereign power. With a legislative ground now formed, Bush's pronouncement served to close one set of possibilities and open another.

The definition of sovereign power whereby an executive formulates and defines the law, and in turn the law conditions the sovereign, closely aligns with Judith Butler's reevaluation of Michel Foucault's definition of governmentality.[59] Butler writes that the methodology of governmentality Foucault proposes—that is, bureaucracy—becomes the generative component of sovereignty; therefore, "the art of government" does not replace sovereignty, but is reinforced by it. Bureaucracy is both sovereign power in its purest form and the framework containing it. Butler writes, "The state *produces*, through the act of withdrawal, a law that is no law, a court that is no court, a process that is no process. The state of emergency returns the operation of power from a set of laws (juridical) to a set of rules (governmental), and the rules reinstate sovereign power."[60] It is in this sense that sovereign power claims greater actionable authority through the removal of its juridical authority, continually claiming new structures of territory and jurisdiction based on self-reinforcing and self-limiting legal reasoning. In Guantánamo Bay, sovereign power is instantiated by claiming it does not exist.

When the memos declare "al Qaeda is not a state,"[61] or "The mere fact that U.S. criminal law applies, however, does not bring a place within the territorial jurisdiction of a federal district court,"[62] or that "a federal district court ought to be reluctant to extend habeas jurisdiction to GBC [Guantanamo Bay, Cuba], when not clearly called for by statute, if doing so would interfere with matters solely within the discretion of the political branches of government,"[63] a sovereign territory is being defined by rewriting legal definitions as opposed to passing laws. The legislative is bypassed via the bureaucratic. In parallel with Butler's definition, we might say the state generates itself by producing a space that is no space.

Henri Lefebvre claims, "Sovereignty implies 'space,' and what is more, it implies a space against which violence, whether latent or overt, is directed—a space established and constituted by violence. . . . Every state is born of violence, and state power endures only by virtue of violence directed towards a space."[64] With the Bush administration policies crafted in the early days of the War on Terror, violence became operative as a means of exerting sovereign power against nation states, failed states, and prisoners in spaces beyond America's internationally recognized borders. The War on Terror, a supposedly new type of war, continues to have its own set of legal maneuvers and spatial conditions. Likewise, the war has its own forms of violence.

59. Butler uses Foucault's definition of governmentality as her starting point. Very broadly, Foucault described governmentality as the way in which individuals, goods, and capital are managed. Or, more directly, as a bureaucratic management of biopolitics. Within Foucault's definition, the sovereign, strictly speaking, is complemented by a governing bureaucracy and has its own logic of operation. See Michel Foucault, "Governmentality," in *The Essential Foucault,* eds. Paul Rabinow and Nikolas Rose (New York: New Press, 2003), 234.

60. Judith Butler, *Precarious Life: The Powers of Mourning and Violence* (New York: Verso, 2006), 61–62.

61. US Department of Justice, *RE: Treaties and Laws,* 14. See memo from November 30, 2001, Selection 6.

62. US Department of Justice, *RE: Possible Habeas Jurisdiction,* 7. See memo from December 28, 2001, Selection 7.

63. Ibid., 7. See memo from December 28, 2001, Selection 7.

64. Henri Lefebvre, *Production of Space,* trans. Donald Nicholson-Smith (Malden: Blackwell Publishing, 1991), 280, 112.

As the state of emergency oscillated between legal opinions, it produced its own territory of knowable, if not easily definable, space. This exceptional space made demands on the prisoners' bodies. The two standard frameworks governing how detained bodies should be treated—legal and moral—were negated for the stated purposes of intelligence gathering and information extraction. As the memos attest, the body as a signifier of human life deserving of morality was dismissed in favor of its intelligence value. The body of an "enemy alien" was understood as merely a vessel for jihadist ideology and actionable intelligence, each reason enough to dismiss the prisoners' humanity and therefore to deny them human rights.

Management of these now nonhuman bodies occurred in the black sites, camp-like spatial anomalies governed by the expansive logics established through the state of exception. As Agamben writes, the state of exception is given a "permanent spatial arrangement" in the camp.[65] And the bodies contained within the camp become *homo sacer*, a form of life "included in the juridical order solely in the form of its exclusion."[66]

By stripping the detainee bodies of both statehood and humanity, they could be tortured and terrorized under the same exceptional regime that justified the creation of the black sites in the first place. This two-step process of cleaving the prisoners from both state and humanity was also done from a legal position within the United States. In early 2002, opinions began to focus not just on the rights of prisoners in the context of American jurisprudence, but on what could be specifically enacted upon them in the context of their humanity.

In a February 26, 2002, memo from Assistant Attorney General for the Office of Legal Counsel Jay Bybee, prisoners' rights against self-incrimination (Miranda rights) were revoked, and the status of military commissions within the president's authority was guaranteed.[67] The memo states the prisoners are subject to trials that "are entirely creatures of the President's authority."[68] The designation of the trials as creatures placed them into another undefined legal category. The term "creature" is not a predetermined legal designation, although it can point to either animal, things "other than human," or a "creature of statute," which refers to something that would not exist "but for a legislative act."[69] Creatures of statute often refer to corporations or localized forms of government (state, municipal) vested by federal authority. Here, a "creature of the President's authority," is a legal procedure created by the president and "not constrained by the strictures placed on 'criminal case[s].'"[70]

Butler has written extensively on the question of what is considered life and how it is categorized and degraded through the government's treatment of prisoners.[71] Butler's underlying question, "who will be human and who will not?" is highly relevant for prisoners of the War on Terror. The question she poses has an implicit answer in that the status of these prisoners cannot be considered truly human when they are classified "enemy combatants" and not subject to

65. Giorgio Agamben, *Homo Sacer: Sovereign Power and Bare Life*, trans. Daniel Heller-Roazen (Stanford: Stanford University Press, 1998), 169.

66. Ibid., 8.

67. US Department of Justice, *Re: Potential Legal Constraints Applicable to Interrogations of Persons Captured by U.S. Armed Forces in Afghanistan*, Memorandum for William J. Haynes II, General Counsel of the Department of Defense, from Jay S. Bybee, Assistant Attorney General, February 26, 2002, 1. See memo from February 26, 2002, Selection 1.

68. U.S. Department of Justice, *Re: Potential Legal Constraints*, 5. See memo from February 26, 2002, Selection 2.

69. In *Black's Law Dictionary*, the entry for "creature" redirects to animal, defined as "Any living *creature* (besides plants) other than a human being.—Also termed creature." The definitions for "animal" and "creature of statute" are taken from the tenth edition of the dictionary. *Black's Law Dictionary*, 10th ed., ed. Bryan A. Garner (St. Paul, MN: Thomson Reuters, 2014), 106, 448.

70. U.S. Department of Justice, *Re: Potential Legal Constraints*, 5. See memo from February 26, 2002, Selection 2.

71. See Butler, *Precarious Life*.

72. US Department of Justice, *Re: Military Interrogation of Alien Unlawful Combatants Held Outside the United States*, Memorandum for William J. Haynes II, General Counsel of the Department of Defense, from John C. Yoo, Deputy Assistant Attorney General, March 14, 2003, 4. See memo from March 14, 2003, Selection 3.

international humanitarian protections; their nonhuman status is just as constructed as the spaces they inhabit. And if, according to the administration's lawyers, they cannot be considered human, then what are they? The memo of March 14, 2003, gives a partial answer. In it John Yoo writes:

> *Given the ongoing threat of al Qaeda attacks, the capture and interrogation of al Qaeda operatives is imperative to our national security and defense. Because of the asymmetric nature of terrorist operations, information is perhaps the most critical weapon for defeating al Qaeda. Al Qaeda is not a nation-state, and has no single country or geographic area as its base of operations. It has no fixed, large-scale military or civilian infrastructure. It deploys personnel, material, and finances covertly and attacks without warning using unconventional weapons and methods. As the September 11, 2001 attacks and subsequent events demonstrate, it seeks to launch terror attacks against purely civilian targets with the United States, and seeks to acquire weapons of mass destruction for such attacks. Because of the secret nature of al Qaeda's operations, obtaining advanced information about the identity of al Qaeda operatives and their plans may prove to be the only way to prevent direct attacks on the United States. Interrogation of captured al Qaeda operatives could provide that information; indeed, in many cases interrogation maybe the only method to obtain it. Given the massive destruction and loss of life caused by the September 11 attacks, it is reasonable to believe that information gained from al Qaeda personnel could prevent attacks of similar (if not greater) magnitude from occurring in the United States.*[72]

If, as the memo suggests, "information is the most critical weapon for defeating al Qaeda," then the real value of the prisoners lies in their potential to hold and transmit such information. Since the prisoners have been legally rendered as nonhuman—as defined by the emergence of human rights discourse post–World War II—it follows that they should be categorized simply as information, or as abstract containers of information, to be accessed by any means necessary. Furthermore, gaining access to this information "may prove to be the only way to prevent direct attacks on the United States." No longer is the access to information governed by human rights protocols; rather, there exists a temporal imperative. The method chosen by the Bush administration was interrogation: "indeed, in many cases interrogation may be the only method to obtain it." Put within this context,

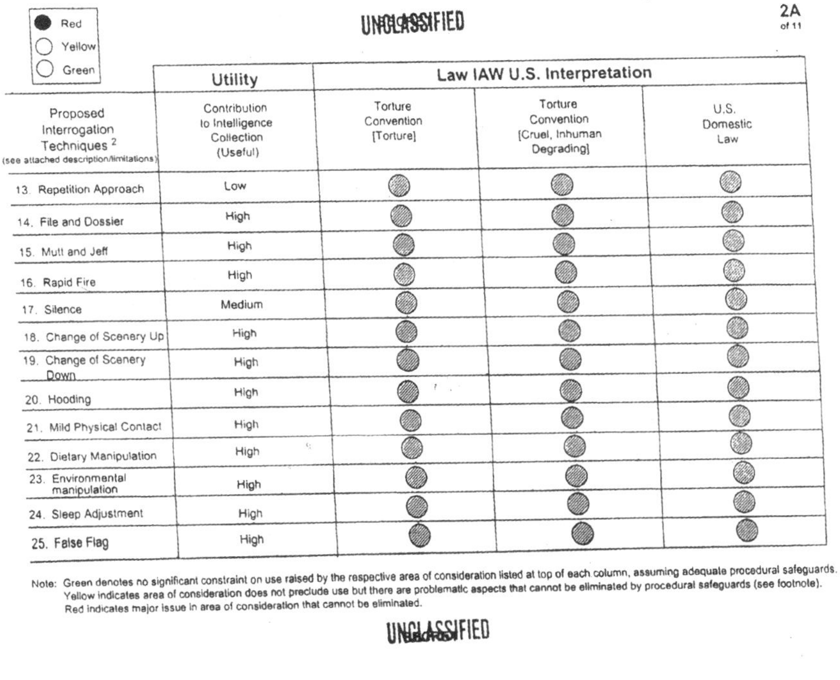

● Red
○ Yellow
○ Green

UNCLASSIFIED

2A
of 11

Proposed Interrogation Techniques [2] (see attached description/limitations)	Utility: Contribution to Intelligence Collection (Useful)	Law IAW U.S. Interpretation: Torture Convention [Torture]	Torture Convention [Cruel, Inhuman Degrading]	U.S. Domestic Law
13. Repetition Approach	Low	●	●	●
14. File and Dossier	High	●	●	●
15. Mutt and Jeff	High	●	●	●
16. Rapid Fire	High	●	●	●
17. Silence	Medium	●	●	●
18. Change of Scenery Up	High	●	●	●
19. Change of Scenery Down	High	●	●	●
20. Hooding	High	●	●	●
21. Mild Physical Contact	High	●	●	●
22. Dietary Manipulation	High	●	●	●
23. Environmental manipulation	High	●	●	●
24. Sleep Adjustment	High	●	●	●
25. False Flag	High	●	●	●

Note: Green denotes no significant constraint on use raised by the respective area of consideration listed at top of each column, assuming adequate procedural safeguards.
Yellow indicates area of consideration does not preclude use but there are problematic aspects that cannot be eliminated by procedural safeguards (see footnote).
Red indicates major issue in area of consideration that cannot be eliminated.

UNCLASSIFIED

Fig. 1.6
A list of proposed interrogation techniques compiled by the Department of Defense. The columns note each technique's usefullness to intelligence gathering and whether it complies to the UN Conventions against Torture and US Domestic Law.

73. US Department of Justice, *Interrogation of al Qaeda Operative,* Memorandum for John Rizzo, Acting General Counsel of the Central Intelligence Agency, from Jay S. Bybee, Assistant Attorney General, August 1, 2002, 2. See memo from August 1, 2002 (B), Selection 1.

74. Ibid., 2. See memo from August 1, 2002 (B), Selection 2.

75. US Department of Defense, *Working Group Report on Detainee Interrogations in the Global War on Terrorism: Assessment of Legal, Historical, Policy, and Operational Considerations,* April 4, 2003. See memo from April 4, 2003, Selection 4.

it's not hard to see how interrogation quickly morphs into "enhanced interrogation" and then into torture.

Removing the constraint of humanity from the obligation to acquire information allows the techniques of interrogation to be evaluated within a rubric of technological effectiveness. Even the most famous memo, the so-called "torture memo" written by Bybee on August 1, 2002, framed various interrogation techniques in terms of their utility in information gathering.[73] The memo described ten techniques, including facial slapping, cramped confinement, stress positions, sleep deprivation, and waterboarding.[74] Later memos expand this list to thirty-five approved techniques, including hooding, environmental manipulation, and threatening transfer to a third country (and with that transfer an implicit threat of torture). The language used in these documents describes interrogation techniques in bureaucratic fashion, listing each technique's "Contribution to Intelligence Collection" along with their status as torture or cruel, inhuman, or degrading treatment under the "Torture Convention" (United National Convention against Torture and Other Cruel, Inhuman or Degrading Treatment) and US domestic law.[75] All thirty-five approved techniques were deemed humane, and all but two (silence and threat of transfer) were noted as having a high intelligence collection value.

The torture techniques became one part of a larger technological regime of the War on Terror, bound to both the constructed territoriality of the black sites and the rendition policies that placed prisoners in them. The black sites are simultaneously displaced and linked through a network of communication infrastructures that allow them to function outside the United States yet within the ever-expanding theater of the War on Terror. The renditions became a means not of bringing prisoners together, but of purposely scattering them apart. The global detention and interrogation program operated as a way of constructing an intelligence network, placing the human-information in strategic positions, and delivering the fruits of the interrogation process across hemispheric communications space.

Thus, interrogation techniques, extraordinary rendition, states of exception, and logistics are bound together through a newly defined theater of war brought about as the result of a highly constructed and radically redefined sovereignty. In the War on Terror, this sovereignty was a complex production, continually evolving and choreographed. The newly sovereign spaces manifest through bureaucratic administration could be negated even as they began to collapse under the immense administrative weight of their own formation.

TECHNOLOGIES OF DISLOCATION

The town of Baldwin, Georgia, is about seventy-five miles northeast of Atlanta. On the southern edge of the local Habersham County airport sits the 115,000-square-foot manufacturing facility of SteelCell of North America, one of largest and most profitable prefabricated prison cell manufacturers in the United States.[1] Often working in tandem with the Atlanta-based architecture firm Rosser International, SteelCell designs and produces over 1,500 prefabricated cells per year, each one specifically configured to the client's needs. The process of ordering and producing a prison cell, as described by SteelCell's Vice President Ray Handte, is as straightforward and unglamorous as one would expect from purchasing any type of mass-produced product.[2]

SteelCell offers three basic cell types, similar to each other but with slight variations in details and amenities. Each unit includes either one or two bunk platforms and a stainless steel combination sink and toilet. Some units have a small desk and seat or a few shelves. The cells used for continual confinement have small showers. Most of the design effort is directed at making the cells as efficient as possible by minimizing material, eliminating hiding spaces, and creating smooth surfaces that can withstand both abuse and cleaning by hoses and power washers. Each cell is roughly 7.5 feet by 12.5 feet and is shipped as a lightweight structure (5,000 pounds, as opposed to 30,000 for a concrete cell), making it perfectly suited for deployment to destinations around the world.[3] The cells manufactured at SteelCell are simple beige boxes, minimally designed and mass-produced to house inmates of any distinction. They proved to be the logical prison material of choice for both the CIA, who shipped them to Eastern Europe, and the government contractors who installed them in Guantánamo Bay.

1. Rob Moore, "SteelCell Caters to Nation's Detention Industry," AccessNorthGa.com, November 27, 2011.

2. I conducted one phone interview with Ray Handte on February 8, 2012. He was proud of his company's work and the role they played in providing prison cells for the US Government. He decline to say what sort of customization requests the government had requested. He also guarded details of his company's construction and shipping process as trade secrets. When asked about reports claiming his cells had been used in "undisclosed locations" around the world, he said that any information made public was done by someone at SteelCell who shouldn't have been discussing it.

3. Moore, "SteelCell Caters."

The Bush administration initiated the black-site detention network, as well as the administrative programs that filled it with prisoners, with the specific aim of dispersing prisoners around the world. It was conceived and constructed in an effort to cloak the prisons' existence behind opaque international logistics and communication. These sites were the physical manifestations of an information-gathering program predicated on "extraordinary rendition," the process of extracting and transferring prisoners across the globe so that whatever information they were suspected of holding could be obtained by any means necessary.

Within this globalized network, a prison's physical existence in one particular location or another mattered less than its legal position within carefully conceived regimes of rendition, detention, and

4. Candice Dyer, "Made in Georgia: Prefab Jail Cells," *Atlanta Journal Constitution*, August 16, 2009.

5. David Johnston and Mark Mazzetti, "A Window Into C.I.A.'s Embrace of Secret Jails," *New York Times*, August 12, 2009.

interrogation. To put it another way, the prisons and the prisoners held within them were contained in many different locations, both geographic and juridical. The movement of prisoners between sites and their confinement within different types of "detention technology"[4] was integral to President Bush's policy of information warfare. The distance between detention spaces—or, for that matter, between Washington and any theater of war—was less important to the administration than the physical act of movement and the psychological effects of rendition. Moving the prisoners beyond any known political or spatial environment caused mental and physical destabilization. This held true whether the detainees were kept at a facility inside a declared war zone or transferred to a third-party state.

Like most of the information pertaining to their existence, the black sites' physical location and other operational details are highly classified. Some of the more infamous locations have been described in news reports, human rights dossiers, and prisoner testimonies. But with the 2014 publication of the Senate Select Committee on Intelligence report on the CIA's use of detention and interrogation, a more fully developed picture of the entire program began to emerge. The report is sweeping in its condemnation of the CIA and is graphic in its descriptions of prisoner interrogations. In terms of the names and locations for the secret prisons where the interrogations took place, however, all information has been redacted.

Crucial to the existence of this international network are the spaces of confinement themselves, a critical form of information technology for the interrogation and torture of detainees. The regime of extraordinary rendition was not just a bureaucratic invention. It was also spatial, predicated on highly contested readings of sovereignty and territory, with the spaces of confinement forming an important link between government action and its strategic objectives. But, like the program as a whole, information about the individual spaces of incarceration—their whereabouts, their aesthetics, their modes of use—exists only in disparate forms of knowledge often in contradiction to the War on Terror's official narratives.

On August 13, 2009, the *New York Times* ran a front-page article reporting the arrest of Kyle "Dusty" Foggo, chief of the CIA's main European supply base, which operates out of Frankfurt, Germany. In a war dominated by logistics, Foggo was the logistics man for the CIA. This "cigar- waving, bourbon-drinking" character was known to be able to make anything happen, and make it happen quickly.[5] Once rumors spread of secret prisons in places like Thailand—and the abuse that occurred within them—the CIA approached Foggo to help quickly set up a series of new detention sites in several countries in Eastern Europe.

The reason for Foggo's arrest—and his subsequent thirty-seven-month jail sentence—was a suspicion of fraud and collusion to game government contracts with his long-time friend, government contractor Brent R. Wilkes. If Foggo was the guy who could get anything, Wilkes was the guy who had everything. Wilkes's company supplied the CIA with many of the materials necessary to run military facilities and therefore secret prisons: plumbing equipment, bedding, earplugs, wrap-around sunglasses, etc.[6] Wilkes secured these contracts by showering Foggo with expensive meals, lucrative job promises, and all-expenses-paid junkets.

Beneath the story of bribery and extortion are details that David Johnston and Mark Mazzetti of the *New York Times* revealed about the construction of black-site prison facilities. "The cells were constructed with special features to prevent injury to the prisoners during interrogations: nonslip floors and flexible, plywood-covered walls to soften the impact of being slammed into the wall."[7] The article further describes how the prisons were intended for a small number of detainees, and there was a need to install many of the cells quickly and at the same time.

Two months after Johnston and Mazzetti's piece in the *Times*, ABC News broke the story of a recently discovered black site near Vilnius, Lithuania. Quoting an unidentified source, ABC News reported the CIA had constructed a "building within a building" using prefabricated cells imported from outside Lithuania, converting what had previously been a horse-riding academy into an interrogation and detention site:

> *On a series of thick concrete pads, [the CIA] installed what a source called "prefabricated pods" to house prisoners, each separated from the other by five or six feet. Each pod included a shower, a bed and a toilet. Separate cells were constructed for interrogations. The CIA converted much of the rest of the building into garage space.*[8]

By using American made, prefabricated modular prison cells, the CIA quickly and quietly installed a detention and interrogation facility in a third-party country. That they did this within an already existing, barn-like structure eliminated the need for constructing extensive infrastructure and building services and meant the facility could be masked from the outside.

Along with the black site located in the riding academy in Lithuania, there were two other reported secret prisons in Eastern Europe, one in a police facility in Bucharest, Romania, and the other at the Stare Kiejkuti military base in northeast Poland. Like Lithuania, the site in Poland was built using prefabricated cells imported from the United States. In his published account of detention and interrogation, collected by the Center for Human Rights and Global Justice, Mohamed Farag Ahmad Bashmilah described his cell in what was believed to be Poland or Romania.[9]

6. Ibid.

7. Ibid.

8. Matthew Cole and Brian Ross, "EXCLUSIVE: CIA Secret 'Torture' Prison Found at Fancy Horseback Riding Academy," ABC News, November 18, 2009, abcnews.go.com/Blotter/cia-secret-prison-found/story?id=9115978.

9. After additional research and documentation, Mohammed Bashmilah's attorneys cannot definitely conclude whether he was renditioned to Europe. His lawyers believe that the final CIA facility he was held in before being transferred to Yemen in 2005 may have been in Afghanistan, and if so, it was most probably the site code named ORANGE in the SSCI report.

10. Center for Human Rights and Global Justice, *Surviving the Darkness* (New York: New York University School of Law, 2007), 35.

11. Bashmilah's experience was told to journalist Mark Benjamin. See Mark Benjamin, "Inside the CIA's Notorious 'Black Sites'," *Salon*, December 15, 2007, www.salon.com/2007/12/15/bashmilah/.

12. Catherine Herridge, "Inside Guantanamo Bay, a Study in Contrasts," Fox News, January 31, 2009, www.foxnews.com/story/2009/01/31/inside-guantanamo-bay-study-in-contrasts.html.

13. US Department of Defense, Contract N62470- 04-D-4017, February 2, 2004, HalliburtonWatch.org (accessed October 16, 2016), www.halliburtonwatch.org/reports/concap04.pdf.

> *[The cell] appeared to be new or refurbished and had a stainless steel toilet and a stainless steel wash basin. In this cell there were two video cameras, one above the door and one on the wall in the corner diagonal to the door. The camera on the wall in the corner was directed at the door, while the camera above the door followed me when I moved in the cell. There was also a speaker next to the camera above the door.*[10]

Bashmilah ended up in Europe as the final stop in a series of extraordinary renditions. He was first captured by Jordanian forces as he flew from Indonesia to Amman in 2003. Jordanian intelligence officials held him at the General Intelligence Department in western Amman and then handed him over to the CIA. The CIA renditioned him to Afghanistan and kept him in "The Hangar," a notorious and quickly constructed black site inside an airplane hangar at the US-operated Bagram Airfield in Afghanistan. After months of captivity, Bashmilah was renditioned to Poland or Romania and finally released to Yemeni custody in May 2005.[11] The Hangar shared a spatial and construction logic with the Lithuanian riding academy in that it was built from modular detention cells arrayed within an open space. But whereas the cells in The Hangar were cage-like structures wrapped in barbed wire or simple concrete boxes sitting on the bare ground, those in Europe were complete and individual units.

The use of prefabricated cells to erect prisons was a technique taken directly from the US prison industry, and the techniques were extended beyond the black sites to the construction of more permanent facilities holding the growing population of prisoners at Guantánamo Bay. Two of the prisons in Camp Delta, Camps V and VI, were built in a similar fashion to the Lithuanian and Polish black sites—quickly and with materials imported from the United States. And, like much of the rest of the War on Terror's logistics and base operations, the two camps were built by Kellogg Brown & Root (KBR), a subsidiary of Halliburton. Camp V was modeled off the maximum security Federal Correctional Complex in Terre Haute, Indiana, and opened in 2004 at a cost of $17.5 million.[12] Camp VI, also constructed by KBR for $30 million, is a 220-bed two-story prison based on a small jail in Lenawee County, Michigan. Camp VI opened in 2006.[13]

Guantánamo Bay and the black site facilities are connected to each other not just by the prisoners who were constantly moved between them, the objectives they served within the larger War on Terror, or their rapid deployment and redeployment as the war moved through different stages of public approval. They are also linked by the spatial and tectonic requirements brought about by mass-produced incarceration technology—the most definitive aesthetic characteristic binding the network together. The development of the post-September 11 security regime was predicated on the swift deployment of facilities and the desire to capture and detain prisoners at any time using any technique deemed appropriate. This efficiency of production converted prison cells from simple detention spaces to a form of information technology. The CIA believed that the many people captured shortly after the attacks had information vital to national security. The EIT program and its black sites were developed and implemented specifically to extract it.

As successive administrations have continued the Bush administration policy of delaying or suspending trials for the detainees thought to have participated in terrorist activities and deferring release for those who never did, what was once an information-gathering operation has now become a warehousing enterprise, holding people that are unwanted and often unacknowledged. By January 2017 there were forty-one prisoners left in Guantánamo Bay, ten of whom have been recommended for transfer and thirty-one held without trial or charges. The thirty-one men held without charges represent the "irreducible minimum," a designation given by the Obama administration to the prisoners not cleared for transfer but unable to be prosecuted because the evidence against them was acquired through torture or other inhumane treatment and is thus inadmissible in court.[14]

The detainees brought into the black sites and later to Guantánamo Bay have been extracted from space and arrested in time, and they remain there as lasting symbols of the War on Terror. One foundational purpose of the black site network was to dislodge the prisoners from a continuous sense of time and place. Guantánamo extends that logic and removes them from time and place altogether, marking temporality in biological terms and space as permanent displacement. The prison cells provide an environment simply capable of *maintaining* life. Only when the final prisoner at Guantánamo succumbs to old age can the "Mission Accomplished" banner be dusted off and hung from one of the concrete slab façades at Camp Delta.

The logic of spatial dislocation was accomplished through technologies used for mass prison cell construction and the architectural detailing required for their production. And yet the particular designs of cells used in Guantánamo Bay, Lithuania, or any of the black sites around the world appear insignificant considering many of the important decisions regarding the prisons took place not in Georgia, Afghanistan, Poland, Syria, Morocco, or Thailand, but in Washington, D.C. To borrow a descriptive phrase made famous by Alberto Gonzales in his dismissal of the Geneva Conventions, the construction methods of the various prisons appear rather "quaint"[15] in relation to the policies they were intended to enforce. Nevertheless, the aesthetic experience of the prisoners held in particular cells played a crucial role in the rendition and detention process.

While many of the architectural decisions were made in offices in Atlanta and Baldwin, the CIA and the White House designed the project's programmatic intent. In describing the secret prison in Poland, reporter Jane Mayer states, "The newer prison, according to well-informed sources, was far more high-tech than the prisons in Afghanistan, and more intensely focused on psychological torment."[16]

14. The term "irreducible minimum" was used by Lisa Monaco, President Obama's top counterterrorism advisor while discussing the challenges to closing Guantánamo Bay. See David Welna, "New Gitmo Plan Would Relocate Some Detainees to U.S.," National Public Radio, July 29, 2015, www.npr.org/sections/parallels/2015/07/29/427318480/new-gitmo-plan-would-relocate-some-detainees-to-u-s.

15. US White House, Decision *Re: Application of the Geneva Convention on Prisoners of War to the Conflict with Al Qaeda and the Taliban,* Memorandum for President George W. Bush, from Alberto R. Gonzales, Counsel to the President, January 25, 2002. See memo from January 25, 2002, Selection 2.

16. Jane Mayer, *The Dark Side: The Inside Story of How the War on Terror Turned into a War on American Ideals* (New York: Doubleday, 2008), 276.

In this case, psychological torment is a specific design constraint predicated on environmental confusion and lack of sensory stimulus. It is no surprise that the American prison industry was well-poised to produce and implement such facilities.

That the black site program was enacted through a specific form of modular architectural production alludes to the nature of a globalized war, where both production and detention are outsourced across national borders as a form of economic rationalization and spatial production is exported as a means of logistical efficiency. Just as the troops are trained domestically and exported, as President Bush claimed, to "Afghanistan and Iraq and beyond so we do not have to face them in the streets of our own cities," the spatial technology of detention is being manufactured in the United States and exported "over there."[17] It is the dream of early modernist architecture—modular production organized around a series of universal design criteria—realized in the nightmare of unending global war.

For at least one hundred years, the architectural fantasy of fast, replicable, and cheap solutions to otherwise complex and costly construction has been the project of architects, urbanists, and engineers. In one early example, Ludwig Mies van der Rohe called for the implementation of new architectural material and technology, arguing for prefabricated modular construction before such a term gained its contemporary imprimatur.[18] The detention facilities of the black site program are cheap, secure, and require little planning to implement or work to install. Like the military itself, the cells were ready to deploy. With the use of modular prison technology the military no longer needed to outsource prisoner detention and interrogation to existing locations in the Middle East. They could be sent to purpose-built sites according to the administration's intent and constructed within states eager to appease American interests, such as Romania, Lithuania, and Poland.

The political demands of the war and the presumed intelligence required to sustain them were fulfilled through the aesthetics and tectonics of confined spaces, created to trigger specific psychological effects. The spaces were designed to break down the prisoners both mentally and physically. It is debatable whether the mental or the physical strain would prove to be more effective. But what was undeniably instrumental was the effect of complete dislocation, of removing the prisoner from any physical point of reference in either time or space. As the visual experience of the cell became less geographically descriptive, and the cell's aesthetics aligned with globalized production techniques, the detainee's knowledge about their specific location became more difficult to discern.

Before the construction of black sites in Eastern Europe and the completion Guantánamo Bay's prison infrastructure, the US military detained suspects with a sense of urgency, housing prisoners in haphazard conditions with little design planning. At the start of the EIT program, the CIA would typically use existing facilities

17. George W. Bush, "Remarks in Greeley, Colorado," George W. Bush White House Archives, October 25, 2004, georgewbush-whitehouse.archives.gov/news/releases/2004/10/20041025-4.html.

18. Mies is used here as an early example of one prominent architect proposing industrialized, prefabricated construction. Detlef Mertins has argued that in practice Mies was less interested in mass-producing entire buildings but in defining a new "*objet type* or standard through a process of developing, refining and perfecting the design." For Mies's original essay, see Ludwig Mies van der Rohe, "Industrial Building," in *G: An Avant-Garde Journal of Art, Architecture, Design and Film 1923–1926,* eds. Detlef Mertins and Michael W. Jennings (Los Angeles: Getty, 2010), 14-15, 120-122. For Mertins's analysis on the *objet type* see Detlef Mertins, *Mies* (London: Phaidon, 2014), 85.

Fig. 1.7
Some of the first prisoners arrive at Camp X-Ray, Guantánamo Bay. January 11, 2002.

in the Middle East as the guest of governments eager to be in America's good graces. These spaces of confinement had their own architectural, visual, and haptic qualities that both reified their location and characterized their mode of use. Reports about proxy prisons in Jordan, Egypt, Syria, and CIA managed sites in Afghanistan depict the types of spaces one might expect: extremely confined, little to no light, damp and cold, few hygienic comforts, and the nearby presence of guards and cries of other inmates that signal persistent threats of physical violence. One facility, located in or near Kabul, Afghanistan, and named "Dark Prison" among the prisoners, was known to hold prisoners in complete darkness, with guards constantly subjecting them to extremely loud music.[19] Similarly, the Palestine Branch, a proxy site located in Damascus, Syria, was notorious in the region well before the War on Terror as a location for torture. One of its most infamous cells, just large enough to hold a single person, was known simply as "the grave."[20]

One of the few organizations with access to the so-called high-value detainees (HVD)—high-ranking officers in al-Qaeda, other prisoners with unique and valuable information, or those with direct and known ties to terrorist plots—was the International Committee of the Red Cross.[21] Many HVD's were held in black sites, both those operated by proxy governments and run by the CIA. Abu Zubaydah, one of the HVDs held by American forces, was detained for four and a half years as a "ghost detainee" in various black sites. "Ghost detainees" were held off the books and could be shuttled between

19. This practice, known as "futility music," was one of the *New York Times* phrases of the year in 2005. See "2005: In a Word," *New York Times*, December 25, 2005, www.nytimes.com/2005/12/25/weekinreview/2005-in-a-word.html.

20. Stephen Grey, *Ghost Plane: The True Story of the CIA Torture Program* (New York: St. Martin's Press, 2006), 2.

21. The existence of fourteen "high-value detainees" was acknowledged by George W. Bush on September 6, 2006, as they were transferred from CIA custody to Defense Department custody and from CIA operated black sites to Guantánamo Bay. In total there have been seventeen prisoners designated as "high value." See Gerry J. Gilmore, "High-Value Detainees Moved to Gitmo; Bush Proposes Detainee Legislation," US Department of Defense, September 6, 2006, archive.defense.gov/news/newsarticle.aspx?id=721. For a full list of high-value detainees, see "The Guantánamo Docket: High Value," *New York Times*, November 2008, www.nytimes.com/interactive/projects/guantanamo/detainees/high-value.

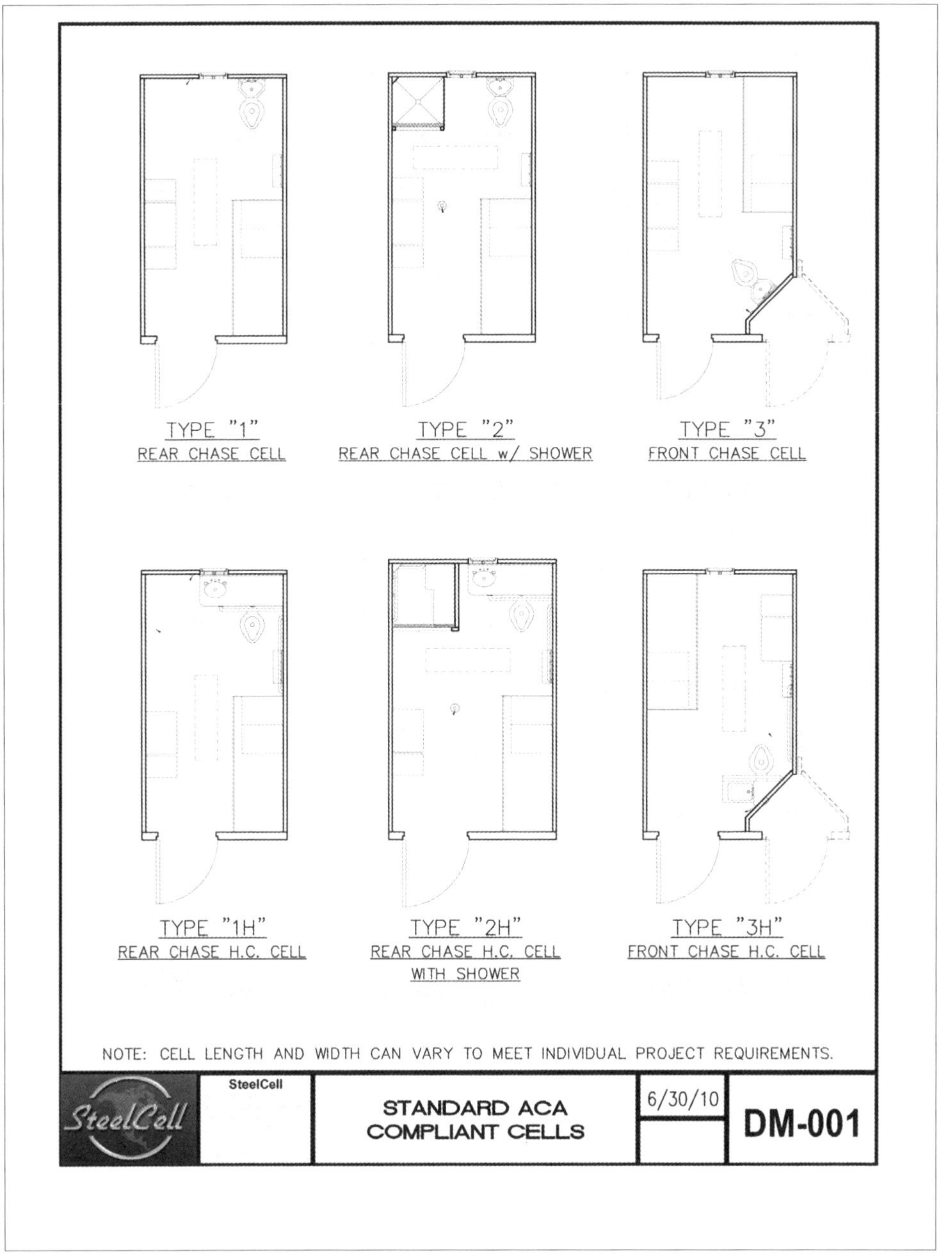

Fig. 1.8
Standard prison cell configurations offered by SteelCell of North America.

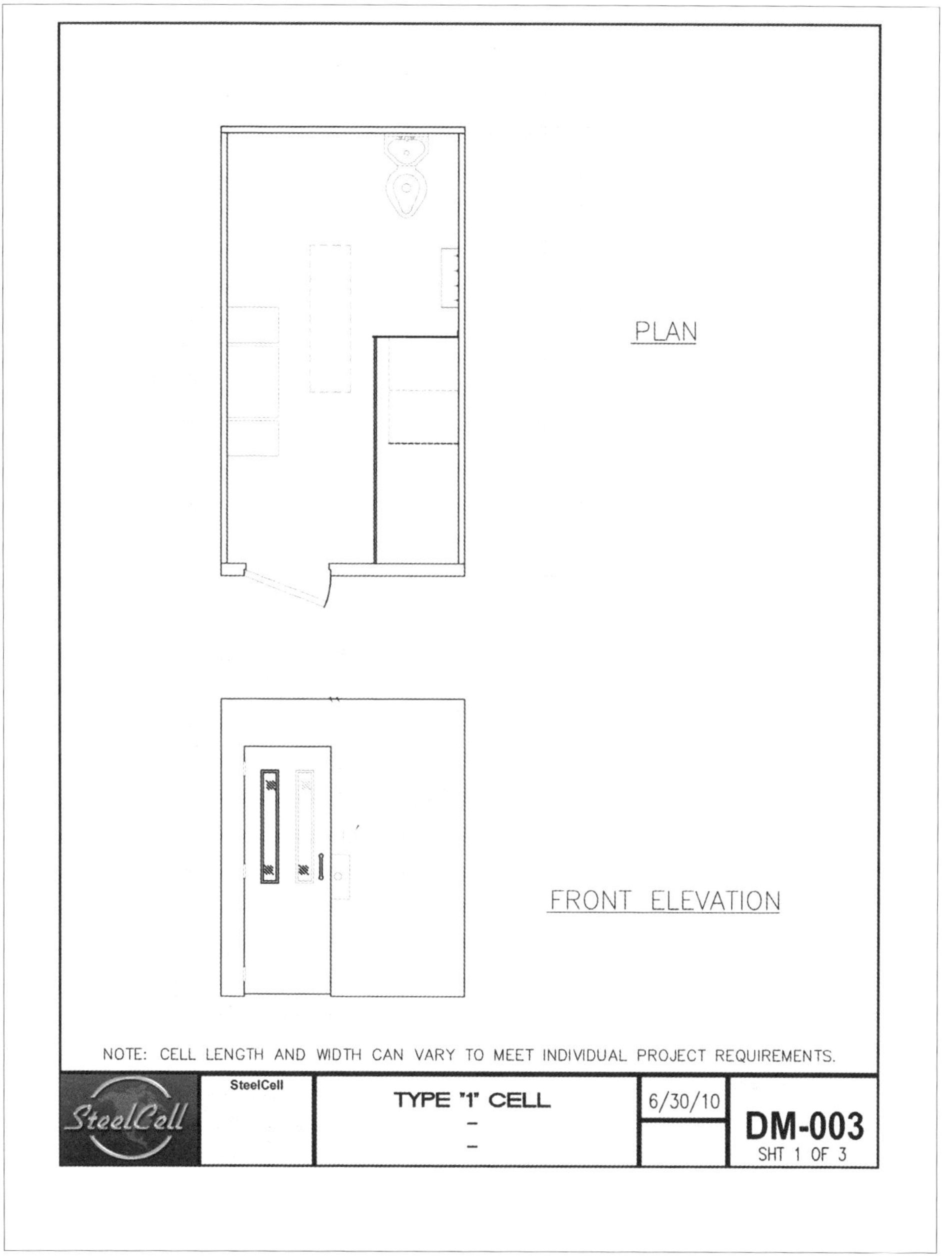

Fig. 1.9
Prefabricated cell similar to those installed at Camp VI, Guantánamo Bay.

22. International Committee of the Red Cross, *ICRC Report on the Treatment of Fourteen "High Value Detainees" in CIA Custody* (Washington, DC: ICRC), 29–32.

23. Carol Rosenberg, "Parole Board Declares Never-Charged Abu Zubaydah a Forever Prisoner," *Miami Herald*, October 26, 2016.

24. Center for Human Rights and Global Justice, *Surviving the Darkness*, 52.

black site locations with little administrative evidence. Zubaydah was one of the first prisoners detained in the war, before many of the later facilities had been erected. He was one of several prisoners taken to Thailand and held in black site "green." During the first stage of his imprisonment he claims to have been confined to boxes of such awkward size he could neither stand nor sit properly in them. To further the effects of claustrophobia and confinement, blankets were often placed around the boxes to restrict airflow. And, at the conclusion of his interrogation, the blankets were left just outside his cell as a constant reminder and thinly veiled threat. The small space, lack of air, and fear of death led Zubaydah to describe his confines as "a coffin."[22] After his interrogation in Thailand he was transferred to Poland and then to Guantánamo Bay, where he remains in captivity. Zubaydah has not been charged with any crime, and he was denied parole in late 2016 by the Guantánamo parole board. He is one of the "forever prisoners" confined to the island indefinitely.[23]

That the design and construction of the black site facilities became more sophisticated while the psychological effects the spaces left on the prisoners remained similar—or in some cases became much worse—speaks to the aesthetics of the prefabricated cell. Describing the conditions in what is believed to be Poland or Romania, Bashmilah states:

> *[T]he ceiling and floor were all painted the same drab grey color and I was not once allowed to see the sun or the sky. . . . As a result I felt sealed in and claustrophobic. I also felt extremely disoriented because I had no idea where I was. The sealed in nature of this facility and the claustrophobia that I experienced contributed to my feeling that this detention facility and the facility in Afghanistan were essentially coffins. It especially felt that way to me because I was innocent. You die a little every day you are in prison because you are in a coffin for the living where you don't see, you don't hear, and there is nothing.*[24]

The switch to prefabricated cells from small concrete rooms or makeshift boxes intensified the loss of visual and environmental stimulation. The generic architectural form of the prefabricated cell led to a decrease of visual detail, as these spaces of confinement were without any unique spatial characteristic that could place the cell in a particular geographic or administrative context. A cell in the Dark Prison, regardless of the treatment, at least conforms to a known type of prison experience: It is loud, dark, wet, cold, and the fear of torture is constant. The mass-produced cell removes all such spatial and territorial markers.

The aesthetic experience of the extraordinary rendition process is one of removal, creating confusion by removing the prisoner from a known context and inhibiting their abilities to process sensory information. Loss of visual information deprives the prisoners of any sort of environmental stimulation so they are, in effect, unable to locate themselves within time, space, or jurisdiction. This architecture simply institutionalized the initial process of arrest and extraction that left prisoners drugged, stripped, diapered, gloved, hooded, goggled, muffled, and bound, to produce total environmental desensitization.

The aesthetic experience of rendition and confinement is a direct result of the production methods used to manufacture the prison cells. Constructed by SteelCell, the cells are produced in a factory designed to maximize material, economic, and logistic efficiencies. These efficiencies produce highly regularized spaces: clean, smooth, and quickly deployed around the world by means of political and economic lubrication. The cells and their political logic minimize the structures of nation-state and international jurisdiction, as well as the cognitive stability of the individual prisoners. Along with their design, governance for these spaces of confinement has been outsourced to the norms and standards of the prison industry. In the end, the same forces that move prisoners around the world also move their spaces of confinement. The complex legal and territorial landscape served as a backdrop to systematically transfer, disperse, and hide both prisoners and prison spaces within a highly designed regime of expansive war powers.

In the end, if Mies's notion of industrialized spatial production can be applied to the black sites, then he had it almost right. In a manifesto-like declaration he pronounced: "The industrial production of all parts can only be truly rationalized during the process of manufacture. Then the work at the building site will be exclusively one of assemblage, and it will be reduced in time to an unsuspected degree."[24]

The process of production *has* created truly rational parts, and with them, seemingly rationalized subjects to be contained therein; subjects reduced to a set of data and information. The unanticipated problem of time was revealed at several scales. Like Mies had championed, the time scale of black site construction was nearly instantaneous, yet their lasting effects would be registered at the temporal scale of human life. His theory of assemblage, however, remains eerily prescient. Assemblage turns out to be both an administrative regime *and* the object of construction. An assemblage of ideologically interpreted laws, recast to disrupt their historical understanding and create spaces beyond their reach. And assembled objects in the form of secret prisons, deployed around the world and used to exploit human bodies rationalized as information.

24. Mies van der Rohe, "Industrial Building," 122.

ACCOUNTABILITY AND ABSTRACTION

1. Conor Friedersdorf, "Dick Cheney Defends the Torture of Innocents," *Atlantic,* December 15, 2014.

2. Shane Harris and Tim Mak, "What the Torture Report Kept Hidden" *Daily Beast,* December 10, 2014, www.thedailybeast.com/articles/2014/12/10/what-the-torture-report-kept-hidden.html.

"The report is seriously flawed."[1]
Former Vice President Dick Cheney, 2014

"How can the public ever decide who is right?"[2]
Mary McCarthy, former CIA officer, Office of the Inspector General, 2014

The long-awaited release of the Senate Select Committee on Intelligence report on the Central Intelligence Agency's EIT program was announced in late 2014 to a flurry of news broadcasts, floor speeches, question dodging, and positioning across the entire political-governmental spectrum. The report promised to be a bombshell, a full reckoning of the illegal and strategically questionable policies that led to prisoners suspected of terrorism, of having knowledge of terrorist-related information, or of supporting terrorist activities, being tortured and possibly killed by US forces, intelligence agencies, or government subcontractors. The report was intended to be a formal acknowledgement of who and what went wrong, of how government policies directly led to prisoner abuse and deaths reported at black sites around the world. The report was supposed to question the "bad apple" theory, which stated only a few rogue and low-level officers went awry and abused some prisoners in contrast to official policy.

The reality of the report was slightly different. It seemed to confirm the critical view that policies regarding the torture of prisoners were formulated at the highest levels of the Bush administration, that certain forms of interrogation were understood to be severe, that the definition of torture was itself open to debate, and that the approved techniques were to be used as needed. Supporters and promoters of the war and defenders of its tactics claimed that the report was seriously flawed, the result of a one-sided political process intent on further discrediting an administration already discredited by unpopular wars. For them, the report was evidence that Democrats were intent on relitigating an episode of America's recent past that had seemingly been forgotten by the public.

That many politicians could read the report and find evidence to fit their prevailing ideology was either proof of their own partisan worldview or that the report was produced in an even-handed and neutral manor. But the political and media reaction to the report's publication showed that it was less a historically accurate compendium of truth and government accountability and more an object open to deep and considered interpretation. In other words, the report had escaped from any sort of governmental communication strategy and landed in the world of interpretive criticism, as an abstracted piece of government communication, purposely opaque and inherently lacking in clarity. The abstract nature of the document was formalized through redaction and missing information—the visual traces of government secrecy. Throughout the report, the black boxes of redaction do more than obscure text, they obscure objective accountability and dislodge the report from any stable, epistemologically verifiable ground on which it might be read.

On December 9, 2014 Dianne Feinstein, the senior senator from California, stood on the senate floor and gave a speech to commemorate the release of the Intelligence Committee's report. Officially titled the *Committee Study of the Central Intelligence Agency's Detention and Interrogation Program* (known as the "Torture Report" in media coverage), the report is the most comprehensive government study of the covert extraordinary rendition and interrogation program instigated by President Bush and administered by the CIA following the September 11 attacks. "The report released today" Feinstein said, "examines the CIA's secret overseas detention of at least 119 individuals and the use of coercive interrogation techniques—in some cases amounting to torture."[3] The report was the culmination of more than five years of research from the Intelligence Committee and its staff, and its release had been anticipated by journalists and Democracts—and feared by former members of the Bush administration and members of the intelligence community.

The Senate Select Committee on Intelligence (SSCI) initiated the report in March 2009. According to Feinstein, the investigation began after a *New York Times* article reported the CIA had destroyed ninety-two videotapes containing evidence of CIA agents conducting "enhanced interrogations"—interrogations defined as torture by the international community that were renamed and designated legal under the Bush administration.

Jose Rodriguez, a CIA agent in Latin America who became head of the agency's Clandestine Service, was found responsible for the destruction of the tapes. Rodriguez claimed the agency waffled in its decision to destroy, or not destroy, some ninety-two tapes documenting suspected terrorist interrogations—including those of Abu Zubaydah, who had been held by the CIA in a black site in Thailand—so he destroyed them without specific directives from CIA director George Tenet. Zubaydah had been waterboarded no less than eighty-three times, and it is likely the tapes contained evidence of the proceedings. In an interview on *60 Minutes*, Rodriguez told correspondent Lesley Stahl that he destroyed all ninety-two interrogation tapes to protect the identities of CIA interrogators. He was concerned that "the distinction between a legally-authorized program as our enhanced interrogation program was, and illegal activity by a bunch of psychopaths would not be made."[4] That is, terrorists would fail to recognize that waterboarding, a practice internationally recognized as torture, had been made

3. Dianne Feinstein, "Senate Intelligence Committee Chairman Dianne Feinstein Remarks on Committee Report on CIA Detention, Interrogation Program," US Senate, December 9, 2014, www.feinstein.senate.gov/public/index.cfm/files/serve/?File_id=c0710e63-f518-40f5-a90d-7e788c9c91a3.

4. "Hard Measures: Ex-CIA Head Defends Post-9/11 Tactics," *60 Minutes*, April 29, 2012, www.cbsnews.com/news/hard-measures-ex-cia-head-defends-post-9-11-tactics/.

Fig. 1.10
Senator Dianne Feinstein presents the executive summary of the SSCI's Central Intelligence Agency's Detention and Interrogation Program. December 9, 2014.

legal by the Bush administration. Rodriguez claims he was worried the tapes could fall into the hands of al-Qaeda or another sympathetic terrorist organization *and* that the CIA could be held accountable for their actions interrogating prisoners.

After several requests to his superiors for permission to destroy the tapes went unanswered, Rodriguez took it upon himself to do so. In his own account, Rodriguez contextualizes the tapes' destruction within the furor surrounding the Abu Ghraib photographs. He claims that journalists were closing in on the location of black site Green, the CIA's secret interrogation site in northern Thailand, and that destroying the tapes was simply "getting rid of some ugly visuals." And so, Rodriguez ordered the tapes destroyed in an industrial shredder until his "problem had been reduced to confetti."[5] The content of the tapes and the dramatic nature in which they were destroyed imbued them with the quality of evidentiary certitude to the existence of torture at the CIA black sites. The lack of transparency surrounding the tapes' destruction compounded by years of reported torture and malfeasance gave Feinstein and the SSCI momentum to begin their investigation.

In the article tipping Feinstein off to Rodriguez's actions, journalist Mark Mazzetti quoted government sources as saying, "The videotapes showed agency operatives in 2002 subjecting terror suspects—including Abu Zubaydah, the first detainee in C.I.A. custody—to severe interrogation techniques. They were destroyed in part because officers were concerned that tapes documenting controversial interrogation methods could expose agency officials to greater risk of legal jeopardy."[6] These reports of potential criminal behavior by the CIA to destroy evidence provided the Intelligence Committee political cover for their investigation.

On March 5, 2009, Feinstein and SSCI vice-chairman Kit Bond, Republican Senator from Missouri, formally announced the bipartisan, one-year investigation to "review the CIA's detention and interrogation program," taking special care to note that it would run parallel to Obama's Executive Order 13491, which constrained CIA detention and interrogation methods.[7] In order to proceed with the investigation and make a thorough conclusion, the SSCI requested documents from all branches of the government, chiefly the CIA.

The SSCI had originally asked for materials related to the EIT program to be handed over directly to the committee, but the CIA balked at a direct handover, insisting the documents be uploaded onto a network and made accessible to the SSCI in only one specific location. Then-CIA director Leon Panetta agreed "to provide literally millions of pages of operational cables, internal emails, memos, and other documents pursuant to the committee's document requests at a secure location."[8] The "secure location" used by the SSCI was leased by the CIA in northern Virginia and operated by CIA information technology officers.[9] The network proved to be both a dumping ground and work space for multiple agencies, allowing the CIA to control which documents were available and when—precisely the type of direct CIA

5. For Rodriguez's account of tape destruction, see Jose A. Rodriguez, *Hard Measures: How Aggressive CIA Actions After 9/11 Saved American Lives* (New York: Threshold Editions, 2012), 193–94.

6. Mark Mazzetti, "C.I.A. Destroyed Tapes of Interrogations," *New York Times*, December 6, 2007.

7. Dianne Feinstein, "Feinstein, Bond Announce Intelligence Committee Review of CIA Detention and Interrogation Program," US Senate, March 5, 2009, www.feinstein.senate.gov/public/index.cfm/press-releases?ID=d882ff87-5056-8059-763f-e15d555d5f89. Executive Order 13491 "ensure[s] compliance with the treaty obligations of the United States, including the Geneva Conventions" and firmly states, "All executive directives, orders, and regulations inconsistent with this order, including but not limited to those issued to or by the Central Intelligence Agency (CIA) from September 11, 2001, to January 20, 2009, concerning detention or the interrogation of detained individuals, are revoked." See Executive Order 13491, January 22, 2011, www.gpo.gov/fdsys/pkg/FR-2009-01-27/pdf/E9-1885.pdf.

8. Dianne Feinstein, "Statement on Intel Committee's CIA Detention, Interrogation Report," US Senate, March 11, 2014, http://www.feinstein.senate.gov/public/index.cfm/press-releases?ID=db84e844-01bb-4eb6-b318-31486374a895.

9. Paul Lewis, "The Documents That Disappeared: How a Furious CIA-Senate Row Erupted," *Guardian*, March 12, 2014, www.theguardian.com/world/2014/mar/12/cia-senate-row-documents-feinstein-brennan.

intervention the SSCI had feared and cautioned against.[10]

In February 2010, frustrated with what she viewed as CIA meddling in the investigation process, Feinstein charged the agency with removing over 870 documents from the network.[11] Feinstein claimed, "This was done without the knowledge or approval of committee members or staff, and in violation of our written agreements. Further, this type of behavior would not have been possible had the CIA allowed the committee to conduct the review of documents here in the Senate. In short, this was the exact sort of CIA interference in our investigation that we sought to avoid at the outset."[12]

If the networked nature of the investigation allowed the CIA to disrupt the committee's proceedings, it also allowed the committee to gain access to a crucial and highly classified report generated from the CIA's own internal review. Known as the "Internal Panetta Review," the report remains one of the most important—and highly classified—documents regarding the EIT program. The eponymous review was undertaken by then-director Leon Panetta in 2009 and consists of over 1,000 pages. The exact content of the review has never been made public, and its existence remains highly controversial within the upper echelons of the CIA and the intelligence community. The *Guardian* reported that the review "was a sensitive, internal assessment of the CIA's detention and interrogation program, which included techniques such as water-boarding that most experts say amounts to torture."[13] In other words, it was the CIA version of the Senate investigation, and it was never intended to be accessed by Feinstein and the SSCI investigators lest it give the SSCI an open admission of CIA wrongdoing. Just how the document was loaded to the shared server and made available to SSCI researchers is unknown. The review could have been placed on the shared network by accident, but Feinstein has speculated that a CIA whistleblower could have placed it there with the direct intent that SSCI investigators find it.[14]

Fallout from the leaked Panetta Review document clouded the continuing Senate investigation. The CIA accused the SSCI of hacking into CIA networks—an accusation the Agency presented to the media and one Feinstein and the SSCI vehemently denied. "To be clear, the committee staff did not 'hack' into CIA computers to obtain these documents as has been suggested in the press," Feinstein said to the Senate, "We have no way to determine who made the Internal Panetta Review documents available to the committee. Further, we don't know whether the documents were provided intentionally by the CIA, unintentionally by the CIA, or intentionally by a whistle-blower."[15] That said, the SSCI quickly realized the importance of the Panetta Review. Fearful that the CIA would realize the report had been posted to a shared network and remove it, SSCI staff members saved electronic copies of the report and even printed portions of it for safekeeping (whether Feinstein approved or even knew of the efforts to make copies at the time is unknown). This fear proved to be well founded. Once the CIA realized the committee had access to the Panetta

10. The shared network was a dumping ground in the literal sense: 6.2 million documents, no index, and no discernable organization.

11. She later claimed fifty more were removed that May.

12. Feinstein, "Statement on Intel Committee's CIA Detention, Interrogation Report."

13. Lewis, "The Documents That Disappeared."

14. Ibid.

15. Feinstein, "Statement on Intel Committee's CIA Detention, Interrogation Report."

Review, they quickly removed it from the shared document network.

The existence of the Panetta Review remained a crucial piece of contested evidence when the SSCI published their findings in late 2014. The review continues to be the only publicly acknowledged internal CIA evaluation of the EIT program. And if media reports and the claims made by the SSCI are true, it exists as—at best—a damning admittance of the program's flaws. At worst, it could provide criminal evidence that the CIA willingly tortured prisoners and openly violated international standards of human rights. Since the disagreement in 2010, the CIA and the SSCI have continued to jostle over how the committee gained access to the file, and what to do with the printed copies the committee staff made from it. As recently as 2015 the CIA was still making requests that all printed copies of the report be "returned immediately."[16]

The Panetta Review remains an integral reference point for both the CIA and the SSCI—an important and missing piece that would help complete both of their EIT program accounts. The CIA claims the SSCI investigation was untruthful or exaggerated. The SSCI claims their report simply reinforces what the CIA had already determined. The veracity of each claim relies on the content of the Panetta Review and the undisclosed remainder of the SSCI report. The two form a missing hole in the center of the investigation—a hole that neither the Obama administration nor any of the post-Panetta CIA directors were interested in filling.[17] Beyond being a keystone that could finally shed some light on the "dark side" of the War on Terror, the fact that the Panetta Review remains not only classified, but potentially destroyed, creates a knowledge vacuum at the center of any quest for accountability. Like other vacuums, it has been quickly filled with partisan attacks, talking points, and endless speculation.

President Obama took office in January 2009 partly on the hopes of those wishing he would prosecute the worst allegations concerning the Bush administration's handling of the War on Terror. There was a desire from certain corners of the political landscape for Vice President Dick Cheney to face responsibility for the "dark side" policies he so vigorously advocated. But the newly elected president didn't fully subscribe to the idea of putting Bush administration policies, or the officials who created them, on trial. Shortly after his election Obama summed up his attitude on matters related to the Bush administration by saying, "We need to look forward as opposed to looking backwards."[18] Early in the Obama administration it was clear officials wanted to move beyond the most divisive and politically damning episodes of the Bush years. And yet, once the Intelligence Committee investigation began, the internal machinations of the CIA and the SSCI correlated with rising hyper-partisanship during Obama's tenure to make the SSCI investigation, and their report, intensely divisive.

The timing of the report's release coincided with the 2014 midterm

16. Mark Mazzetti, "C.I.A. Report Found Value of Brutal Interrogation Was Inflated," *New York Times*, January 20, 2015.

17. Upon leaving office Obama included the full, 6,700 page SSCI report in his personal papers to be archived in his presidential library. According to statute, the report will remain secret for twelve years after he leaves office before it can enter the declassification review process. See Spencer Ackerman, "Senate Torture Report to Be Kept from Public for 12 Years after Obama Decision," *Guardian*, December 12, 2016, www.theguardian.com/us-news/2016/dec/12/obama-senate-cia-torture-report-september-11-classified.

18. Obama quoted in an interview with George Stephanopoulos. See Satyam Khanna, "Obama on Appointing Special Prosecutor to Investigate Bush's Crimes: 'We Need to Look Forward,'" *Think Progress*, January 11, 2009, thinkprogress.org/security/2009/01/11/34654/obama-special-prosecutor-torture.

defeat for the Senate Democrats. The Republican Party regained the majority of the senate, which in turn, gave them control of the Intelligence Committee. Worried a change of leadership would allow the committee to vote against issuing the report in any form, Feinstein decided to release it before committee control officially switched parties in January 2015. The partisan climate on the committee was so strong that the Republican members released their own rebuttal to the committee's report. In it they claimed the Republican views and disagreements were "in response to, and at points predicated upon, the research and foundational work that underlie the Study's account of the CIA Detention and Interrogation Program. These views should not be treated as an independent report based upon a separate investigation, but rather our evaluation and critique of the Study's problematic analysis, factual findings, and conclusions."[19] The weight of the committee report was thus countered by the report from its minority, creating a political conflict not just over content, but also over methodology. Once released, Republicans immediately questioned the report's validity and purpose. Committee member Marco Rubio claimed the report put American lives in danger. Pundits at Fox News questioned the report's timing and claimed Americans only need security, not transparency. Liz Cheney, daughter of former Vice President Dick Cheney, went a step further, calling the report a "crock."[20]

The full Intelligence Committee report is said to be nearly 6,700 pages, and the investigation was reported to have cost over $40 million in taxpayer funds.[21] The report, as presented by Feinstein, the committee, and as discussed more broadly in the media, is technically only the executive summary, a 525-page summary of the full-length document. All 525 pages contain at least partial redactions. In addition, the report contains 2,775 footnotes, many of which are also redacted and reference documents and emails that exist outside the body of the report, and which may or may not be available to the public.

Since the early days of the War on Terror, there has been a drive to uncover and report on the misconduct of the CIA EIT program. Yet the amount of available published material about the program is countered by the open secret that very little of the program's details can be confirmed or denied. The SSCI report, while presented as a type of conclusive document, does very little to bring clarity to the enduring opacity of the program. What the report does is establish twenty key "findings and conclusions," most of which pertain to either the CIA's mismanagement of the program, or the agency's later attempts to cover it up.

The committee denounced the CIA for willfully understating the conditions of confinement under which the detainees were held and the types of treatment to which they were subjected. At the same time, the committee claimed the CIA vastly overstated the value of information they were acquiring from interrogations in disrupting

19. US Senate, *Committee Study of the Central Intelligence Agency's Detention and Interrogation Program, Additional Minority Views,* 2014, www.intelligence.senate.gov/sites/default/files/press/additional-minority.pdf.

20. A compilation of reactions was gathered by *Mother Jones* magazine. See AJ Vicens, "Here Are Some of the Worst Conservative Reactions to the CIA Torture Report," *Mother Jones*, December 9, 2014, www.motherjones.com/politics/2014/12/senate-torture-report-dick-cheney-conservative-responses.

21. Page number fact taken from page 1 of the report; expense from Spencer Ackerman, Dominic Rushe, and Julian Borger, "Senate Report on CIA Torture Claims Spy Agency Lied about 'Ineffective' Program," *Guardian*, December 9, 2014, www.theguardian.com/us-news/2014/dec/09/cia-torture-report-released.

terrorist plots, keeping the military safe, or keeping Americans out of harm's way. One of the most damning findings is the combined condemnation of the program's ineffectualness and the CIA's willingness to appear before the media and pretend otherwise. "The Committee reviewed 20 of the most frequent and prominent examples of purported counterterrorism successes that the CIA has attributed to the use of its enhanced interrogation techniques, and found them to be wrong in fundamental respects."[22] This claim directly contradicts the effectiveness many Bush administration and CIA officials cited as the rationale for the interrogation program.[23] Even after the report's release, many in the CIA continued to make claims about the program's effectiveness in spite of the report's findings.

One day after the report was published, former CIA directors Tenet, Porter Goss, and Michael Hayden along with former CIA deputy directors John E. McLaughlin, Albert M. Calland, and Stephen Kappes wrote an opinion piece for the *Wall Street Journal*. In it they cite the capture and interrogation of Zubaydah and the supposed information he provided as proof of the program's effectiveness. Their joint statement contradicts not only the report's findings but the CIA's own conclusion. In the case of Zubaydah, the report notes testimony given by then-CIA Director Hayden to the SSCI on April 12, 2007, and presents it in direct contrast with information taken from the CIA. Under oath Hayden said:

> *Now in June, after about four months of interrogation, Abu Zubaydah* reached a point where he refused to cooperate and he shut down. *He would not talk at all to the FBI interrogators and although he was still talking to CIA interrogators* no significant progress was being made in learning anything of intelligence value. *He was, to our eye, employing classic resistance to interrogation techniques and employing them quite effectively. And it was clear to us that we were unlikely to be able to overcome those techniques without some significant intervention.*[24]

Yet the CIA's internal records found:

> *At no point during or after the use of the CIA's enhanced interrogation techniques did Abu Zubaydah provide the information sought.*[25]

In the committee hearings Hayden insisted Zubaydah was withholding knowledge vitally important to American security and the ongoing military operations in Afghanistan:

> *We began in 2002, in the spring of 2002. We had one very high value detainee, Abu Zubaydah.* We knew he knew

22. US Senate, *Committee Study*, 2.

23. In a 2011 interview with PBS, CIA attorney John Rizzo said, "I continue to believe that the [Enhanced Interrogation] program was necessary and effective and that there was no practical alternative other than the one we chose. I can't think of a single thing I could have done or would have done differently." See Azmat Khan, "John Rizzo: CIA's Enhanced Interrogation 'Necessary and Effective'," *Frontline*, September 13, 2011, www.pbs.org/wgbh/frontline/article/john-rizzo-cias-enhanced-interrogation-necessary-and-effective.

24. US Senate, *Committee Study*, 462. [Emphasis in original]

25. Ibid., 463.

26. Ibid., 465. [Emphasis in original]

27. Ibid.

28. Ibid., 466.

29. Ibid., 471.

30. For the CIA directors' statement, see "Ex-CIA Directors: Interrogations Saved Lives," *Wall Street Journal*, December 10, 2014. Other journalists have correlated Seymour Hersh's account of the walk in but it should be noted that Hersh's use of unnamed sources has been widely criticized by both former administration officials and other journalists. Hersh continues to stand by his informants' claims. For an interview between Hersh and journalist Bob Garfield discussing the journalistic questions raised by Hersh's essay, see "Seymour Hersh, NYC Nail Salons, and Ebola-Free Liberia," *On the Media*, May 15, 2015, www.wnyc.org/story/on-the-media-2015-05-15. For Hersh's original article see, Seymour M. Hersh, "The Killing of Osama bin Laden," *London Review of Books*, May 21, 2015.

> a lot. He would not talk. We were going nowhere with him. *The decision was made, we've got to do something. We've got to have an intervention here. What is it we can do?*[26]

In contrast, the internal CIA documents questioned the value of the intelligence garnered from interrogating Zubaydah, acknowledged the enhanced interrogation techniques did not yield any further useful information, and revealed that the CIA's own interrogators objected to the techniques:

> *As detailed elsewhere, numerous individuals had been detained and subjected to the CIA's enhanced interrogation techniques, despite doubts and questions surrounding their knowledge of terrorist threats and the location of senior al-Qa'ida [sic] leadership.*[27]

> *A quantitative review of Abu Zubaydah's disseminated intelligence reporting indicates that more intelligence reports were disseminated from Abu Zubaydah's first two months of interrogation—prior to the use of the CIA's enhanced interrogation techniques—than were derived during the two-month period during and after the use of the CIA' s enhanced interrogation techniques.*[28]

> *During the interrogation of Abu Zubaydah, CIA personnel at DETENTION SITE GREEN objected to the continued use of the CIA's enhanced interrogation techniques against Abu Zubaydah, stating that it was "highly unlikely" Abu Zubaydah possessed the threat information CIA Headquarters was seeking.*[29]

In addition to claiming the program's effectiveness, in their joint statement the former CIA heads reaffirm their stance that the CIA interrogations revealed information locating Osama bin Laden: "Specifically, information developed in the interrogation program piqued the CIA's interest in the courier, placing him at the top of the list of leads to bin Laden." This claim has been widely disputed and was vigorously challenged by journalist Seymour Hersh in an essay in the *London Review of Books*. According to Hersh, bin Laden was located through a simple informant, "It began with a walk-in. In August 2010 a former senior Pakistani intelligence officer approached Jonathan Bank, then the CIA's station chief at the US embassy in Islamabad. He offered to tell the CIA where to find bin Laden in return for the reward that Washington had offered in 2001."[30]

With the CIA withholding the Panetta Review, and large sections

UNCLASSIFIED

~~TOP SECRET//~~[redacted]~~//NOFORN~~

X. Appendix 3: Example of Inaccurate CIA Testimony to the Committee-April 12, 2007

Testimony of Michael V. Hayden, Director, Central Intelligence Agency to the Senate Select Committee on Intelligence, April 12, 2007[2553]

CIA Testimony	Sampling of Information in CIA Records
The Interrogation of Abu Zubaydah	
DIRECTOR HAYDEN: "Now in June, after about four months of interrogation, Abu Zubaydah *reached a point where he refused to cooperate and he shut down.* He would not talk at all to the FBI interrogators and although he was still talking to CIA interrogators *no significant progress was being made in learning anything of intelligence value.* He was, to our eye, employing classic resistance to interrogation techniques and employing them quite effectively. And it was clear to us that we were unlikely to be able to overcome those techniques without some significant intervention."	Abu Zubaydah was rendered to CIA custody on March [redacted], 2002. The CIA representation that Abu Zubaydah stopped cooperating with debriefers who were using traditional interrogation techniques is not supported by CIA records. In early June 2002, Abu Zubaydah's interrogators recommended that Abu Zubaydah spend several weeks in isolation from interrogation while the interrogation team members traveled [redacted] "as a means of keeping [Abu Zubaydah] off-balance and to allow the team needed time off for a break and to attend to personal matters [redacted]," as well as to discuss "the endgame" for Abu Zubaydah [redacted] with officers from CIA Headquarters. As a result, Abu Zubaydah spent much of June 2002 and all of July 2002, 47 days in total, in isolation. When CIA officers next interrogated Abu Zubaydah, they immediately used the CIA's enhanced interrogation techniques, including the waterboard. Prior to the 47 day isolation period, Abu Zubaydah provided information on al-Qa'ida activities, plans, capabilities, and relationships, in addition to information

[redacted]

[2553] Transcript at DTS #2007-3158. The CIA's June 2013 Response states: "We disagree with the *Study's* conclusion that the Agency actively impeded Congressional oversight of the CIA Detention and Interrogation Program. …As discussed in our response to Conclusion 9, we also disagree with the assessment that the information CIA provided on the effectiveness of the program was largely inaccurate. Finally, we have reviewed DCIA Hayden's testimony before SSCI on 12 April, 2007 and do not find, as the *Study* claims, that he misrepresented virtually all aspects of the program, although a few aspects were in error.…The testimony contained some inaccuracies, and the Agency should have done better in preparing the Director, particularly concerning events that occurred prior to his tenure. However, there is no evidence that there was any intent on the part of the Agency or Director Hayden to misrepresent material facts." The CIA's June 2013 Response states that the CIA has "identified a number of broad lessons learned" and includes eight recommendations. The CIA's only recommendation related to Congress was: "Recommendation 8: Improve recordkeeping for interactions with Congress. Direct the Director of the Office of Congressional Affairs (OCA) and the Chief Information Officer to develop a concrete plan to improve recordkeeping on CIA's interactions with Congress. OCA's records going forward should reflect each interaction with Congress and the content of that interaction. OCA should work with the oversight committees to develop better access to transcripts of CIA testimony and briefings. This plan should be completed within 90 days of the arrival of a new Director of OCA."

~~TOP SECRET//~~[redacted]~~//NOFORN~~

Page 462 of 499

UNCLASSIFIED

Fig. 1.11
Page 462 of the SSCI report showing the difference between testimony given by CIA Director Michael Hayden to the Intelligence Committee and the CIA's own findings.

of the SSCI report redacted, there will continue to be competing claims about the veracity of CIA and Intelligence Committee claims about the interrogation program. But the report does present certain bits of concrete evidence. Of the 119 listed individuals known to have been captured and interrogated by the CIA, twenty had not been acknowledged previously, and at least thirty-nine are now known to have been subject to enhanced interrogation. Most of the detainees were captured in 2002 and 2003, with the last detained in 2007. Some details pertaining to specific CIA interrogations are documented, in particular those related to the abuse suffered by Zubaydah and Khalid Sheikh Mohammed. But for the most part, the report confirms what had already been widely reported: prisoners held by the CIA were tortured, their interrogations resulted in very little useful information or actionable intelligence, and whatever information was obtained could have been acquired through traditional interrogation procedures.

Another aspect of the EIT program the report keeps classified is the locations of black-site facilities, referring to them only by color-coded names. In all there were ten or eleven acknowledged sites (and their unconfirmed locations): Cobalt (Salt Pit, Afghanistan), Blue—also known as Quartz—(Poland), Black (Romania), Violet (Lithuania), Brown (Afghanistan), Grey (Afghanistan), Green (Thailand), Orange (Afghanistan), Red (location unknown), Indigo (Guantanámo Bay), and Maroon (Guantánamo Bay).[31] Journalists and human-rights experts had already reported most of this information, but the list of sites given in the investigation is narrower than longer lists of presumed sites offered elsewhere, such as the General Intelligence Department site in Amman used to hold Mohamed Farag Ahmad Bashmilah. The color-coded sites refer not to the complete network, but only to sites run by the CIA. Proxy locations operated by third-party governments like the General Intelligence Department, the Palestinian Branch in Syria, al-Tamara Prison in Morocco, or the Tora Prison in Egypt are not included, nor is there any mention of their existence. The only reference to outsourcing in the report regards CIA contractors. It is clear from the redactions that the exact locations of the prisons, the individual prisoners held in each, and the agents administering the interrogations will remain classified. The committee members themselves best summed up the limits to the report's efficacy, "A full accounting of CIA detentions and interrogations may be impossible, as records in some cases are non-existent, and, in many other cases, are sparse and insufficient."[32]

Beyond the partisan spectacle into which it was released, the report does not express any admittance of CIA wrongdoing, nor is it a fully formed account of the rendition and interrogation program. With the redactions and acknowledgement of a larger, more complete finding, the report marks a continuation of black site information management. In contrast to its intended purpose, the report amplifies the

31. Proposed locations from the online archive Cryptome, see "CIA Torture Pseudonyms Update," Cryptome, December 15, 2014, www.cryptome.org/2014/12/cia-torture-nyms.htm. There are ongoing questions about the existence of site Red, it appears only once in the report (on footnote 848, page 140). It is speculated that it is a separate location within another site. I might also propose that it is a typo, and "RED" is the first part of "REDACTED."

32. US Senate, *Committee Study*, 13.

noise surrounding the extraordinary rendition and detention program to the detriment of any discernable signal. This is not to say the report was made in vain, nor that the information it does contain is without purpose. But its use does not derive from bringing accountability to any of the seemingly illegal actions executed in the name of security and freedom. What the report accomplishes, despite its drawbacks, is to illuminate the inner workings of governance and the bureaucratic apparatus established to *perform* transparency and accountability, while in reality doing no such thing. The report can be seen as an object-form of the "antiepistemology" of secrecy that asks not how information can be openly shared and disseminated but "how knowledge can be covered and obscured."[33]

At the time of its publication, the report was only the latest in a long lineage of government investigations and publications purporting to reveal the deeper truth about a contested history. The most famous of these is likely the Warren Commission Report that confirmed the prevailing government account stating Lee Harvey Oswald was the lone gunman responsible for President John F. Kennedy's assassination. However, the Warren Commission has done very little to silence the conspiracy industry that continues to flourish around Kennedy's death. Daniel Patrick Moynihan claims that conspiracies are born together with secrets.[34] Other commissions that performed a similar role to the Senate Intelligence Committee report include the Roberts Commission, established to investigate the attacks on Pearl Harbor; the Rockefeller Commission, established to examine alleged CIA activities inside the US; the Church Committee, another investigation into internal CIA spying; the Tower Commission, which investigated the Iran-Contra affair; and of course the 9/11 Commission, which investigated the attacks of the day and ended in its own controversial report. In many ways the 9/11 Commission is a specter haunting the Intelligence Committee work and its subsequent publication. The Senate Intelligence report is slightly different from most of these previous publications in that the investigation originated in the Senate and not the executive office (with the exception of the Church Commission), but the outcome—a daunting, difficult to read, bound report—is the same: putting to rest an issue in a way that appears exhaustive and uncontestable, but in reality is neither.

The work of the 9/11 Commission was released in July 2004 as *The 9/11 Commission Report*. It was widely available for purchase and became an industry bestseller. A year later, W.W. Norton & Company announced that over a million copies of the paperback had been sold. It was even named a finalist for the National Book Award, one of the highest honors for American publishing. The literary success of *The 9/11 Commission Report* was not lost on publishers as the release date for the SSCI report on the CIA approached. But whereas Norton won a contract from the commission to sell the publication in return for a modest $10 cover price and a release date coinciding with the commission's public release, no such deal was made by the Intelligence

33. Galison, "Removing Knowledge": 237.

34. Daniel Patrick Moynihan, *Secrecy: The American Experience* (New Haven, CT: Yale University Press, 1998), 98–99.

UNCLASSIFIED

~~TOP SECRET//~~[redacted]~~//NOFORN~~

intelligence on KSM's [redacted],[1855] and sought other opportunities to gain access to KSM through [redacted].[1856] In July 2002, a detainee in foreign government custody provided extensive information on KSM's [redacted] and confirmed that KSM was "very close" to [redacted] who "should know how to contact KSM."[1857]

(~~TS//~~[redacted]~~//NF~~) When the CIA finally located and met again with ASSET X on [redacted], 2002, ASSET X stated that "he could [redacted] within a few weeks," and was "willing to travel [redacted] to locate [redacted]."[1858] ASSET X was recruited as a source by the CIA, but, despite his offer to track KSM's [redacted], ASSET X was dispatched by the CIA to [redacted].[1859] [redacted].[1860]

[1855] *See* CIA [redacted] [redacted], disseminated as [redacted].

[1856] CIA officers proposed recontacting a 1995 asset with possible access to KSM through [redacted]. (*See* email from: [REDACTED]; to: Jose Rodriguez, [redacted], [redacted], [redacted], [redacted], [REDACTED], [REDACTED]; cc: [REDACTED], [REDACTED], [REDACTED], [REDACTED], [REDACTED], [REDACTED]; subject: Finding Khalid Sheikh Muhammad; date: [redacted], 2002, at 06:49:13 PM.) The email was resent, on [redacted], 2002, to additional addressees. (*See* email from: [REDACTED]; to: [REDACTED], [REDACTED], [REDACTED], [redacted]; cc: subject: Finding Khalid Sheikh Muhammad; date: [redacted], 2002, at 3:46:13 PM.) At this point, the nefarious activities of KSM's [redacted] were of significant interest to the Intelligence Community and policymakers. KSM's [redacted] terrorism were briefed to the President and were the subject of a direct tasking by the Deputy Secretary of Defense. *See* ALEC [redacted]; ALEC [redacted].

[1857] The detainee was [redacted] [DETAINEE S], [redacted]. *See* [redacted] 66193 [redacted]; [redacted] 31049 [redacted]; [redacted] 31223 [redacted], disseminated as [redacted]; [redacted] 31088 [redacted]; [redacted] 31140 [redacted]; DIRECTOR [redacted]; [redacted] 31221 [redacted], disseminated as [redacted]; [redacted] 31339 [redacted]; [redacted] 31049 [redacted]; [redacted] 31424 [redacted], disseminated as [redacted]).

[1858] [redacted] 2770 [redacted]; [redacted] 2773 [redacted]; [redacted] 2778 [redacted]. At this time, the CIA offered a compensation package that was increased from the CIA's previous offer.

[1859] [redacted] 1062 [redacted]; [redacted] 1107 [redacted]; [redacted] 1101 [redacted]; DIR [redacted]; [redacted] 37701 [redacted]; [redacted] 41495 [redacted]; Interview of [REDACTED], by [REDACTED], 14 October 2004, CIA Oral History Program; Interview of [REDACTED], by [REDACTED], 14 September 2004, CIA Oral History Program. During this time period, ASSET X reported that he had made contact with KSM's [redacted] (*See* [redacted] 10084 [redacted]; [redacted] 10090 [redacted]; [redacted] 1088 [redacted]; DIRECTOR [redacted].) Also during this period, CIA officers [redacted] continued to note that ASSET X had offered to locate KSM's [redacted]. (*See* [redacted] 2812 [redacted] 481096 [redacted].) [redacted] *See* email from: [redacted]; to: [REDACTED]; cc: [REDACTED], [redacted], [redacted]; subject: another for the highlights; date: [redacted], 2002, at 4:14:24 PM.

[1860] [redacted] 37701 [redacted]; [redacted] 41495 [redacted]

~~TOP SECRET//~~[redacted]~~//NOFORN~~

Page 330 of 499

UNCLASSIFIED

Fig. 1.12
Page 330 of the SSCI report. A heavily redacted page of the report on the interrogation of Khalid Sheikh Mohammed, noted here at "KSM."

Committee for its report.[35] Instead Melville House, a small publisher in downtown Brooklyn, took it upon themselves to take the publicly available PDF, retype it, reformat it, and then publish it as a standalone book. Dennis Johnson, cofounder and copublisher of Melville House, understood his desire to publish the report not as an opportunity to acquire public documents and flip them for profit, but as a patriotic and important duty along the lines of providing troops in the Revolutionary War with copies of Thomas Paine's "Common Sense."[36] Luckily for Johnson, like *The 9/11 Commission Report*, there was an audience for the SSCI report. The initial 50,000 copy print run sold out almost immediately.

The commercial success of the report illuminates a public desire to read about the government's covert interrogation practices, although it is impossible to compare book sales with PDF downloads or to those who actually *read* the document. In a *New Yorker* article about Melville House's all-nighter publication quest, Alexandra Schwartz suggests why it's important for an independent publisher to take on such a thankless task: "The report is in the public domain and freely available online, but, for reasons of form as well as of content, it's hell to read."[37] As released by the committee, the report appeared to be a scan of a document. It was low-resolution and unsearchable. It was filled with redactions and footnotes and redactions *in* footnotes. By downloading and opening the report, it was clear the report existed not just as a useable document—which is to say as text and information, easily discernable facts and a coherent story—but as an object, meant to be pored over and analzyed, deciphered, and questioned. The report appeared more as an abstract idea of a report, since it contained within it all the aesthetic signifiers of an important government transmission. In reality, it was presented less like an objective and dispassionate truth on the given subject and more like an object of abstract art—difficult to access and receptive to politically and ideologically weighted criticism.

In her introduction to a survey of writings on abstraction and visual art, Maria Lind notes that certain power structures have taken on "the artistic gesture of abstraction." She goes on to claim, "We are beyond the aestheticization of politics—now politics are closer to pure perception and become aesthetics as such."[38] Lind makes a claim that politics is a predominantly affective experience governed not by empirical truth, shared knowledge, or established fact but an experience mediated through aesthetic practices. Thus, abstraction, with its foundation in unstable meaning, becomes a primary aesthetic register for the affective experiences mediating the relationship between subject and state.

Art historian Kirk Varnedoe claims that abstraction is "most successful and effective when association and meaning appear out of touch." He continues, "The absence of resemblance allows the work to embrace a great range of intuitions barely imaginable before the work was done, and only marginally present in the artist's conscious

35. For details on *The 9/11 Commission Report* publication, including Norton's announcement to donate $600,000 in profits to charity, see Edward Wyatt, "Publisher Names 9/11 Charities," *New York Times*, July 21, 2005.

36. For details on Melville House and their process publishing the report, see Alexandra Schwartz, "Turning the Torture Report into a Book," *New Yorker*, December 19, 2014.

37. Schwartz, "Turning the Torture Report into a Book."

38. Lind is referencing a work by Hito Steyerl and quotes a comment by Brian Massumi on the post-September 11 color-coded security alerts. See Maria Lind, "Introduction," in *Abstraction*, ed. Lind (Cambridge, MA: MIT Press, 2013), 19.

39. Kirk Varnedoe, "Why Abstract Art," in Lind, *Abstraction*, 59.

40. The *Oxford English Dictionary* defines abstraction as, "The action of taking something away; the action or process of withdrawing or removing something from a larger quantity or whole." See "abstraction, n.," OED Online, Oxford University Press, December 2016, www.oed.com/view/Entry/766?redirectedFrom=abstraction#eid.

41. Jacques Rancière, *The Politics of Aesthetics: The Distribution of the Sensible* (London: Continuum, 2004), 13.

intention."[39] Varnedoe is describing one of the underlying dictates of abstraction in its aesthetic form, that there is some type of artistic intention, but through the formal composition of nonrepresentation, meaning and association become disconnected. To go one step further, meaning might be nonexistent. In other words, the work of abstraction may simply result in aesthetic form—even highly intentional form—without any sort of underlying semiotic or symbolic referent.

At its root, abstraction does not mean to hide or obscure but to withdraw, to divert. The logic of abstract rationality claims withdrawal not as a vestige of the author's aesthetic will, but as a driving logic behind a work's creation.[40] This thinking can be applied to abstract art and government reports alike, with the same result: the cloaking of meaning and a purposeful obfuscation of underlying intent—an aesthetic antiepistemology.

Through abstraction, withdrawing information, displacing the historical record, and withholding verifiable facts, become the *desired* outcomes behind certain methods of government communication and the performance of accountability. Jacques Rancière claims that this is simply what politics is: the management of the aesthetic. The management of what is seen and what is not. "Politics revolves around what can be seen and what can be said about it, around who has the ability to see and the talent to speak."[41]

The methods of visual obfuscation available to government bureaucracies and nation states, including redaction and secrecy, are administrative methodologies and bureaucratic structures established to remove information from sight and control discourse through the management of facts. Both redaction and secrecy were routinely deployed in the SSCI report. The black boxes of redaction serve as aesthetic signifiers that a withdrawal has taken place. If obfuscation is one goal of redaction, then instigating a discourse without established knowledge and agreeable facts is the driving logic behind the charade of accountability registered through abstract aesthetic practices. In the case of government-sponsored torture and any attempt to bring clarity and accountability to the rendition program instigated by the CIA, formal abstraction through heavily redacted and endlessly footnoted reports serves many purposes. Publication-with-redaction maintains the useful ignorance of plausible deniability. It entrenches the mechanics of bureaucracy as a substitute for due diligence and accountability. And, most important of all, it portends to a thorough uncovering of knowns, all the while presenting and validating only unknowns.

PART 2

AN ATLAS OF EXTRAORDINARY RENDITION

Countries with Known Black Site Facilities
Guantánamo Bay
Indigo
Maroon

Source: US Senate, *SSCI Report*.

Countries with Reported Black Site Operations
Morocco
Algeria
Mauritania
Gambia

Source: Ross, "Rendition and the 'Global War on Terrorism'."

Bagram Airfield, Afghanistan

Site Codename
"Gray"

Location
34°56′41.96″ N
69°15′48.62″ E

Fig. 2.1
Bagram Airfield, Afghanistan. October 7, 2004.

Site Unknown, Afghanistan

Site Codename
"Brown" or "Orange"

Location Unknown

Dark Prison, Afghanistan (possibly same as Salt Pit)

Site Codename
"Brown" or "Orange"

Location Unknown

Salt Pit, Afghanistan

Site Codename
"Cobalt"

Location
34°34′38.27″ N
69°17′11.60″ E

Fig. 2.2
Salt Pit, outside Kabul, Afghanistan. May 19, 2004.

Guantánamo Bay, Cuba
Site Codenames
"Indigo" and "Maroon"
Possible Aliases
"Camp VII", "Camp No", "Strawberry Fields"
Possible Locations
19°54′50.51″ N
75° 7′19.71″ W
19°54′25.37″ N
75° 6′36.98″ W
1. Camp I
2. Camp II/III
3. Camp IV
4. Camp V
5. Camp VI
6. Camp VII, Camp No, Strawberry Fields (Possible Locations)
7. Camp Echo
6
6

Fig 2.3
Guantánamo Bay, Cuba. September 19, 2016.

Fig. 2.4
Site Violet prior to prison renovation, outside Antaviliai, Lithuania. July, 27, 2002.

Fig. 2.5
Site Blue, Stare Kiejkuty, Poland. April 14, 2004.

Bucharest, Romania

Site Codename
"Black"

Alias
"Bright Light"

Location
44°28′4.05″ N
26° 2′45.40″ E

Fig 2.6
Site Black, North Bucharest, Romania.
April 5, 2009.

Site Unknown, Thailand

Site Codename
"Green"

Alias
"Cat's Eye"

Possible Locations
Udon Thani Voice of America broadcast facility
17°40′26″ N
103°12′8″ E

Near Chiang Mai International Airport
18°46′00″ N
98°57′45″ E

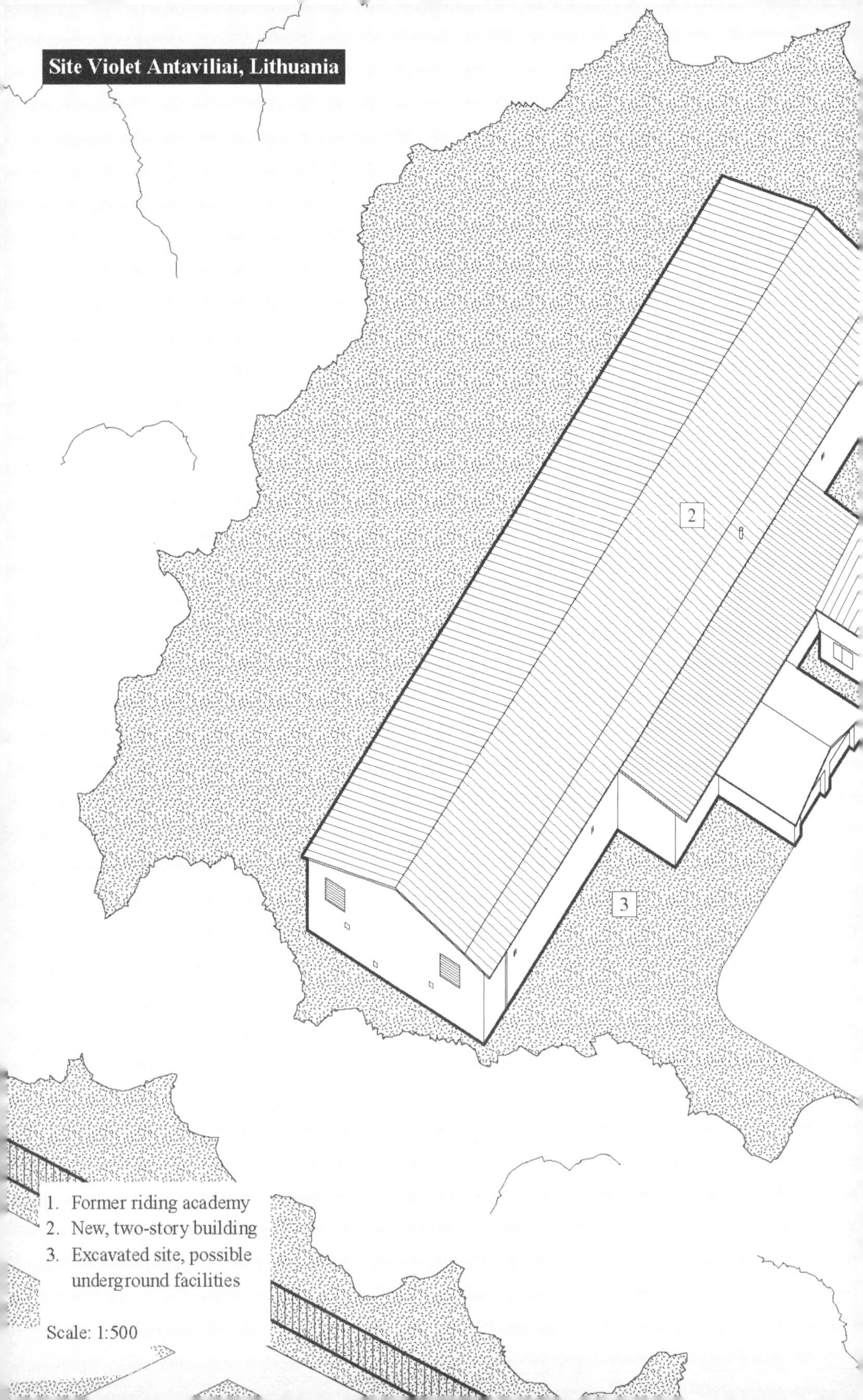
Site Violet Antaviliai, Lithuania
2
3
1. Former riding academy
2. New, two-story building
3. Excavated site, possible underground facilities
Scale: 1:500

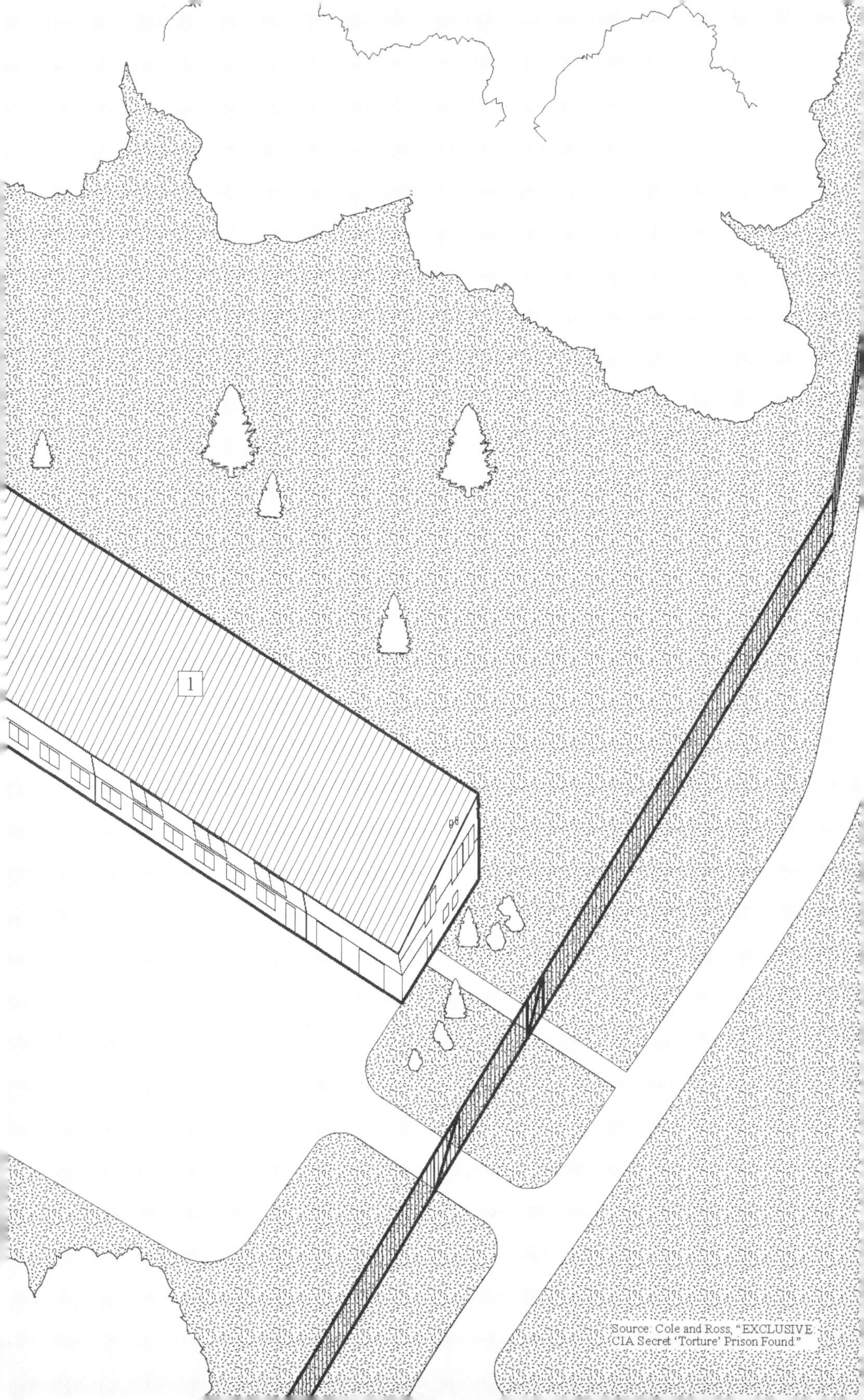

Source: Cole and Ross, "EXCLUSIVE: CIA Secret 'Torture' Prison Found."

Site Black Bucharest, Romania

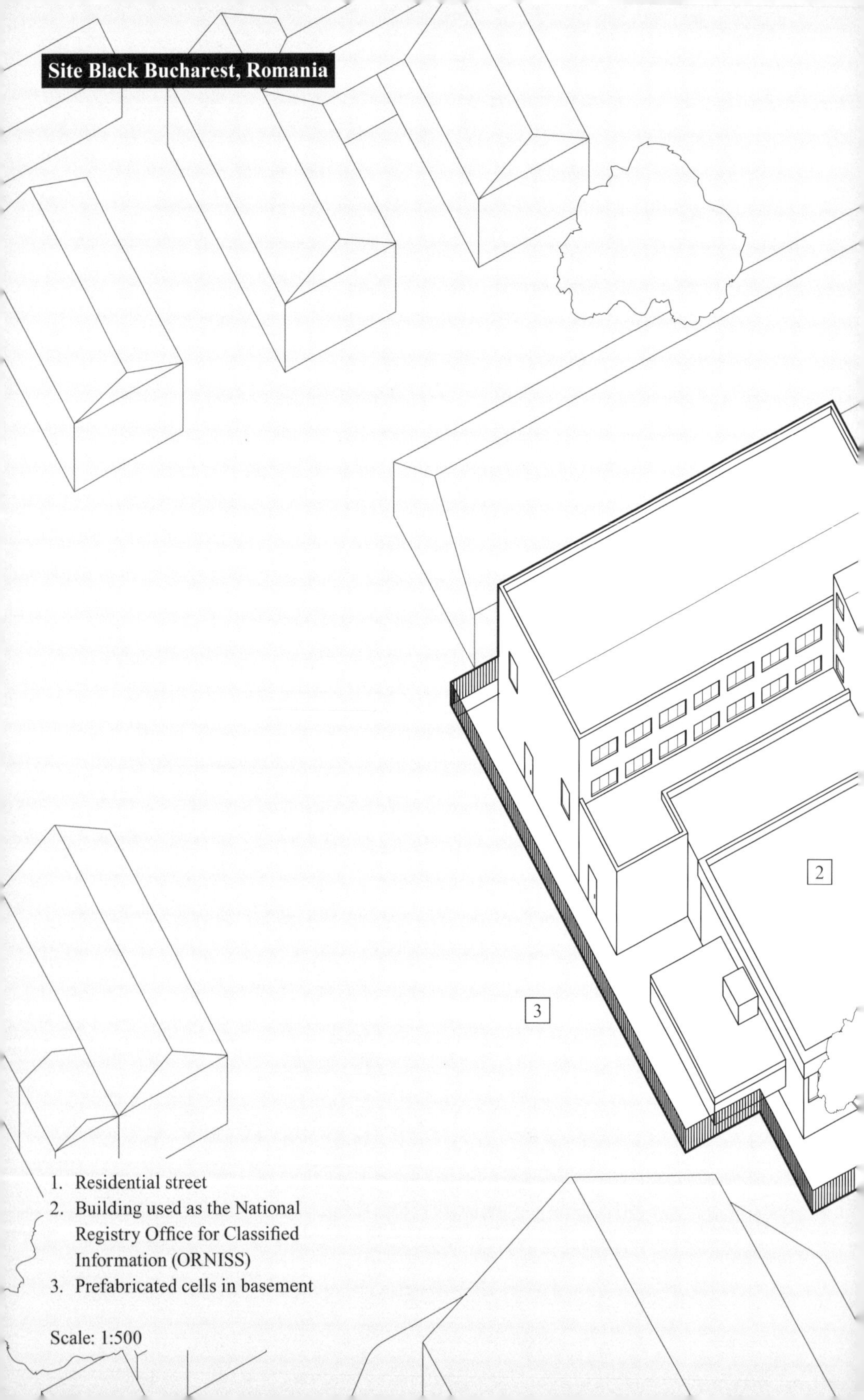

1. Residential street
2. Building used as the National Registry Office for Classified Information (ORNISS)
3. Prefabricated cells in basement

Scale: 1:500

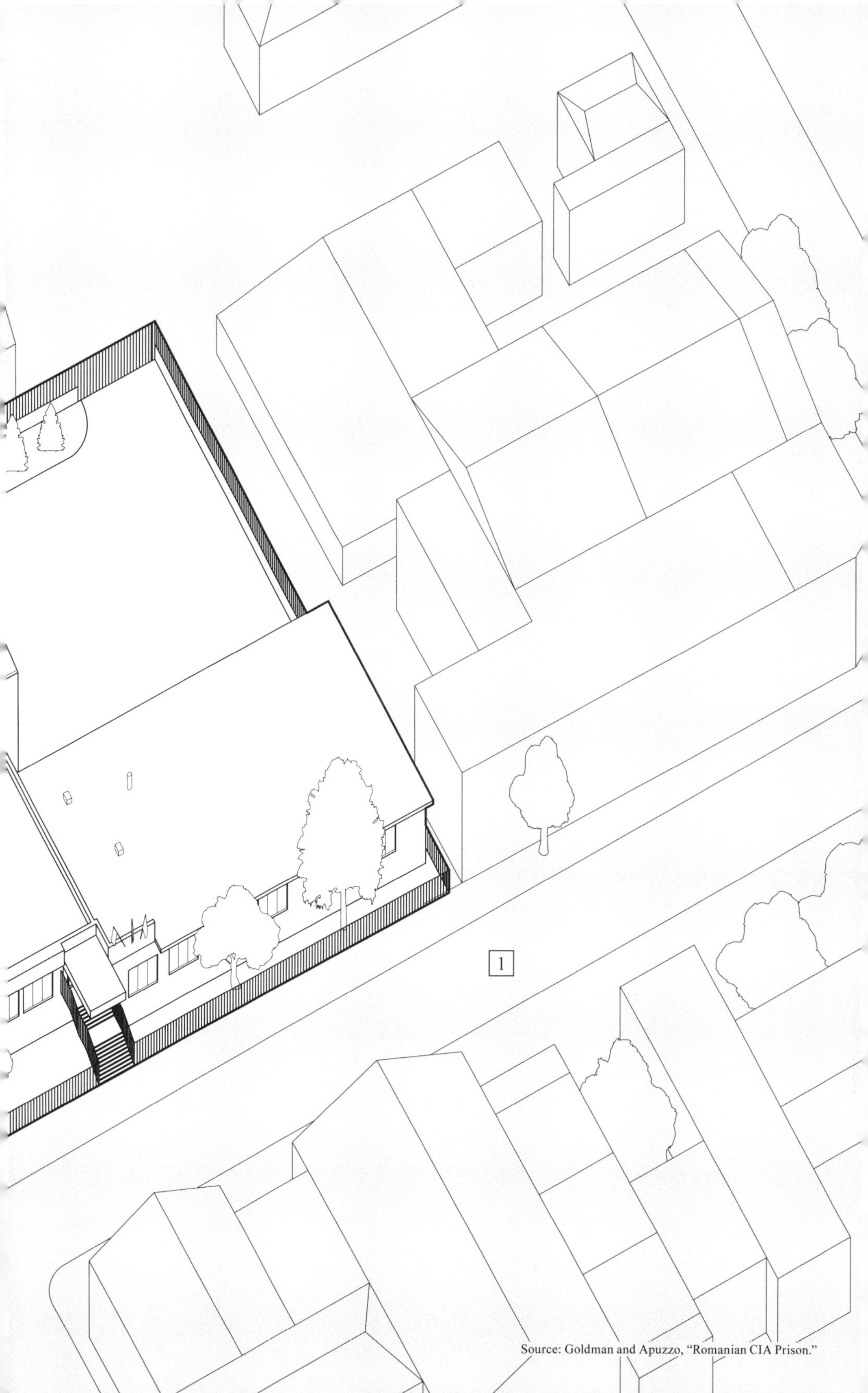

Source: Goldman and Apuzzo, “Romanian CIA Prison.”

Salt Pit, Afghanistan

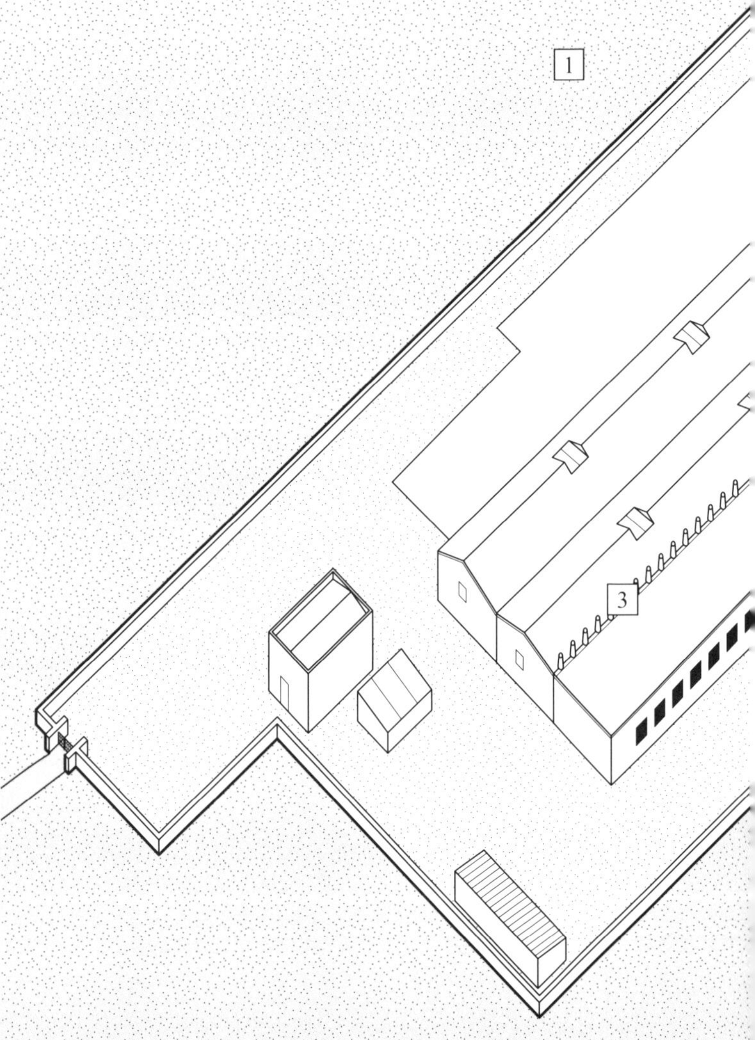

1. Former brick factory north of Kabul
2. Twenty cells inside prison
3. No insulation, no heating or cooling systems
4. Windows covered with two coats of black paint and curtains

Scale: 1:2200

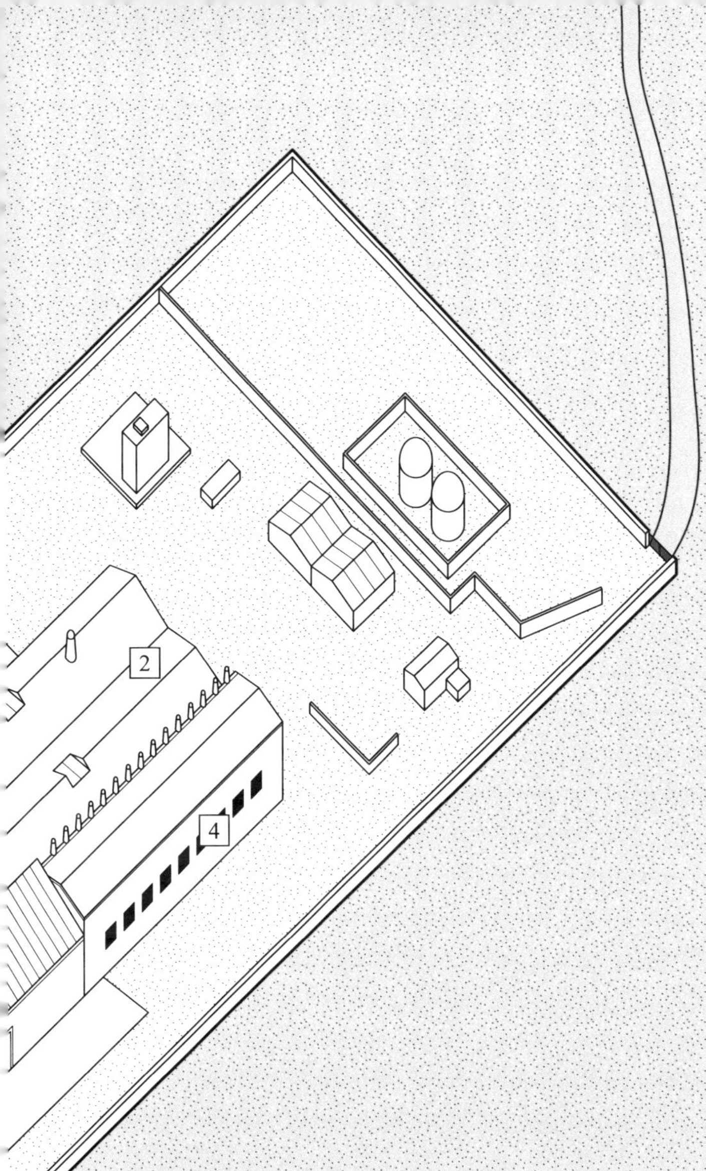

Source: Central Intelligence Agency,
Death Investigation—Gul RAHMAN.

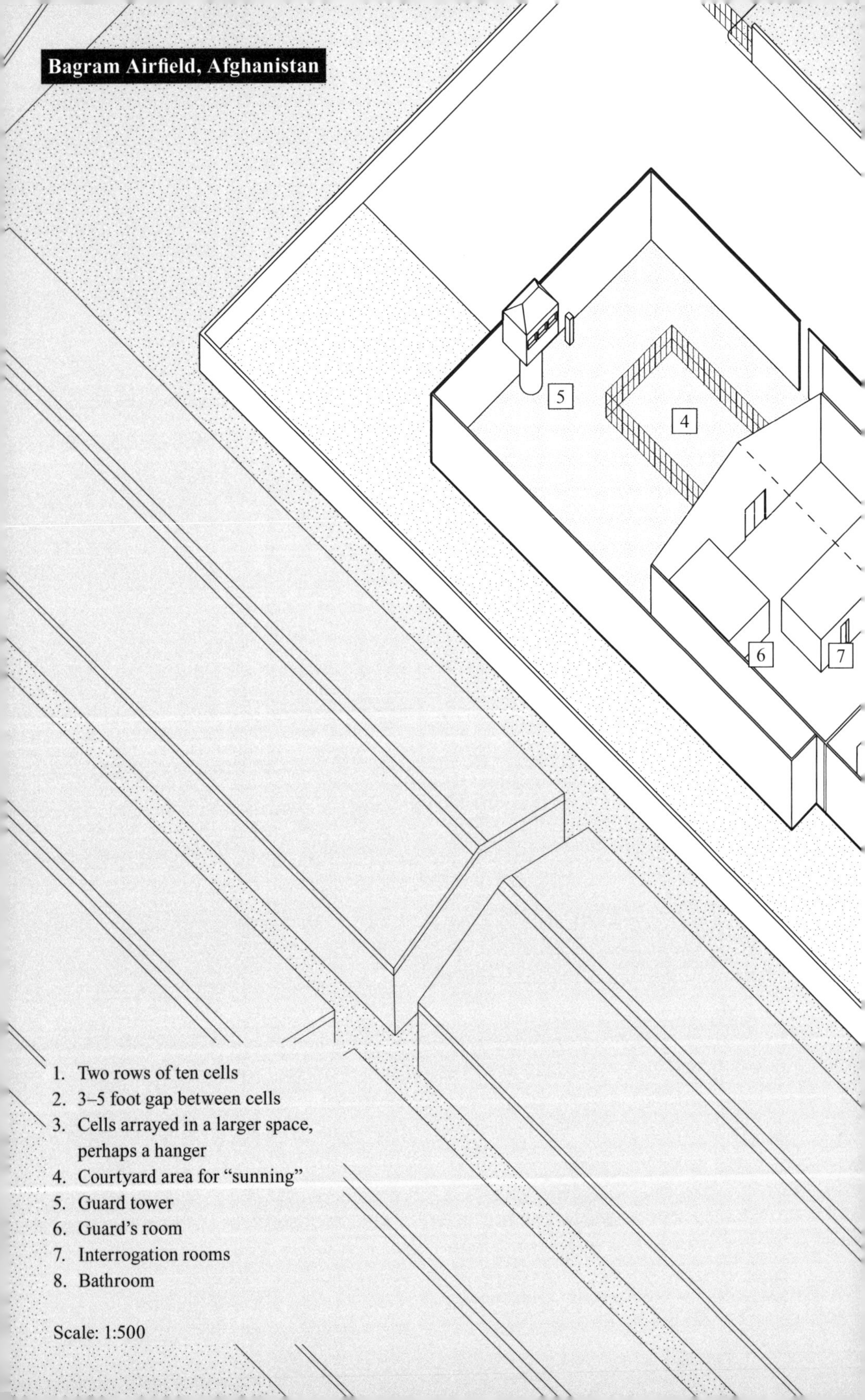

Bagram Airfield, Afghanistan

1. Two rows of ten cells
2. 3–5 foot gap between cells
3. Cells arrayed in a larger space, perhaps a hanger
4. Courtyard area for “sunning”
5. Guard tower
6. Guard’s room
7. Interrogation rooms
8. Bathroom

Scale: 1:500

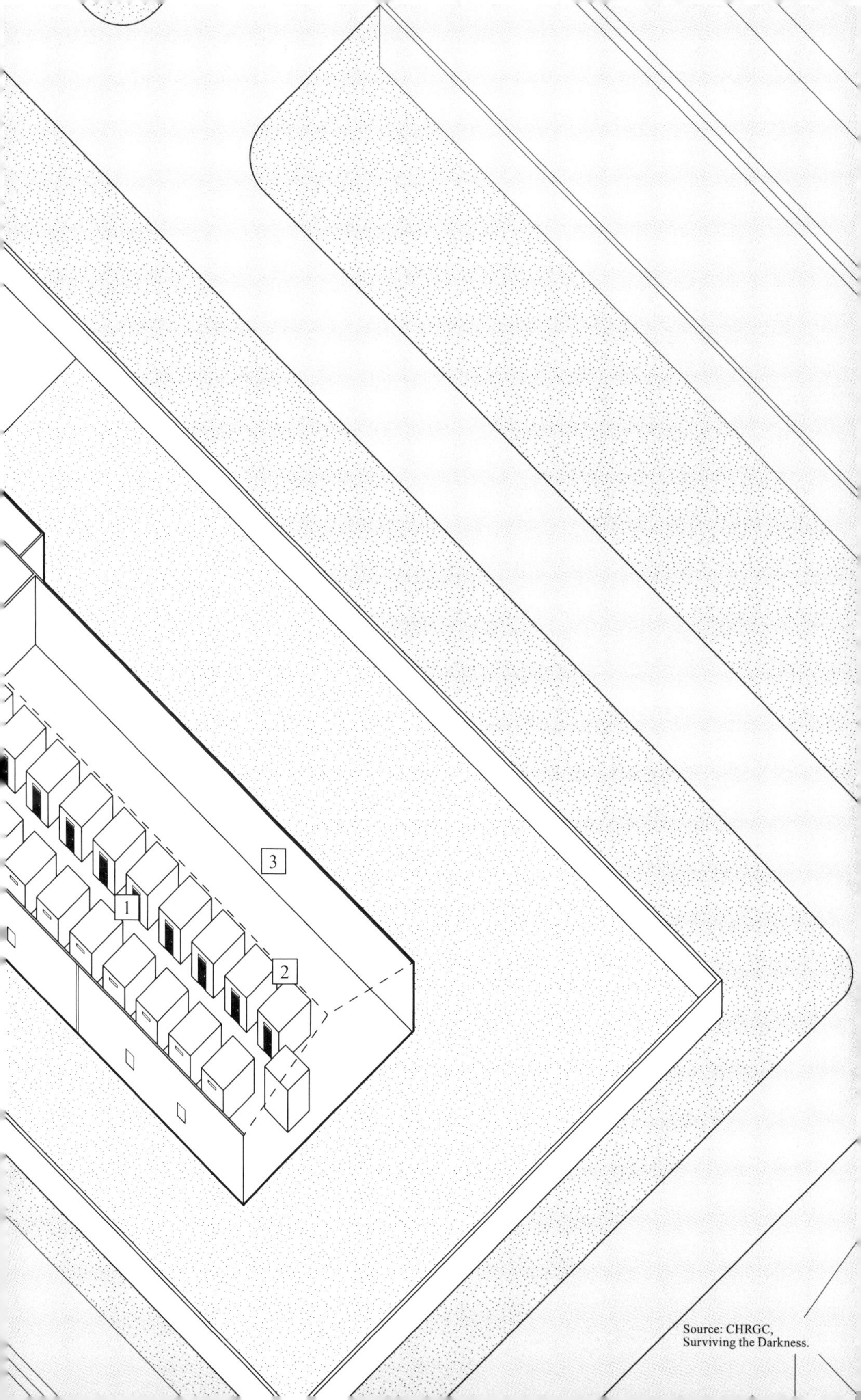

Source: CHRGC,
Surviving the Darkness.

Interrogation Room, Bagram Airfield, Afghanistan

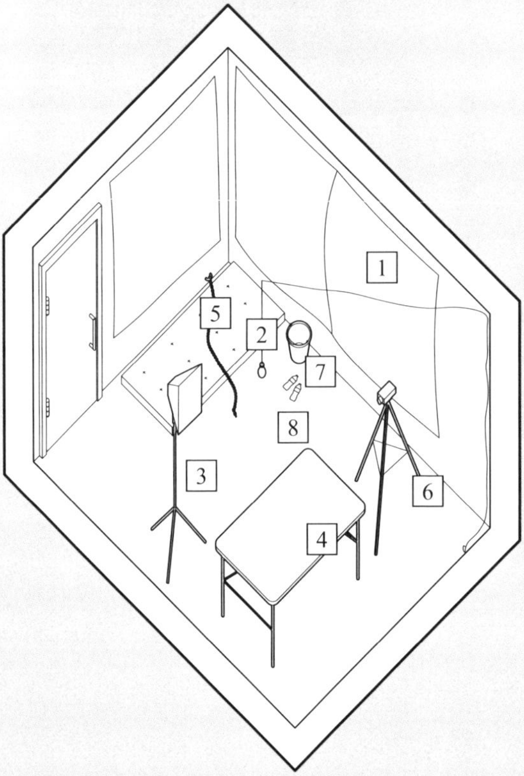

1. Cloth hanging from wall
2. Bare lightbulb
3. Interrogation lights
4. Table
5. Shackle attached to wall
6. Camera on tripod
7. Bucket for toilet
8. Nestlé water for drinking and ablutions

Scale: 1:80

Source: CHRGC, *Surviving the Darkness,* 24.

Interrogation Room, Site Violet, Lithuania

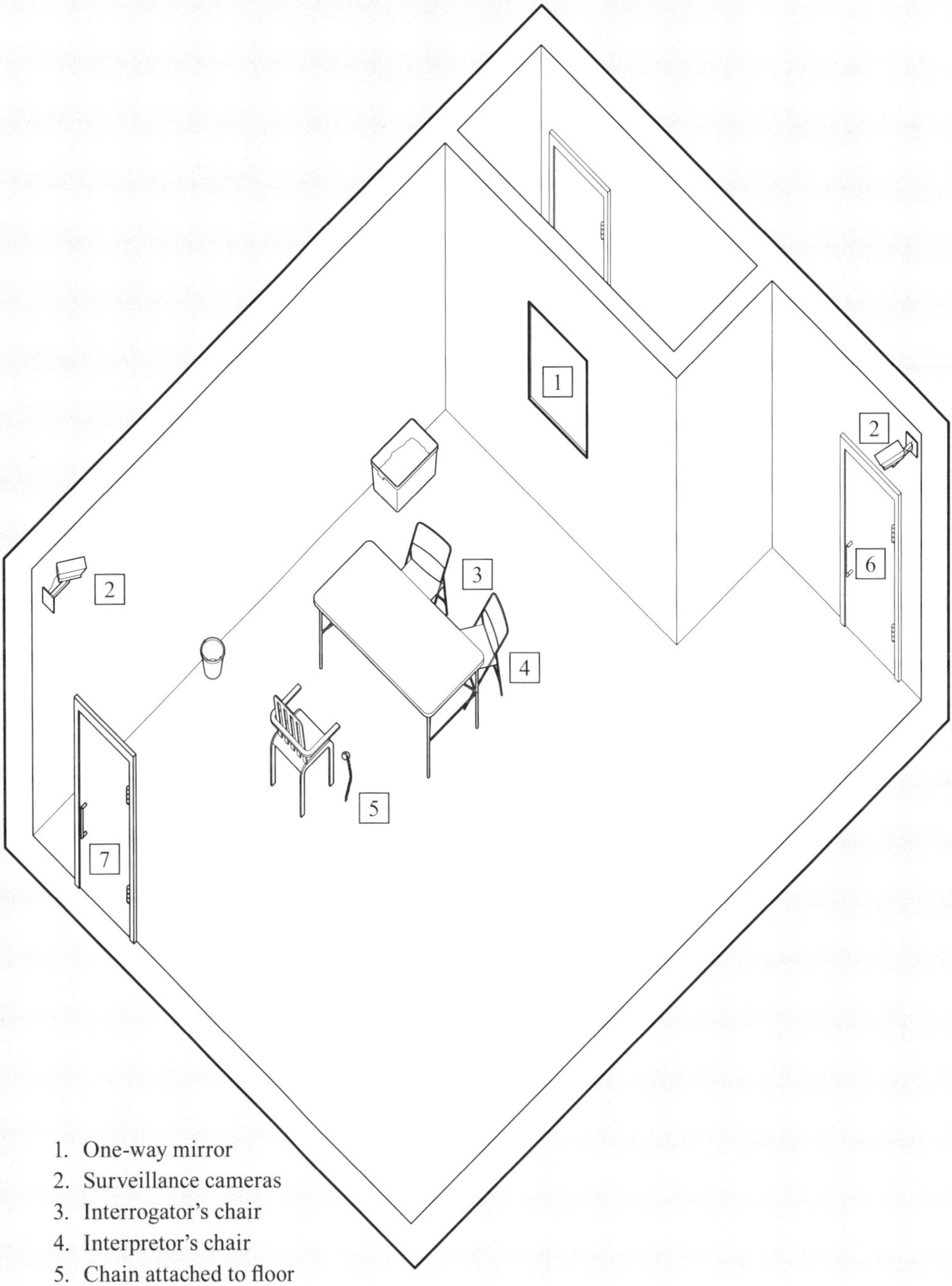

1. One-way mirror
2. Surveillance cameras
3. Interrogator's chair
4. Interpretor's chair
5. Chain attached to floor
6. Guard entrance
7. Prisoner entrance

Scale: 1:80

Source: CHRGC, *Surviving the Darkness,* 42.

Holding Cell, Site Green, Thailand

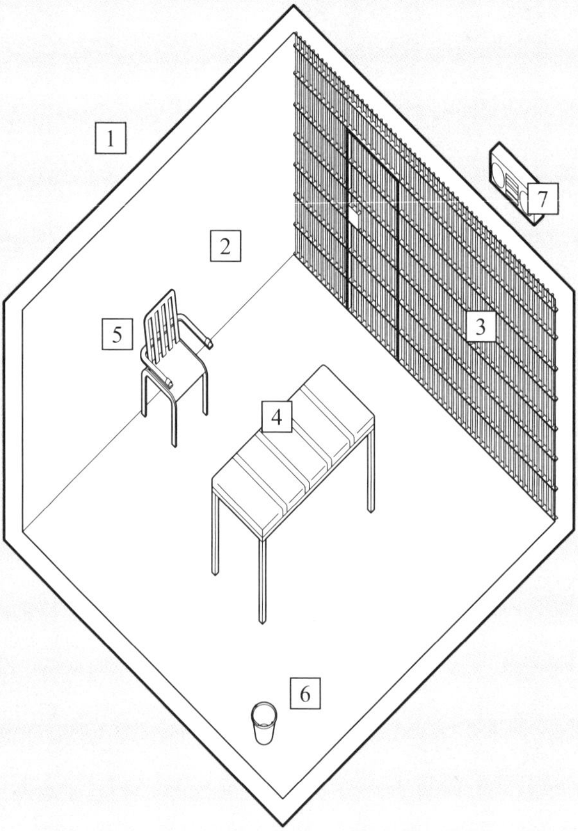

1. Approximately 12′ x 12′ room
2. Room painted white
3. Three solid walls, one with bars
4. Bed with restraints
5. Chair with restraints
6. Bucket for toilet
7. Constant music playing

Scale: 1:80

Source: ICRC, *ICRC Report*, 28.

Detention Cell, Site Violet, Lithuania

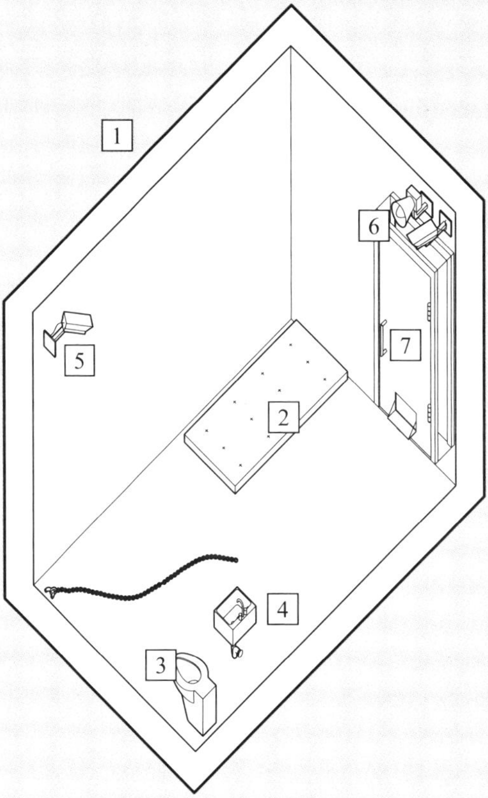

1. Approximately 8′ x 13′ cell
2. Mattress
3. Stainless steel toilet
4. Stainless steel washbasin
5. Camera
6. Camera and speaker
7. Double door

Scale: 1:80

Source: CHRGC, *Surviving the Darkness*, 43–45.

Bathroom, Site Violet, Lithuania

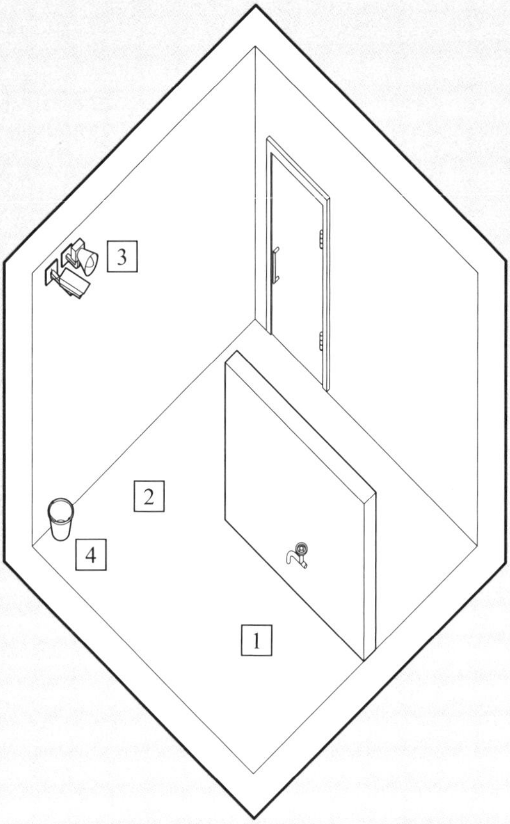

1. Shower area
2. Guard position
3. Camera and speaker
4. Trashcan

Scale: 1:80

Source: CHRGC, *Surviving the Darkness,* 43–45.

Detention Cell, Site Black, Romania

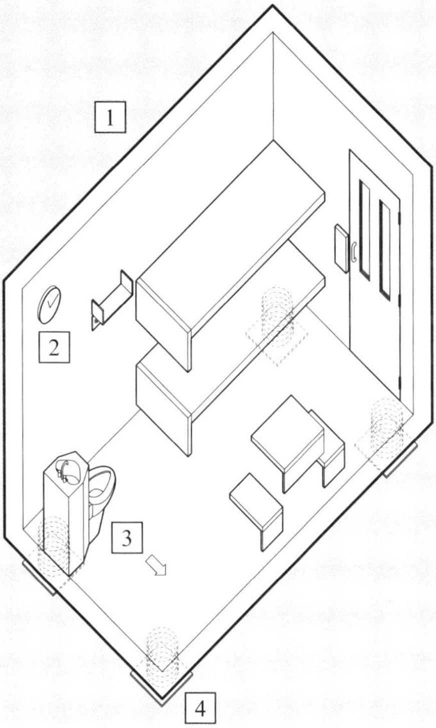

1. Prefabricated cell
2. Clock
3. Arrow pointing to Mecca
4. Springs to destabilize prisoners

Scale: 1:80

Source: Goldman and Apuzzo, "Romanian CIA Prison."

Detention Cell, Bagram Airfield, Afghanistan

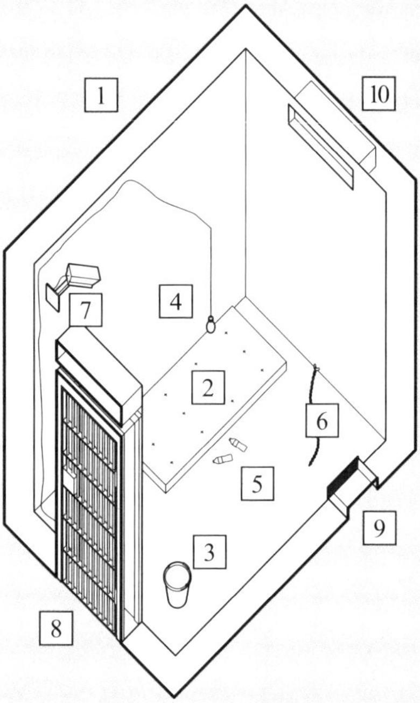

1. Approximately 10′ x 13.25′ cell
2. Foam mattress
3. Bucket for toilet
4. Bare light bulb
5 Nestlé water for drinking
6. Chain attached to wall and prisoner wrist
7. Camera
8. Double door
9. Opening at floor level
10. Opening at ceiling level

Scale: 1:80

Source: CHRGC, *Surviving the Darkness*, 22–23.

Razor Wire Cell, Bagram Airfield, Afghanistan

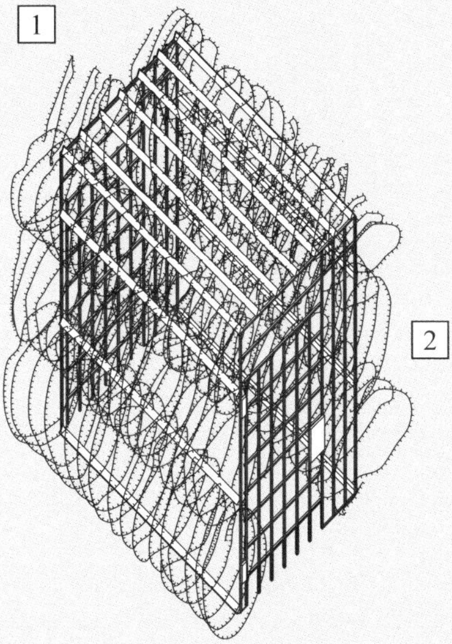

1. “Sally port” temporary detention cell
2. Razorwire

Scale: 1:80

Source: Rose, “Why Bagram is Guantanamo’s Evil Twin.”

Detention Cell, Site Cobalt, Afghanistan

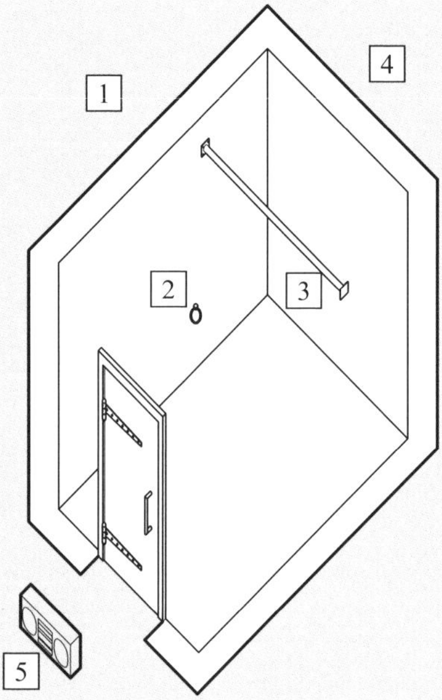

1. Stand alone concretete box
2. Metal ring on wall for tying prisoners
3. Metal bar for hanging
4. Cell block windows covered with two coats of black paint and heavy curtains
5. Constant music playing

Scale: 1:80

Source: Central Intelligence Agency, *Death Investigation—Gul RAHMAN.*

Detention Cell, Dark Prison, Afghanistan

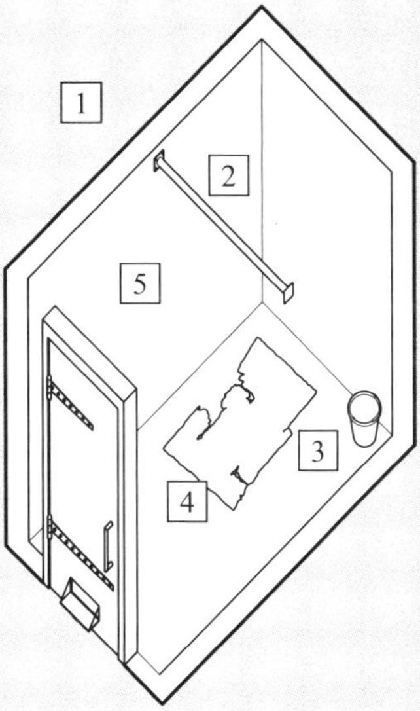

1. Approximately 3′ x 6.5′ cell
2. Metal bar for hanging
3. Bucket for toilet
4. Tattered blanket on ground
5. No natural or artificial light

Scale: 1:80

Source: ICRC, *ICRC Report*, 31.

Interrogation Cell, Guantánamo Bay

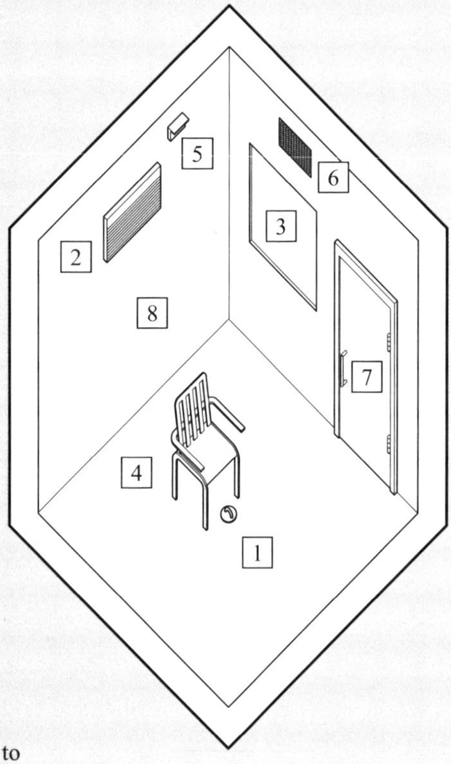

1. Anchor on floor attached to prisoner ankles
2. Air conditioner vent
3. One-way mirror
4. Easily cleaned plastic chair
5. Strobe lights
6. Speakers
7. Completely sealed door
8. Walls painted white or covered in paper to reduce stimulation

Scale: 1:80

Source: Human Rights Watch, *Guantanamo: Detainee Accounts,* 11–12; US Senate, *SSCI Report,* 137–138.

False Wall, Site Unknown, Afghanistan

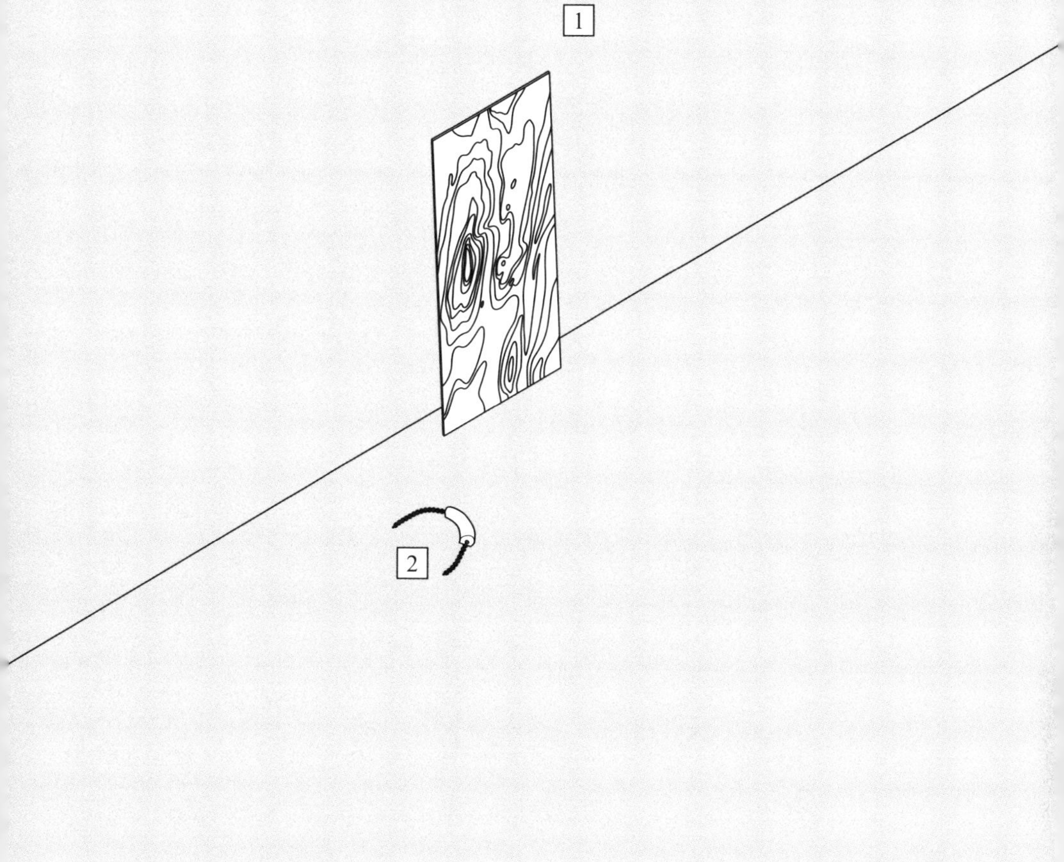

1. Room with wooden wall
2. Ring with foam placed around prisoner neck and used to swing prisoner into wood wall

Scale: 1:80

Source: Human Rights Watch, *Delivered Into Enemy Hands,* 52.

Confinement Box, Site Unknown, Afghanistan

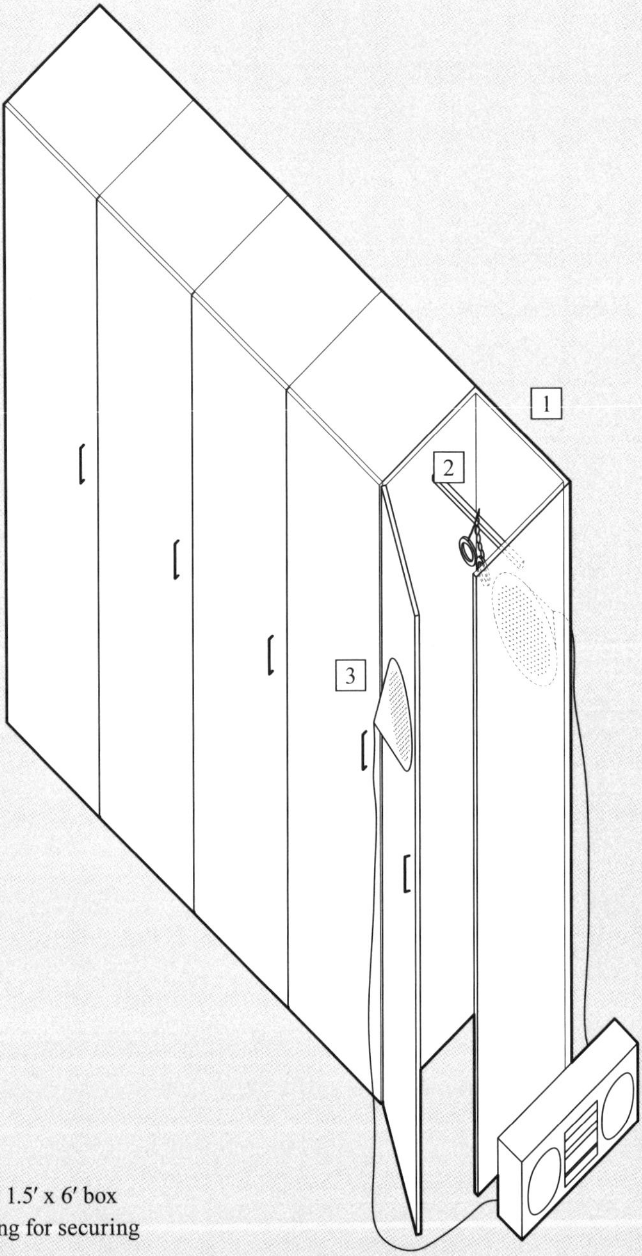

1. Approximately 1.5′ x 6′ box
2. Bar along ceiling for securing prisoner wrists
3. Speaker built into side of box

Scale: 1:30

Source: Human Rights Watch, *Delivered Into Enemy Hands*, 45.

Confinement Box, Site Unknown, Afghanistan

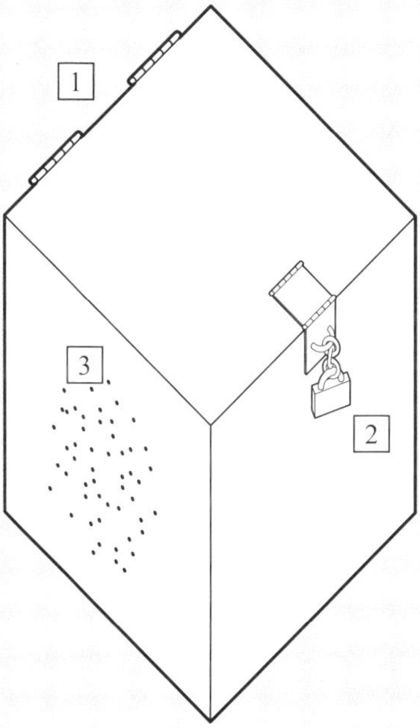

1. Approximately 3′ x 3′ box
2. Secured with lock
3. Holes for air and prodding

Scale: 1:30

Human Rights Watch, *Delivered Into Enemy Hands*, 52.

Confinement Boxes, Site Green, Thailand

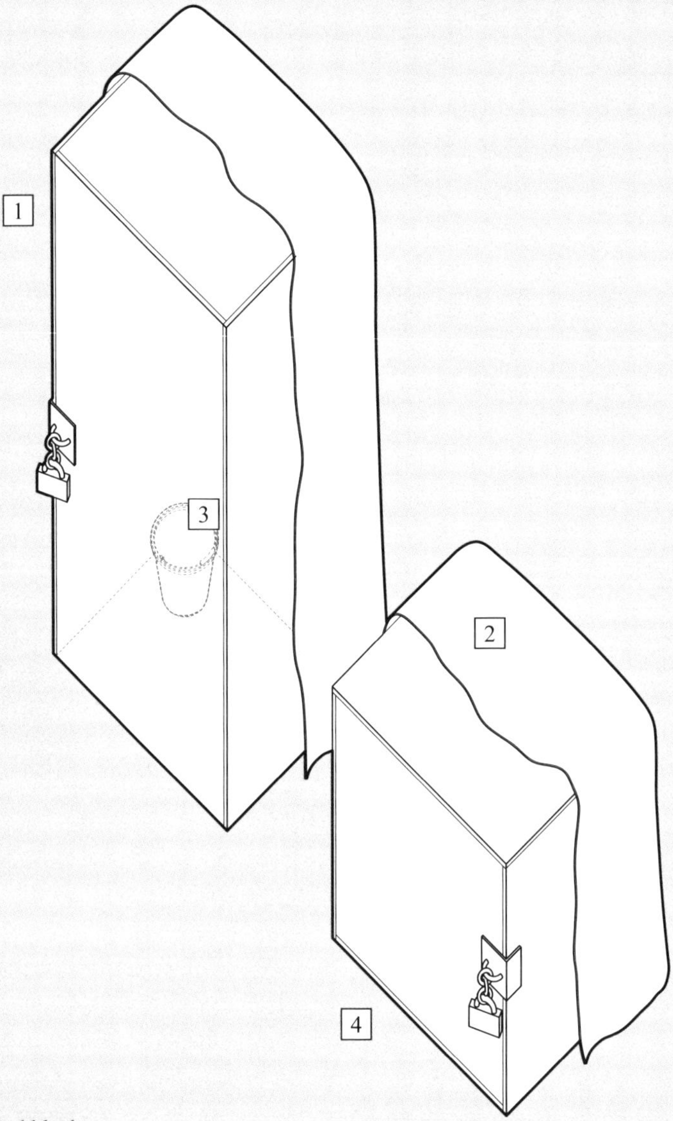

1. Boxes painted black
2. Cloth to restrict light and air
3. Bucket for toilet
4. Small box, too small to sit upright

Scale: 1:30

Source: ICRC, *ICRC Report,* 29–30.

Water Boarding/Water Bath, Site Unknown, Afghanistan

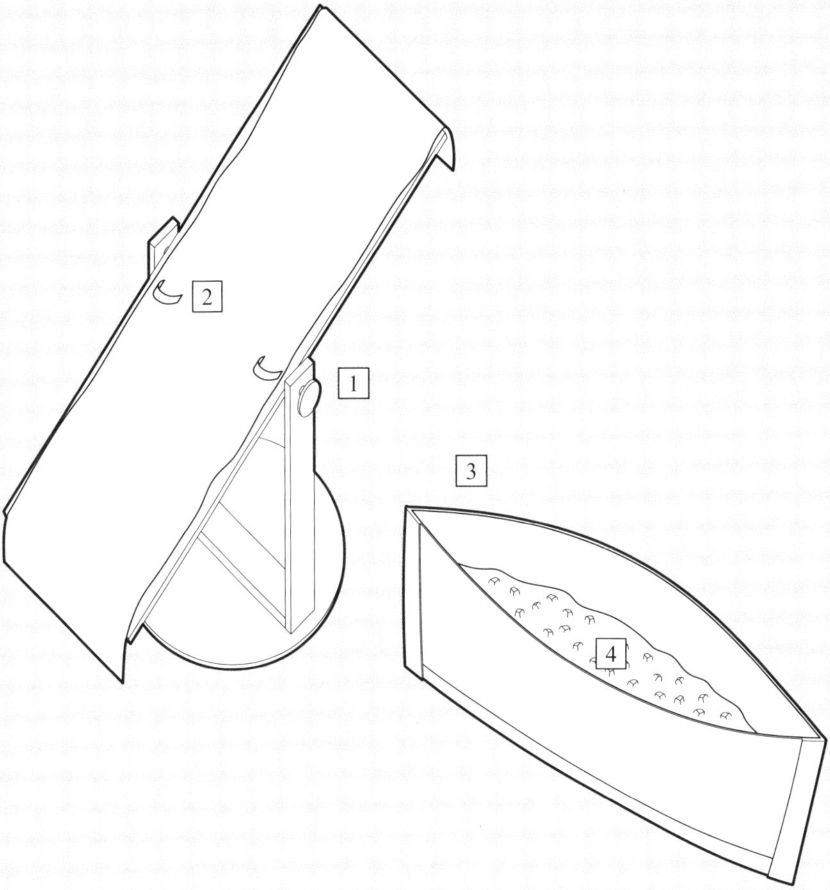

1. Hinge to turn prisoner upside down
2. Restraints
3. Plastic sheeting formed into "basin"
4. Ice water

Scale: 1:30

Source: Human Rights Watch, *Delivered Into Enemy Hands,* 49–50.

"Electric Chair," Site Cobalt, Afghanistan

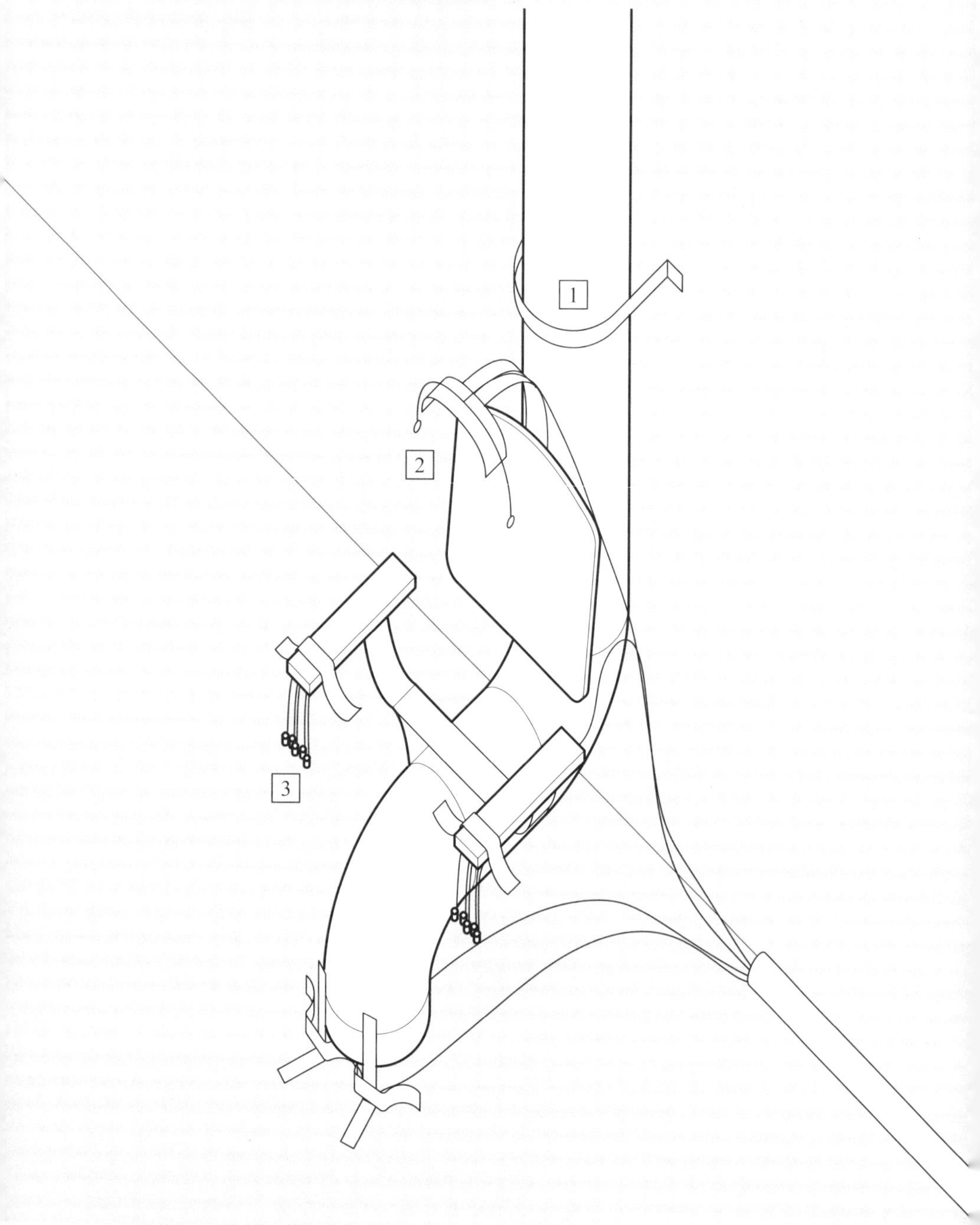

1. Created from an existing pipe
2. Makeshift headset
3. Wires attached to fingers and head

Scale: 1:15

Source: Human Rights Watch, "US: Ex-Detainees Describe Unreported CIA Torture."

Force Feeding Device, Guantánamo Bay

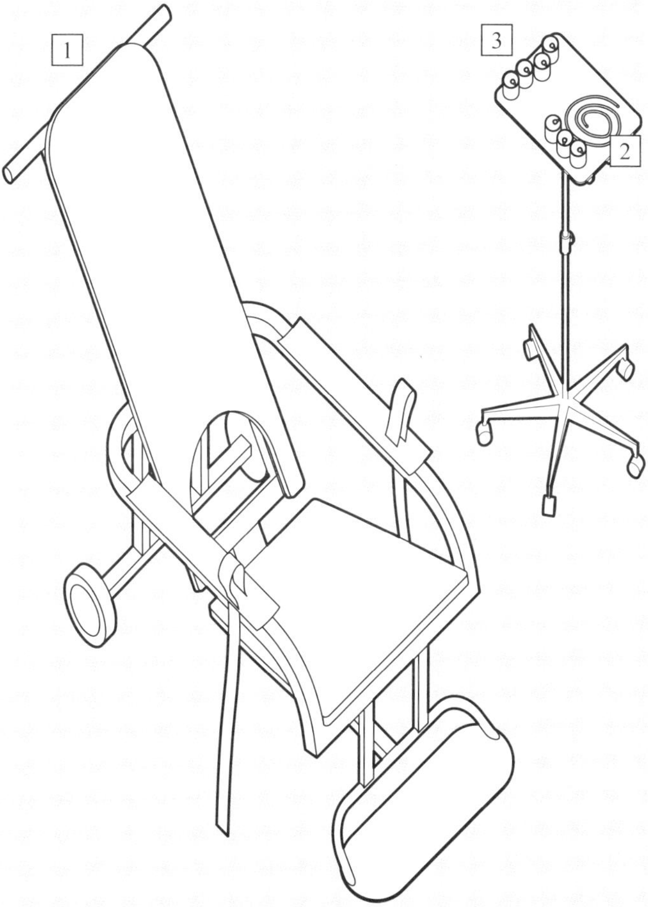

1. Mobile medical chair with restraints
2. Tube for inserting into prisoner's nose
3. Ensure dietary supplement

Scale: 1:15

Source: Fisher, "Photos from Guantanamo's Force-Feeding Facilities."

Extraordinary Rendition Sensory Deprivation Materials

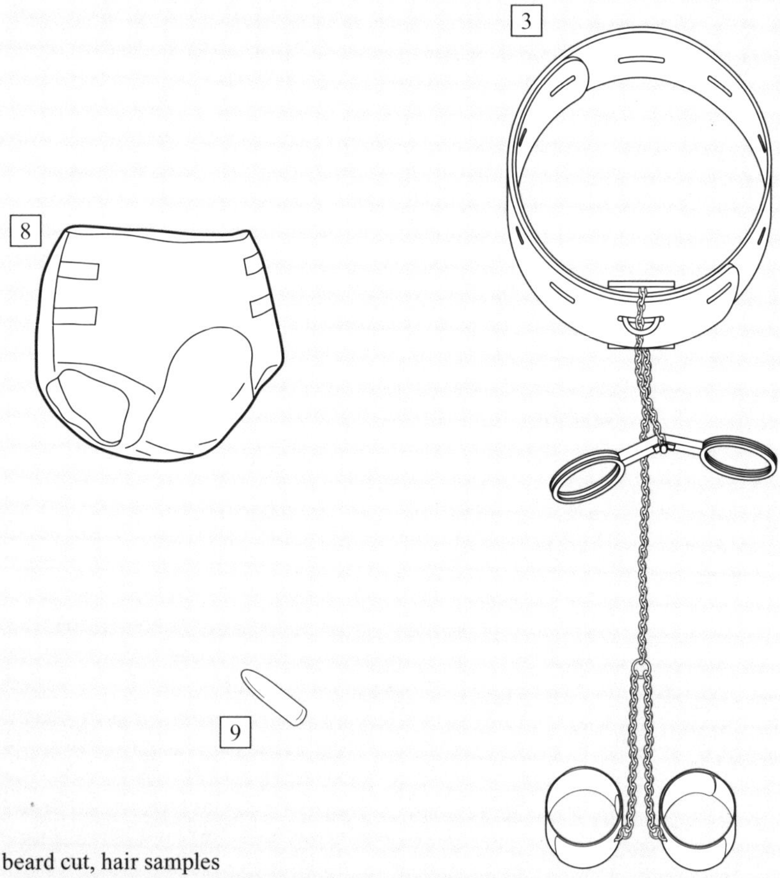

1. Hair and beard cut, hair samples saved
2. Prisoners strip searched, given orange jumpsuits
3. Belt with hand shackles and leg irons
4. Black-out goggles
5. Earmuffs
6. Face mask
7. Gloves and/or mittens
8. Diaper
9. Suppository

Scale: NTS

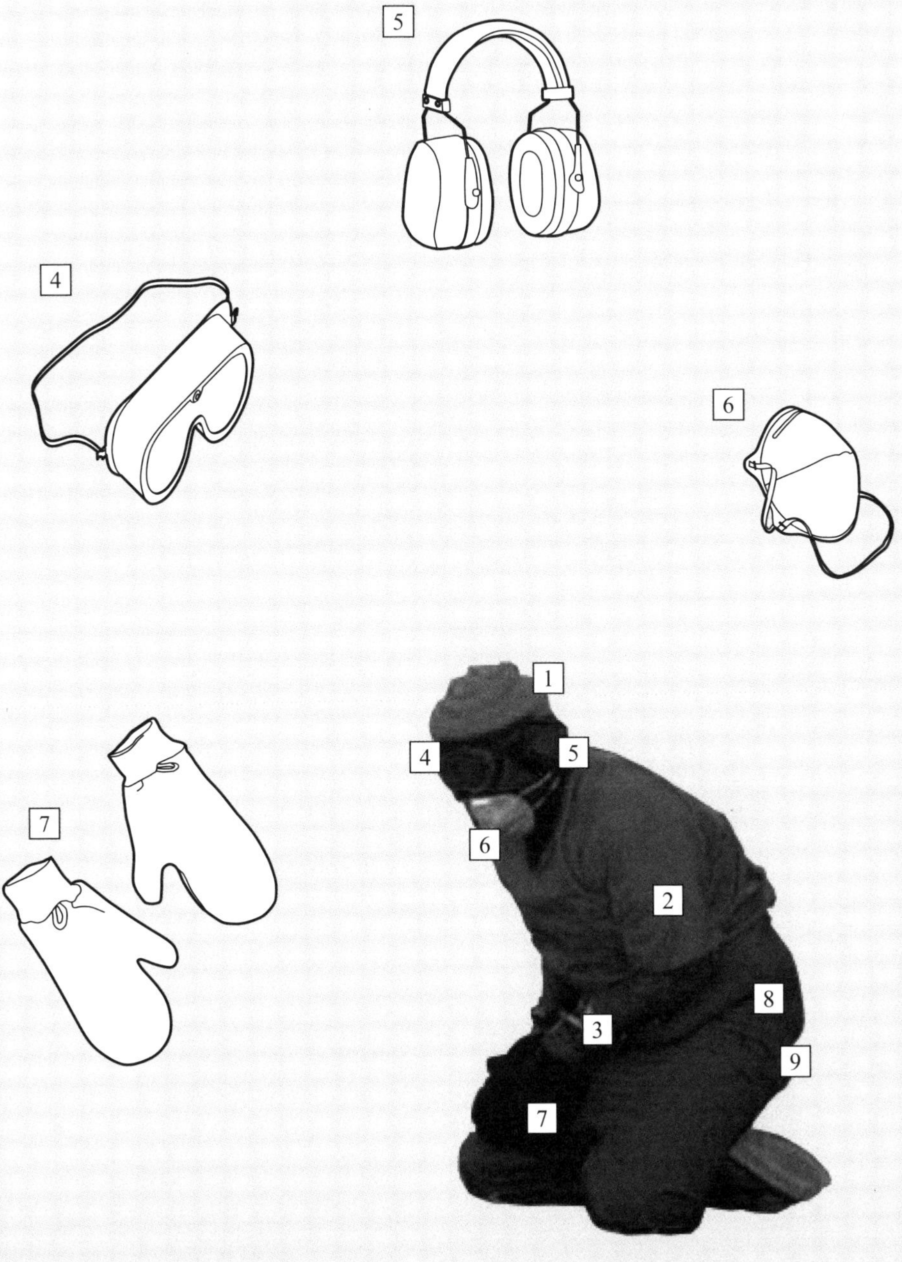

Source: Human Rights Watch. *Guantanamo: Detainee Accounts*, 4; Priest, "Wrongful Imprisonment."

Force Feeding Meal Replacement, Guantánamo Bay

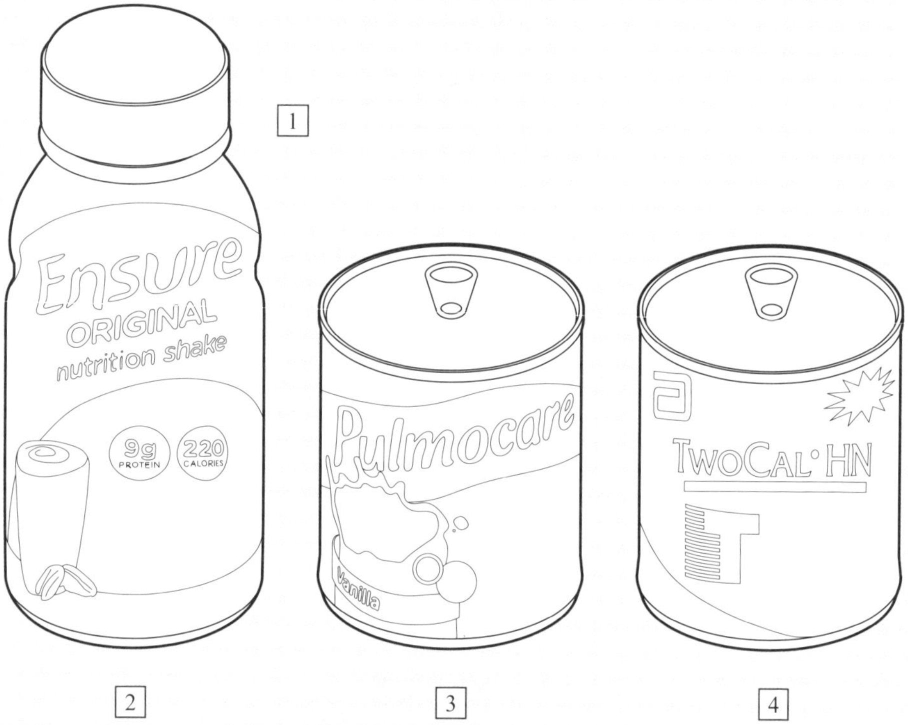

1. 3,875 cases of Ensure purchased for $142,345 to use at Guantánamo Bay, mostly between March and May, 2013 during a mass hunger strike
2. Ensure, "complete, balanced nutrition"
3. Pulmocare designed for "tube or oral feeding"
4. TwoCal "to help patients gain and maintain healthy weight"

Scale: NTS

Source: Leopold, "Gitmo Spent $300,000 on Liquid Supplements," Abbott Nutrition.

BLACK SITE EVIDENCE

Spelling and formating from the original publications has been preserved.

BAGRAM AIRFIELD, AFGHANISTAN

I was then placed in a cell, about 2m x 4m, naked, where I was kept in a standing position with my hands cuffed and chained to a bar above my head. My feet were flat on the floor. …Also during this period I was on four occasions taken to a separate room away from the main interrogation room. Here cold water from buckets was thrown onto me for about forty minutes. Not constantly as it took time to refill the buckets. After which I would be taken back to the interrogation room. …I was not allowed to pray. I could not bathe or wash. I was not provided with any time outdoors.

Account given by Khalid Sheikh Mohammed to ICRC. ICRC, *ICRC Report,* 34.

After the initial medical examination and photographing I was taken to be interrogated, but I was in such an inconsolable state that the interrogator recognized he couldn't get any information from me.

After this failed interrogation, I was taken to the first of the three different cells in which I would be held in this facility in Afghanistan. My first cell was Cell No. 6. I worked this out because on one occasion when I was taken from my cell to the interrogation room my blindfold slipped and I could see the number "6" painted in white on the door. I also knew that I was in Cell No. 6 because after I arrived I heard the other prisoners talk about me as the new person in Cell No. 6.

By listening to the other prisoners, and through careful observation when I was taken out of my cell for interrogation or to go to the bathroom, I worked out that there were two rows of cells in the area where Cell No. 6 was located. While I never saw that there were two rows, I believe that in one row, the cells were numbered evenly from "2" to "20" and in the other row the cells were numbered with odd numbers from "1" to "19," such that I was in between cells "4" and "8" and across from cell "5." I believe that the cells were numbered in this way because I heard people in my row call out even numbers and people in the other row call out odd ones when they said what cell they were in. I understand that some of the detainees who were in these cells are still missing.

CHRGJ, *Surviving the Darkness,* 18.

In the cell there was a bucket that I used as a toilet, which was emptied out only once a day. There was a foam mattress and one thick blanket. I was given Nestlé bottles—they had their outside wrapper removed but still had the Nestlé logo embossed on the bottle—that were filled with water from a container outside the cells…

CHRGJ, *Surviving the Darkeness,* 20–24.

There were no windows in the cell. The only ventilation came through an opening in the wall near the floor that was about the size of a computer keyboard and had a grate over it, and two openings near the ceiling, one above the door and one directly across from the door, through which they would pipe music into my cell. This cell had two doors, one right after the other. The interior door was made of metal and the exterior one was a door with metal bars.

Between my cell and the neighboring cell there was a gap of about one meter to one meter and a half (3.28 to 4.92 feet) that I could see through the keyboard-sized opening. The ceiling of the cell was low, much lower than the ceiling outside the cell. The ceiling of the cell was about two to two and a half meters (6.56 to 8.2 feet) high in contrast to the ceiling outside the cell which seemed to be very high, as if we were in a hangar. The cell seemed to be made of stone and had a dirt floor with a red covering.

...The entire time I was in this cell I was also shackled to the wall by a chain attached to my leg. I counted that the leg chain had twenty-four links in it and it was just long enough to enable me to reach the bucket I used as a toilet.

...Initially the only light in the cell was a brief flicker every half hour when the guards came in to wake me and turned the lights on. After the first week or ten days, the bare light bulb in the cell was turned on and left on at all times, except that when the guards came to the cell and the lights would be turned off briefly.

...I was subject to constant surveillance by the camera that sat above the cell door. There was no heating in the cell and it was very cold.

When the weather got colder an electric heater was placed in front of the door of my cell. In the evening they would open the little grate in the cell door that they used to pass food to me and heat would pass through.

...I think that once it became clear that my mental state was very bad, I was transferred to another cell that was not part of the two rows of cells of which my first cell was a part. Here there was still constant noise twenty-four hours a day, seven days a week but it was not as loud as it had been in the first cell because there was not a speaker and it was not directly piped in. This cell was approximately three by four meters (9.84 by 13.12 feet). Inside the cell there was a bucket which I used as a toilet, Nestlé bottles filled with water, a foam mattress, and a camera above the door. This was to be my home for about one and a half to two months.

In this second cell the bare light bulb was kept on all the time except when guards brought food or entered the cell for some other reason. My hands and feet were constantly shackled. In addition to my hands being chained, there was a chain attached to an iron post in the wall that attached to my right hand. The chain that held me was long enough to allow me to reach the bucket I used for a toilet. It was very heavy, which made it hard to move. The chain was so heavy that I could not even lift my right hand to my chest during prayer. I was kept under constant surveillance by the camera above the cell door.

Shortly afterwards I was moved from this second cell to a cell right across the corridor. Once I left the second cell they began to use it as a torture and interrogation room

The constant light that was on for the majority of my time here meant that I could not tell what time of day it was, or keep to a prayer schedule. Sometimes I could see light through cracks in the window outside of Cell No. 6…

During the entire period of my detention here, I was held in solitary confinement and saw no one other than my guards, interrogators, and other prison personnel. The only time I was taken out of my cell was for interrogations, for washing once a week, for medical and psychiatric visits when they were needed, and to be "sunned" once a week. This means that about once a week I was blindfolded, hooded and shackled and taken to an outside courtyard to sit on a metal chair facing a wall for about ten minutes. I believe the purpose of this "sunning" was to give detainees like me some exposure to the sun to ensure we did not get sick.

CHRGJ, *Surviving the Darkeness,* 25–26.

During these "sunning" sessions, the guards would remove my hood and stand behind me to ensure that I did not turn my head away from the approximately two meter-high (6.56 feet) wall that was directly in front of me. They would then give me nail clippers so that I could cut my nails. While I wasn't allowed to see anything except the wall, I could hear planes taking off and landing, and I always heard children's voices speaking outside the wall in a language I believe was Pashto. I could also hear some light traffic.

On one occasion while I was in this position I turned my head slightly without letting the guards know, to try and feel the sun on my face, and saw a guards' watchtower just to the left of my chair.

CHRGJ, *Surviving the Darkeness,* 26.

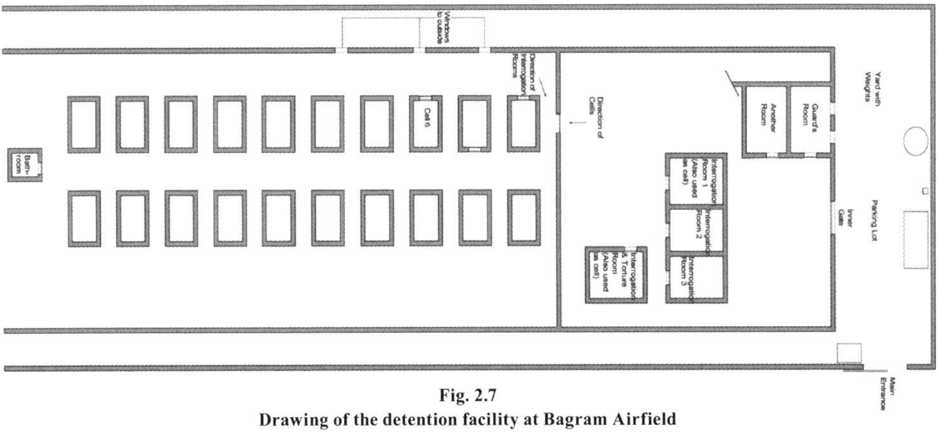

Fig. 2.7
Drawing of the detention facility at Bagram Airfield from the account of Mohamed Farag Ahmed Bashmilah.

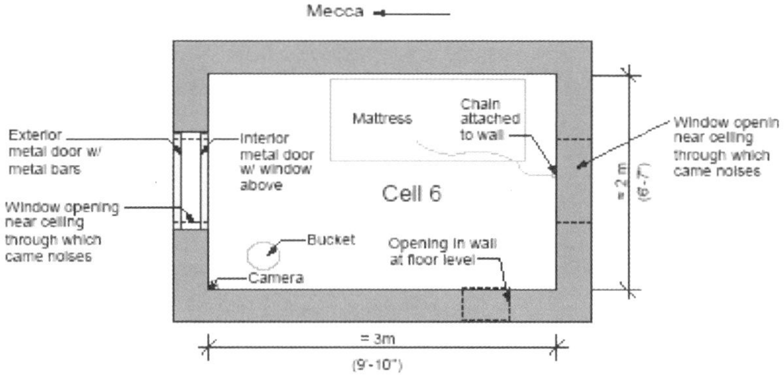

Fig. 2.8
Drawing of "cell 6" from the account of Mohamed Farag Ahmed Bashmilah.

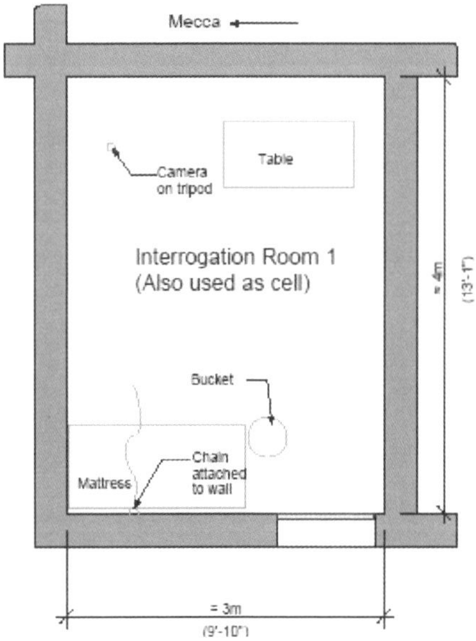

Fig. 2.9
Drawing of interrogation room and detention cell from the account of Mohamed Farag Ahmad Bashmilah.

Fig. 2.10
Drawing of detention facility bathroom from the account of Mohamed Farag Ahmad Bashmilah.

The tower was raised about two and a half meters (8.2 feet) and had two floors. The entrance was on the lower floor but the guards were upstairs. These guards were dressed in military uniforms and their faces were unmasked. They appeared to be Afghan. In the same way I was also able to see a few things in the courtyard, such as a broken down Russian-looking vehicle and water tank.

Deep inside the forbidden zone at the U.S.-occupied Bagram air base in Afghanistan, around the corner from the detention center and beyond the segregated clandestine military units, sits a cluster of metal shipping containers protected by a triple layer of concertina wire.

Priest and Barton, "U.S. Decries Abuse but Defends Interrogations."

An airplane hangar, vast and bright with artificial lights, was Umarov's third prison: Bagram, Afghanistan. "Our cages were in a two-story building inside the bigger building," he tells us. "They had high fences and were surrounded by sharp wires." All the windows were covered. "The whole place," he says, "was blocked from daylight and man's sight." Each cell held as many as 15 men; each man was issued blue prison dungarees, a wooden platform to serve as a bed, and two blankets. Umarov used one of the blankets as a mattress, the other to cover himself—though it wasn't enough.

From the account of Muhibullo Abdulkarim Umarov. Funk, "A Detainee's Story."

DARK PRISON, KABUL, AFGHANISTAN

During an interview held with the experts Bishar al-Rawi indicated that, in the dark prison, there were no lights, heating or decoration.

His cell was about 5x9 feet with a solid steel door and a hatch towards the bottom of it. He only had a bucket to use as a toilet, an old piece of carpet and a rusty steel bar across the width of the cell to hang people from. All the guards wore hoods with small eye holes, and they never spoke. Very loud music was played continuously. He also indicated that he had been subjected to sleep deprivation for up to three days and received threats. Binyam Mohamed provided a similar account to the experts as did the lawyer for Khaled El-Masri and Suleiman Abdallah.

United Nations Human Rights Council, *Joint Study*, 60.

"There was a hall with rooms apart from each other. I am guessing there were about twenty rooms."

Quote from Binyam Mohamed. Paglen and Thompson, *Torture Taxi*, 28.

Quote from Binyam Mohamed. Paglen and Thompson, *Torture Taxi,* 29.

"They knocked my head against a wall a few times until I could feel blood, then I was thrown into a cell. It was cell number sixteen or seventeen, the second or third last room from the shower room. The room was about two meters by 2.5 meters. The cell had a heavy metal door, all sold, then a second door with bars. There were speakers near the ceilings at both ends of the room. There was a watching hole low down on one wall. There was a hanging pole for people left there in a kneeling position. There was a bucket in the corner for a toilet."

Mohamed described a prison so dark that he couldn't see his hand in from of his face: "It was pitch black, and no lights on the rooms for most of the time. They used to turn the light on for a few hours, but that only made it worse when they turned it back off."

Account given by Waleed Bin Attash. ICRC, *ICRC Report,* 31–32.

On arrival at the place of detention in Afghanistan I was stripped naked. I remained naked for the next two weeks. I was put in a cell measuring approximately 1m x 2m. I was kept in a standing position, feet flat on the floor, but with my arms above my head and fixed with handcuffs and a chain to a metal bar running across the width of the cell. The cell was dark with no light, artificial or natural. …Loud music was playing twenty-four hours each day through- out the three weeks I was held there.

After some time of being held in this position my stump began to hurt so I removed my artificial leg to relieve the pain. Of course my one good leg then began to ache and soon started to give way so that I was left hanging with all my weight on my wrists. I shouted for help but at first nobody came. Finally, after about one hour a guard came and my artificial leg was given back to me and I was again placed in the standing position with my hands above my head. After that the interrogators sometimes deliberately removed my artificial leg in order to add extra stress to the position. For the first two weeks I was held in this position apart for two or three times when I was allowed to lie down, but I cannot remember for how long.

Human Rights Watch, "U.S. Operated Secret 'Dark Prison' in Kabul."

[From Binyam Mohamed] There was loud music, [Eminem's] "Slim Shady" and Dr. Dre for 20 days.... [Then] they changed the sounds to horrible ghost laughter and Halloween sounds. [At one point, I was] chained to the rails for a fortnight.... The CIA worked on people, including me, day and night.... Plenty lost their minds. I could hear people knocking their heads against the walls and the doors, screaming their heads off.

Human Rights Watch, "U.S. Operated Secret 'Dark Prison' in Kabul."

They described being held in complete darkness for weeks on end, shackled to rings bolted into the walls of their cells, with loud music or other sounds played continuously. Some detainees said they were shackled in a manner that made it impossible to lie down or sleep, with restraints that caused their hands and wrists to swell up or bruise. The detainees said they were deprived of food for days at a time, and given only filthy water to drink. ...Afghan guards told some of them that the facility was located near Kabul. ...Human Rights Watch said that the "dark prison" may have been closed after several detainees were transferred to the Bagram facility in late 2004.

SITE COBALT (THE SALT PIT), KABUL, AFGHANISTAN

The Salt Pit was the top-secret name for an abandoned brick factory, a warehouse just north of the Kabul business district that the CIA began using shortly after the United States invaded Afghanistan in October 2001. The 10-acre facility included a three-story building, eventually used by the U.S. military to train the Afghan counterterrorism force, and several smaller buildings, which were off-limits to all but the CIA and a handful of Afghan guards and cooks who ran the prison, said several current and former military and intelligence officers.

Priest, "CIA Avoids Scrutiny of Detainee Treatment."

The CIA wanted the Salt Pit to be a "host-nation facility," an Afghan prison with Afghan guards. Its designation as an Afghan facility was intended to give U.S. personnel some insulation from actions taken by Afghan guards inside, a tactic used in secret CIA prisons in other countries, former and current CIA officials said.

The CIA, however, paid the entire cost of maintaining the facility, including the electricity, food and salaries for the guards, who were all vetted by agency personnel. The CIA also decided who would be kept inside, including some "high-value targets," senior al Qaeda leaders in transit to other, more secure secret CIA prisons.

"We financed it, but it was an Afghan deal," one U.S. intelligence officer said.

Fig. 2.11
The Salt Pit in January, 2001. This facility has since been destroyed, with others constructed nearby.

Quote From Khaled El-Masri. Grey, *Ghost Plane*, 87.

"I awoke in a small, dirty cell," he said. "It was like a basement room with a tiny window. ...The cell he was in had a small window at the top of the wall. The light of a setting sun came through. (87)

Goldman and Gannon, "Death shed light on CIA 'Salt Pit' near Kabul."

Baheer said he was flown to Afghanistan and taken to the Salt Pit, the code name for the abandoned brick factory turned CIA prison. In small, windowless cells, detainees were subjected to harsh treatment and at least one mock execution, according to several former CIA officials.

"I was left naked, sleeping on the barren concrete," said Baheer. His toilet was a bucket. Loudspeakers blared. Guards concealed their identity with masks and carried torches.

SITE UNKNOWN, AFGHANISTAN

Human Rights Watch, "Delivered Into Enemy Hands."

Shoroeiya and Sharif each said they were kept in almost total darkness the entire time they were in the first facility in Afghanistan. Their cells, as well as the rooms where they were interrogated, were dark. Guards and interrogators would come to them with flashlights and in some cases strong spotlights they would shine in their eyes. In addition to the darkness, there was loud, Western music blaring constantly. Both said they were denied clothing during the first few months of their detention. Shoroeiya had a thin mat in his cell, while Sharif said he had a carpet, perhaps a mat, in his cell. Both had a bucket in their cell they were to use as a toilet. The men said that chemicals were in the bucket that, when mixed with their urine and excrement, gave off a terrible stench.

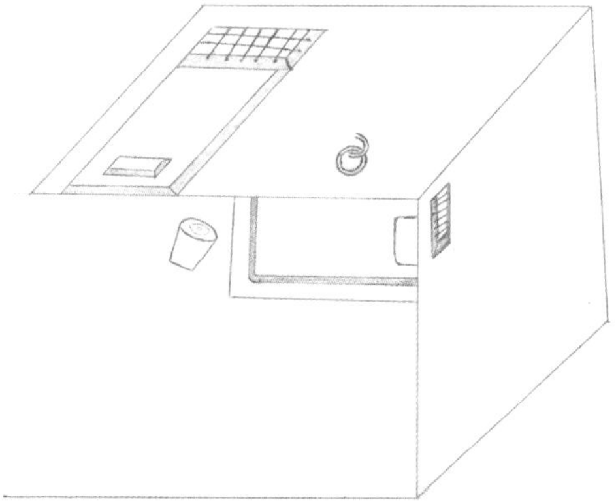

Fig. 2.12
Detention cell sketch by Mohammed Shoroeiya.

Sharif said his cell was about 4 x 3 meters. It had a steel door in the middle and a window with steel bars over the door. On what he described as the backside of the cell there was also another small window. Shoroeiya did not provide measurements for his cell, but he said it was slightly bigger, and drew it as slightly bigger than Sharif's cell. Shoroeiya's cell also had a door with a window at the top with bars on it and a slot in the middle of the door that the guards used to pass food through and check on him occasionally. There was a small window, about 10 x 30 centimeters that had bars on it too, was about 13 centimeters from the ground, and provided some ventilation.[152] He added that it also "was a very good entrance for rats."

Human Rights Watch, "Delivered Into Enemy Hands."

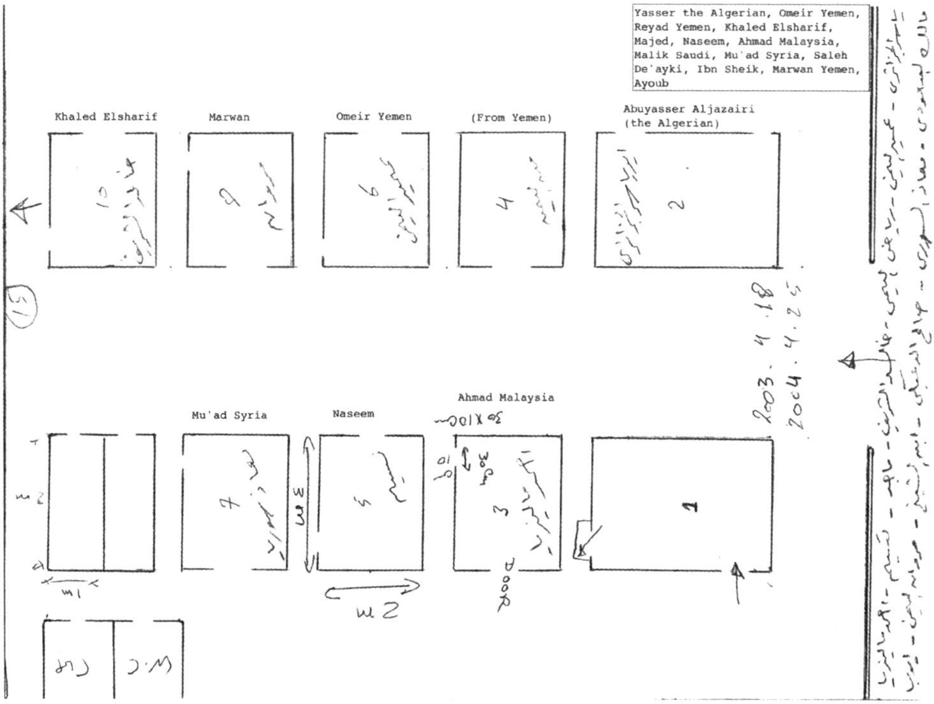

Fig. 2.13
Detention facility sketch by Mohammed Shoroeiya.

Human Rights Watch, "Delivered Into Enemy Hands."

On another occasion he said he was in a room that was about 1.5 x 1.5 meters. Again his hands were suspended above his head from an iron bar that went between the walls. His feet could touch the ground but he also could only stand on one foot because his broken foot was still not healed. There were no windows and it was dark, but there were small, "yellow" holes. He could see a small red light that made him think there may have been a camera in there. They left him there for several hours.

Human Rights Watch, "Delivered Into Enemy Hands."

Shoroeiya said the board was made of wood and could turn around 360 degrees. Sometimes they would strap him onto the board and spin him around while wearing a hood that covered his nose and mouth. This would completely disorient him. While he was strapped to the board with his head lower than his feet, they would pour buckets of extremely cold water over his nose and mouth to the point that he felt he was going to suffocate. After the hood was put over his face, he said, "then there is the water pouring…. They start to pour water to the point where you feel like you are suffocating." When asked how many times this was done to him, he said "a lot …a lot … it happened many times …. They pour buckets of water all over you."

Fig. 2.14
Detention box sketch by Mohammed Shoroeiya.

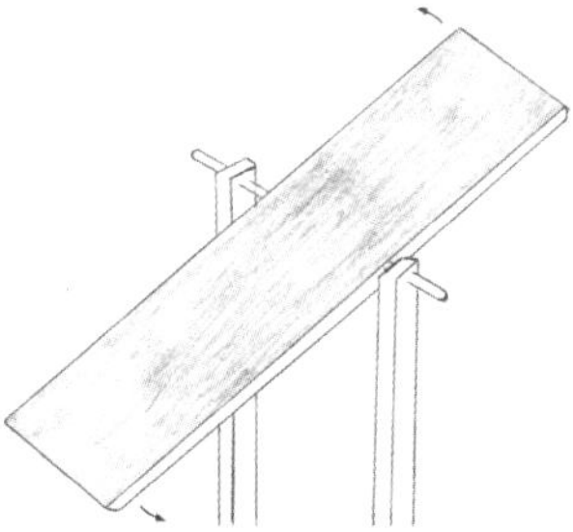

Fig. 2.15
Waterboard sketch by Mohammed Shoroeiya.

BLACK SITES AT GUANTÁNAMO BAY, CUBA

Figs. 2.16, 2.17
Possible interrogation sites, Guantánamo Bay, Cuba. 2012.

At the outset, in early 2002, detainees arriving at Guantánamo were held in the open air, barbed-wire-enclosed Camp X-ray—a site that became the iconic image of Guantánamo. But Camp X-ray closed that April, and was replaced by a series of much less makeshift and generally more-restrictive prison facilities.

In February 2003 the military opened Camp 4 in an effort to ease restrictions and allow detainees who do not pose disciplinary problems to congregate more freely. Designed to resemble a prisoner-of-war lockup, Camp 4 includes 10-cot bunkhouses, communal showers and toilets, a soccer field, and a common outdoor area where detainees eat, pray, and play games together.

...Camp 4 has space for approximately 175 detainees, but was virtually emptied in May 2006 after a group of detainees reportedly attacked the guards with improvised weapons, including broken pieces of light bulbs, and caused significant damage to the facility. Other facilities include an interrogation center known as "Camp No," reportedly another name for camp 7, and "Strawberry Fields" a secret interrogation and detention center.

Human Rights Watch, *Locked Up Alone,* 7–8.

Johnston and Mazzetti, "A Window Into C.I.A.'s Embrace of Secret Jails."

Eventually, the agency's network would encompass at least eight detention centers, including one in the Middle East, one each in Iraq and Afghanistan and a maximum-security long-term site at Guantánamo Bay, Cuba, that was dubbed Strawberry Fields, officials said. (It was named after a Beatles song after C.I.A. officials joked that the detainees would be held there, as the lyric put it, "forever.")

Miami Herald, "'Platinum' Captives Held at Off-Limits Gitmo Camp."

Somewhere on this isolated outpost, strictly off-limits from the Pentagon's media tour, is a secret prison camp housing 15 alleged senior al Qaeda captives called "high-value detainees." It is Camp 7, and run by a special unit code-named Task Force Platinum.

No reporter has seen Camp 7 on the weekly tours for U.S. and foreign media that showcase a U.S. program of "safe and humane detention" while the Pentagon decides whether to try them at "full, fair and open" trials.

"Quite frankly, for security reasons and policies that come down from the Secretary of Defense, we cannot divulge the location of where it is," said Army Lt. Col. Ed Bush, a prison camps spokesman on Tuesday's media tour.

Interview with Army Sergeant Joe Hickman and Army Specialist Tony Davila. Horton, "The Guantánamo 'Suicides'."

It looked like other camps within Camp America, Davila said, only it had no guard towers and it was surrounded with concertina wire. They saw no activity, but Hickman guessed the place could house as many as eighty prisoners. One part of the compound, he said, had the same appearance as the interrogation centers at other prison camps.

The compound was not visible from the main road, and the access road was chained off. The Guardsman who told Davila about the compound had said, "This place does not exist," and Hickman, who was frequently put in charge of security for all of Camp America, was not briefed about the site. Nevertheless, Davila said, other soldiers—many of whom were required to patrol the outside perimeter of Camp America—had seen the compound, and many speculated about its purpose. One theory was that it was being used by some of the non-uniformed government personnel who frequently showed up in the camps and were widely thought to be CIA agents.

A friend of Hickman's had nicknamed the compound "Camp No," the idea being that anyone who asked if it existed would be told, "No, it doesn't."

From the account of Muhibullo Abdulkarim Umarov. Funk, "A Detainee's Story."

They threw him into isolation for 10 days. "I was taken to the dark room," he says. "The soldiers took all my clothes and left me there." The room was made of iron; it measured three feet by five feet. At night, frigid air was pumped through a hole in its ceiling, and its small window was covered by Plexiglas so the air couldn't leave. Two electric coils provided dim light, and during the day, they were turned up to heat the cell to a very high temperature.

SITE VIOLET, ANTAVILIAI, LITHUANIA

The CIA has been hiding and interrogating some of its most important al Qaeda captives at a Soviet-era compound in Eastern Europe, according to U.S. and foreign officials familiar with the arrangement.

Priest, "CIA Holds Terror Suspects in Secret Prisons."

By mid-2002, the CIA had worked out secret black-site deals with two countries, including Thailand and one Eastern European nation, current and former officials said. An estimated $100 million was tucked inside the classified annex of the first supplemental Afghanistan appropriation.

In March 2004, the family sold the property to Elite, LLC, a now-defunct company registered in Delaware and Panama and Washington, D.C. That same month, Lithuania marked its formal admission to NATO.

Cole and Ross, "EXCLUSIVE: CIA Secret 'Torture' Prison Found."

The CIA constructed the prison over the next several months, apparently flying in prefabricated elements from outside Lithuania. The prison opened in Sept. 2004.

According to sources who saw the facility, the riding academy originally consisted of an indoor riding area with a red metallic roof, a stable and a cafe. The CIA built a thick concrete wall inside the riding area. Behind the wall, it built what one Lithuanian source called a "building within a building."

On a series of thick concrete pads, it installed what a source called "prefabricated pods" to house prisoners, each separated from the other by five or six feet. Each pod included a shower, a bed and a toilet. Separate cells were constructed for interrogations. The CIA converted much of the rest of the building into garage space.

Intelligence officers working at the prison were housed next door in the converted stable, raising the roof to add space. Electrical power for both structures was provided by a 2003 Caterpillar autonomous generator. All the electrical outlets in the renovated structure were 110 volts, meaning they were designed for American appliances. European outlets and appliances typically use 220 volts.

The prison pods inside the barn were not visible to locals. They describe seeing large amounts of earth being excavated during the summer of 2004. Locals who saw the activity at the prison and approached to ask for work were turned away by English-speaking guards. The guards were replaced by new guards every 90 days.

Former CIA officials directly involved or briefed on the highly classified secret prison program tell ABC News that as many as eight suspects were held for more than a year in the Vilnius prison. Flight logs viewed by ABC News confirm that CIA planes made repeated flights into Lithuania during that period. In November 2005, after public disclosures about the program, the prison was closed, as was another "black site" in Romania.

Fig. 2.18
Site Violet, Antaviliai, Lithuania.

Fig. 2.19
Site Violet, Antaviliai, Lithuania.

SITE BLUE, STARE KIEJKUTY, POLAND

Account given by Walid Mohammed bin Attash. ICRC, *ICRC Report,* 32–33.

After approximately three weeks in Afghanistan I was transferred to another place. …I arrived in the next place of detention during June 2003. I think I was detained underground as I had to walk down some stairs in order to reach the cell. My blindfold was then removed. The cell was about 4m x 5m. I was kept chained by my ankle shackles to a pin fixed in the floor.

Account given by Mohamed Farag Ahmad Bashmilah. CHRGJ, *Surviving Darkness,* 33–34.

On arrival at the detention facility, I was forced up several stairs and then I was shackled and made to wait. I was then forced to walk down a ramp inside the facility. I think I was made to wait after climbing the stairs because they were taking the detainees down the ramp one by one. The ramp was a steep metal slope with a special surface, one that is designed for traction.

Account given by Walid Mohammed bin Attash. ICRC, *ICRC Report,* 35–37.

After arrival my clothes were again cut off of me, the bag and blindfold were removed and photographs were again taken of me naked. I was put in a cell with cameras where I was later informed by an interrogator that I was monitored 24 hours a day by a doctor, psychologist and interrogator. I think the cell was underground. I had to go down steps to get to it. It was about 3m x 4m with wooden walls.

…I wasn't given any clothes for the first month. Artificial light was on 24 hours a day, but I never saw sunlight. I was never taken outdoors.

After about one month I was moved to another cell. I was given clothes to wear. I was no longer kept in a standing position. I was only shackled by the ankles. I could shower once a week. The interrogation

Fig. 2.20
Security fence at Site Blue, Stare Kiejkuty, Poland.

became less harsh. No more physical assault, but threats along the lines of "we will take you to another room" or by having the plastic collar put on the table in front of me during the questioning.

...On June 4th I was moved to a third cell. This move occurred after I complained about the constant music that was still being played outside my cell. The new cell was a cage like structure built inside an underground room. I preferred it as there was no music and, as it was a cage structure instead of solid walls, the ventilation was better. I was again kept shackled by the feet, but not the wrists. Water was provided in two bottles. One for drinking, one for the toilet. Toilet paper was provided. Toilet still consisted of a bucket inside the cell. It was removed on a daily basis.

During the harshest period of my interrogation I gave a lot of false information in order to satisfy what I believed the interrogators wished to hear in order to make the ill-treatment stop. I later told the interrogators that their methods were stupid and counterproductive. I'm sure that the false information I was forced to invent in order to make the ill-treatment stop wasted a lot of their time and led to several false red-alerts being placed in the US.

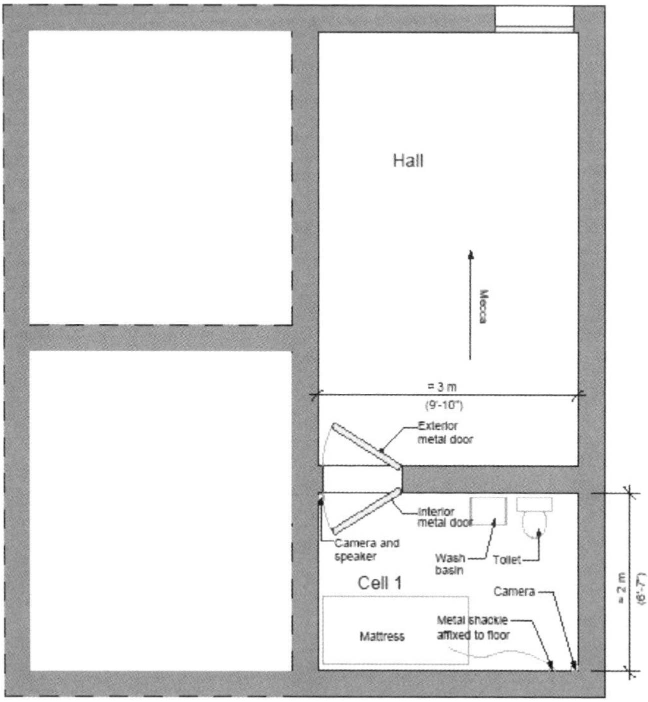

Fig. 2.21
Drawing of cell layout from the account of Mohamed Farag Ahmad Bashmilah.

CHRGJ, *Surviving Darkness*, 35.

This cell appeared to be new or refurbished and had a stainless steel toilet and a stainless steel wash basin. In this cell there were two video cameras, one above the door and one on the wall in the corner diagonal to the door. The camera on the wall in the corner was directed at the door, while the camera above the door followed me when I moved in the cell. There was also a speaker next to the camera above the door.

The speaker above the cell door blasted white noise much like the sound of radio interference into my cell twenty-four hours a day except for when the guards came in and the noise was shut off. There was also a large stereo near the entrance of the shower room that was used to blast music into the room. I was taken to this shower room once a week to wash for about two minutes.

CHRGJ, *Surviving Darkness*, 36–37.

During my first three to four weeks in this cell my hands were cuffed all of the time. Additionally, there was a metal ring in the floor with a heavy chain on it that was attached to my ankle. This heavy chain had one hundred and ten links on it and constricted my movement in the tiny cell. The metal ring was located below the camera on the wall and the chain was only long enough for me to reach the mattress and the toilet. This cell was roughly two by three meters (6.56 by 9.84 feet).

To enter and exit the cell you had to pass through two doors, one right after the other. As the guards would enter my cell they would open the first exterior door outward toward them and then the second inner door inward into the cell. The inner door had an opening at the bottom which they would use to pass me food or anything else they wanted to give me without coming into my cell. Above this opening

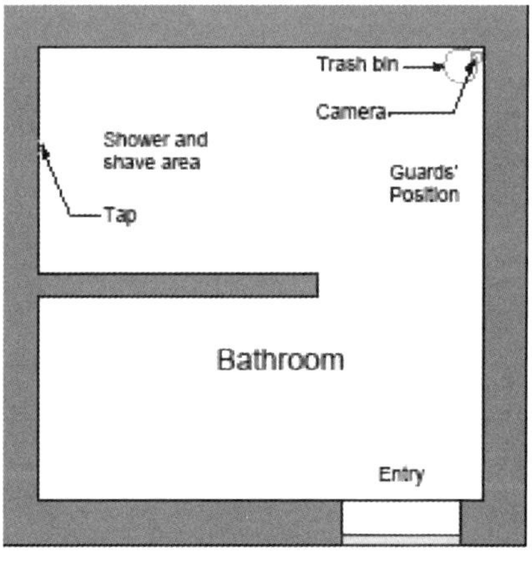

Fig. 2.22
Drawing of bathroom layout from the account of Mohamed Farag Ahmad Bashmilah.

there was a narrow pane of clear glass which extended about a foot above the floor of the cell.

My cell was part of a cluster of three cells. In addition to the double doors that led to my cell there was another door at the entrance to the cluster.

The cell's condition—its newness, the stainless steel sink and toilet, the cameras and the sophisticated double doors—immediately made me think that I was in a western country.

When the interrogator eventually came into my cell he indicated the direction of Mecca as being the same direction that the toilet faced, which is something that would not happen in a Muslim country. This confirmed my suspicion that I was being held in a prison that had been built by westerners or in a western country.

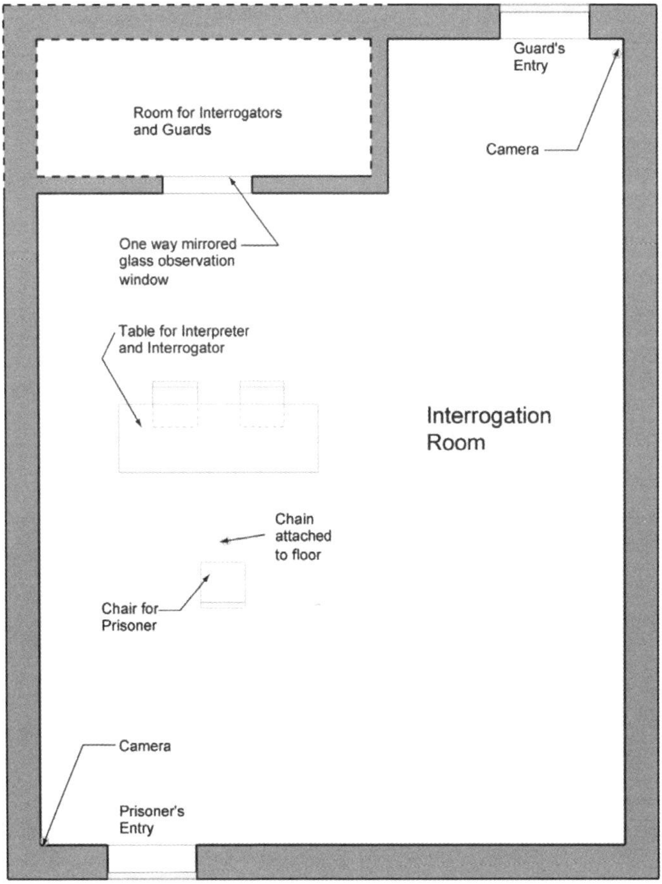

Fig. 2.23
Drawing of interrogation room layout from the account of Mohamed Farag Ahmad Bashmilah.

Mayer, *Darkside,* 275.

While the prisons in Afghanistan were primitive, a later CIA facility to which [Khalid Sheikh] Mohammed was transferred was troubling in a different way. Designed exclusively for the highest-value detainees, it was sleeker and more Orwellian. The special facility appears to have been in Eastern Europe, probably Poland, according to a source who studied the details closely, although the Polish government denies this.

CHRGJ, *Surviving Darkness,* 40.

Ten or eleven days after I arrived at this facility, I was given a digital Casio watch made in either Japan or Malaysia, which displayed a map of the earth. When I pushed a button on the watch it indicated that it was set to Greenwich Mean Time. The watch also had the date on it, and on the day I received it, the date read 05 May 04. Using this date I was able to verify, based on knowing how many days I had been in this facility, that I had been transferred out of Afghanistan on or around April 24, 2004.

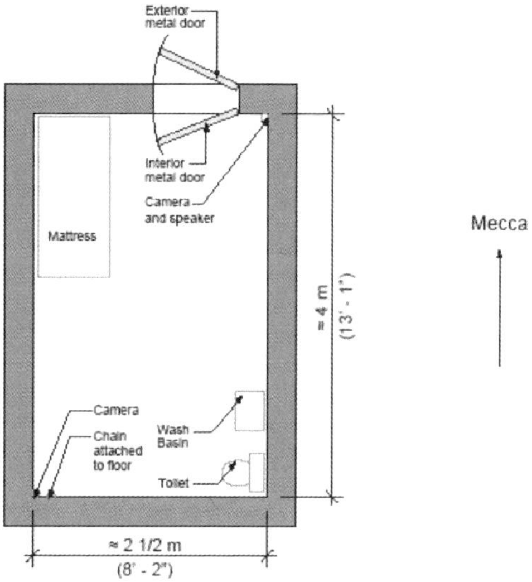

Fig. 2.24
Drawing of second detention cell from the account of Mohamed Farag Ahmad Bashmilah.

CHRGJ, *Surviving Darkness,* 42.

In the interrogation room there was me, the doctor with the disfigured hand, an interpreter, an interrogator, and three guards. I was weighed on a scale that used pounds as its unit of measure and the scale showed that I was about ninety pounds. Then the guards untied my hands and sat me in a chair and strapped my arms to the arms of the chair. They then used a chain to connect the shackles on my feet to a metal ring in the floor. I saw blue cans on the table that contained what looked like pink colored liquid. There were also tubes like those used for IVs and a metal IV pole.

Around September 2004, I was cuffed and blindfolded and walked to a run-down cell with a filthy mattress where I stayed until I was transferred to Yemen in May 2005.

...This second cell was approximately two and a half by four meters (8.2 by 13.12 feet) and contained the same camera and speaker arrangement as the previous cell. Again, there was a mattress, a stainless steel toilet, and a stainless steel wash basin. At some point, I was told by an interrogator who came into my cell that Mecca was in the direction of the door. This cell was also in a cluster of three. Although there was also a metal shackle in this cell, I was not chained to the floor as in the previous cell, but instead had shackles on my ankles chaining my legs together. Although there was a speaker in this cell as in the other cell, no noise came out of the speaker except for during the last month or month and a half when Quranic verses were played about once a week.

CHRGJ, *Surviving Darkness,* 43-44.

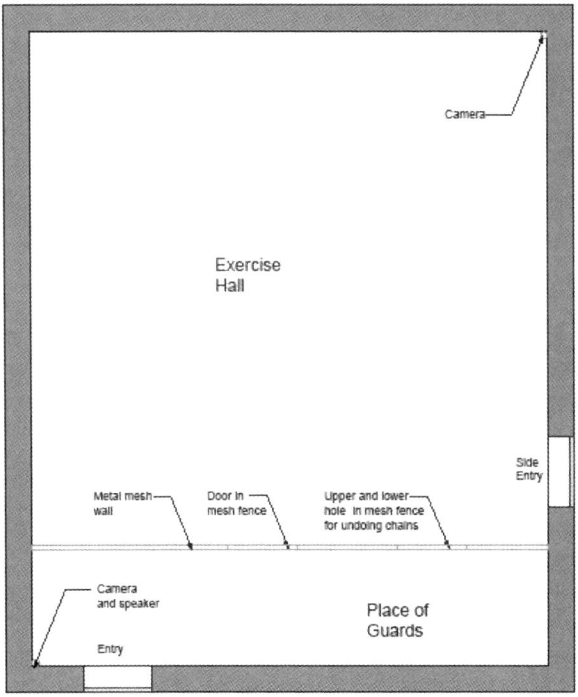

Fig. 2.25
Drawing of exercise hall layout from the account of Mohamed Farag Ahmad Bashmilah.

The newer prison, according to well-informed sources, was far more high-tech than the prisons in Afghanistan, and more intensely focused on psychological torment. The cells had hydraulic doors and air-conditioning. Multiple cameras in each cell provided video surveillance of the detainees.

Mayer, *Darkside,* 276.

CHRGJ, *Surviving Darkness*, 45-50.

Toward the end of my detention, I was given a list of books about five pages long with about a hundred books on it. …The books seemed brand new and each one had a page that was imprinted with a stamp from a Bookshop in Washington D.C.

…This facility also had an exercise hall in which I was allowed to exercise for about fifteen to twenty minutes once a week in the month or two before I was sent to Yemen. Three guards would come to my cell and we would go through the usual hooding and shackling procedure before they would take me to a large empty hall with balls in it. …To enter the exercise hall I would first pass through an outer door and then go through a door in the metal mesh fence that ran the length of the room. The fence separated the main part of the exercise hall with the balls in it from the place the guards stood watching me while I exercised. Once I was in the main part of the exercise hall I would put my hands through a metal opening in the fence and a guard would remove my cuffs. I would do the same with my feet, and then I would play by myself by kicking and bouncing the balls off of the walls.

Fig. 2.26
Guard tower at Stare Kiejkuty, Poland.

CHRGJ, *Surviving Darkness*, 52.

In both cells, the ceiling and floor were all painted the same drab grey color and I was not once allowed to see the sun or the sky for the more than twelve months I was in this facility. As a result I felt sealed in and claustrophobic. I also felt extremely disoriented because I had no idea where I was.

The sealed in nature of this facility and the claustrophobia that I experienced contributed to my feeling that this detention facility and the facility in Afghanistan were essentially coffins. It especially felt that way to me because I was innocent. You die a little every day you are in prison because you are in a coffin for the living where you don't see, you don't hear, and there is nothing.

Senator Jozef Pinior, a member of Poland's upper house, said he has information showing that a local contractor was commissioned to build a cage to be supplied to Stare Kiekuty, a Polish army base that also played host to a CIA "black site" used to house terrorism suspects enroute to Guantánamo Bay. The senator said that the cage "was not used for exotic birds" at the base in northeastern Poland.

Day, "CIA 'Ordered Cage to Hold Prisoners in Poland'."

SITE BLACK (BRIGHT LIGHT), BUCHAREST, ROMANIA

One of the CIA's most important secrets in the war on terrorism was hiding in plain sight, on a leafy residential street along a busy set of train tracks in Romania's capital. There, tucked in the basement of a government building, the CIA ran a clandestine prison, former U.S. intelligence officials said.

For years, the building—codenamed Bright Light—housed some of the CIA's most important terror suspects, including Khalid Sheik Mohammad, the mastermind of 9/11.

... The basement consisted of six prefabricated cells, each with a clock and arrow pointing to Mecca, the officials said. The cells were on springs, keeping them slightly off balance and causing disorientation among some detainees.

Goldman and Apuzzo, "Romanian CIA Prison."

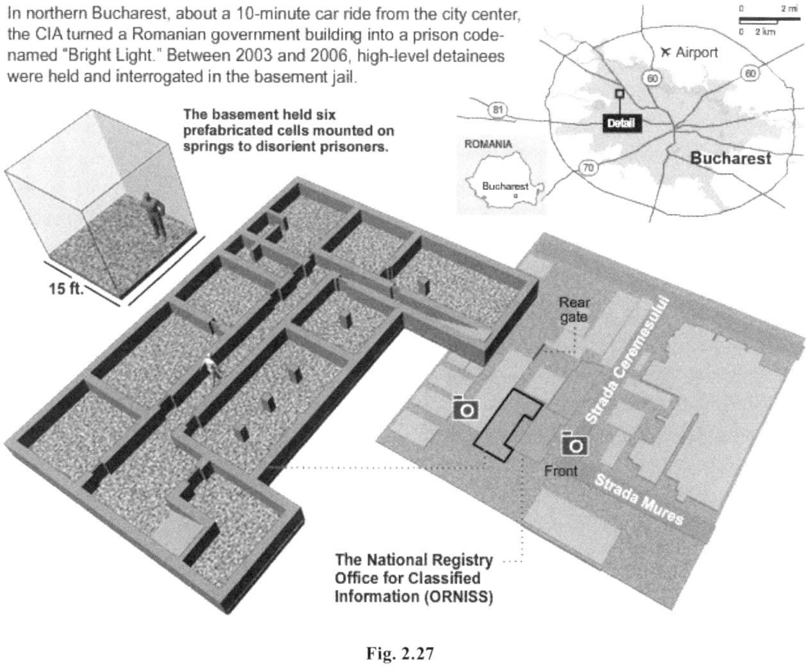

Fig. 2.27
Basement plan, Site Black, Bucharest, Romania.

Horton, “Inside the CIA’s Black Site in Bucharest.”

The facility’s address is Strada Mureș 4, according to the German account.

Figs. 2.28–2.30
Video stills of Site Black, Bucharest, Romania. Associated Press.

SITE GREEN, THAILAND

Mayer, *Darkside,* 149.

…the CIA installed Zubayda in a new facility in Thailand. The Thai government’s only stipulation was that there must be absolutely no publicity about its cooperation. If the operation could be kept completely covered up, however, the CIA could have the run of the Thai facility. It boasted, among other features, subterranean cells.

Mayer, *Darkside,* 165-166.

Zubayda’s “hard time” began when he was locked into the “tiny coffin” for hours on end, which he described as excruciatingly painful. It was too small for him to stand or stretch out, so small he said he had to double up his limbs in the fetal position. …He described the box as black, both inside and out, and said that it was covered in towels, which he thought was an effort to construct the flow of air inside. ...A source familiar with Zubayda's account described the tiny coffin box as "unbearable, most terrible." Article 21 of the Third Geneva Convention—which applies to all prisoners of war—specifically prohibits such forms of cruelty, which are classified as "close confinement."

Political analysts and diplomats in Thailand suspect that the prison was, and perhaps still is, situated at a military base in the northeastern province of Udon Thani from where the US launched its bombers during the Vietnam War and is currently believed to monitor regional radio communications, including inside China.

Crispin, "US and Thailand: Allies in Torture."

Wherever the CIA-run interrogation facilities are situated, the torture of suspects in Thailand apparently represents the latest US violation of the Geneva Conventions and also controversially violates Thai law and sovereignty.

The government of Thailand denied the existence of a secret prison facility in Thailand in 2002/3, stating that international and local media had visited the suspected places and found no evidence of such a facility. In the light of the detailed nature of the allegations, however, the experts believe it credible that a CIA black site existed in Thailand, and calls on the domestic authorities to launch an independent investigation into the matter.

United Nations Human Rights Council, *Joint Study,* 50.

Fig. 2.31
QSL card for the International Broadcasting Bureau (IBB) Udonthani (Thailand) relay station. Possible Site Green location.

Account of Abu Zubaydah. IRCR, *ICRC Report,* 28–31.

I woke up, naked, strapped to a bed, in a very white room. The room measured approximately 4m x 4m. The room had three solid walls, with the fourth wall consisting of metal bars separating it from a larger room. I am not sure how long I remained in the bed. After some time, I think it was several days, but can't remember exactly, I was transferred to a chair where I was kept, shackled by hands and feet for what I think was the next 2 or 3 weeks.

...The cell and room were air-conditioned and were very cold. Very loud, shouting type music was constantly playing. It kept repeating about every fifteen minutes twenty-four hours a day. Sometimes the music stopped and was replaced by a loud hissing or crackling noise.

...Then, about two and a half or three months after I arrived in this place, the interrogation began again, but with more intensity than before. Then the real torturing started. Two black wooden boxes were brought into the room outside my cell. One was tall, slightly higher than me and narrow. Measuring perhaps in area 1m x 0.75m and 2m in height. The other was shorter, perhaps only 1m in height. I was taken out of my cell and one of the interrogators wrapped a towel around my neck, they then used it to swing me around and smash me repeatedly against the hard walls of the room. I was also repeatedly slapped in the face. As I was still shackled, the pushing and pulling around meant that the shackles pulled painfully on my ankles.

I was then put into the tall back box for what I think was about one and a half to two hours. The box was totally black on the inside as well as the outside. It had a bucket inside to use as a toilet and had water to drink provided in a bottle. They put a cloth or cover over the outside of the box to cut out the light and restrict my air supply. It was difficult to breathe. When I was let out of the box I saw that one of the walls of the room had been covered with plywood sheeting. From now on it was against this wall that I was then smashed with the towel around my neck. I think that the plywood was put there to provide some absorption of the impact of my body. The interrogators realized that smashing me against the hard wall would probably quickly result in physical injury.

...Then, little by little, things started to get better. I was again given rice to eat. Then my mattress was returned. I was allowed to clean my cell. The tall box was removed, but the short one remained in the room outside my cell, I think as a deliberate reminder as to what my interrogators were capable of.

"UN Secret Detention Report."

In January 2008, the *Asia Times* reported that political analysts and diplomats in Thailand suspected that the detention facility was "situated at a military base in the northeastern province of Udon Thani".

The *New York Times* alleged later that local officials were said to be growing uneasy about "a black site outside Bangkok code-named Cat's Eye" and that this was a reason for the CIA to want "its own, more permanent detention centers."

"UN Secret Detention Report."

APPENDICES

A. EXTRAORDINARY RENDITIONS

B. PROXY SITE EVIDENCE

C. THE MEMOS

APPENDIX A: EXTRAORDINARY RENDITIONS

Spelling and formatting of prisoner names has been preserved from their original publication.
Information marked with asterisk is inferred from incomplete evidence.
High Value Detainees marked with (HVD) and prisoners subject to the Enhanced Interrogation Techniques program marked with (EIT).

Abu Zubaydah (HVD, EIT)

SSCI Prisoner Number:	1
Nationality:	Palestinian
Entered CIA Custody:	Pakistan, 3/31/02
Released by CIA to:	Guantánamo Bay, 9/5/06
Facilities Detained in:	Green, Blue, Indigo and/or Maroon, Violet, Brown, Morocco
Current Status:	Detained, Guantánamo Bay

Zakariya

SSCI Prisoner Number:	2
Nationality:	Yemeni
Entered CIA Custody:	Georgia, 4/30/02–5/2/02
Released by CIA to:	Bagram, 5/3/03–5/16/03
Facilities Detained in:	Cobalt and/or Grey, Afghanistan (other)
Current Status:	Detained, Guantánamo Bay

Jamal Eldin Boudraa

SSCI Prisoner Number:	3
Nationality:	Algerian
Entered CIA Custody:	Georgia, 4/30/02–5/2/02
Released by CIA to:	Algeria, 1/20/04–1/31/04
Facilities Detained in:	Cobalt and/or Gray, Afghanistan (other)
Current Status:	Released, 2010

Abbar al-Hawari, aka Abu Sufiyan

SSCI Prisoner Number:	4
Nationality:	Algerian
Entered CIA Custody:	Georgia, 4/30/02–5/2/02
Released by CIA to:	Bagram, 5/5/03–5/16/03
Facilities Detained in:	Cobalt and/or Gray, Afghanistan (other)
Current Status:	Transferred, Algeria 11/10/08

Hassan Muhammad Abu Bakr Qa'id

SSCI Prisoner Number:	5
Nationality:	Libyan
Entered CIA Custody:	Pakistan, 6/1/02–6/9/02
Released by CIA to:	Bagram*, 11/3/03–11/20/03
Facilities Detained in:	Cobalt and/or Gray, Afghanistan (other)
Current Status:	Deceased, 6/12

Ridha Ahmad Najar, aka Najjar (EIT)

SSCI Prisoner Number:	6
Nationality:	Tunisian
Entered CIA Custody:	Pakistan, 6/1/02–6/9/02
Released by CIA to:	Bagram, 5/1/04–5/18/04
Facilities Detained in:	Cobalt and/or Gray, Orange*, Afghanistan (other)
Current Status:	Detained, Afghanistan

Ayub Marshid Ali Salih

SSCI Prisoner Number:	7
Nationality:	Yemeni
Entered CIA Custody:	Pakistan, 9/14/02–9/15/02
Released by CIA to:	Bagram, 10/14/02–10/24/02
Facilities Detained in:	Cobalt and/or Gray
Current Status:	Detained, Guantánamo Bay

Bashir Nasir Ali al-Marwalah

SSCI Prisoner Number:	8
Nationality:	Yemeni
Entered CIA Custody:	Pakistan, 9/14/02–9/15/02
Released by CIA to:	Bagram, 10/14/02–10/24/02
Facilities Detained in:	Cobalt and/or Gray
Current Status:	Detained, Guantánamo Bay

Ha'il Aziz Ahmad al-Mithali

SSCI Prisoner Number:	9
Nationality:	Yemeni
Entered CIA Custody:	Pakistan, 9/14/02–9/15/02
Released by CIA to:	Bagram, 10/14/02–10/24/02
Facilities Detained in:	Cobalt and/or Gray
Current Status:	Detained, Guantánamo Bay

Hassan bin Attash

SSCI Prisoner Number:	10
Nationality:	Saudi
Entered CIA Custody:	Pakistan, 9/14/02–9/15/02
Released by CIA to:	Bagram, 5/4/04–5/14/04
Facilities Detained in:	Cobalt and/or Gray, Orange*, Jordan
Current Status:	Detained, Guantánamo Bay

Musab Umar Ali al-Mudwani

SSCI Prisoner Number:	11
Nationality:	Yemeni
Entered CIA Custody:	Pakistan, 9/14/02–9/15/02
Released by CIA to:	Bagram, 10/14/02–10/24/02
Facilities Detained in:	Cobalt and/or Gray
Current Status:	Detained, Guantánamo Bay

UNCLASSIFIED

~~TOP SECRET//~~[redacted]~~//NOFORN~~

IX. Appendix 2: CIA Detainees from 2002 – 2008

#	*CIA Detainees*	*Date of Custody*	*Days in CIA Custody*
1	**Abu Zubaydah**	[redacted] 2002	1,59[redacted]
2	Zakariya	[redacted]2002	36[redacted]
3	Jamal Eldin Boudraa	[redacted]2002	62[redacted]
4	Abbar al-Hawari, aka Abu Sufiyan	[redacted]2002	36[redacted]
5	Hassan Muhammad Abu Bakr Qa'id	[redacted]2002	51[redacted]
6	**Ridha Ahmad Najar, aka Najjar**	[redacted]2002	69[redacted]
7	Ayub Murshid Ali Salih	[redacted]2002	4[redacted]
8	Bashir Nasir Ali al-Marwalah	[redacted]2002	4[redacted]
9	Ha'il Aziz Ahmad al-Mithali	[redacted]2002	4[redacted]
10	Hassan bin Attash	[redacted]2002	59[redacted]
11	Musab Umar Ali al-Mudwani	[redacted]2002	4[redacted]
12	Said Saleh Said, aka Said Salih Said	[redacted] 2002	4[redacted]
13	Shawqi Awad	[redacted]2002	4[redacted]
14	Umar Faruq, aka Abu al-Faruq al-Kuwaiti	[redacted]2002	41[redacted]
15	Abd al-Salam al-Hilah	[redacted]2002	59[redacted]
16	*Karim, aka Asat Sar Jan*	[redacted]2002	6[redacted]
17	*Akbar Zakaria, aka Zakaria Zeineddin*	[redacted]2002	5[redacted]
18	***Rafiq bin Bashir bin Halul al-Hami***	[redacted]2002	5[redacted]
19	***Tawfiq Nasir Awad al Bihani***	[redacted]2002	5[redacted]
20	**Lutfi al-Arabi al-Gharisi**	[redacted]2002	38[redacted]
21	***Dr. Hikmat Nafi Shaukat***	[redacted]2002	7[redacted]
22	*Yaqub al-Baluchi aka Abu Talha*	[redacted]2002	8[redacted]
23	Abd al-Rahim Ghulam Rabbani	[redacted]2002	54[redacted]
24	**Gul Rahman**	[redacted]2002	1[redacted]
25	**Ghulam Rabbani aka Abu Badr**	[redacted]2002	54[redacted]
26	**Abd al-Rahim al-Nashiri**	[redacted]2002	1,37[redacted]
27	*Haji Ghalgi*	[redacted]2002	18[redacted]
28	*Nazar Ali*	[redacted]2002	3[redacted]
29	*Juma Gul*	[redacted]2002	8[redacted]
30	*Wafti bin Ali aka Abdullah*	[redacted]2002	8[redacted]
31	*Adel*	[redacted]2002	6[redacted]
32	*Qari Mohib Ur Rehman*	[redacted]2002	6[redacted]
33	*Shah Wali Khan*	[redacted]2002	2[redacted]
34	*Hayatullah Haqqani*	[redacted]2002	8[redacted]
35	Bisher al-Rawi	[redacted]2002	[redacted]
36	Jamil el-Banna, aka Abu Anas	[redacted]2002	[redacted]

~~TS~~[redacted]~~NF~~

KEY

Bold Text: Detainees in bold text were subjected to the CIA's enhanced interrogation techniques.

Italics Text: Detainees in italics have not been previously acknowledged by the CIA to the SSCI.

#: Detainee number on main detainee spreadsheet; based on date of CIA custody. Number is based on a designation made by the Committee, not the CIA.

Note on Redaction: The last digit of days in CIA custody is redacted.

SOURCE INFORMATION

CIA Fax to SSCI Committee Staff, entitled, "15 June Request for Excel Spreadsheet," June 17, 2009. DTS #2009-2529.

CIA detainee charts provided to the Committee on April 27, 2007. Document in Committee Records entitled, "Briefing Charts provided to committee members from CIA Director Michael Hayden at the closed Hearing on April 12, 2007, concerning EITs used with CIA detainees, and a list of techniques." DTS #2007-1594.

CIA operational cables and other records produced for the Committee's Study of the CIA's Detention and Interrogation Program.

~~TOP SECRET//~~[redacted]~~//NOFORN~~

Page 458 of 499

UNCLASSIFIED

Fig. A.1

Above and right. Pages from the SSCI report listing all 119 publicly acknowledged extraordinary renditions. Prisoners previously unknown and the use of "Enhanced Interrogation Techniques" (EIT) were noted by the committee.

UNCLASSIFIED
TOP SECRET//[redacted]//NOFORN

#	CIA Detainees	Date of Custody	Days in CIA Custody
37	**Ghairat Bahir**	[redacted]2002	5[redacted]
38	Pacha Wazir	[redacted] 2002	3[redacted]
39	Muhammad Amein al-Bakri	[redacted] 2003	4[redacted]
40	*Abdullah Midhat Mursi*	[redacted]2003	1[redacted]
41	**Ramzi bin al-Shibh**	[redacted]2002	12[redacted]
42	**Ibn Shaykh al-Libi**	[redacted]2002	11[redacted]
43	**Muhammad Umar 'Abd al-Rahman, aka Asadallah**	[redacted]2003	1[redacted]
44	***Abu Khalid***	[redacted]2003	[redacted]
45	**Khalid Shaykh Mohammad**	[redacted]2003	12[redacted]
46	**Mustafa Ahmad al-Hawsawi**	[redacted]2003	12[redacted]
47	**Abu Yasir al-Jaza'iri**	[redacted]2003	12[redacted]
48	**Suleiman Abdullah**	[redacted]2003	4[redacted]
49	Hamid Aich	[redacted]2003	[redacted]
50	Sayed Habib	[redacted]2003	4[redacted]
51	**Abu Hazim, aka Abu Hazim al-Libi**	[redacted]2003	7[redacted]
52	**Al-Shara'iya, aka Abd al-Karim**	[redacted]2003	4[redacted]
53	Muhammad Khan (son of Sabbat)	[redacted]2003	5[redacted]
54	*Ibrahim Haqqani*	[redacted]2003	[redacted]
55	**Ammar al-Baluchi**	[redacted]2003	11[redacted]
56	**Khallad bin Attash**	[redacted]2003	11[redacted]
57	**Laid Ben Dohman Saidi, aka Abu Hudhaifa**	[redacted]2003	4[redacted]
58	**Majid Khan**	[redacted]2003	11[redacted]
59	Muhammad Dinshah	[redacted]2003	2[redacted]
60	Muhammad Jafar Jamal al-Qahtani	[redacted]2003	3[redacted]
61	Abu Naim al-Tunisi	[redacted]2003	3[redacted]
62	**Mohd Farik bin Amin, aka Abu Zubair**	[redacted]2003	11[redacted]
63	*Zarmein*	[redacted]2003	1[redacted]
64	Hiwa Abdul Rahman Rashul	[redacted]2003	1[redacted]
65	Adel Abu Radwan Ben Hamlili	[redacted]2003	3[redacted]
66	Shawqat Habibullah Khan	[redacted]2003	2[redacted]
67	**Samr Hilmi Abdul Latif al-Barq**	[redacted]2003	[redacted]
68	Ali Jan	[redacted] 2003	3[redacted]
69	Muhammad Khan (son of Amir)	[redacted]2003	[redacted]
70	Modin Nik Muhammad	[redacted]2003	7[redacted]
71	Abdullah Ashami	[redacted]2003	2[redacted]
72	**Bashir bin Lap, aka Lillie**	[redacted]2003	11[redacted]
73	**Ridwan bin Isomuddin, aka Hambali**	[redacted]2003	12[redacted]

TS[redacted]NF

KEY

Bold Text: Detainees in bold text were subjected to the CIA's enhanced interrogation techniques.

Italics Text: Detainees in italics have not been previously acknowledged by the CIA to the SSCI.

#: Detainee number on main detainee spreadsheet, based on date of CIA custody. Number is based on a designation made by the SSCI, not the CIA.

SOURCE INFORMATION

CIA Fax to SSCI Committee Staff, entitled, "15 June Request for Excel Spreadsheet," June 17, 2009 (DTS #2009-2529)

CIA detainee charts provided to the Committee on April 27, 2007. Document in Committee Records entitled, "Briefing Charts provided to committee members from CIA Director Michael Hayden at the closed Hearing on April 12, 2007, concerning EITs used with CIA detainees, and a list of techniques." DTS #2007-1594.

CIA operational cables and other records produced for the Committee's Study of the CIA's Detention and Interrogation Program.

TOP SECRET//[redacted]//NOFORN
Page 459 of 499

UNCLASSIFIED

Fig. A.2

UNCLASSIFIED
TOP SECRET//[redacted]//NOFORN

#	CIA Detainees	Date of Custody	Days in CIA Custody
74	Sanad 'Ali Yislam al-Kazimi	[redacted]2003	3[redacted]
75	Salah Nasir Salim 'Ali, aka Muhsin	[redacted]2003	9[redacted]
76	Abd Qadir Allah Muhi Amar al-Hadi	[redacted]2003	[redacted]
77	Bismullah	[redacted]2003	[redacted]
78	Sa'id Allam	[redacted]2003	[redacted]
79	Sa'ida Gul	[redacted]2003	[redacted]
80	Shah Khan Wali	[redacted]2003	[redacted]
81	Yahya, aka Raqallah	[redacted]2003	[redacted]
82	*Zakariya 'abd al-Rauf*	[redacted]2003	[redacted]
83	*Zamann Nur Muhammad Jomu Khan*	[redacted]2003	[redacted]
84	*Abdullah Salim al-Qahtani*	[redacted]2003	[redacted]
85	*Arwad Sabhan al-Shammari*	[redacted]2003	[redacted]
86	Nasir Jalal	[redacted]2003	2[redacted]
87	**Majid Bin Muhammad Bin Sulayman Khayyil, aka Arsala Khan**	[redacted]2003	[redacted]
88	*Ayu Hendeci*	[redacted]2003	[redacted]
89	Mohd al-Shomirale	[redacted]2003	5[redacted]
90	Ali Saeed Awadh	[redacted]2003	1[redacted]
91	**Adnan al-Libi**	[redacted] 2003	2[redacted]
92	Muhammad Abdullah Saleh	[redacted] 2004	4[redacted]
93	Riyadh the Facilitator	[redacted]2004	1[redacted]
94	Abu Abdullah al-Zalaytini	[redacted]2004	2[redacted]
95	Binyam Ahmed Muhamed	[redacted]2004	1[redacted]
96	Firas al-Yemeni	[redacted]2004	9[redacted]
98	Khalid 'Abd al-Razzaq al-Masri	[redacted]2004	1[redacted]
97	**Hassan Ghul**	[redacted]2004	9[redacted]
99	**Muhammad Qurban Sayyid Ibrahim**	[redacted]2004	2[redacted]
100	Saud Memon	[redacted]2004	7[redacted]
101	*Gul Rahman (2)*	[redacted]2004	[redacted]
102	Hassan Ahmed Guleed	[redacted]2004	9[redacted]
103	Abu 'Abdallah	[redacted]2004	8[redacted]
104	**ABU BAHAR AL-TURKI**	[REDACTED] 2004	Approximately 1[redacted]
105	**ABU TALHA AL-MAGREBI**	[REDACTED] 2004	Approximately 1[redacted]
106	Abd al-Bari al-Filistini	[redacted] 2004	7[redacted]
107	Ayyub al-Libi	[redacted]2004	9[redacted]
108	Marwan al-Jabbur	[redacted]2004	7[redacted]
109	Qutal al-Uzbeki	[redacted]2004	8[redacted]

TS[redacted]NF

KEY

Bold Text: Detainees in bold text were subjected to the CIA's enhanced interrogation techniques.

Italics Text: Detainees in italics have not been previously acknowledged by the CIA to the SSCI.

#: Detainee number on main detainee spreadsheet, based on date of CIA custody. Number is based on a designation made by the SSCI, not the CIA.

SOURCE INFORMATION

CIA Fax to SSCI Committee Staff, entitled, "15 June Request for Excel Spreadsheet," June 17, 2009 (DTS #2009-2529)

CIA detainee charts provided to the Committee on April 27, 2007. Document in Committee Records entitled, "Briefing Charts provided to committee members from CIA Director Michael Hayden at the closed Hearing on April 12, 2007, concerning EITs used with CIA detainees, and a list of techniques." DTS #2007-1594.

CIA operational cables and other records produced for the Committee's Study of the CIA's Detention and Interrogation Program.

TOP SECRET//[redacted]//NOFORN
Page 460 of 499

UNCLASSIFIED

Fig. A.3

UNCLASSIFIED
TOP SECRET//[redacted]//NOFORN

#	CIA Detainees	Date of Custody	Days in CIA Custody
110	**Janat Gul**	[redacted]2004	9[redacted]
111	**Ahmed Khalfan Ghailani**	[redacted]2004	1[redacted]
112	**Sharif al-Masri**	[redacted]2004	9[redacted]
113	*Abd Rashid Samaan*	[redacted] 2004	6[redacted]
114	**Abu Faraj al-Libi**	[redacted] 2005	4[redacted]
115	*Abu Munthir al-Magrebi*	[redacted]2005	4[redacted]
116	Ibrahim Jan	[redacted]	3[redacted]
117	**Abu Ja'far al-Iraqi**	[redacted] 2005	2[redacted]
118	*Abd al-Hadi al-Iraqi*	[redacted] 2006	1[redacted]
119	**Muhammad Rahim**	[redacted] 2007	2[redacted]

TS[redacted]NF

KEY

Bold Text: Detainees in bold text were subjected to the CIA's enhanced interrogation techniques.

Italics Text: Detainees in italics have not been previously acknowledged by the CIA to the SSCI.

#: Detainee number on main detainee spreadsheet, based on date of CIA custody. Number is based on a designation made by the SSCI, not the CIA.

Sources: CIA Fax to SSCI Committee Staff, entitled, "15 June Request for Excel Spreadsheet," June 17, 2009 (DTS #2009-2529); CIA detainee charts provided to the Committee on April 27, 2007; document in Committee records entitled, "Briefing Charts provided to committee Members from CIA Director Michael Hayden at the closed Hearing on April 12, 2007, concerning EITs used with CIA detainees, and a list of techniques" (DTS #2007-1594, hearing transcript at DTS# 2007-3158); and CIA operational cables and other records produced for the Committee's Study of the CIA's Detention and Interrogation Program.

** Gul Rahman, listed as detainee 24, was the subject of a notification to the Senate Select Committee on Intelligence following his death at DETENTION SITE COBALT; however, he has not appeared on lists of CIA detainees provided to Committee.

TOP SECRET//[redacted]//NOFORN
Page 461 of 499

UNCLASSIFIED

Fig. A.4

Said Saleh Said, aka Said Salih Said

SSCI Prisoner Number: 12
Nationality: Yemeni
Entered CIA Custody: Pakistan, 9/14/02–9/15/02
Released by CIA to: Bagram, 10/14/02–10/24/02
Facilities Detained in: Cobalt and/or Gray
Current Status: Detained, Guantánamo Bay

Shawqi Awad

SSCI Prisoner Number: 13
Nationality: Yemeni
Entered CIA Custody: Pakistan, 9/14/02–9/15/02
Released by CIA to: Bagram, 10/14/02–10/24/02
Facilities Detained in: Cobalt and/or Gray
Current Status: Detained, Guantánamo Bay

Umar Faruq, aka Abu al-Faruq al-Kuwaiti

SSCI Prisoner Number: 14
Nationality: Kuwaiti
Entered CIA Custody: Indonesia, 9/14/02–9/29/02
Released by CIA to: Bagram, 10/29/03–11/22/03
Facilities Detained in: Cobalt and/or Gray
Current Status: Deceased, 9/25/06

Abd al-Salam al-Hilah

SSCI Prisoner Number: 15
Nationality: Yemeni
Entered CIA CustodyA: Egypt, 9/29/02
Released by CIA to: Bagram, 5/11/04–5/20/04
Facilities Detained in: Cobalt and/or Gray, Orange, Afghanistan (other)
Current Status: Detained, Guantánamo Bay

Karim, aka Asat Sar Jan

SSCI Prisoner Number: 16
Nationality: Not known
Entered CIA Custody: Not known, 9/29/02–10/28/02
Released by CIA to: Not known, 11/28/02–1/5/03
Facilities Detained in: Cobalt and/or Gray
Current Status: Not known

Akbar Zakaria, aka Zakaria Zeineddin

SSCI Prisoner Number: 17
Nationality: Not known
Entered CIA Custody: Not known, 9/29/02–10/28/02
Released by CIA to: Not known, 11/18/02–12/26/02
Facilities Detained in: Cobalt and/or Gray
Current Status: Not known

Rafiq bin Bashir bin Halul al-Hami (EIT)
SSCI Prisoner Number: 18
Nationality: Tunisian
Entered CIA Custody: Iran, 9/29/02–10/28/02
Released by CIA to: Bagram, 11/18/02–12/26/02
Facilities Detained in: Cobalt and/or Gray, Afghanistan (other)
Current Status: Released, 2011

Tawfiq Nasir Awad al Bihani (EIT)
SSCI Prisoner Number: 19
Nationality: Yemeni
Entered CIA Custody: Iran, 9/29/02–10/28/02
Released by CIA to: Bagram, 11/18/02–12/26/02
Facilities Detained in: Cobalt and/or Gray, Afghanistan (other)
Current Status: Detained, Guantánamo Bay

Lutfi al-Arabi al-Gharisi (EIT)
SSCI Prisoner Number: 20
Nationality: Tunisian
Entered CIA Custody: Not known, 9/29/02–10/28/02
Released by CIA to: Bagram, 10/14/03–11/21/03
Facilities Detained in: Cobalt and/or Gray
Current Status: Detained, Afghanistan

Dr. Hikmat Nafi Shaukat (EIT)
SSCI Prisoner Number: 21
Nationality: Iraqi
Entered CIA Custody: Pakistan, 9/29/02–10/30/02
Released by CIA to: Not known, 12/8/02–1/17/03
Facilities Detained in: Cobalt and/or Gray
Current Status: Not known

Yaqub al-Baluchi aka Abu Talha
SSCI Prisoner Number: 22
Nationality: Not known
Entered CIA Custody: Not known, 9/29/02–11/9/02
Released by CIA to: Not known, 12/18/02–2/6/03
Facilities Detained in: Cobalt and/or Gray
Current Status: Not known

Abd al-Rahim Ghulam Rabbani
SSCI Prisoner Number: 23
Nationality: Pakistani
Entered CIA Custody: Pakistan, 11/1/02–11/9/02
Released by CIA to: Bagram, 5/4/04–5/21/04
Facilities Detained in:x Cobalt and/or Gray, Orange*, Afghanistan (other)
Current Status: Detained, Guantánamo Bay

Gul Rahman (1) (EIT)
SSCI Prisoner Number: 24
Nationality: Afghan
Entered CIA Custody: Pakistan, 11/1/02–11/9/02
Released by CIA to: Killed in CIA custody, 11/20/02
Facilities Detained in: Cobalt and/or Gray
Current Status: Deceased in CIA detention, 10/2002

Ghulam Rabbani aka Abu Badr (EIT)
SSCI Prisoner Number: 25
Nationality: Pakistani
Entered CIA Custody: Pakistan, 11/1/02–11/9/02
Released by CIA to: Bagram, 5/4/04–5/21/04
Facilities Detained in: Cobalt and/or Gray, Orange*, Afghanistan (other)
Current Status: Detained, Guantánamo Bay

Abd al-Rahim al-Nashiri (HVD, EIT)
SSCI Prisoner Number: 26
Nationality: Saudi
Entered CIA Custody: UAE, 11/10/02–11/11/02
Released by CIA to: Guantánamo Bay, 9/5/06
Facilities Detained in: Green, Cobalt and/or Gray, Blue, Black, Indigo and/or Maroon, Morocco
Current Status: Detained, Guantánamo Bay

Haji Ghalgi
SSCI Prisoner Number: 27
Nationality: Not known
Entered CIA Custody: Not known, 11/10/02–12/9/02
Released by CIA to: Not known, 5/19/03–6/26/03
Facilities Detained in: Cobalt and/or Gray
Current Status: Not known

Nazar Ali
SSCI Prisoner Number: 28
Nationality: Not known
Entered CIA Custody: Not known, 11/10/02–12/9/02
Released by CIA to: Not known, 12/10/02–1/17/03
Facilities Detained in: Cobalt and/or Gray
Current Status: Not known

Juma Gul
SSCI Prisoner Number: 29
Nationality: Not known
Entered CIA Custody: Not known, 11/10/02–12/9/02
Released by CIA to: Released, 2/8/03–3/18/03
Facilities Detained in: Cobalt and/or Gray
Current Status: Released, 2003

Wafti bin Ali aka Abdullah

SSCI Prisoner Number:	30
Nationality:	Not known
Entered CIA Custody:	Not known, 11/10/02–12/9/02
Released by CIA to:	Not known, 1/29/03–3/8/03
Facilities Detained in:	Cobalt and/or Gray
Current Status:	Not known

Adel

SSCI Prisoner Number:	31
Nationality:	Not known
Entered CIA Custody:	Not known, 11/10/02–12/9/02
Released by CIA to:	Not known, 1/9/03–2/16/03
Facilities Detained in:	Cobalt and/or Gray
Current Status:	Not known

Qari Mohib Ur Rehman

SSCI Prisoner Number:	32
Nationality:	Afghan
Entered CIA Custody:	Pakistan, 11/10/02–12/9/02
Released by CIA to:	Released, 1/9/03–2/16/03
Facilities Detained in:	Cobalt and/or Gray
Current Status:	Released, 2/11/03

Shah Wali Khan

SSCI Prisoner Number:	33
Nationality:	Afghan
Entered CIA Custody:	Not known, 11/15/02–12/9/02
Released by CIA to:	Bagram, 12/5/02–1/7/03
Facilities Detained in:	Cobalt and/or Gray
Current Status:	Not known

Hayattulah Haqqani

SSCI Prisoner Number:	34
Nationality:	Not known
Entered CIA Custody:	Not known, 11/15/02–12/9/02
Released by CIA to:	Not known, 2/3/03–3/8/03
Facilities Detained in:	Cobalt and/or Gray
Current Status:	Not known

Bisher al-Rawi

SSCI Prisoner Number:	35
Nationality:	Iraqi
Entered CIA Custody:	Gambia, 12/9/02
Released by CIA to:	Bagram, 12/10/02–12/18/02
Facilities Detained in:	Cobalt and/or Gray
Current Status:	Released, 30 March 2007

Jamil el-Banna, aka Abu Anas

SSCI Prisoner Number:	36
Nationality:	Jordanian
Entered CIA Custody:	Gambia, 12/9/02
Released by CIA to:	Bagram, 12/10/02–12/18/02
Facilities Detained in:	Cobalt and/or Gray
Current Status:	Released, 12/19/07

Ghairat Bahir (EIT)

SSCI Prisoner Number:	37
Nationality:	Afghan
Entered CIA Custody:	Pakistan, 12/9/02–12/31/02
Released by CIA to:	Bagram, 5/2/04–6/2/04
Facilities Detained in:	Cobalt and/or Gray, Orange*
Current Status:	Released, 05/08

Pacha Wazir

SSCI Prisoner Number:	38
Nationality:	Afghan
Entered CIA Custody:	UAE, Morocco, 12/9/02–12/31/02
Released by CIA to:	Bagram, 11/4/03–12/5/03
Facilities Detained in:	Cobalt and/or Gray
Current Status:	Released, 2/10

Muhammad Amein al-Bakri

SSCI Prisoner Number:	39
Nationality:	Yemeni
Entered CIA Custody:	Thailand, 1/1/03–2/8/03
Released by CIA to:	Bagram, 5/5/04–6/21/04
Facilities Detained in:	Green*, Cobalt and/or Gray, Orange*
Current Status:	Released, 09/14

Abdullah Midhat Mursi

SSCI Prisoner Number:	40
Nationality:	Not known
Entered CIA Custody:	Not known, 1/1/03–2/8/03
Released by CIA to:	Not known, 4/21/03–6/7/03
Facilities Detained in:	Cobalt and/or Gray
Current Status:	Not known

Ramzi bin al-Shibh (HVD, EIT)

SSCI Prisoner Number:	41
Nationality:	Yemeni
Entered CIA Custody:	Pakistan, 2/8/03
Released by CIA to:	Guantánamo Bay, 9/5/06
Facilities Detained in:	Cobalt and/or Gray, Blue, Black, Indigo and/or Maroon, Orange, Morocco, Jordan*
Current Status:	Detained, Guantánamo Bay

Ibn Shaykh al-Libi (HVD)

SSCI Prisoner Number: 42
Nationality: Libyan
Entered CIA Custody: Pakistan; Afghanistan (DoD); Egypt, 2/9/03–2/9/03
Released by CIA to: Libya (?), 4/14/06–4/23/06
Facilities Detained in: Cobalt and/or Gray, Indigo and/or Maroon, Morocco
Current Status: Deceased, 5/9/09

Muhammad Umar 'Abd al-Rahman, aka Asadallah (EIT)

SSCI Prisoner Number: 43
Nationality: Egyptian
Entered CIA Custody: Pakistan, 2/9/03–2/28/03
Released by CIA to: Egypt*, 7/9/03–8/6/03
Facilities Detained in: Cobalt and/or Gray
Current Status: Released, 2010

Abu Khalid (EIT)

SSCI Prisoner Number: 44
Nationality: Not known
Entered CIA Custody: Not known, 2/9/03–3/5/03
Released by CIA to: Not known, 3/1/03–4/3/03
Facilities Detained in: Cobalt and/or Gray
Current Status: Not known

Khalid Shaykh Mohammad (HVD, EIT)

SSCI Prisoner Number: 45
Nationality: Pakistani
Entered CIA Custody: Pakistan, 3/3/03–3/5/03
Released by CIA to: Guantánamo Bay, 9/5/06–9/5/06
Facilities Detained in: Cobalt and/or Gray, Blue, Black, Violet, Brown
Current Status: Detained in Guantánamo Bay

Mustafa Ahmad al-Hawsawi (HVD, EIT)

SSCI Prisoner Number: 46
Nationality: Saudi
Entered CIA Custody: Pakistan, 3/3/03–3/5/03
Released by CIA to: Guantánamo Bay, 9/4/06–9/5/06
Facilities Detained in: Cobalt and/or Gray, Indigo and/or Maroon, Violet, Brown, Morocco
Current Status: Detained, Guantánamo Bay

Abu Yasir al-Jaza'iri (EIT)

SSCI Prisoner Number: 47
Nationality: Algerian
Entered CIA Custody: Pakistan, 3/3/03–3/26/03
Released by CIA to: Foreign custody, 8/14/06–9/6/06
Facilities Detained in: Cobalt and/or Gray, Blue, Black*, Indigo and/or Maroon*, Orange, Morocco*
Current Status: Not known

Suleiman Abdullah (EIT)

SSCI Prisoner Number:	48
Nationality:	Tanzanian
Entered CIA Custody:	Somalia, Kenya, Somalia, Djibouti, 3/28/03–3/28/03
Released by CIA to:	Bagram, 5/31/04–6/9/04
Facilities Detained in:	Cobalt and/or Gray, Orange
Current Status:	Released, 10/08

Hamid Aich

SSCI Prisoner Number:	49
Nationality:	Not known
Entered CIA Custody:	Not known, 3/28/03–4/18/03
Released by CIA to:	Not known, 5/7/03–6/6/03
Facilities Detained in:	Afghanistan (other)
Current Status:	Not known

Sayed Habib

SSCI Prisoner Number:	50
Nationality:	Not known
Entered CIA Custody:	Not known, 4/1/03 4/18/03
Released by CIA to:	Released, 8/13/04–8/31/04
Facilities Detained in:	Cobalt and/or Gray, Orange
Current Status:	Released, 8/04

Abu Hazim, aka Abu Hazim al-Libi (EIT)

SSCI Prisoner Number:	51
Nationality:	Libyan
Entered CIA Custody:	Pakistan, 4/13/03–4/18/03
Released by CIA to:	Libya, 4/21/05
Facilities Detained in:	Cobalt and/or Gray, Orange
Current Status:	Released, 3/23/10

Al-Shara'iya, aka Abd al-Karim (EIT)

SSCI Prisoner Number:	52
Nationality:	Libyan
Entered CIA Custody:	Pakistan, 4/13/03–4/18/03
Released by CIA to:	Libya, 8/22/04
Facilities Detained in:	Cobalt and/or Gray, Orange
Current Status:	Released, 2/16/11

Muhammad Khan (son of Suhbat)

SSCI Prisoner Number:	53
Nationality:	Not known
Entered CIA Custody:	Not known, 4/13/03–5/16/03
Released by CIA to:	Not known, 5/7/04–6/18/04
Facilities Detained in:	Cobalt and/or Gray, Orange*
Current Status:	Not known

Ibrahim Haqqani

SSCI Prisoner Number: 54
Nationality: Not known
Entered CIA Custody: Not known, 4/13/03–5/16/03
Released by CIA to: Not known, 5/3/03–6/14/03
Facilities Detained in: Cobalt and/or Gray
Current Status: Not known

Ammar al-Baluchi (HVD, EIT)

SSCI Prisoner Number: 55
Nationality: Kuwaiti
Entered CIA Custody: Pakistan, 5/15/03–5/16/03
Released by CIA to: Guantánamo Bay, 9/4/06–9/5/06
Facilities Detained in: Cobalt and/or Gray, Black, Morocco
Current Status: Detained, Guantánamo Bay

Khallad bin Attash (HVD, EIT)

SSCI Prisoner Number: 56
Nationality: Yemeni
Entered CIA Custody: Pakistan, 5/15/03–5/16/03
Released by CIA to: Guantánamo Bay, 9/4/06–9/5/06
Facilities Detained in: Cobalt and/or Gray, Blue, Black
Current Status: Detained, Guantánamo Bay

Laid Ben Dohman Saidi, aka Abu Hudhaifa (EIT)

SSCI Prisoner Number: 57
Nationality: Algerian
Entered CIA Custody: Tanzania; Malawi, 5/15/03–5/24/03
Released by CIA to: Algeria, 8/26/04–8/26/04
Facilities Detained in: Cobalt and/or Gray, Orange, Afghanistan (other)
Current Status: Released, 08/04

Majid Khan (HVD, EIT)

SSCI Prisoner Number: 58
Nationality: Pakistani
Entered CIA Custody: Pakistan, 5/15/03–5/24/03
Released by CIA to: Guantánamo Bay, 9/4/06–9/5/06
Facilities Detained in: Cobalt and/or Gray, Orange, Afghanistan (other)
Current Status: Detained, Guantánamo Bay

Mohammad Dinshah

SSCI Prisoner Number: 59
Nationality: Not known
Entered CIA Custody: Not known, 5/15/03–6/20/03
Released by CIA to: Not known, 1/30/04–3/15/04
Facilities Detained in: Afghanistan (other)
Current Status: Not known

Muhammad Jafar Jamal al-Qahtani
SSCI Prisoner Number: 60
Nationality: Saudi
Entered CIA Custody: Not known, 5/15/03–6/20/03
Released by CIA to: Bagram, 4/19/04–6/3/04
Facilities Detained in: Cobalt and/or Gray, Orange*
Current Status: Not known

Abu Nasim al-Tunisi
SSCI Prisoner Number: 61
Nationality: Not known
Entered CIA Custody: Not known, 5/15/03–6/20/03
Released by CIA to: Bagram, 4/9/04–5/24/04
Facilities Detained in: Cobalt and/or Gray, Orange*
Current Status: Not known

Mohd Farik bin Amin, aka Abu Zubair (HVD, EIT)
SSCI Prisoner Number: 62
Nationality: Malaysian
Entered CIA Custody: Thailand, 6/18/03–6/20/03
Released by CIA to: Guantánamo Bay, 9/4/06–9/5/06
Facilities Detained in: Cobalt and/or Gray
Current Status: Detained, Guantánamo Bay

Zarmein
SSCI Prisoner Number: 63
Nationality: Not known
Entered CIA Custody: Not known, 6/18/03–7/24/03
Released by CIA to: Released, 1/4/04–2/18/04
Facilities Detained in: Cobalt and/or Gray
Current Status: Released, 01/04–02/04

Hiwa Abdul Rahman Rashul
SSCI Prisoner Number: 64
Nationality: Iraqi
Entered CIA Custody: Iraq, 6/18/03–7/24/03
Released by CIA to: Iraq, 10/6/03–11/20/03
Facilities Detained in: Cobalt and/or Gray
Current Status: Not known

Adel Abu Redwan Ben Hamlili
SSCI Prisoner Number: 65
Nationality: Algerian
Entered CIA Custody: Pakistan, 6/18/03–7/24/03
Released by CIA to: Bagram, 4/13/04–5/28/04
Facilities Detained in: Cobalt and/or Gray, Orange*
Current Status: Released, 1/22/10

Shaistah Habibullah Khan

SSCI Prisoner Number:	66
Nationality:	Not known
Entered CIA Custody:	Not known, 7/1/03–7/24/03
Released by CIA to:	Released, 2/6/04–2/29/04
Facilities Detained in:	Cobalt and/or Gray
Current Status:	Released, 2/04

Samr Hilmi Abdul Lalif al-Barq (EIT)

SSCI Prisoner Number:	67
Nationality:	Palestinian
Entered CIA Custody:	Pakistan, 7/29/03–8/1/03
Released by CIA to:	Jordan, 10/17/03–10/29/03
Facilities Detained in:	Cobalt and/or Gray, Blue, Black
Current Status:	Detained, Israel

Ali Jan

SSCI Prisoner Number:	68
Nationality:	Not known
Entered CIA Custody:	Afghanistan, 8/1/03–8/14/03
Released by CIA to:	Bagram, 5/7/04–5/29/04
Facilities Detained in:	Cobalt and/or Gray, Orange*
Current Status:	Released, 07/04

Muhammad Khan (son of Amir)

SSCI Prisoner Number:	69
Nationality:	Not known
Entered CIA Custody:	Not known, 8/1/03–8/14/03
Released by CIA to:	Not known, 2/17/04–3/10/04
Facilities Detained in:	Cobalt and/or Gray
Current Status:	Not known

Modin Nik Muhammad

SSCI Prisoner Number:	70
Nationality:	Not known
Entered CIA Custody:	Not known, 8/1/03–8/14/03
Released by CIA to:	Released, 11/29/03–12/21/03
Facilities Detained in:	Cobalt and/or Gray
Current Status:	Released, 11/03–12/03

Abdullah Ashami

SSCI Prisoner Number:	71
Nationality:	Syrian
Entered CIA Custody:	Afghanistan, 8/1/03–8/14/03
Released by CIA to:	Bagram, 4/27/04–5/19/04
Facilities Detained in:	Cobalt and/or Gray, Orange*
Current Status:	Deceased, 7/08

Bashir bin Lap, aka Lillie (HVD, EIT)

SSCI Prisoner Number:	72
Nationality:	Malaysian
Entered CIA Custody:	Thailand, 8/13/03–8/14/03
Released by CIA to:	Guantánamo Bay, 9/4/06–9/5/06
Facilities Detained in:	Cobalt and/or Gray
Current Status:	Detained, Guantánamo Bay

Riduan bin Isomuddin, aka Hambali (HVD, EIT)

SSCI Prisoner Number:	73
Nationality:	Indonesian
Entered CIA Custody:	Thailand, 8/13/03–8/14/03
Released by CIA to:	Guantánamo Bay, 9/4/06
Facilities Detained in:	Cobalt and/or Gray, Black, Morocco
Current Status:	Detained, Guantánamo Bay

Sanad 'Ali Yislam al-Kazimi

SSCI Prisoner Number:	74
Nationality:	Yemeni
Entered CIA Custody:	UAE, 8/13/03–8/17/03
Released by CIA to:	Bagram, 5/13/04
Facilities Detained in:	Cobalt and/or Gray, Orange*
Current Status:	Detained, Guantánamo Bay

Salah Nasir Salim Ali, aka Muhsin

SSCI Prisoner Number:	75
Nationality:	Yemeni
Entered CIA Custody:	Indonesia, Jordan, 8/28/03–9/15/03
Released by CIA to:	Yemen, 4/28/05–5/7/05
Facilities Detained in:	Cobalt and/or Gray, Orange
Current Status:	Released, 3/27/06–3/28/06

Abd Qudra Allah Mala Azrat al-Hadi

SSCI Prisoner Number:	76
Nationality:	Not known
Entered CIA Custody:	Not known, 9/16/03–10/20/03
Released by CIA to:	Not known, 12/15/03–1/27/04
Facilities Detained in:	Not known
Current Status:	Not known

Bismullah

SSCI Prisoner Number:	77
Nationality:	Not known
Entered CIA Custody:	Not known, 9/16/03–10/20/03
Released by CIA to:	Released, 9/17/03–10/29/03
Facilities Detained in:	Not known
Current Status:	Released, 9/03–10/03

Sa'id Allam
SSCI Prisoner Number: 78
Nationality: Not known
Entered CIA Custody: Not known, 9/16/03–10/20/03
Released by CIA to: Not known, 12/15/03–1/27/04
Facilities Detained in: Not known
Current Status: Not known

Sa'ida Gul
SSCI Prisoner Number: 79
Nationality: Not known
Entered CIA Custody: Not known, 9/16/03–10/20/03
Released by CIA to: Not known, 12/15/03–1/27/04
Facilities Detained in: Not known
Current Status: Not known

Shah Khan Wali
SSCI Prisoner Number: 80
Nationality: Not known
Entered CIA Custody: Not known, 9/16/03–10/20/03
Released by CIA to: Not known, 12/15/03–1/27/04
Facilities Detained in: Not known
Current Status: Not known

Yahya, aka Rugollah
SSCI Prisoner Number: 81
Nationality: Not known
Entered CIA Custody: Not known, 9/16/03–10/20/03
Released by CIA to: Not known, 12/15/03–1/27/04
Facilities Detained in: Not known
Current Status: Not known

Zakariya 'abd al-Rauf
SSCI Prisoner Number: 82
Nationality: Not known
Entered CIA Custody: Not known, 9/16/03–10/20/03
Released by CIA to: Not known, 12/15/03–1/27/04
Facilities Detained in: Not known
Current Status: Not known

Zamarai Nur Muhammad Juma Khan
SSCI Prisoner Number: 83
Nationality: Not known
Entered CIA Custody: Not known, 9/16/03–10/20/03
Released by CIA to: Not known, 12/15/03–1/27/04
Facilities Detained in: Not known
Current Status: Not known

Abdullah Salim al-Qahtani

SSCI Prisoner Number: 84
Nationality: Not known
Entered CIA Custody: Not known, 9/16/03–10/20/03
Released by CIA to: Not known, 10/6/03–11/18/03
Facilities Detained in: Not known
Current Status: Not known

Awwad Sabhan al-Shammari

SSCI Prisoner Number: 85
Nationality: Not known
Entered CIA Custody: Not known, 9/16/03–10/20/03
Released by CIA to: Not known, 10/6/03–11/18/03
Facilities Detained in: Not known
Current Status: Not known

Noor Jalal

SSCI Prisoner Number: 86
Nationality: Not known
Entered CIA Custody: Not known, 9/16/03–10/20/03
Released by CIA to: Bagram, 5/3/04–6/15/04
Facilities Detained in: Orange*
Current Status: Not known

Majid Bin Muhammad Bin Sulayman Khayil, aka Arsala Khan (EIT)

SSCI Prisoner Number: 87
Nationality: Afghan
Entered CIA Custody: Not known, 9/16/03–10/20/03
Released by CIA to: Bagram, 11/5/03–12/18/03
Facilities Detained in: Cobalt and/or Gray
Current Status: Released, 2007

Aso Hawleri

SSCI Prisoner Number: 88
Nationality: Kurdish
Entered CIA Custody: Iraq, 9/16/03–10/26/03
Released by CIA to: Not known, 9/26/03–11/14/03
Facilities Detained in: Not known
Current Status: Not known

Mohd al-Shomaila, Mohamed Farag Ahmad Bashmilah

SSCI Prisoner Number: 89
Nationality: Yemeni
Entered CIA Custody: Jordan, 10/26/03–10/26/03
Released by CIA to: Yemen, 4/28/05–5/7/05
Facilities Detained in: Cobalt and/or Gray, Orange
Current Status: Released, 3/27/06

Ali Saeed Awadh

SSCI Prisoner Number:	90
Nationality:	Not known
Entered CIA Custody:	Not known, 10/26/03–12/26/03
Released by CIA to:	Released, 4/13/04–6/22/04
Facilities Detained in:	Cobalt and/or Gray
Current Status:	Released, 04/04–06/04

Adnan al-Libi (EIT)

SSCI Prisoner Number:	91
Nationality:	Libyan
Entered CIA Custody:	Pakistan, 12/17/03–12/26/03
Released by CIA to:	Libya, 8/22/04
Facilities Detained in:	Cobalt and/or Gray, Orange
Current Status:	Released, 2/16/11

Muhammad Abdullah Saleh

SSCI Prisoner Number:	92
Nationality:	Yemeni
Entered CIA Custody:	Djibouti, 01/04
Released by CIA to:	Yemen, 5/5/05
Facilities Detained in:	Afghanistan
Current Status:	Deceased

Riyadh the Facilitator, Ali al-Hajj al-Sharqawi

SSCI Prisoner Number:	93
Nationality:	Yemeni
Entered CIA Custody:	Pakistan, 1/8/04
Released by CIA to:	Bagram, 5/10/04–5/16/04
Facilities Detained in:	Cobalt and/or Gray, Orange*, Jordan
Current Status:	Detained, Guantánamo Bay

Abu Abdallah al-Zulaytini

SSCI Prisoner Number:	94
Nationality:	Libyan
Entered CIA Custody:	Mauritania, Morocco, 1/16/04–1/22/04
Released by CIA to:	Libya, 8/22/04
Facilities Detained in:	Cobalt and/or Gray, Orange
Current Status:	Released, 2/16/11

Binyam Ahmed Mohamed

SSCI Prisoner Number:	95
Nationality:	Ethiopian/British
Entered CIA Custody:	Pakistan, Morocco, 1/22/04
Released by CIA to:	Bagram, 5/11/04–5/20/04
Facilities Detained in:	Cobalt and/or Gray, Orange*
Current Status:	Released, 2/23/09

Firas al-Yemeni

SSCI Prisoner Number: 96
Nationality: Yemeni
Entered CIA Custody: Iraq, 1/22/04
Released by CIA to: Yemen, 8/29/06–9/6/06
Facilities Detained in: Cobalt and/or Gray, Orange
Current Status: Released, 5/07

Khalid ‘Abd al-Razzaq al-Masri

SSCI Prisoner Number: 97
Nationality: Kuwaiti/German
Entered CIA Custody: Macedonia, 1/24/04
Released by CIA to: Released, 5/28/04
Facilities Detained in: Afghanistan (other)
Current Status: Released, 5/28/04

Hassan Ghul (EIT)

SSCI Prisoner Number: 98
Nationality: Pakistani
Entered CIA Custody: Iraq, 1/24/04
Released by CIA to: Pakistan*, 8/21/06–8/30/06
Facilities Detained in: Cobalt and/or Gray, Black
Current Status: Released, 5/1007–5/31/07; Deceased, 10/12

Muhammad Qurban Sayyid Ibrahim (EIT)

SSCI Prisoner Number: 99
Nationality: Not known
Entered CIA Custody: Not known, 1/24/04–1/27/04
Released by CIA to: Not known, 10/10/04–10/22/04
Facilities Detained in: Not known
Current Status: Not known

Saud Memon

SSCI Prisoner Number: 100
Nationality: Pakistani
Entered CIA Custody: South Africa; Pakistan, 1/24/04–3/12/04
Released by CIA to: Pakistan*, 2/2/06–3/31/06
Facilities Detained in: Not known
Current Status: Deceased, 2007

Gul Rahman (2)

SSCI Prisoner Number: 101
Nationality: Afghan
Entered CIA Custody: Afghanistan, 3/1/04–3/12/04
Released by CIA to: Released, 3/31/04–4/20/04
Facilities Detained in: Not known
Current Status: Released, 03/04–04/04

Hassan Ahmed Guleed (HVD)

SSCI Prisoner Number:	102
Nationality:	Somalian
Entered CIA Custody:	Djibouti, 3/10/04–3/12/04
Released by CIA to:	Guantánamo Bay, 9/4/06–9/5/06
Facilities Detained in:	Cobalt and/or Gray*, Indigo and/or Maroon*, Morocco
Current Status:	Detained, Guantánamo Bay

Abu 'Abdallah

SSCI Prisoner Number:	103
Nationality:	Not known
Entered CIA Custody:	Not known, 3/10/04–4/19/04
Released by CIA to:	Not known, 7/28/06–9/6/06
Facilities Detained in:	Cobalt and/or Gray
Current Status:	Not known

Abu Bahar Al-Turki [Pseud.] (EIT)

SSCI Prisoner Number:	104
Nationality:	Not known
Entered CIA Custody:	Not known, 3/10/04–6/16/04
Released by CIA to:	Released, 7/23/04–10/29/04
Facilities Detained in:	Not known
Current Status:	Released

Abu Talha Al-Magrebi [Pseud.] (EIT)

SSCI Prisoner Number:	105
Nationality:	Not known
Entered CIA Custody:	Not known, 3/10/04–6/16/04
Released by CIA to:	Released, 7/23/04–10/29/04
Facilities Detained in:	Not known
Current Status:	Released

Abd al-Bari al-Filistini

SSCI Prisoner Number:	106
Nationality:	Palestinian
Entered CIA Custody:	Pakistan, 6/16/04
Released by CIA to:	Not known, 7/26/06–8/4/06
Facilities Detained in:	Orange
Current Status:	Not known

Ayyub al-Libi, Mustafa al-Mehdi

SSCI Prisoner Number:	107
Nationality:	Libyan
Entered CIA Custody:	Pakistan, 6/16/04
Released by CIA to:	Libya, 4/21/05
Facilities Detained in:	Orange
Current Status:	Released, 2/16/11

Marwan al-Jabbur

SSCI Prisoner Number:	108
Nationality:	Palestinian
Entered CIA Custody:	Pakistan, 6/16/04
Released by CIA to:	Jordan, 7/26/06–8/4/06
Facilities Detained in:	Orange
Current Status:	Released, 10/06

Qattal al-Uzbeki

SSCI Prisoner Number:	109
Nationality:	Not known
Entered CIA Custody:	Not known, 6/16/04
Released by CIA to:	Not known, 8/25/06–9/3/06
Facilities Detained in:	Orange
Current Status:	Not known

Janat Gul (EIT)

SSCI Prisoner Number:	110
Nationality:	Not known
Entered CIA Custody:	Not known, 7/10/04–7/22/04
Released by CIA to:	Foreign custody, 7/30/06–8/20/06
Facilities Detained in:	Black, Orange
Current Status:	Released, date unknown

Ahmed Khalfan Ghailani (HVD, EIT)

SSCI Prisoner Number:	111
Nationality:	Tanzanian
Entered CIA Custody:	Pakistan, 9/1/04–9/5/04
Released by CIA to:	Guantánamo Bay, 9/4/06–9/5/06
Facilities Detained in:	Not known
Current Status:	Detained, United States

Sharif al-Masri (EIT)

SSCI Prisoner Number:	112
Nationality:	Egyptian
Entered CIA Custody:	Pakistan, 9/17/04–9/30/04
Released by CIA to:	Egypt, 12/6/04–12/28/04
Facilities Detained in:	Orange
Current Status:	Released, 2011

Abdi Rashid Samatar

SSCI Prisoner Number:	113
Nationality:	Not known
Entered CIA Custody:	Not known, 9/17/04–11/25/04
Released by CIA to:	Not known, 6/29/06–9/6/06
Facilities Detained in:	Not known
Current Status:	Not known

Abu Faraj al-Libi (HVD, EIT)
SSCI Prisoner Number: 114
Nationality: Libyan
Entered CIA Custody: Pakistan, 5/24/05–5/25/05
Released by CIA to: Guantánamo Bay, 9/4/06–9/5/06
Facilities Detained in: Black, Orange
Current Status: Detained, Guantánamo Bay

Abu Munthir al-Magrebi
SSCI Prisoner Number: 115
Nationality: Not known
Entered CIA Custody: Not known, 5/24/05–6/3/05
Released by CIA to: Not known, 8/27/06–9/6/06
Facilities Detained in: Black
Current Status: Not known

Ibrahim Jan
SSCI Prisoner Number: 116
Nationality: Not known
Entered CIA Custody: Not known, 9/1/05–10/31/05
Released by CIA to: Not known, 7/8/06–9/6/06
Facilities Detained in: Not known
Current Status: Not known

Abu Ja'far al-Iraqi (EIT)
SSCI Prisoner Number: 117
Nationality: Iraqi
Entered CIA Custody: Not known, 11/16/05–11/30/05
Released by CIA to: Not known, 9/1/06–9/6/06
Facilities Detained in: Not known
Current Status: Not known

Abd al-Hadi al-Iraqi (HVD)
SSCI Prisoner Number: 118
Nationality: Iraqi
Entered CIA Custody: Turkey, 11/1/06–11/9/06
Released by CIA to: Guantánamo Bay, 4/20/07–4/27/07
Facilities Detained in: Brown
Current Status: Detained, Guantánamo Bay

Muhammad Rahim (HVD, EIT)
SSCI Prisoner Number: 119
Nationality: Afghan
Entered CIA Custody: Pakistan, 7/10/07–7/14/07
Released by CIA to: Guantánamo Bay, 3/6/08–3/14/08
Facilities Detained in: Brown
Current Status: Detained, Guantánamo Bay

RENDITIONS NOT NOTED IN THE SSCI REPORT

Shaker Aamer
SSCI Prisoner Number: N/A
Nationality: Saudi
Entered CIA Custody: Afghanistan, 11/24/01
Released by CIA to: Guantánamo Bay, 2002
Facilities Detained in: Afghanistan (Dark Prison), Afghanistan (Bagram)
Current Status: Transferred, Britain, 10/30/15

Ahmed Hussein Mustafa Kamil Agiza
SSCI Prisoner Number: N/A
Nationality: Egyptian
Entered CIA Custody: Sweden, 12/18/01
Released by CIA to: Not known
Facilities Detained in: Sweden, Egypt
Current Status: Released, 8/2/11

Amanatullah Ali
SSCI Prisoner Number: N/A
Nationality: Pakistani
Entered CIA Custody: Iraq, 2/04
Released by CIA to: Not known
Facilities Detained in: Iraq, Afghanistan, Pakistan
Current Status: Released, 10/14

Fahad al Bahli
SSCI Prisoner Number: N/A
Nationality: Saudi
Entered CIA Custody: Malawi, 6/22/03
Released by CIA to: Sudan, 07/05
Facilities Detained in: Zimbabwe, Sudan
Current Status: Released, Sudan 07/05

Moazzam Begg
SSCI Prisoner Number: N/A
Nationality: British, Pakistani decent
Entered CIA Custody: Pakistan, 2/02
Released by CIA to: Guantánamo Bay, 2/2/03
Facilities Detained in: Afghanistan (Bagram)
Current Status: Released, Britain, 1/25/05

Abdel Hakim Belhadj

SSCI Prisoner Number:	N/A
Nationality:	Libyan
Entered CIA Custody:	Thailand, 3/7/04
Released by CIA to:	Not known
Facilities Detained in:	Thailand, Libya (Tajoura Prison), Libya (Abu Salim Prison)
Current Status:	Released, 3/23/10

Bensayah Belkacem

SSCI Prisoner Number:	N/A
Nationality:	Algerian
Entered CIA Custody:	Bosnia, 1/19/02
Released by CIA to:	Guantánamo Bay, 1/02
Facilities Detained in:	Bosnia
Current Status:	Transferred, 12/5/13

Richard Belmar

SSCI Prisoner Number:	N/A
Nationality:	British
Entered CIA Custody:	Pakistan, 2/7/02
Released by CIA to:	Guantánamo Bay, 10/28/02
Facilities Detained in:	Afghanistan (Bagram)
Current Status:	Released, Britain, 1/25/05

Fatima Bouchar

SSCI Prisoner Number:	N/A
Nationality:	Moroccan
Entered CIA Custody:	Thailand, 3/7/04
Released by CIA to:	Not known
Facilities Detained in:	Thailand, Libya (Tajoura Prison)
Current Status:	Released, 6/21/04

Hadj Boudella

SSCI Prisoner Number:	N/A
Nationality:	Algerian and Bosnian
Entered CIA Custody:	Bosnia, 1/19/02
Released by CIA to:	Guantánamo Bay, 1/02
Facilities Detained in:	Bosnia
Current Status:	Transferred, Bosnia and Herzegovina, 12/16/08

Lakhdar Boumediene

SSCI Prisoner Number:	N/A
Nationality:	Bosnian
Entered CIA Custody:	Bosnia, 1/19/02
Released by CIA to:	Guantánamo Bay, 1/02
Facilities Detained in:	Bosnia
Current Status:	Released, 5/15/09

Abou Elkassim Britel
SSCI Prisoner Number: N/A
Nationality: Moroccan
Entered CIA Custody: Pakistan, 3/10/02
Released by CIA to: Not known
Facilities Detained in: Pakistan (Lahore and Islamabad), Morocco (Témara and Salè)
Current Status: Released, 4/14/11

Abdul Halim Dalak
SSCI Prisoner Number: N/A
Nationality: Not known
Entered CIA Custody: 11/01
Released by CIA to: Not known
Facilities Detained in: Syria (Palestinian Branch)
Current Status: Not known

Ahmed Muhammed Haza al-Darbi
SSCI Prisoner Number: N/A
Nationality: Saudi
Entered CIA Custody: Azerbaijan, 6/02
Released by CIA to: Guantánamo Bay, 03/03
Facilities Detained in: Afghanistan (Bagram)
Current Status: Detained, Guantánamo Bay

Wesam Abdulrahman Ahmed al-Deemawi
SSCI Prisoner Number: N/A
Nationality: Jordanian
Entered CIA Custody: Iran, Afghanistan, 2002
Released by CIA to: Guantánamo Bay, 5/8/03
Facilities Detained in: Afghanistan (Dark Prison), Afghanistan (other), Afghanistan (Bagram)
Current Status: Released 03/04–04/04

Mouad al Fizani, Abou Naseem
SSCI Prisoner Number: N/A
Nationality: Libyan or Tunisian
Entered CIA Custody: Pakistan, 6/03
Released by CIA to: Not known
Facilities Detained in: Not known
Current Status: Not known

Ibrahim Habaci
SSCI Prisoner Number: N/A
Nationality: Turkish
Entered CIA Custody: Malawi, 6/22/03
Released by CIA to: Sudan, 07/05
Facilities Detained in: Zimbabwe, Sudan
Current Status: Released, Sudan 07/05

Mamdouh Ahmed Habib

SSCI Prisoner Number:	N/A
Nationality:	Egyptian
Entered CIA Custody:	Pakistan, 10/4/01
Released by CIA to:	Not known
Facilities Detained in:	Pakistan, Egypt, Afghanistan, Guantánamo Bay
Current Status:	Released, 1/05

Khalifa Abdi Hassan

SSCI Prisoner Number:	N/A
Nationality:	Kenyan
Entered CIA Custody:	Malawi, 6/22/03
Released by CIA to:	Sudan, 07/05
Facilities Detained in:	Zimbabwe, Sudan
Current Status:	Released, Sudan 07/05

Mustafa Ait Idr

SSCI Prisoner Number:	N/A
Nationality:	Algerian and Bosnian
Entered CIA Custody:	Bosnia, 1/19/02
Released by CIA to:	Guantánamo Bay, 1/02
Facilities Detained in:	Bosnia
Current Status:	Transferred, Bosnia and Herzegovina, 12/16/08

Mahmud Sardar Issa

SSCI Prisoner Number:	N/A
Nationality:	Sudanese
Entered CIA Custody:	Malawi, 6/22/03
Released by CIA to:	Sudan, 07/05
Facilities Detained in:	Zimbabwe, Sudan
Current Status:	Released, Sudan 07/05

Bahaa Mustafa Jaghel

SSCI Prisoner Number:	N/A
Nationality:	Syrian
Entered CIA Custody:	Afghanistan, 1/02
Released by CIA to:	Not known, 2005
Facilities Detained in:	Syria (Palestinian Branch)
Current Status:	Arrested, 2005

Sabir Mahfouz Lahmar

SSCI Prisoner Number:	N/A
Nationality:	Algerian
Entered CIA Custody:	Bosnia, 1/19/02
Released by CIA to:	Guantánamo Bay, 1/02
Facilities Detained in:	Bosnia
Current Status:	Transferred, France, 11/3-/09

Barah Abdul Latif

SSCI Prisoner Number:	N/A
Nationality:	Syrian
Entered CIA Custody:	Pakistan, 02/02–03/02
Released by CIA to:	Not known
Facilities Detained in:	Syria (Palestinian Branch)
Current Status:	Not known

Mohammed Saad Iqbal Madni

SSCI Prisoner Number:	N/A
Nationality:	Egyptian with Pakistani citizenship
Entered CIA Custody:	Indonesia, 1/9/02
Released by CIA to:	Not known
Facilities Detained in:	Indonesia; Egypt; Cobalt and/or Gray*; Afghanistan (other); Guantánamo Bay
Current Status:	Released, 8/08

Jamal Muhammed Alawi Mari

SSCI Prisoner Number:	N/A
Nationality:	Yemeni
Entered CIA Custody:	Pakistan, 9/23/01
Released by CIA to:	Guantánamo Bay, 2002
Facilities Detained in:	Jordan
Current Status:	Released, Yemen, 12/19/2009

Abdul Karim Mehmood, Abu Musab al-Baluchi, Musaab Aruchi

SSCI Prisoner Number:	N/A
Nationality:	Pakistani
Entered CIA Custody:	Pakistan, 6/04
Released by CIA to:	Not known
Facilities Detained in:	Not known
Current Status:	Not known

Jamal Qasim Saeed Mohammad

SSCI Prisoner Number:	N/A
Nationality:	Yemeni
Entered CIA Custody:	Pakistan, 10/01
Released by CIA to:	Not known
Facilities Detained in:	Pakistan, Jordan
Current Status:	Not known

Mohammed Nechle

SSCI Prisoner Number:	N/A
Nationality:	Algerian and Bosnian
Entered CIA Custody:	Bosnia, 1/19/02
Released by CIA to:	Guantánamo Bay, 1/02
Facilities Detained in:	Bosnia
Current Status:	Transferred, Bosnia and Herzegovina, 12/16/08

Abu Omar, Hassan Mustafa Osama Nasr
SSCI Prisoner Number: N/A
Nationality: Egyptian
Entered CIA Custody: Italy, 2/17/03
Released by CIA to: Not known
Facilities Detained in: Torah Prison, Egypt
Current Status: Released, 2/17/07

Saifullah Paracha
SSCI Prisoner Number: N/A
Nationality: Pakistani
Entered CIA Custody: Thailand, 7/8/03
Released by CIA to: Guantánamo Bay, 9/19/04
Facilities Detained in: Afghanistan
Current Status: Detained, Guantánamo Bay

Walid Muhammad Shahir al-Qadasi
SSCI Prisoner Number: N/A
Nationality: Yemeni
Entered CIA Custody: Afghanistan, 2002
Released by CIA to: Guantánamo Bay, 5/9/03
Facilities Detained in: Afghanistan (Dark Prison), Afghanistan (Bagram)
Current Status: Transferred, Yemen, 04/04

Yunus Rahmatullah
SSCI Prisoner Number: N/A
Nationality: Pakistani
Entered CIA Custody: Iraq, 2/04
Released by CIA to: Not known
Facilities Detained in: Iraq, Afghanistan
Current Status: Released,5/14

Sami Mostefa al-Sadi
SSCI Prisoner Number: N/A
Nationality: Libyan
Entered CIA Custody: Hong Kong, 3/15/04
Released by CIA to: Not known
Facilities Detained in: Hong Kong, Libya
Current Status: Released, 8/11

Mohamedou Ould Slahi
SSCI Prisoner Number: N/A
Nationality: Mauritanian
Entered CIA Custody: Mauritania,11/01
Released by CIA to: Guantánamo Bay, 8/4/02
Facilities Detained in: Jordan, Afghanistan (Bagram), Indigo and/or Maroon
Current Status: Released, 10/17/16

Yasser Tinawi

SSCI Prisoner Number:	N/A
Nationality:	Syrian
Entered CIA Custody:	Somalia, 7/17/02
Released by CIA to:	Syria, 03/03
Facilities Detained in:	Ethiopia, Egypt, Syria (Palestinian Branch)
Current Status:	Released, 2/05

Arif Ulusam

SSCI Prisoner Number:	N/A
Nationality:	Turkish
Entered CIA Custody:	Malawi, 6/22/03
Released by CIA to:	Sudan, 07/05
Facilities Detained in:	Zimbabwe, Sudan,
Current Status:	Released, Sudan 07/05

Mullah Abdul Salam Zaeef

SSCI Prisoner Number:	N/A
Nationality:	Pakistani
Entered CIA Custody:	Pakistan, 1/2/02
Released by CIA to:	Guantánamo Bay, 5/1/02
Facilities Detained in:	Afghanistan (Bagram), USS Bataan
Current Status:	Transferred, Afghanistan, 9/11/05

Mohamed Sulelman Ibrahim el-Zery

SSCI Prisoner Number:	N/A
Nationality:	Egyptian
Entered CIA Custody:	Sweden, 12/18/01
Released by CIA to:	Not known
Facilities Detained in:	Sweden, Egypt
Current Status:	Released, 10/27/03

Mohammed Haydar Zammar

SSCI Prisoner Number:	N/A
Nationality:	German, Syrian decent
Entered CIA Custody:	Morocco, 12/8/01
Released by CIA to:	Syria, 2007
Facilities Detained in:	Syria (Palestinian Branch)
Current Status:	Released, Syria 2013

B. PROXY SITE EVIDENCE

Spelling and formating from the original publications has been preserved.

FAR FALESTIN (THE PALESTINIAN BRANCH), DAMASCUS, SYRIA

With an "invitation" you could enter what is a large complex. Keep going through, across a courtyard into a building on your right, go through an office (the prison manager's), into a corridor, and then turn left down a short flight of winding stairs to the basement. In this imaginary journey you would now be in Syria's most feared interrogation center, the Palestinian Branch.

Grey, *Ghost Plane,* 1-2.

Go farther down the corridor, past five large communal cells on each side. If the metal doors were open you would see men squatting on the concrete floors, and women and children in the final right-hand cell. Keep going, right to the end of the building, and you'll come to a sort of T junction. Ahead are two small toilets, and to your left and right are minicorridors where you will find a series of what look like monastic cells on either side. On each side there are five of them facing another five opposite, except in the far left corner, where one cell is missing and a door leads onward to some forbidden room. The makes a total of nineteen little cells. As you stand at the T junction, the cells are numbered counterclockwise, beginning with cell number 1 on your immediate right and ending with cell number 19 on your immediate left.

At this point, you'll notice the smell of uncleared toilets and the sweat of men crammed together. As you're a new visitor, it is likely you will go to an empty cell. The last cell, number 19, has recently been used for people coming in and out, so it's probably empty. As

Fig. A.5
The Palestinian Branch, Damascus, Syria. May 4, 2011.

you're pushed through the door you will see that, if you of average height and width, you can barely fit inside. The cell is three feet wide, six feet long, and seven feet high.

Welcome to the Grave, as this place is known to the inmates of a global network of prisons.

Grey, *Ghost Plane,* 2–4.

…on this day, December 17, 2002, are at least seven prisoners who claim to have arrived courtesy of the United States. …In cell number 2 is Maher Arar, a Canadian. …Next door to Maher in cell number 3, is a fellow Canadian named Abdullah Almalki. …Another prisoner is Mohammed Haydar Zammar, a forty-two-year-old German businessman from Hamburg. …His cell, number 13, is shorter than his body length. …In cell number 5 is a man in his thirties called Abdel; in cell number 8 is someone called Omar; and in cell number 12 is a teenager with a brother in Guantánamo. …In cell number 17 is a prisoner called Barah; in cell number 7 is Bahaa, age twenty-nine.

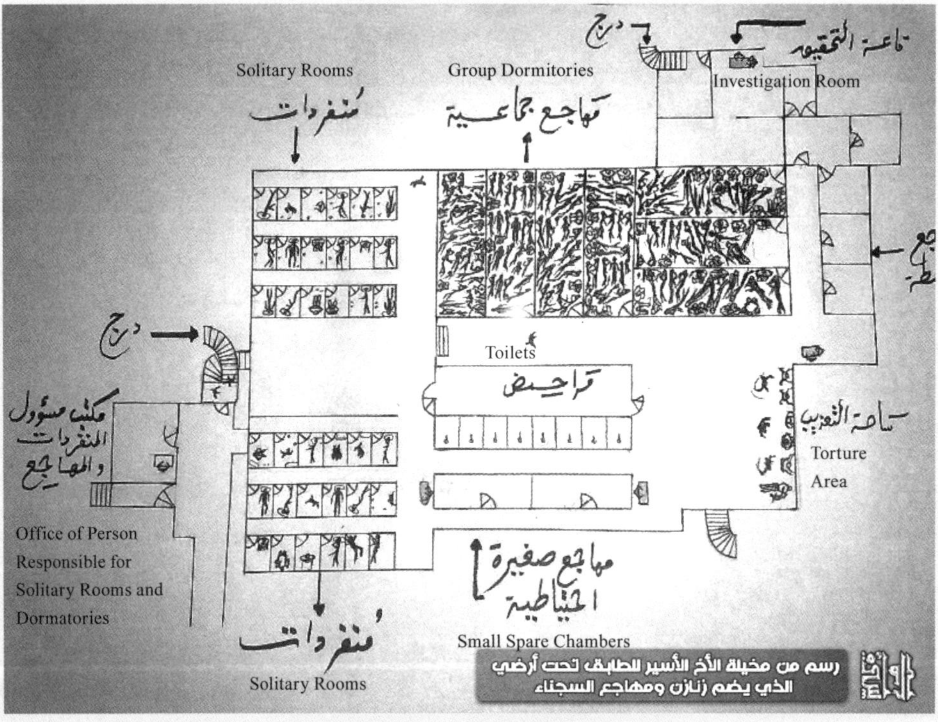

Fig. A.6
Drawing of the Palestinian Branch by a former prisoner.
Translation by Dalia Hamati.

In its response to the questionnaire sent by the experts, the Government of the Syrian Arab Republic stated that the country had no secret prisons or detention centres. There were no cases of secret detention, and no individuals had been arrested without the knowledge of competent authorities. No authorization has been granted to the security service of any foreign State to establish secret detention facilities in the Syrian Arab Republic.

United Nations Human Rights Council, *Joint Report,* 76.

BOSNIA AND HERZEGOVINA

"For three or four days they were very bad – they were making noise, they were hitting the walls of the container – they put me through lots of sleep deprivation. They told me that I had to remain standing all day long."

From the account of Almin Hardaus. Cageprisoners, "Citizens No More," 7.

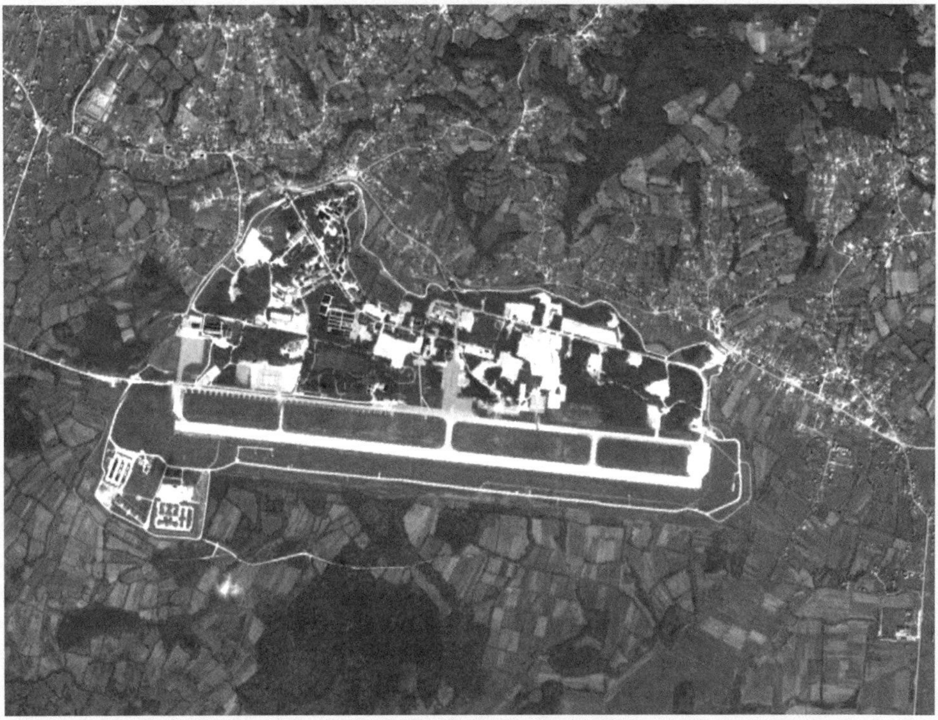

Fig. A.7
Eagle Camp, outside Tuzla, Bosnia and Herzegovina.
Exact location of detention facility unknown. July 19, 2007.

From the account of Nihad Karsic. Cageprisoners, "Citizens No More," 7.

"They were putting me through sleep deprivation. This went on for many days. The first few days it was very intensive, soldiers were coming, they were shouting at me terrorist and so on...One other agent came, in the late evening, because I did not have daylight, but I assumed it was late evening. All this time I didn't have access to daylight. From my instinct I could tell when it was day and night, due to noise and my own drowsiness...They fed me very badly—they brought us very little amount of food, and this was timetabled—in the first two or three I didn't have anything to eat."

German Foreign Policy, "Examined and Interrogated."

...the interrogation container had been insulated against all incoming daylight, to deprive the prisoner of a sense for space and time. This is a typical method explored by the CIA in the 1950s, aimed at systematically breaking a prisoner's resistance. This method falls into the category of psychological torture.

TORA PRISON, EGYPT

Grey, *Ghost Plane,* 19.

As I took a sunset cruise from downtown Cairo up the Nile in a felucca sailboat in 2003, I might have spotted the watchtowers on the riverbank. But I would not know the reality of life inside the Torah Prison that lay behind, nor in its fear inner sanctum, known as Al-Aqrab, the Scorpion.

Quoted from Agiza's mother based on a phone call she had with her son. Grey, *Ghost Plane* 32.

"When he arrived in Egypt, they took him, while hooded and handcuffed, to a building. He was led to an underground facility, going down a staircase. Then, they started interrogation, and torture."

Account of Agiza from a redacted United Nations report by Swedish ambassador Sven Linder. Grey, *Ghost Plane,* 35.

...forced to be blindfolded during interrogation period; detention in too small cells 1.5 x 1.5 meters during the same period; lack of sleep due to surveillance in the cells...

Fig. A.8
Tora Prison, Egypt. July 23, 2009.

When the plane landed, he was told he was in Cairo, he said. He was assigned a basement room like "a grave," about 6 feet by 4 feet, he said, and was kept there for 92 days, according to the transcript of his tribunal hearing. On Jan. 11, 12 and 20, 2002, he was interrogated for 12 to 15 hours on each occasion, he said during the interviews here.

Perlez, Bonner, and Masood, "An Ex-Detainee of the U.S."

Fig. A.9
Watchtower, Tora Prison, Egypt.

Fig. A.10
Main Gate, Tora Prison, Egypt.

Fig. A.11
Tora Prison and surrounding neighborhood, Egypt.

AL JAFR PRISON, JORDAN

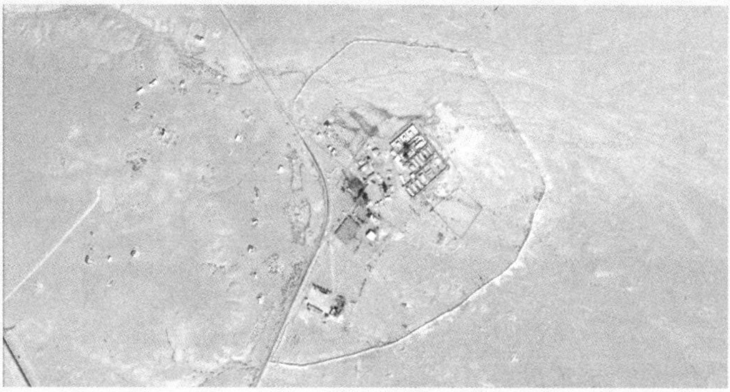

Fig. A.12
Al Jafr Prison, Jordan. February 17, 2002.

Al Jafr Prison doesn't appear on maps of Jordan. There are no photographs of the place available from the world's news services. The remote prison appears out of the southern desert as if some medieval apparition, with two towers anchoring a circular stone wall. Barbed wire is everywhere. The notorious prison was closed in the 1970s, but it reopened in the 1990s as a maximum security jail. "This is a prison," a Jordanian intelligence officer explains bluntly, "for terrorist detainees."

U.S. News & World Report, "Al Qaeda's Desert Inn."

It's also the place where the CIA has used a secret interrogation center since 9/11, U.S. News has learned. As many as 100 al Qaeda prisoners have passed through al Jafr, according to U.S. and Jordanian intelligence sources. Among them are some of the biggest catches in the war on terror: al Qaeda operations head Khalid Shaikh Mohammed and Persian Gulf chief Abd al-Rahim al Nashiri. Most stay just a few days before being shipped out to longer-term facilities.

Fig. A.13
Al Jafr Prison, Jordan. ***The Arab American News.***

GENERAL INTELLIGENCE DEPARTMENT, AMMAN, JORDAN

Whitlock, "Jordan's Spy Agency: Holding Cell for the CIA."

Over the past seven years, an imposing building on the outskirts of this city has served as a secret holding cell for the CIA.

The building is the headquarters of the General Intelligence Department, Jordan's powerful spy and security agency. Since 2000, at the CIA's behest, at least 12 non-Jordanian terrorism suspects have been detained and interrogated here, according to documents and former prisoners, human rights advocates, defense lawyers and former U.S. officials.

In most of the cases, the spy center served as a covert way station for CIA prisoners captured in other countries. It was a place where they could be hidden after being arrested and kept for a few days or several months before being moved on to Guantánamo Bay, Cuba, or CIA prisons elsewhere in the world.

United Nations Human Rights Council, *Joint Report*, 70.

At least 15 prisoners, mostly seized in Karachi, Pakistan, or in the Pankisi Gorge in Georgia, claim to have been rendered by the CIA to the main headquarters of the General Intelligence Department of Jordan in Amman, between September 2001 and 2004.

Fig. A.14
General Intelligence Department Headquarters, Wadi As-Seir, Amman, Jordan. September 29, 2017.

While the exact number of transfers cannot be ascertained, Human Rights Watch has found that at least 14 non-Jordanian prisoners were sent from United States to Jordanian custody during this three-year period, and the actual figure may be much higher. While a few other countries have received individuals rendered by the United States in recent years (that is, transferred without formal legal process), no country is known to have detained as many as Jordan.

Human Rights Watch, "Double Jeopardy."

The headquarters, which appear to cover nearly an acre of land, contain a large four-story detention facility that Human Rights Watch visited in August 2007.

Human Rights Watch, "Double Jeopardy."

The building that holds the detention facility is in the shape of two triangles that together form a square; the facility itself takes up approximately half of the building, i.e., one of the triangles. Each floor of the detention facility, except the top floor, consists of three main corridors (the sides of the triangle) running around a central courtyard. The administrative offices and interrogation rooms are on the second floor of the building, while visiting rooms are on the ground floor. During the period that Human Rights Watch inspected the facility, all of the detainees in custody were held on the second floor. There are also many cells on the ground floor and third floor, however, as well as a small number of cells on the fourth floor, which includes a few collective cells and what the director called the "women's section" of the facility. In addition, the facility has a basement where many prisoners have claimed that they were brought for the most violent treatment.

Prisoners in GID detention at Wadi Sir are kept in single-person cells and are prohibited from speaking with one another, but some have managed to communicate via the back window of their cells. (Each cell faces onto the central courtyard, and has a window looking out on the yard.)

CAMP BONDSTEEL, KOSOVO

"From a tower, I saw a place which looked like a replica of Guantánamo, but on a smaller scale," Robles tells Le Monde. "Small rudimentary wooden shelters were surrounded by a tall barbed wire fence. I saw between fifteen and twenty prisoners inside huts, dressed in orange jumpsuits like those used at Guantánamo. The prisoners I saw were not shackled. Most of them were sitting down, some isolated from the others. Some prisoners had beards. Others read the Koran. There were walkways around the cells for the guards. A female U.S. soldier who worked at the prison explained to me that she had just been transferred there from Guantánamo," Robles continued.

Nougayrede, "NATO Base in Kosovo Home to 'Secret' American Prison."

...Camp Bondsteel is a zone of "non-law." As it was being built in 1999, the camp was described as the largest U.S. base since the Vietnam War.

Interview with Alvaro Gil Robles, Human Rights Commissioner for the Council of Europe. *Spiegel Online,* "Everyone Knew What Was Going On in Bondsteel."

Robles: The prisoners were housed in little wooden huts, some alone, others in pairs or threes. Each hut was surrounded with barbed wire, and guards were patrolling between them. Around all of this was a high wall with watchtowers

...At the time of my visit, there were 15 prisoners. Most of them were Kosovo Albanians or Serbs, and there were four or five North Africans. Some of them wore beards and read the Koran.

Deutsche Welle, "Questions Arise Over US Base in Kosovo."

"There can be no doubt that for years there has been a prison in the Bondsteel base with no external civilian or judicial oversight," Marek Antoni Nowicki [U.N. ombudsman to Kosovo] told Berliner Zeitung. "The prison looks like the pictures we have seen of Guantánamo Bay."

Fig. A.15
Camp Bondsteel, near Ferizaj, Kosovo.
Exact location of detention facility unknown. July 6, 2010.

TEMARA PRISON, MOROCCO

Mohamed was put in a cell in a house that he described as being 'dug down, almost underground.' There were six rooms: three for prisoners, one for the guards, one for interrogation, and one was empty. He saw that there were already to prisoners in the other cells."

...A week later, Mohammed was transferred to a different prison and help in a white room with a hook on the wall.

Paglan and Thompson, *Torture Taxi* 26-27.

In Morocco, visitors to the city zoo at Rabat might notice a nearby collection of houses, surrounded by an ordinary-looking chain-link fence and high trees. How could they have imagined the types of torture with razor blades or broken glass bottles that were perpetuated inside, not just one their own nationals, but upon foreigners sent there from abroad.

Grey, *Ghost Plane,* 19.

He [Binyam Mohamed] was taken to a prison outside Rabat that was made up of a cluster of houses—each with six rooms and a basement. Three were for prisoners, one for interrogation, one for the guards, and one stood empty. The houses were surrounded by a metal fence and high trees, up to thirty feet tall. At first he was placed in a large room with white-washed walls and a large but shuttered window. Three weeks later he was moved to an end room by a toilet. This had wooden paneling. It was the torture room.

Grey, *Ghost Plane,* 55.

The center was just off the main highway to Casablanca, close to the Rabat zoo, and some inmates reported even hearing sounds of the animals. It was officially under the control of the Moroccan internal security service (the Direction de la Surveillance du Territoire, or DST) then headed by Hamidou Laanigiri. (60)

Grey, *Ghost Plane,* 60.

Walker and Baxter, "Revealed: The Terror Prison U.S. is Helping Build in Morocco."

The United States is helping Morocco to build a new interrogation and detention facility for Al-Qaeda suspects near its capital, Rabat, according to Western intelligence sources.

The sources confirmed last week that building was under way at Ain Aouda, above a wooded gorge south of Rabat's diplomatic district. Locals said they had often seen American vehicles with diplomatic plates in the area.

The construction of the new compound, run by the Direction de la Securité du Territoire (DST), the Moroccan secret police, adds to a substantial body of evidence that Morocco is one of America's principal partners in the secret "rendition" programme in which the CIA flies prisoners to third countries for interrogation.

ACLU, "Biography of Plaintiff Abou Elkassim Britel."

Following his arrival in Rabat, U.S. officials transferred Britel to the custody of agents of the Moroccan intelligence services who took him to the notorious Témara prison. At the Témara prison, Britel was cut off entirely from the world for nearly eight and a half months. He was denied access to family, friends, counsel and the Italian consulate. Not once was he permitted outside the four walls of the prison. He was held in total isolation in a tiny cell, deprived of both sleep and adequate food. He was forced to undergo intensive interrogations about his private life and the people he associated with in Italy and pressured to act as an informant. While being interrogated, Britel was subjected to brutal forms of physical torture, including repeated, severe beatings, and threats against his own life and those of his family as well as "bottle torture"— a technique commonly used by Moroccan intelligence services whereby a bottle is forced into the detainee's anus.

Fig. A.16
Temara Prison, Rabat, Morocco. June, 11, 2011.

AIN AOUDA, MOROCCO

United Nations Human Rights Council, *Joint Study.*

Credible reports have also emerged that the United States was helping Morocco to build another interrogation and detention facility for Al-Qaeda suspects at Ain Aouda, near the capital Rabat. Although Moroccan authorities deny that detention and interrogation of "terrorist" suspects occur outside the ordinary legal framework, there is a strong sense that the intelligence services act in a climate of total impunity.

Walker and Baxter, "Revealed: The Terror Prison US is Helping Build in Morocco."

The sources confirmed last week that building was under way at Ain Aouda, above a wooded gorge south of Rabat's diplomatic district. Locals said they had often seen American vehicles with diplomatic plates in the area.

The construction of the new compound, run by the Direction de la Securité du Territoire (DST), the Moroccan secret police, adds to a substantial body of evidence that Morocco is one of America's principal partners in the secret "rendition" programme in which the CIA flies prisoners to third countries for interrogation.

There are no public access roads leading to the site, which can be seen at the moment only from a bend above the Korifla Gorge. The secluded forest setting is similar to that of Temara, 10 miles to the north.

ABU SALIM, LIBYA

Hubbard, "Liberated inmates tell of 'dark age' under Gadhafi."

When the uprising broke out in February, Abdullah was sharing a five-by-six yard cell with four others, one of whom had gone insane from the treatment inside, he said.

...The cells range in size, with thin mattresses, a squat toilet, basin, shower and heavy metal door. Some have carpet and hanging milk boxes to hold toiletries.

Human Rights Watch, "Delivered Into Enemy Hands."

In his final weeks at Abu Salim, al-Libi was held in a separate wing of the facility. Some said he was placed there by the prison administration and others said he had requested the isolation. The section had about 20 cells in one corridor, with 10 cells on each side. The corridor began with an open entrance from a courtyard and ended with a big metal door. Al-Libi was in one of the first two cells near the entrance by the courtyard.

From August 28, 2008 until his release, he was kept in solitary confinement in small cell, about 1 x 2 meters with just a bucket for a toilet. They forced him to shave his beard against his religious beliefs.

From the account of Mafud al-Sadiq Embaya Abdullah. Human Rights Watch, "Delivered Into Enemy Hands."

C. THE MEMOS

Note: Title, formatting, and spelling from the original documents has been preserved.

September 18, 2001
Proclamation 7463 of September 14, 2001. Declaration of National Emergency by Reason of Certain Terrorist Attacks

September 25, 2001
The President's Constitutional Authority to Conduct Military Operations Against Terrorists and Nations Supporting Them

November 6, 2001
Legality of the Use of Military Commissions to Try Terrorists

November 16, 2001
Military Order of November 13, 2001. Detention, Treatment, and Trial of Certain Non-Citizens in the War Against Terrorism

November 30, 2001
Re: Treaties and Laws Applicable to the Conflict in Afghanistan And to the Treatment of Persons Captured by U.S. Armed Forces in that Conflict

December 28, 2001
RE: Possible Habeas Jurisdiction over Aliens Held in Guantánamo Bay, Cuba

January 9, 2002
RE: Application of Treaties and Laws to al Qaeda and Taliban Detainees

January 19, 2002
Status of Taliban and Al Qaida

January 22, 2002
Re: Application of Treaties and Laws to al Qaeda and Taliban Detainees

January 25, 2002
Decision Re: Application of the Geneva Convention on Prisoners of War to the Conflict with al Qaeda and the Taliban

February 1, 2002
Department of Justice position on why the Geneva Convention did not apply to al Qaeda and Taliban detainees

February 7, 2002 (A)
Humane Treatment of al Qaeda and Taliban Detainees

February 7, 2002 (B)
Re: Status of Taliban Forces Under Article 4 of the Third Geneva Convention of 1949

February 26, 2002
Re: Potential Legal Constraints Applicable to Interrogations of Persons Captured by U.S. Armed Forces in Afghanistan

March 13, 2002
Re: The President's power as Commander in Chief to transfer captured terrorists to the control and custody of foreign nations

August 1, 2002 (A) [1]
Re: Standards of Conduct for Interrogation under 18 U.S.C. §§ 2340–2340A

1. The three memos dated August 1, 2002 are commonly referred to as the "torture memos."

August 1, 2002 (B)
Interrogation of al Qaeda Operative

August 1, 2002 (C)
Letter to Alberto Gonzales from John Yoo

March 14, 2003
Re: Military Interrogation of Alien Unlawful Combatants Held Outside the United States

April 4, 2003
Working Group Report on Detainee Interrogations in the Global War on Terrorism: Assessment of Legal, Historical, Policy, and Operational Considerations

April 16, 2003
Counter-Resistance Techniques in the War on Terrorism

August 14, 2003
RE: FW: Taskers ("Interrogation Wish List")

September 18, 2001

Proclamation 7463 of September 14, 2001. Declaration of National Emergency by Reason of Certain Terrorist Attacks

By George W. Bush

By the President of the United States of America

A Proclamation

A national emergency exists by reason of the terrorist attacks at the World Trade Center, New York, New York, and the Pentagon, and the continuing and immediate threat of further attacks on the United States.

September 18, 2001, Selection 1

September 25, 2001

The President's Constitutional Authority to Conduct Military Operations Against Terrorists and Nations Supporting Them

By John C. Yoo

The President may deploy military force preemptively against terrorist organizations or the States that harbor or support them, whether or not they can be linked to the specific terrorist incidents of September 11.

September 25, 2001, Selection 1

November 6, 2001

Legality of the Use of Military Commissions to Try Terrorists

By Patrick F. Philbin

We conclude that under 10 U.S.C. § 821 and his inherent powers as Commander in Chief, the President may establish military commissions to try and punish terrorists apprehended as part of the investigation into, or the military and intelligence operations in response to, the September 11 attacks.* As we outline in Part I, ample precedent establishes that military commissions may

November 6, 2001, Selection 1

required that the United States be engaged in armed conflict with another nation. The terrorists' actions in this case are sufficient to create a state of war *de facto* that allows application of the laws of war.

November 6, 2001, Selection 2

A military commission is a form of military tribunal typically used in three scenarios: (i) to try individuals (usually members of enemy forces) for violations of the laws of war; (ii) as a general court administering justice in occupied territory; and (iii) as a general court in an area where martial law has been declared and the civil courts are closed. *See generally* William

November 6, 2001, Selection 3

Military commissions are not courts within Article III of the Constitution, nor are they subject to the jury trial requirements of the Fifth and Sixth Amendments of the Constitution. *See Quirin*, 317 U.S. at 40. Unlike Article III courts, the powers of military commissions are derived not from statute, but from the laws of war. *See Ex parte Vallandigham*, 68 U.S. (1 Wall.) 243, 249-53 (1863). That is, their authority derives from the Constitution's vesting of the power of Commander in Chief in the President. "Neither their procedure nor their jurisdiction has been prescribed by statute. [Instead,] [i]t has been adapted in each instance to the need that called it forth." *Madsen*, 343 U.S. at 347-48. "In general ... [Congress] has left it to the President, and the military commanders representing him, to employ the commission, as occasion may require, for the investigation and punishment of violations of the laws of war." *Id.* at 346 n.9 (quoting Winthrop, *supra* at 831).

November 6, 2001, Selection 4

present circumstances. As noted above, Congress has endorsed the pre-existing practice of permitting military commissions to try "all offenses which are defined as such by the law of war." *Quirin*, 317 U.S. at 30. It is important, nevertheless, to note that the President has inherent authority as Commander in Chief to convene such tribunals even without authorization from Congress.

November 6, 2001, Selection 5

successfully"). One of the necessary incidents of authority over the conduct of military operations in war is the power to punish enemy belligerents for violations of the laws of war. The laws of war exist in part to ensure that the brutality inherent in war is confined within some limits. It is essential for the conduct of a war, therefore, that an army have the ability to enforce the laws of war by punishing transgressions by the enemy.[4]

November 6, 2001, Selection 6

The most likely constitutional issue to be raised concerning military commissions would be an objection to the denial of the rights to trial by jury in criminal cases and grand jury indictment as provided in Article III, Section 2 and the Fifth and Sixth Amendments.[7] Such objections would most likely be raised with respect to military commissions convened within the territorial United States, and we address them in that context. We believe that if a particular use of military commissions to try offenses against the laws of war is constitutionally permissible within the United States, it follows *a fortiori* that such a use is permissible to deal with enemy belligerents overseas, where many constitutional protections would not apply in any event.

November 6, 2001, Selection 7

339 U.S. at 774. As the Court in *Eisentrager* explained, since an alien citizen of an enemy nation may constitutionally be deprived of liberty by Executive action solely on the basis of his citizenship during time of war, "no reason is apparent why an alien enemy charged with having committed a crime should have greater immunities from Executive action." *Id.* at 784. As the Court concluded, the "Constitution does not confer a right of personal security or an immunity from military trial and punishment upon an alien enemy engaged in the hostile service of a government at war with the United States." *Id.* at 785. Although there is no "government at

November 6, 2001, Selection 8

commission contemplated by the common law of war."). The critical question for determining whether military commissions can properly be used here, therefore, is whether the terrorist attacks have created a situation to which the laws of war apply.[16] That is, are the terrorist acts subject to the laws of war at all, or are they solely criminal matters to be treated under the municipal criminal law of the United States or a particular State?

November 6, 2001, Selection 9

We conclude that, even without any action by Congress to acknowledge a state of war, the President, in his constitutional role as Commander in Chief, and through his broad authority in the realm of foreign affairs, *see, e.g., United States v. Curtiss-Wright Export Corp.*, 299 U.S. 304, 320 (1936), also has full authority to determine when the Nation has been thrust into a conflict that must be recognized as a war and treated under the laws of war. In *The Prize Cases*,

November 6, 2001, Selection 10

By making the President Commander in Chief of the armed forces, the Constitution must be understood to grant him the full authorities required for him to effectively defend the Nation in the event of an armed attack. Necessarily included among those powers must be the ability to determine whether persons responsible for an attack should be subject to punishment under the laws of war. We outlined above our conclusion that the President's powers as Commander in

November 6, 2001, Selection 11

originate and carry it on." *The Prize Cases*, 67 U.S. at 666. Where an organized force is carrying on a campaign of violence that reaches a sufficient level of intensity, it may be deemed an "armed conflict" by the President, thereby justifying application of the laws of armed conflict, including trials for the violation of those laws.[19] As explained below, the terrorist attacks meet

November 6, 2001, Selection 12

It is true that many situations involving application of the laws of war in the past have involved conflicts between sovereigns or quasi-sovereign entities (including, for example, rebel movements attempting to establish governments). But that fact should not be understood as in any way precluding application of the laws of armed conflict to widespread terrorist violence. In the past, usually only a sovereign or quasi-sovereign entity attempting to establish itself as a government over a substantial territory could have the resources to mount and sustain a series of attacks of sufficient intensity to raise the question of "war" or "armed conflict." The terrorist

network now facing the United States has found other means to finance its campaign while operating from the territory of several different nations at once. That change, however, cannot be considered to somehow exempt terrorist networks from the standards demanded by the laws of armed conflict and the punishments that would apply when the terrorists undertake violent attacks in violation of those laws. Simply by operating outside the confines of the traditional concepts of nation-states, terrorists cannot shield themselves from the prohibitions universally commanded by the laws of armed conflict and trial for violations of those laws. The examples

November 6, 2001, Selection 13

Moreover, there is nothing in the logic of the laws of armed conflict that in any way restricts them from applying to a campaign of hostilities carried on by a non-state actor with a trans-national reach. To the contrary, the logic behind the laws suggests that they apply here. Generally speaking, the laws are intended to confine within certain limits the brutality of armed conflict, which might otherwise go wholly unchecked. *Cf. The Prize Cases*, 67 U.S. at 667 (the laws of war "all tend to mitigate the cruelties and misery produced by the scourge of war"). The ability to punish violations of the laws of armed conflict is critical for deterring all foreign entities from undertaking any acts that violate those laws. If terrorists could somehow be exempt from being tried for violations of the laws of war simply because they do not need to rely upon a government—or a quasi-sovereign structure controlling territory—the purposes of the laws of war would be defeated.[25]

November 6, 2001, Selection 14

The precedents under American law outlined above are sufficient to establish conclusively that at least as of September 11, terrorist attacks on the United States had created a situation that would justify a conclusion that the laws of war properly apply. We realize that

November 6, 2001, Selection 15

The critical question for determining whether the laws of armed conflict apply here, therefore, is whether the terrorist attacks were a sufficiently organized and systematic set of violent actions that they crossed a sufficient level of intensity to be considered "armed conflict." There can be no doubt that, whatever the "level of intensity" required to create an armed conflict, the gravity and scale of the violence inflicted on the United States on September 11 crossed that threshold. To use the words of the 1996 Amended Protocol II to the 1980 UN Convention on

November 6, 2001, Selection 16

III. Under the Laws of War, the Terrorists are Unlawful Combatants Subject To Trial and Punishment for Violations of the Laws of War.

We stress at the outset that determining that the terrorist attacks can be treated under the rubric of the "laws of war" does *not* mean that terrorists will receive the protections of the Geneva Conventions or the rights that the laws of war accord to lawful combatants. To the contrary, as the U.S. Army Field Manual *The Law of Land Warfare* makes clear, persons who do not comply with the conditions prescribed for recognition as lawful combatants (which include wearing a fixed insignia and bearing arms openly) are not entitled to status as prisoners of war and may punished for hostile acts in violation of the laws of armed conflict.[34] The Supreme

November 6, 2001, Selection 17

As noted above, the terrorists involved in the attacks did not meet even the minimal conditions required to be recognized as lawful combatants. It is open to some doubt whether

November 6, 2001, Selection 18

November 16, 2001

Military Order of November 13, 2001. Detention, Treatment, and Trial of Certain Non-Citizens in the War Against Terrorism

By George W. Bush

(g) Having fully considered the magnitude of the potential deaths, injuries, and property destruction that would result from potential acts of terrorism against the United States, and the probability that such acts will occur, I have determined that an extraordinary emergency exists for national defense

November 16, 2001, Selection 1

purposes, that this emergency constitutes an urgent and compelling government interest, and that issuance of this order is necessary to meet the emergency.

Sec. 2. *Definition and Policy.*

(a) The term "individual subject to this order" shall mean any individual who is not a United States citizen with respect to whom I determine from time to time in writing that:

(1) there is reason to believe that such individual, at the relevant times,

(i) is or was a member of the organization known as al Qaida;

(ii) has engaged in, aided or abetted, or conspired to commit, acts of international terrorism, or acts in preparation therefor, that have caused, threaten to cause, or have as their aim to cause, injury to or adverse effects on the United States, its citizens, national security, foreign policy, or economy; or

(iii) has knowingly harbored one or more individuals described in subparagraphs (i) or (ii) of subsection 2(a)(1) of this order; and

(2) it is in the interest of the United States that such individual be subject to this order.

November 16, 2001, Selection 2

November 30, 2001

RE: Treaties and Laws Applicable to the Conflict in Afghanistan And to the Treatment of Persons Captured by U.S. Armed Forces in that Conflict

By John C. Yoo

former with sanctuary in Afghanistan. We conclude that these treaties do not protect the al Qaeda organization, which as a non-State actor cannot be a party to the international agreements governing war. We further conclude that the President has reasonable grounds to find that these treaties do not apply to the Taliban militia. This memorandum expresses no view as to whether

November 30, 2001, Selection 1

agreements. Because al Qaeda is merely a violent political movement or organization, it is not a Nation State, and hence is ineligible to be a signatory to any treaty. Because of the novel nature of this conflict, moreover, we do not believe that al Qaeda would be included in non-international forms of armed conflict to which some provisions of the Geneva Conventions might apply. Therefore, the Hague Convention IV, the Geneva Conventions, and the WCA do not apply to the conflict with al Qaeda.

November 30, 2001, Selection 2

Hague Convention IV, and so cannot receive its protections. In regard to the treatment of Taliban prisoners, we believe that the Geneva Conventions do not apply here because the Taliban is and was not a government and Afghanistan is not -- and even prior to the beginning of the present conflict was not -- a functioning State. Even if this were not the case, however, it is clear that the President has the constitutional authority to declare treaties with Afghanistan suspended pending the restoration of a legitimate government to that country. We emphasize

November 30, 2001, Selection 3

Thus, the WCA does not criminalize all breaches of the Geneva Conventions. Failure to follow some of the regulations regarding the treatment of POWs, such as difficulty in meeting all of the conditions set forth for POW camp conditions, does not constitute a grave breach within the meaning of Geneva Convention III, art. 130. Only by causing great suffering or serious bodily injury to POWs, killing or torturing them, depriving them of access to a fair trial, or forcing them to serve in the Armed Forces, could the United States actually commit a grave breach of the Geneva Convention III. Similarly, unintentional, isolated collateral damage on civilian targets would not constitute a grave breach within the meaning of Geneva Convention

November 30, 2001, Selection 4

territory of one of the High Contacting Parties." In conjunction with common Article 2, the text of Article 3 simply does not reach international conflicts where both parties are not Nation States. If we were to read the Geneva Conventions as applying to all forms of armed conflict, we would expect the High Contracting Parties to have used broader language, which they easily could have done. To interpret common Article 3 by expanding its scope well beyond the meaning borne by the text is effectively to amend the Geneva Conventions without the approval of the State Parties to the agreements.

November 30, 2001, Selection 5

II. *Application of WCA and Associated Treaties to al Qaeda*

It is clear from the foregoing that members of the al Qaeda terrorist organization do not receive the protections of the laws of war, and hence that actions taken by the U.S. Armed Forces with respect to captured members of al Qaeda are not covered by the WCA. There are four reasons, examined in detail below, that support this conclusion. First, al Qaeda's status as a non-State actor renders it ineligible to claim the protections of the treaties specified in the WCA. Second, the nature of the conflict precludes application of common Article 3 of the Geneva Conventions. Third, al Qaeda members fail to satisfy the eligibility requirements for treatment as POWs under Geneva Convention III. Fourth, even if al Qaeda were covered, its conduct on September 11, if not before, removes any Hague Convention protections its members might have had.

First, al Qaeda's status as a non-State actor renders it ineligible to claim the protections of the treaties specified by the WCA. Al Qaeda is not a State. It is a non-governmental terrorist organization composed of members from many nations, with ongoing operations in dozens of nations, who seem united in following a radical brand of Islam that seeks to attack Americans throughout the world. No non-governmental organizations are, or could be, parties to any of the international agreements here governing the laws of war. Thus, al Qaeda is not eligible to sign the Hague Convention IV or the Geneva Conventions -- and even if it were eligible, it has not done so. As a result, the U.S. military's treatment of al Qaeda members is not governed by the Hague Convention IV, which by its terms explicitly applies only to the High Contracting Parties to the agreement. Further, al Qaeda cannot claim the protections of the bulk of the Geneva Conventions, whose scope in common Article 2 is limited only to cases of declared war or armed conflict "between two or more of the High Contracting Parties." Conduct towards captured members of al Qaeda, therefore, cannot constitute a violation of 18 U.S.C. § 2441(c)(1) or § 2441(c)(2).

November 30, 2001, Selection 6

Second, the nature of the conflict precludes application of the common Article 3 of the Geneva Conventions. Al Qaeda is not covered by common Article 3, which does not apply to the current conflict. As discussed in Part I, the text of Article 3, when read in harmony with common Article 2, shows that the Geneva Conventions were intended to cover either: a) traditional wars between Nation States (Article 2), or non-international civil wars (Article 3). Our conflict with al Qaeda does not fit into either category. That conflict is not an international war between Nation States, but rather a conflict between a Nation State and a non-governmental organization. At the same time, the conflict is not a civil war under Article 3, because it *is* a conflict of "an international character," rather than an internal armed conflict between parties contending for control over a government or territory. Therefore, the military's treatment of al Qaeda members captured in that conflict is not limited either by common Article 3 of the Geneva Conventions or 18 U.S.C. § 2441(c)(3), the provision of the WCA incorporating that article.

November 30, 2001, Selection 7

Third, al Qaeda members fail to satisfy the eligibility requirements for treatment as POWs under Geneva Convention III. It might be argued that, even though it is not a State

November 30, 2001, Selection 8

Even if Article 4, however, were considered somehow to be jurisdictional as well as substantive, captured members of al Qaeda still would not receive the protections accorded to POWs. Article 4(A)(2), for example, further requires that the militia or volunteers follow the requirements of the Hague Convention IV in that they are under the command of a responsible person, that they wear recognizable insignia, that they carry arms openly, and that they obey the laws and customs of war. In attacking the Pentagon and the World Trade Centers by disguising themselves and then hijacking airplanes, al Qaeda terrorists violated all four of the Hague Convention IV standards. Article 4(A)(3) also is inapt: al Qaeda are not members of "regular armed forces."

Fourth, even if al Qaeda were covered, its conduct on September 11, if not before, removes any Hague Convention protections its members might have had. Even if al Qaeda were somehow eligible for some protections under the relevant treaties, it has forfeited those rights by its own conduct. As discussed earlier, Hague Convention IV declares that the "laws, rights and duties of war" only apply to armies, militia, and volunteer corps when they fulfill four conditions: command by responsible individuals, wearing insignia, carrying arms openly, and obeying the laws of war. Al Qaeda has never obeyed these requirements in *any* of its attacks on the United States and its citizens, as exemplified by its September 11, 2001 attack on a purely civilian target, the World Trade Center, by using disguised hijackers to turn civilian airliners into guided missiles. By conducting itself in this manner, al Qaeda is deprived of any protections it could claim under the Hague Convention IV. Actions affecting al Qaeda members, then, still would be unregulated by Hague Convention IV or by the corresponding provision of the WCA.

November 30, 2001, Selection 9

States and Afghanistan, and thereby to the Taliban militia. Nonetheless, the President has the constitutional authority to determine that Afghanistan is a "failed State," so that the Conventions are currently inoperative as to that country.[17] Alternatively, even if the President found that Afghanistan is not in a condition of statelessness, the President would be acting within the scope

November 30, 2001, Selection 10

conflict with respect to the Taliban militia, which would then trigger the WCA. Nonetheless, we believe that the President has the constitutional authority to find that Afghanistan was a failed State during the period in which the Taliban exercised control over most of the country and that it remains so at present. Should the President make such a determination, it would follow that the Taliban militia, like al Qaeda, is not entitled to the protections of the Geneva Conventions.

Constitutional Authority. It is clear that, under the Constitution, the President has the plenary authority to determine that Afghanistan is no longer an operating State and therefore that members of the Taliban are not protected by the Geneva Conventions.[18] As an initial matter,

November 30, 2001, Selection 11

Part of the President's plenary power over the conduct of the Nation's foreign relations is the interpretation of treaties and of international law. Interpretation of international law includes the determination whether a territory has the necessary political structure to qualify as a Nation State for purposes of treaty implementation. In *Clark v. Allen*, 331 U.S. 503 (1947), for

November 30, 2001, Selection 12

A "failed State" is generally characterized by the collapse or near-collapse of State authority, by the inability of central authorities to maintain government institutions, ensure law and order or engage in normal dealings with other governments, and by the prevalence of violence that destabilizes civil society and the economy. The President could find that from the

November 30, 2001, Selection 13

We want to make clear that this Office does not have access to all of the facts necessary to make a fully informed decision on whether Afghanistan was and remains a failed State. Nonetheless, the available facts in the public record would support such a decision by the President -- including facts that pre-existed the recent military reversals suffered by the Taliban in the past several weeks. Secretary of Defense Donald Rumsfeld, for example, declared at a November 2, 2001 press conference that the "Taliban is not a government. The government of Afghanistan does not exist today. The Taliban never was a government as such. It was a force in the country that is not substantially weakened – in many cases cloistered away from the people." *Secretary Rumsfeld Media Availability en Route to Moscow* (Nov. 2, 2001), available at http://www.yale.edu/lawweb/avalon/sept.11/dod_brief64.htm (visited Nov. 8, 2001). Indeed, in finding Afghanistan to be a failed State, the President would only be affirming the State Department's view, expressed near the start of the current conflict, that "[t]here is no functioning central government [in Afghanistan]. The country is divided among fighting factions. . . . The Taliban [is] a radical Islamic movement [that] occupies about 90% of the country."[20] It should also be noted that prominent authorities agree that Afghanistan is a failed State. As one leading scholar of international law has written, "[t]he most dramatic examples of the decline in state authority can be found in countries where government and civil order have virtually disappeared. Recent examples are Liberia, Somalia, and Afghanistan. The term 'failed states' has come to be used for these cases and others like them." Oscar Schachter, *The Decline of the Nation-State and Its Implications for International Law*, 36 Colum. J. Transnat'l L. 7, 18 (1997). Lakhdar Brahimi, the United Nations mediator in Afghanistan and a former Algerian Foreign Minister, described Afghanistan under the Taliban as a "failed state which looks like an infected wound." Ahmed Rashid, *Taliban: Militant Islam, Oil & Fundamentalism in Central Asia* 207 (2001).

November 30, 2001, Selection 14

economy.[21] A failed State will not satisfy some or all of the three traditional tests for "statehood" under international law:

November 30, 2001, Selection 15

i) Does the entity have a defined territory and population?

ii) Are the territory/population under the control of its own government?

iii) Does the entity engage in or have the capacity to engage in formal relations with other States?

See Restatement (Third) of the Foreign Relations Law of the United States, at § 201; *see also* 1933 Montevideo Convention on Rights and Duties of States, art. I, 49 Stat. 3097, 28 Am. J. Int'l L. Supp. 75 (1934). In another version of the traditional formulation, the State Department has identified four tests for "statehood":

i) Does the entity have effective control over a clearly defined territory and population?

ii) Is there an organized governmental administration of the territory?

iii) Does the entity have the capacity to act effectively to conduct foreign relations and to fulfill international obligations?

iv) Has the international community recognized the entity?

November 30, 2001, Selection 16

First, even at the outset of the current conflict, the Taliban militia did not have effective control over a clearly defined territory and population. Even before the United States air strikes

November 30, 2001, Selection 17

Second, again even before the United States air strikes and the successes of the Northern Alliance, an organized governmental administration did not exist in Afghanistan. One expert on

November 30, 2001, Selection 18

Third, the Taliban militia was arguably unable to conduct normal foreign relations or to fulfill its international legal obligations. Indeed, information available to the President might

November 30, 2001, Selection 19

Qaeda that it could not pursue independent policies with respect to the outside world. Certainly, publicly known facts demonstrate that the Taliban was unwilling and perhaps unable to obey its international obligations and to conduct normal diplomatic relations. Thus, the Taliban has consistently refused to comply with United Nations Security Council Resolutions 1333 (2000) and 1267 (1999), which called on it to surrender Osama bin Laden to justice and to take other actions to abate terrorism based in Afghanistan.[26] Those resolutions also called on all

November 30, 2001, Selection 20

Fourth, the Taliban militia was not recognized as the legitimate government of Afghanistan by the United States or by any member of the international community except Pakistan. The only two other States that had maintained diplomatic relations with it before the current conflict began (Saudi Arabia and the United Arab Emirates) soon severed them.[29]

Based on the foregoing, we conclude that a reasonable basis exists for the President to find that Afghanistan (even when largely controlled by the Taliban) failed some, and perhaps all, of the ordinary tests of statehood. Nor do we think that the recent military successes of the Northern Alliance change that outcome: the President could find that Afghanistan both *was* and *remains* stateless.[30] If the President finds that Afghanistan is presently in a condition of statelessness, it cannot be considered to remain, at present, a High Contracting Party to the Geneva Conventions. This conclusion would have two immediate ramifications.

November 30, 2001, Selection 21

C. *Suspension of The Geneva Conventions as to Afghanistan*

Even if the President were not to find that Afghanistan is a failed State, the President could still temporarily suspend the Geneva Conventions during the current military action. As a constitutional matter, the President has the power to suspend performance of some or all of the obligations of the United States under the Conventions towards Afghanistan. Such a decision could be based on presidential findings that Afghanistan lacks the capacity to fulfill its treaty obligations or (if supported by the facts) on findings that Afghanistan is in material breach of its obligations.

November 30, 2001, Selection 22

D. Suspension Under International Law

Although the President has the constitutional authority to determine either that Afghanistan is a failed State or that the Geneva Conventions should be suspended under the present circumstances, there remains the distinct question whether such Presidential actions would be valid as a matter of international law.[40] We emphasize that the resolution of the

November 30, 2001, Selection 23

any suspension decision by the President in the world of international politics. While a close question, we believe that the better view is that, in certain circumstances, countries can suspend the Geneva Conventions consistently with international law.

November 30, 2001, Selection 24

presume that the State parties did not intend to preclude suspension. Indeed, if the drafters and ratifiers of the Geneva Conventions believed the treaties could not be suspended, while allowing for withdrawal and denunciation, they could have said so explicitly and easily in the text.

November 30, 2001, Selection 25

militia, we turn to your question concerning the effect, if any, of customary international law. Some may take the view that even if the Hague Convention IV and the Geneva Conventions, by their terms, do not govern the conflict in Afghanistan, the substance of these agreements has received such universal approval that it has risen to the status of customary international law. Regardless of its substance, however, customary international law cannot bind the executive branch under the Constitution because it is not federal law. This is a view that this Office has

November 30, 2001, Selection 26

Conclusion

For the foregoing reasons, we conclude that, based on appropriate presidential determinations, the neither the federal War Crimes Act, the Hague Convention IV, nor the Geneva Conventions would apply to the operations of the U.S. Armed Forces against the al Qaeda terrorist organization or the Taliban militia, or to the treatment of members of those groups captured by U.S. Armed Forces in this conflict. We also conclude that customary international law has no binding legal effect on either the President or the military because it is not federal law, as recognized by the Constitution. Nonetheless, we also believe that the President, as Commander in Chief, has the constitutional authority to impose the customary laws of war on both the al Qaeda and Taliban groups and the U.S. Armed Forces.

Please let us know if we can provide further assistance.

November 30, 2001, Selection 27

December 28, 2001
RE: Possible Habeas Jurisdiction over Aliens Held in Guantánamo Bay, Cuba
By Patrick F. Philbin, John C. Yoo

military commission. If a federal district court were to take jurisdiction over a habeas petition, it could review the constitutionality of the detention and the use of a military commission, the application of certain treaty provisions, and perhaps even the legal status of al Qaeda and Taliban members.

We conclude that the great weight of legal authority indicates that a federal district court could not properly exercise habeas jurisdiction over an alien detained at GBC. Nonetheless, we cannot say with absolute certainty that any such petition would be dismissed for lack of jurisdiction. A detainee could make a non-frivolous argument that jurisdiction does exist over aliens detained at GBC, and we have found no decisions that clearly foreclose the existence of habeas jurisdiction there. On the other hand, it does not appear that any federal court has allowed a habeas petition to proceed from GBC, either. While we believe that the correct answer is that federal courts lack jurisdiction over habeas petitions filed by alien detainees held outside the sovereign territory of the United States, there remains some litigation risk that a district court might reach the opposite result.

December 28, 2001, Selection 1

of this district court does not per se bar this court's jurisdiction over his [habeas] petition."). As this memorandum explains, however, under *Eisentrager* different rules apply to enemy aliens held outside the United States.

December 28, 2001, Selection 2

The analysis from *Eisentrager* should apply to bar any habeas application filed by an alien held at GBC. In the critical passage that most nearly summarizes the Court's holding, the *Eisentrager* Court based its conclusion on the fact that the prisoners were seized, tried, and held in territory that was outside the sovereignty of the United States and outside the territorial jurisdiction of any court of the United States. We do not believe that the Court intended to establish a two-part test, distinguishing between "sovereign" territory and territorial "jurisdiction." Instead, we believe that the Court used the latter term interchangeably with the former to explain *why* an alien has no right to a writ of habeas corpus when held outside the sovereign territory of the United States. The same reasoning applies to GBC because it is outside the sovereign territory of the United States.

The United States holds GBC under a lease agreement with Cuba entered into in 1903. *See* Agreement Between the United States of America and the Republic of Cuba for the Lease to the United States of Lands in Cuba for Coaling and Naval Stations, Feb. 16-23, 1903, U.S.-Cuba, T.S. No. 418, 6 Bevans 1113 ("Lease Agreement").[3] That agreement expressly provides that "the United States recognizes the continuance of the ultimate sovereignty of the Republic of Cuba over the" lands and waters subject to the lease. *Id.* art. III. Although the agreement goes on to state that the United States "shall exercise complete jurisdiction and control over and within" the leased areas, it specifically reserves sovereignty to Cuba. *Id.*

December 28, 2001, Selection 3

should not be subject to question in the courts. The Supreme Court has acknowledged that "the determination of sovereignty over an area is for the legislative and executive departments" – that

December 28, 2001, Selection 4

All nine believed, however, that neither Bermuda nor GBC was subject to the sovereignty of the United States.

December 28, 2001, Selection 5

jurisdiction" of any federal court. *Id.* If an alien detainee is both outside the United States' sovereign territory and outside the territorial jurisdiction of a federal court, then it is clear that no habeas jurisdiction exists. We have explained above that we believe GBC meets those conditions. A non-frivolous argument might be constructed, however, that GBC, while not part of sovereign territory of the United States, *is* within the territorial jurisdiction of a federal court. In that scenario, the application of *Eisentrager* might not be as clear. This is because "sovereignty" over territory and "jurisdiction" over territory could mean different things. A nation, for example, can retain its sovereignty over its territory, yet at the same time allow another nation to exercise limited jurisdiction within it.

December 28, 2001, Selection 6

18 U.S.C. § 7 (1994). The mere fact that U.S. criminal law applies, however, does not bring a place within the territorial jurisdiction of a federal district court. As the Supreme Court explained in *Vermilya-Brown*, a nation may extend its statutes to regulate conduct "on areas under the control, though not within the territorial jurisdiction or sovereignty, of the nation enacting the legislation." 335 U.S. at 381. Laws are frequently applied extraterritorially to conduct occurring *outside* a nation's territorial jurisdiction, but the mere application of law in

December 28, 2001, Selection 7

Fourth, and perhaps most importantly, a federal district court ought to be reluctant to extend habeas jurisdiction to GBC, when not clearly called for by statute, if doing so would interfere with matters solely within the discretion of the political branches of government. Detention and trial of al Qaeda and Taliban members is undertaken pursuant to the President's Commander in Chief and foreign affairs powers. Without a clear statement from Congress extending jurisdiction to GBC, a court should defer to the executive branch's activities and decisions prosecuting the war in Afghanistan.[7]

December 28, 2001, Selection 8

January 9, 2002
RE: Application of Treaties and Laws to al Qaeda and Taliban Detainees
By John C. Yoo, Robert J. Delahunty

Nearly identical in language to the November 30, 2001 memo, this memo concerns the policies covering US jurisdiction over Guantánamo Bay in relation to the Geneva Conventions and other international treaties. Importantly, it applies the opinions regarding the battlefields of Afghanistan to Guantánamo Bay.

Conclusion

For the foregoing reasons, we conclude that neither the federal War Crimes Act nor the Geneva Conventions would apply to the detention conditions in Guantanamo Bay, Cuba, or to trial by military commission of al Qaeda or Taliban prisoners. We also conclude that customary international law has no binding legal effect on either the President or the military because it is not federal law, as recognized by the Constitution. Nonetheless, we also believe that the President, as Commander in Chief, has the constitutional authority to impose the customary laws of war on both the al Qaeda and Taliban groups and the U.S. Armed Forces.

Please let us know if we can provide further assistance.

January 9, 2002, Selection 1

<u>January 19, 2002</u>

Status of Taliban and Al Qaida

By Donald H. Rumsfeld

(U) Transmit the following to the Combatant Commanders:

(S) The United States has determined that Al Qaida and Taliban individuals under the control of the Department of Defense are not entitled to prisoner of war status for purposes of the Geneva Conventions of 1949.

January 19, 2002, Selection 1

<u>January 22, 2002</u>

Re: Application of Treaties and Laws to al Qaeda and Taliban Detainees

By Jay S. Bybee

Like the January 9, 2001 memo, this memo is nearly identical in language to the one issued November 30, 2001. In addition, this memo clearly outlines the Bush administration policy for dealing with Taliban detainees in regards to the Geneva Conventions.

<u>I. Background and Overview of the War Crimes Act and the Geneva Conventions</u>

It is our understanding that your Department is considering two basic plans regarding the treatment of members of al Qaeda and the Taliban militia detained during the Afghanistan conflict. First, the Defense Department intends to make available a facility at the U.S. Navy base at Guantanamo Bay, Cuba ("GTMO"), for the long-term detention of these individuals, who have come under our control either through capture by our military or transfer from our allies in Afghanistan. At the present moment, your Department has confined these individuals in temporary facilities, pending the construction of a more permanent camp at GTMO. While it is conceivable that some might argue that these facilities are not fully in keeping with the terms of Geneva III, we understand that they meet minimal humanitarian requirements consistent with the need to prevent violence and for force protection. We understand that GTMO authorities are

January 22, 2002, Selection 1

A. *Justified Deviations from Geneva Convention Requirements*

We should make clear that as we understand the facts, the detainees currently are being treated in a manner consistent with common article 3 of Geneva III. This means that they are housed in basic humane conditions, are not being physically mistreated, and are receiving adequate medical care. They have not yet been tried or punished by any U.S. court system. As a result, the current detention conditions in GTMO do not violate common article 3, nor do they present a grave breach of Geneva III as defined in article 130. For purposes of domestic law, therefore, the GTMO conditions do not constitute a violation of the WCA, which criminalizes only violations of common article 3 or grave breaches of the Conventions.

That said, some very well may argue that detention conditions currently depart from Geneva III requirements. Nonetheless, not all of these deviations from Geneva III would amount to an outright violation of the treaty's requirements. Instead, some departures from the text can be justified by some basic doctrines of legal excuse. We believe that some deviations would not amount to a treaty violation, because they would be justified by the need for force protection. Nations have the right to take reasonable steps for the protection of the armed forces guarding prisoners. At the national level, no treaty can override a nation's inherent right to self-defense.

January 22, 2002, Selection 2

Other deviations from Geneva III, which do not involve force protection, may still be justified as a domestic legal matter on the ground that immediate compliance is infeasible. Certain conditions, we have been informed, are only temporary until the Defense Department can construct permanent facilities that will be in compliance with Geneva. We believe that no treaty breach would exist under such circumstances. The State Department has informed us that

January 22, 2002, Selection 3

Here, Geneva III contains no strict deadlines for compliance. Indeed, it would be illogical to require immediate compliance, particularly if a nation were suddenly attacked and had no warning that POW facilities would be needed. Further, it might not be immediately practicable, given the conditions in the field where POWs would first be detained, to provide conditions that fully comply with Geneva III. Given that Geneva III has no mandated timetable, the armed forces have a reasonable time to satisfy their obligations of treatment with regard to POWs and are not guilty of breach when it is infeasible to achieve immediate compliance.

B. *Status of Taliban Prisoners Under Article 4.*

Even if the President declines to suspend our obligations under Geneva III toward Afghanistan, it is possible that Taliban detainees still might not receive the legal status of POWs. Geneva III provides that once a conflict falls within common article 2, combatants must fall within one of several categories in order to receive POW status. Article 4(A)(1)-(3) sets out the three categories relevant here: i) members of the armed forces of a party to the conflict, along with accompanying militia and volunteer forces; ii) members of militia or volunteer corps who are commanded by an individual responsible to his subordinates, who have a distinctive sign recognizable from a distance, who carry arms openly, and who obey the laws of war; and iii) members of regular armed forces who profess allegiance to a government or authority that is not recognized by the detaining power. Should "any doubt arise as to whether persons, having committed a belligerent act and having fallen into the hands of the enemy," article 5 of Geneva III requires that these individuals "enjoy the protections of" the Convention until a tribunal has determined their status. As we understand it, as a matter of practice prisoners are presumed to have article 4 POW status until a tribunal determines otherwise.

Although these provisions seem to contemplate a case-by-case determination of an individual detainee's status, the President could determine categorically that all Taliban prisoners fall outside article 4. Under Article II of the Constitution, the President possesses the power to

January 22, 2002, Selection 4

Further, if the President were to find that all Taliban prisoners did not enjoy the status of POWs under article 4, they would not be legally entitled to the standards of treatment in common article 3. As the Afghanistan war is international in nature, involving as it does the use of force

January 22, 2002, Selection 5

<u>*Conclusion*</u>

For the foregoing reasons, we conclude that neither the federal War Crimes Act nor the Geneva Conventions would apply to the detention conditions of al Qaeda prisoners. We also conclude that the President has the plenary constitutional power to suspend our treaty obligations toward Afghanistan during the period of the conflict. He may exercise that discretion on the basis that Afghanistan was a failed state. Even if he chose not to, he could interpret Geneva III to find that members of the Taliban militia failed to qualify as POWs under the terms of the treaty. We also conclude that customary international law has no binding legal effect on either the President or the military because it is not federal law, as recognized by the Constitution.

We should make clear that in reaching a decision to suspend our treaty obligations or to construe Geneva III to conclude that members of the Taliban militia are not POWs, the President need not make any specific finding. Rather, he need only authorize or approve policies that would be consistent with the understanding that al Qaeda and Taliban prisoners are not POWs under Geneva III.

Please let us know if we can provide further assistance.

Jay S. Bybee
Assistant Attorney General

January 22, 2002, Selection 6

<u>January 25, 2002</u>

Decision Re: Application of the Geneva Convention on Prisoners of War to the Conflict with Al Qaeda and the Taliban

By Alberto R. Gonzales

international and domestic law, GPW does not apply to the conflict with al Qaeda. OLC has further opined that you have the authority to determine that GPW does not apply to the Taliban. As I discussed with you, the grounds for such a determination may include:

- **A determination that Afghanistan was a failed state because the Taliban did not exercise full control over the territory and people, was not recognized by the international community, and was not capable of fulfilling its international obligations (e.g., was in widespread material breach of its international obligations).**
- **A determination that the Taliban and its forces were, in fact, not a government, but a militant, terrorist-like group.**

January 25, 2002, Selection 1

- **As you have said, the war against terrorism is a new kind of war. It is not the traditional clash between nations adhering to the laws of war that formed the backdrop for GPW. The nature of the new war places a high premium on other factors, such as the ability to quickly obtain information from captured terrorists and their sponsors in order to avoid further atrocities against American civilians, and the need to try terrorists for war crimes such as wantonly killing civilians. In my** judgment, this new paradigm renders obsolete Geneva's strict limitations on questioning of enemy prisoners and renders quaint some of its provisions requiring that captured enemy be afforded such things as commissary privileges, scrip (i.e., advances of monthly pay), athletic uniforms, and scientific instruments.

January 25, 2002, Selection 2

February 1, 2002

Department of Justice position on why the Geneva Convention did not apply to al Qaeda and Taliban detainees

By John Ashcroft

There are two basic theories supporting the conclusion that Taliban combatants are not legally entitled to Geneva Convention protections as prisoners of war:

1. During relevant times of the combat, Afghanistan was a failed state. As such it was not a party to the treaty, and the treaty's protections do not apply;

2. During relevant times, Afghanistan *was* a party to the treaty, but Taliban combatants are not entitled to Geneva Convention III prisoner of war status because they acted as unlawful combatants.

February 1, 2002, Selection 1

In sum, Option 1, a determination that the Geneva Convention does not apply, will provide the United States with the highest level of legal certainty available under American law.

February 1, 2002, Selection 2

February 7, 2002 (A)

Humane Treatment of al Qaeda and Taliban Detainees

By George W. Bush

a. I accept the legal conclusion of the Department of Justice and determine that none of the provisions of Geneva apply to our conflict with al Qaeda in Afghanistan or elsewhere throughout the world because, among other reasons, al Qaeda is not a High Contracting Party to Geneva.

February 7, 2002 (A), Selection 1

c. I also accept the legal conclusion of the Department of Justice and determine that common Article 3 of Geneva does not apply to either al Qaeda or Taliban detainees, because, among other reasons, the relevant conflicts are international in scope and common Article 3 applies only to "armed conflict not of an international character."

d. Based on the facts supplied by the Department of Defense and the recommendation of the Department of Justice, I determine that the Taliban detainees are unlawful combatants and, therefore, do not qualify as prisoners of war under Article 4 of Geneva. I note that, because Geneva does not apply to our conflict with al Qaeda, al Qaeda detainees also do not qualify as prisoners of war.

February 7, 2002 (A), Selection 2

February 7, 2002 (B)
Re: Status of Taliban Forces Under Article 4 of the Third Geneva Convention of 1949
By Jay S. Bybee

Department of Defense ("DoD"), we conclude that the President has reasonable factual grounds to determine that no members of the Taliban militia are entitled to prisoner of war ("POW") status under GPW. First, we explain that the Taliban militia cannot meet the requirements of

February 7, 2002 (B), Selection 1

4(A)(2). Based on the facts presented to us by DoD, we believe that the President has the factual basis on which to conclude that the Taliban militia, as a group, fails to meet three of the four GPW requirements, and hence are not legally entitled to POW status.

February 7, 2002 (B), Selection 2

First, there is no organized command structure whereby members of the Taliban militia report to a military commander who takes responsibility for the actions of his subordinates. The Taliban lacks a permanent, centralized communications infrastructure. Periodically, individuals

February 7, 2002 (B), Selection 3

Moreover, when the armed groups organized, the core of the organization was often al Qaeda, a multinational terrorist organization, whose existence was not in any way accountable to or dependent upon the sovereign state of Afghanistan. We have previously concluded, as a

February 7, 2002 (B), Selection 4

Second, there is no indication that the Taliban militia wore any distinctive uniform or other insignia that served as a "fixed distinctive sign recognizable at a distance." DoD has

February 7, 2002 (B), Selection 5

Third, the Taliban militia carried arms openly. This fact, however, is of little significance because many people in Afghanistan carry arms openly. Although Taliban forces did not generally conceal their weapons, they also never attempted to distinguish themselves from other individuals through the arms they carried or the manner in which they carried them. Thus, the

February 7, 2002 (B), Selection 6

Finally, there is no indication that the Taliban militia understood, considered themselves bound by, or indeed were even aware of, the Geneva Conventions or any other body of law.

February 7, 2002 (B), Selection 7

We conclude, however, that the four basic conditions that apply to militias must also apply, at a minimum, to members of armed forces who would be legally entitled to POW status.

In other words, an individual cannot be a POW, even if a member of an armed force, unless forces also are: (a) "commanded by a person responsible for his subordinates"; (b) "hav[e] a fixed distinctive sign recognizable at a distance"; (c) "carry[] arms openly"; and (d) "conduct[] their operations in accordance with the laws and customs of war." Thus, if the President has the factual basis to determine that Taliban prisoners are not entitled to POW status under Article 4(A)(2) as members of a militia, he therefore has the grounds to also find that they are not entitled to POW status as members of an armed force under either Article 4(A)(1) or Article 4(A)(3).

February 7, 2002 (B), Selection 8

<u>February 26, 2002</u>
Re: Potential Legal Constraints Applicable
to Interrogations of Persons Captured by U.S. Armed
Forces in Afghanistan
By Jay S. Bybee

As we explain below, the Self-Incrimination Clause (and hence *Miranda)* does not apply in the context of a trial by military commission for violations of the laws of war. Accordingly, military commissions may admit statements made by a defendant in a custodial interrogation conducted without *Miranda* warnings. Therefore, to the extent that the only trial-related use of statements obtained in an interrogation will be before a military commission, there is no need to provide *Miranda* warnings.

February 26, 2002, Selection 1

Finally, in response to your other inquiries, we explain that the Sixth Amendment right to counsel does not apply prior to the initiation of adversary judicial criminal proceedings, and thus is not likely to apply to persons seized in Afghanistan and held overseas. In addition, the Citizens Protection Act, 28 U.S.C. § 530B (Supp. IV 1998), commonly known as the McDade Act – which places restrictions on government attorneys' conduct with respect to interrogations – does not apply to Defense Department lawyers.

February 26, 2002, Selection 2

that the *Miranda* procedures be followed in order for a custodial statement to be deemed admissible. For example, in *New York v. Quarles*, the Court held that when the police arrest a suspect under circumstances presenting an imminent danger to the public safety, they may, without informing him of his *Miranda* rights, ask questions necessary to elicit information that would neutralize the threat. The Court concluded that in such circumstances, the need to ensure public safety outweighed any benefit that might be gained from the ordinary rule of requiring *Miranda* warnings. 467 U.S. at 657.

February 26, 2002, Selection 3

II. Trials by Military Commissions.

The Self-Incrimination Clause does not apply to trials by military commissions for violations of the laws of war. The Clause is limited by its terms to "any criminal case," U.S. Const., amend. V, and the Supreme Court has long understood the rights guaranteed by the amendment to be limited to the scope they had at common law in criminal prosecutions at the time of the founding. *See, e.g.*,

February 26, 2002, Selection 4

Self-Incrimination Clause also does not constrain the evidence that military commissions may receive. Trials by military commissions are not "criminal case[s]" within the terms of the Amendment. Rather, they are entirely creatures of the President's authority as Commander in Chief under Article II and are part and parcel of the conduct of a military campaign.[2] As a result, they are not constrained by the strictures placed on "criminal case[s]" by the Self-Incrimination Clause (or other provisions in the Bill of Rights). As the *Quirin* Court stated broadly (albeit in *dicta*), "the Fifth

February 26, 2002, Selection 5

Moreover, with respect to trials of foreign nationals conducted outside U.S. territory, our conclusion is additionally supported by the well-established fact that the Fifth Amendment does not confer rights upon aliens outside the sovereign territory of the United States. *See Verdugo-Urquidez*,

February 26, 2002, Selection 6

in Mexico but [that he could] contact the American Consul on their behalf"). Even where, as here, the suspects are held by the United States government abroad, other factors may make the burdens of *Miranda* outweigh any benefits that *Miranda* may provide in deterring misconduct in run-of-the-mill prosecutions. In particular, it seems likely that when a battlefield detainee is being interrogated for military and intelligence information – a process that may extend over many days or weeks – the provision of *Miranda* warnings by *other* U.S. personnel who may wish to question the same detainee during the same time period for purposes of building a criminal case will make the detainee less likely to provide information vital to the objectives of military and intelligence questioning. In such a scenario, there is a sound argument that the disadvantages that will result from providing *Miranda* warnings (in terms of lost information of military and intelligence value) outweigh any benefits to be gained from applying *Miranda* as a device for regulating police conduct.

February 26, 2002, Selection 7

March 13, 2002

Re: The President's power as Commander in Chief to transfer captured terrorists to the control and custody of foreign nations

By Jay S. Bybee

control of the United States armed forces, to other countries. We conclude that the President has plenary constitutional authority, as the Commander in Chief, to transfer such individuals who are captured and held outside the United States to the control of another country. Individuals who are detained within the United States, however, may be subject to a more complicated set of rules established by both treaty and statute.

March 13, 2002, Selection 1

to third countries. GPW does not restrict the President's discretion because the President has determined that the al Qaeda or Taliban detainees are not legally entitled to prisoner of war ("POWs") status within the meaning of the Conventions. The Torture Convention poses no obstacle to transfer because the treaty does not apply extraterritorially. As removal applies only to the transfer of individuals already within the territorial jurisdiction of the United States, and as extradition is rarely if ever applied to individuals held abroad, those methods of transfer do not apply to the detainees held either in Afghanistan or at the U.S. Naval Base at Guantanamo Bay, Cuba.

March 13, 2002, Selection 2

restrictions on the operation of the President's Commander-in-Chief authority. The GPW imposes some limitations on the transfer of United States-held POWs to other nations. These limitations, however, apply only to individuals who are legally entitled to POW status, and leave the President considerable discretion as to when such transfers are permissible. Further, as this Office has explained elsewhere, the members of non-state terrorist organizations such as al Qaeda are not entitled to POW status as a matter of law because the GPW's protections for POWs apply only to international armed conflicts between state parties. *See* Memorandum for Alberto R. Gonzales, Counsel to the President and William J. Haynes, II, General Counsel, Department of Defense, from Jay S. Bybee, Assistant Attorney General, Office of Legal Counsel, *Re: Application of Treaties and Laws to al Qaeda and Taliban Detainees* at 9-10 (Jan. 22, 2002) ("GPW Memo"). Therefore, there are no GPW constraints on the President's ability to transfer al Qaeda prisoners to third countries. The Torture Convention also imposes limitations on transfer, but those restrictions have no extraterritorial effect and thus are not applicable to prisoners who are captured and detained abroad.[1]

March 13, 2002, Selection 3

of war. This view of the President's war powers is supported by the Constitution's text and a comprehensive understanding of its structural allocation of powers, but also by an unbroken chain of historical practice dating back to the Founding era. In tandem, these factors conclusively demonstrate that the Commander-in-Chief Clause constitutes an independent grant of substantive authority to engage in the detention and transfer of prisoners captured in armed conflicts.

1. Constitutional text and structure

The text, structure, and history of the Constitution establish that the Founders entrusted the President with the primary responsibility, and therefore the power, to control and conduct military operations engaged in by the United States. Article II, Section 2 states that the

March 13, 2002, Selection 4

Moreover, as the courts have consistently recognized, the President's discretion in exercising the Commander-in-Chief power is complete, and his military decisions are not subject to challenge in the courts. In the *Prize Cases*, 67 U.S. (2 Black) 635, 670 (1862), for example,

March 13, 2002, Selection 5

Hamilton) (Jacob E. Cooke ed., 1982 reprint) (1961). The centralization of authority in the President alone is particularly crucial in matters of national defense, war, and foreign policy, where a unitary executive can evaluate threats, consider policy choices, and make command decisions affecting operations in the field with a speed and energy that is far superior to any other branch. As Hamilton noted. "Of all the cares or concerns of government the direction of

March 13, 2002, Selection 6

Second, the constitutional structure requires that any ambiguity in the allocation of a power that is executive in nature must be resolved in favor of the executive branch. As this

March 13, 2002, Selection 7

Government and Regulation of the land and naval Forces"). Even if the Constitution's entrustment of the Commander-in-Chief power to the President did not bestow upon him the authority to make unilateral determinations regarding the disposition of captured enemies, the President would nevertheless enjoy such a power by virtue of the broad sweep of the Vesting Clause. Thus, the power to dispose of the liberty of individuals captured and brought under the control of United States armed forces during military operations remains in the hands of the President alone unless the Constitution specifically commits the power to Congress.

March 13, 2002, Selection 8

conduct warfare.[4] The treatment of captured enemy soldiers is but one of the many facets of the conduct of war, entrusted by the Constitution in plenary fashion to the President by virtue of the Commander-in-Chief Clause. Moreover, it is an area in which the President appears to enjoy exclusive authority, as the power to handle captured enemy soldiers is not reserved by the Constitution in whole or in part to any other branch of the government.

March 13, 2002, Selection 9

In sum, the power of the President to set forth and establish all aspects of the prisoner of war policy of the United States, including the power to transfer prisoners of war to the custody and control of other nations, has always been understood as being within the Commander-in-Chief power. Further, it has never been challenged or called seriously into question by the coordinate branches of the government.

March 13, 2002, Selection 10

Vietnam.[78] In sum, historical practice firmly supports the power of the President to transfer and otherwise dispose of the liberty of *all* individuals captured incident to military operations, and not merely those individuals who may technically be classified as prisoners of war under relevant treaties.

March 13, 2002, Selection 11

war. On February 7, 2002, the President exercised this authority and found that none of the Taliban prisoners are entitled to POW status. Consequently, GPW's limitations on the ability to transfer POWs do not apply. GPW establishes no minimum standards regulating the transfer of combatants who do not meet the definition of a POW under Article 4.

Thus, although the transfer provisions of GPW are inapplicable to members of al Qaeda or the Taliban militia, the President could, of course, decide to transfer members of al Qaeda or the Taliban consistent with GPW. If the President were to decide to apply GPW, it would govern POW transfer in the following fashion. Article 12 provides that "[p]risoners of war may only be transferred by the Detaining Power to a Power which is a party to the Convention and after the Detaining Power has satisfied itself of the willingness and ability of such transferee Power to apply the Convention." The GPW thus imposes two initial limitations on transfers of prisoners of war. The first requirement, which holds that the Transferee Power must be a party to the GPW, is both easy to understand and relatively unproblematic, as virtually every nation in the world has signed it.[83] The requirement that the Detaining Power "satisfy itself" that the Transferee Power is "willing" to apply the GPW, however, is considerably more vague. The International Committee of the Red Cross ("ICRC") has expressed the opinion that the Detaining Power can fulfill its obligation only through a prior investigation, which it suggests be conducted under the auspices of the Power assigned to protect the prisoners. *See* 3 *The Geneva Conventions of 12 August 1949: Commentary* 136 (Jean S. Pictet ed., ICRC 1960). We do not agree, however, that Article 12 requires that the Detaining Power have actual knowledge of the conditions in which the other power will keep a transferred POW, or that the other power guarantee a certain kind of treatment. The phrase "satisfy[y] itself," certainly does not require a prior investigation of the sort contemplated by the ICRC, but instead suggests that whether the receiving nation will meet with GPW is for the transferring country to determine. Further, Article 12 does not state that the Detaining Power must satisfy itself that the transferee nation will honor the strict letter of the GPW in every respect. Rather, a separate sentence of Article 12 indicates that the Detaining Power's responsibility is limited to ascertaining that the transferee nation will not breach the GPW "in any *important* respect."[84] The ICRC has interpreted that phrase to mean "systematic violations of the Convention," breaches causing "serious prejudice to the prisoners," and "grave breaches of the Convention" as defined by Article 130. Pictet, *supra*, at 138. Even the ICRC, therefore, acknowledges that the Detaining Power need not satisfy itself that the transferee nation will meet every requirement of GPW in its treatment of POWs.

Once a POW is formally transferred, GPW establishes that the Detaining Power is no longer responsible for the treatment that the POW receives.[85] If, however, the "Protecting Power" – typically the ICRC – complains that the Transferee Nation is not honoring GPW's limitations, the Detaining Power must investigate the Protecting Power's claim, and might even be required to request the return of the prisoner. Like the up-front limitations on POW transfers, however, these back-end GPW requirements are entirely self-enforcing and subject to interpretation, and the manner in which the United States elects to uphold its treaty obligations is left entirely to its own discretion. Your Department would likely have more information that the Department of Justice concerning United States practice, if any, under this provision.

C. Limitations Imposed on the Transfer Of Detainees By the Torture Convention

In addition to GPW, the Torture Convention establishes certain restrictions on the ability of state parties to transfer individuals within its control. The Torture Convention prohibits contracting parties from transferring individuals who are in their custody within their territory to the control of foreign governments that are more likely than not to torture them. Article 3 of the Torture Convention specifies that "[n]o State Party shall expel, return ("refouler") or extradite a person to another State where there are substantial grounds for believing that he would be in danger of being subjected to torture."[86] Article 2 provides that "[n]o exceptional circumstances whatsoever, whether a state of war or a threat of war, internal political instability or any other

public emergency, may be invoked as a justification of torture."[87] The United States is a party to the Convention. President Reagan signed the Convention on April 18, 1988, and the Senate consented to it on October 27, 1990.

Two of the Senate's reservations, understandings, and declarations accompanying the Convention are worth mentioning here. First, the United States expressed the understanding that the phrase "substantial grounds for believing that he would be in danger of being subjected to torture" in Article 3 means that "it is more likely than not that he would be tortured."[88] Second, the United States expressly declared that Article 3 of the Convention is not self-executing.[89] As a non-self-executing treaty, the Torture Convention does not, without implementing legislation, provide a private cause of action in federal court for an individual to oppose his expulsion or extradition. *See generally* Memorandum for Mary B. DeRosa, Legal Adviser, National Security

March 13, 2002, Selection 12

Foreign Relations Law of the United States § 111 & cmt. h (1987). Thus, the Torture Convention does not itself provide a prisoner with the legal grounds to ask a federal court to block his transfer to another country.

March 13, 2002, Selection 13

been promulgated pursuant to it are applicable to military transfers.[90] Congress has also broadly proclaimed, however, that "[i]t shall be the policy of the United States not to expel, extradite, or otherwise effect the involuntary return of any person to a country in which there are substantial grounds for believing the person would be in danger of being subjected to torture, regardless of whether the person is physically present in the United States." *Id.* § 2242(a), 112 Stat. at 2681-822; 18 U.S.C. § 1231 note. This provision largely tracks the language of the Torture Convention, but it significantly extends the Convention's protections to persons who are not physically present in the United States. Congress expressly referred to this proclamation as a "policy statement," *id.*, indicating that it should not be construed as an actual interpretation of the treaty language or as a provision creating judicially enforceable rights. *See Lyng v. Northwest Indian Cemetery Protective Assn.*, 485 U.S. 439, 454-55 (1988) (holding with respect to statutory language similarly setting forth the "policy of the United States" that "[n]owhere in the law is there so much as a hint of any intent to create a cause of action or any judicially enforceable individual rights"); *Attakai v. United States*, 746 F. Supp 1395, 1405 (D. Arizona 1990) (same). Furthermore, even if it were an interpretation of the Convention, the interpretation would not be binding on the Executive, and indeed it would arguably constitute unconstitutional interference with the President's constitutional authority over treaties. *See generally* Memorandum for John

March 13, 2002, Selection 14

The non-self-executing nature of the Torture Convention does not answer the question whether the executive branch has a legal obligation to enforce the treaty by refusing to transfer individuals, held in custody in United States territory, to foreign governments under circumstances where it is more likely than not that they will be tortured.[91] But we need not address this latter issue because the Torture Convention has no extraterritorial effect (except in the case of extradition) and, hence, cannot apply to al Qaeda and Taliban prisoners detained *outside* of United States territory at Guantanamo Bay or in Afghanistan. Although the United States Supreme Court has never interpreted the scope of Article 3, under which the United States cannot "expel," "return," or "extradite" individuals to countries in which it is more likely than not that they will be tortured, it has interpreted identical language elsewhere. As the Supreme Court has held, a treaty's use of the words "return" and "expel" means that the treaty's requirements apply only to individuals being held within the territory of the United States. *See Sale v. Haitian Centers Council, Inc.*, 509 U.S. 155 (1993) (construing the same words as used in the Conventions Relating to the Status of Refugees). The Court explained that the word *expel* "refers to the deportation or expulsion of an alien who is already present in the host country." *Id.* at 180. The word *return*, on the other hand, which the treaty defines in part by a parenthetical reference to the French word "refouler," "has a legal meaning [that is] narrower than its common meaning." *Id.* "Refouler" is not a synonym for the English word "return," but rather means to "repulse," "repel," or "drive back." *Id.* at 180-81. Thus, in the context of international treaties such as the Torture Convention, the word "return" refers to the involuntary removal of individuals who have not been legally admitted into the territory of the host country, but rather have been turned back or detained at the border.[92] *Id.* at 181-82. "A treaty cannot impose uncontemplated extraterritorial obligations on those who ratify it through no more than its general humanitarian intent." *Id.* at 183.[93]

Given the Supreme Court's interpretation of identical language in the Refugee Convention, it makes no sense to view the Torture Convention as affecting the transfer of prisoners held outside the United States to another country.[94] Our conclusion receives further

March 13, 2002, Selection 15

Dep't of Justice, 491 U.S. 440, 466 (1989). Here, reading the Torture Convention to apply extraterritorially would interfere with the President's powers as Commander in Chief and Chief Executive to direct the operations of the military. We do not read the Torture Convention to have such an effect without a clear statement in the text of the treaty or any implementing legislation.

March 13, 2002, Selection 16

Thus, the United States is free from any constraints imposed by the Torture Convention in deciding whether to transfer detainees that it is holding abroad to third countries.

D. Criminal Penalties for Conspiring to Commit Acts of Torture Abroad

Although the President is free from *ex ante* constitutional and domestic law constraints on his ability to transfer military detainees held outside the United States to the custody of foreign nations, criminal penalties could apply to such transfers if they were deemed to be part of a conspiracy to commit an act of torture abroad. 18 U.S.C. § 2340A(a) (1994), provides:

> Whoever outside the United States commits or attempts to commit torture shall be fined under this title or imprisoned not more than 20 years, or both, and if death results to any person from conduct prohibited by this subsection, shall be punished by death or imprisoned for any term of years or for life.

18 U.S.C.A. § 2340A(c) (2000), *amended by* USA Patriot Act, Pub. L. No. 107-56, sec. 811(g), 115 Stat. 272, 381 (2001), provides that the same penalties are applicable to "[a] person who conspires to commit an offense under this section." This law applies to official conduct engaged

March 13, 2002, Selection 17

The statute therefore would provide criminal penalties for any transfer that is found to be part of a conspiracy to commit torture abroad. Under the general federal criminal conspiracy statute, to establish the existence of a criminal conspiracy a prosecutor must demonstrate beyond a reasonable doubt :

> (1) that two or more people agreed to pursue an unlawful objective; (2) that the defendant voluntarily agreed to join the conspiracy; and (3) that one or more members of the conspiracy committed an overt act in furtherance of the conspiracy.

United States v. Loe, 262 F.3d 427, 432-33 (5th Cir. 2001) (referring to 18 U.S.C. § 371), *cert. denied*, No. 01-919, 2002 WL 233060 (Feb. 19, 2002). The Supreme Court has read the first two of these general requirements into other statutes criminalizing "conspiracies" without further defining the term. *See, e.g., Salinas v. United States*, 522 U.S. 52, 63-65 (1997) (reading the requirements into the RICO statute, 18 U.S.C. § 1962(d)). The Court has ruled, however, that the requirement of an overt act is a statutory creation that should not be read into statues that do not expressly provide for it. *See id.* at 64; *Fiswick v. United States*, 329 U.S. 211, 216 n.4 (1946). It is irrelevant for present purposes whether an overt act is required under the criminal torture statute, however, as the transfer of an individual would almost certainly itself be sufficient to qualify as the requisite overt act.

Thus, to fully shield our personnel from criminal liability, it is important that the United States not enter into an agreement with a foreign country, explicitly or implicitly, to transfer a detainee to that country for the purpose of having the individual tortured. Such an agreement would not have to be explicit to be prosecuted, as an agreement "can instead be inferred from the facts and circumstances of the case." *Iannelli v. United States*, 420 U.S. 770, 777 n.10 (1975). So long as the United States does not intend for a detainee to be tortured post-transfer, however, no criminal liability will attach to a transfer, even if the foreign country receiving the detainee does torture him. For criminal liability to attach, the accused must be shown to have intended to effectuate the criminal object of the conspiracy. *United States v. U.S. Gypsum Co.*, 438 U.S. 422, 443 n.20 (1978). Thus, so long as the United States personnel who agree to transfer a detainee do not intend to effectuate the criminal object that is forbidden by the criminal torture statute – here, the torturing of the detainee – they cannot be prosecuted under the statute.

II. DOMESTIC RULES GOVERNING EXTRADITION

Extradition is "the normal process by which individuals charged with or convicted of a crime against the law of one state and found in a second state are returned by the second state to the first for trial or punishment."[95] It is a highly specialized process, the basic characteristics of which are outlined below, and it is accordingly subject to its own particularized set of rules and limitations. Thus, the more generic restrictions that the Geneva Convention places on transfers of prisoners of war do not apply to requests for extradition, and, reciprocally, the specialized rules and requirements that are applicable to the extradition process do not restrict other methods of transfer. Extradition requests typically relate to individuals being held within a nation's territorial jurisdiction, and it is therefore unlikely that the process can be invoked with respect to alien combatants captured in Afghanistan and detained in Guantanamo Bay or Afghanistan. *See*

March 13, 2002, Selection 18

III. DOMESTIC RULES GOVERNING REMOVAL

Removal rules govern only aliens who are being held within the territory of the United States. Thus, the following discussion is not applicable to the Taliban and al Qaeda detainees presently being held at Guantanamo Bay. Nevertheless, we provide an analysis of the removal

March 13, 2002, Selection 19

tortured or otherwise persecuted. The removal statute provides that "the Attorney General may not remove an alien to a country if the Attorney General decides that the alien's life or freedom would be threatened in that country because of the alien's race, religion, nationality, membership in a particular social group, or political opinion." 8 U.S.C. § 1231(b)(3)(A), INA § 241(b)(3)(a). This provision should not present an obstacle to removing an alien terrorist to a country of the Attorney General's choice, however. First, any persecution that a terrorist might suffer would likely be attributable not to his "race, religion, nationality, membership in a particular social group, or political opinion," but to his participation in an illegal terrorism campaign. *Id.* Second, the provision is expressly made inapplicable to an alien if, among other things, the alien "ordered, incited, assisted, or otherwise participated in the persecution of an individual because of the individual's race, religion, nationality, membership in a particular social group, or political opinion." *Id.* § 1231(b)(3)(B), INA § 241(b)(3)(B). This provision could cover virtually every alien terrorist who is apprehended in the United States, as it is the express goal of al Qaeda terrorists to persecute United States citizens because of their nationality. Even where that exception is inapplicable, however, an exemption is also provided where "there are reasonable grounds to believe that the alien is a danger to the security of the United States." *Id.* This second provision provides the Attorney General with a flexible catch-all that should cover virtually any alien who is involved in planning terrorist activities.

March 13, 2002, Selection 20

<u>*Conclusion*</u>

We conclude that as Commander in Chief and Chief Executive, the President has the plenary constitutional power to detain and transfer prisoners captured in war. We also conclude that neither the GPW nor the Torture Convention restrict the President's legal authority to transfer prisoners captured in the Afghanistan conflict to third countries. Although the GPW places conditions on the transfer of POWs, neither al Qaeda nor Taliban prisoners are legally entitled to POW status, and hence there are no GPW conditions placed on their transfer. While the Torture Convention arguably might govern transfer of these prisoners, it does not apply extraterritorially. If detainees in the future are held within the territory of the United States, however, a more complex set of rules would apply.

Please let us know if we can provide any further assistance.

Jay S. Bybee
Assistant Attorney General

March 13, 2002, Selection 21

Code. As we understand it, this question has arisen in the context of the conduct of interrogations outside of the United States. We conclude below that Section 2340A proscribes acts inflicting, and that are specifically intended to inflict, severe pain or suffering, whether mental or physical. Those acts must be of an extreme nature to rise to the level of torture within the meaning of Section 2340A and the Convention. We further conclude that certain acts may be cruel, inhuman, or degrading, but still not produce pain and suffering of the requisite intensity to fall within Section 2340A's proscription against torture. We conclude by examining possible defenses that would negate any claim that

August 1, 2002 (A), Selection 1

In Part I, we examine the criminal statute's text and history. We conclude that for an act to constitute torture as defined in Section 2340, it must inflict pain that is difficult to endure. Physical pain amounting to torture must be equivalent in intensity to the pain accompanying serious physical injury, such as organ failure, impairment of bodily function, or even death. For purely mental pain or suffering to amount to torture under Section 2340, it must result in significant psychological harm of significant duration, e.g., lasting for months or even years. We conclude that the mental harm also must result

August 1, 2002 (A), Selection 2

consequences." *Vacco v. Quill*, 521 U.S. 793, 802–03 (1997). Thus, even if the defendant knows that severe pain will result from his actions, if causing such harm is not his objective, he lacks the requisite specific intent even though the defendant did not act in good faith. Instead, a defendant is guilty of torture only if he acts with the express purpose of inflicting severe pain or suffering on a person within his custody or physical control. While as a theoretical matter such knowledge does not constitute specific intent,

August 1, 2002 (A), Selection 3

a whole" to ascertain a statute's meaning). Each component of the definition emphasizes that torture is not the mere infliction of pain or suffering on another, but is instead a step well removed. The victim must experience intense pain or suffering of the kind that is equivalent to the pain that would be associated with serious physical injury so severe that death, organ failure, or permanent damage resulting in a loss of significant body function will likely result. If that pain or suffering is psychological, that suffering must result from one of the acts set forth in the statute. In addition, these acts must cause long-term mental harm. Indeed, this view of the criminal act of torture is consistent with the term's

August 1, 2002 (A), Selection 4

the United Kingdom (1978).[15] In that case, the European Court of Human Rights examined interrogation techniques somewhat more sophisticated than the rather rudimentary and frequently obviously cruel acts described in the TVPA cases. Careful attention to this case is worthwhile not just because it examines methods not used in the TVPA cases, but also because the Reagan administration relied on this case in reaching the conclusion that the term torture is reserved in international usage for "extreme, deliberate, and unusually cruel practices." S. Treaty Doc. 100-20, at 4.

The methods at issue in *Ireland* were:

(1) Wall Standing. The prisoner stands spread eagle against the wall, with fingers high above his head, and feet back so that he is standing on his toes such that his all of his weight falls on his fingers.
(2) Hooding. A black or navy hood is placed over the prisoner's head and kept there except during the interrogation.
(3) Subjection to Noise. Pending interrogation, the prisoner is kept in a room with a loud and continuous hissing noise.
(4) Sleep Deprivation. Prisoners are deprived of sleep pending interrogation.
(5) Deprivation of Food and Drink. Prisoners receive a reduced diet during detention and pending interrogation.

The European Court of Human Rights concluded that these techniques used in combination, and applied for hours at a time, were inhuman and degrading but did not amount to torture. In analyzing whether these methods constituted torture, the court

August 1, 2002 (A), Selection 5

V. The President's Commander-in-Chief Power

Even if an interrogation method arguably were to violate Section 2340A, the statute would be unconstitutional if it impermissibly encroached on the President's constitutional power to conduct a military campaign. As Commander-in-Chief, the President has the constitutional authority to order interrogations of enemy combatants to gain intelligence information concerning the military plans of the enemy. The demands of the Commander-in-Chief power are especially pronounced in the middle of a war in which the nation has already suffered a direct attack. In such a case, the information gained from interrogations may prevent future attacks by foreign enemies. Any effort to apply Section 2340A in a manner that interferes with the President's direction of such core war matters as the detention and interrogation of enemy combatants thus would be unconstitutional.

August 1, 2002 (A), Selection 6

B. Interpretation to Avoid Constitutional Problems

As the Supreme Court has recognized, and as we will explain further below, the President enjoys complete discretion in the exercise of his Commander-in-Chief authority and in conducting operations against hostile forces. Because both "[t]he executive power and the command of the military and naval forces is vested in the President," the Supreme Court has unanimously stated that it is "*the President alone* [] who is constitutionally invested with the *entire charge of hostile operations*." *Hamilton v. Dillin*, 88 U.S. (21 Wall.) 73, 87 (1874) (emphasis added). That authority is at its height in the middle of a war.

In light of the President's complete authority over the conduct of war, without a clear statement otherwise, we will not read a criminal statute as infringing on the President's ultimate authority in these areas. We have long recognized, and the Supreme

August 1, 2002 (A), Selection 7

In order to respect the President's inherent constitutional authority to manage a military campaign against al Qaeda and its allies, Section 2340A must be construed as not applying to interrogations undertaken pursuant to his Commander-in-Chief authority.

August 1, 2002 (A), Selection 8

Authorization Act (Sep. 15, 1995). As we discuss below, the President's power to detain and interrogate enemy combatants arises out of his constitutional authority as Commander in Chief. A construction of Section 2340A that applied the provision to regulate the President's authority as Commander-in-Chief to determine the interrogation and treatment of enemy combatants would raise serious constitutional questions. Congress may no more regulate the President's ability to detain and interrogate enemy combatants than it may regulate his ability to direct troop movements on the battlefield. Accordingly, we would construe Section 2340A to avoid this constitutional difficulty, and conclude that it does not apply to the President's detention and interrogation of enemy combatants pursuant to his Commander-in-Chief authority.

August 1, 2002 (A), Selection 9

interrogations of enemy combatants ordered by the President pursuant to his Commander-in-Chief power would be unconstitutional. Even if an interrogation method, however, might arguably cross the line drawn in Section 2340, and application of the statute was not held to be an unconstitutional infringement of the President's Commander-in-Chief authority, we believe that under the current circumstances certain justification defenses might be available that would potentially eliminate criminal liability. Standard criminal law defenses of necessity and self-defense could justify

August 1, 2002 (A), Selection 10

Conclusion

For the foregoing reasons, we conclude that torture as defined in and proscribed by Sections 2340–2340A, covers only extreme acts. Severe pain is generally of the kind difficult for the victim to endure. Where the pain is physical, it must be of an intensity akin to that which accompanies serious physical injury such as death or organ failure. Severe mental pain requires suffering not just at the moment of infliction but it also requires lasting psychological harm, such as seen in mental disorders like posttraumatic stress disorder. Additionally, such severe mental pain can arise only from the predicate acts listed in Section 2340. Because the acts inflicting torture are extreme, there is significant range of acts that though they might constitute cruel, inhuman, or degrading treatment or punishment fail to rise to the level of torture.

Further, we conclude that under the circumstances of the current war against al Qaeda and its allies, application of Section 2340A to interrogations undertaken pursuant to the President's Commander-in-Chief powers may be unconstitutional. Finally, even if an interrogation method might violate Section 2340A, necessity or self-defense could provide justifications that would eliminate any criminal liability.

Please let us know if we can be of further assistance.

Jay S. Bybee
Assistant Attorney General

August 1, 2002 (A), Selection 11

August 1, 2002 (B)

Interrogation of al Qaeda Operative

By Jay S. Bybee

As part of this increased pressure phase, Zubaydah will have contact only with a new interrogation specialist, whom he has not met previously, and the Survival, Evasion, Resistance, Escape ("SERE") training psychologist who has been involved with the interrogations since they began. This phase will likely last no more than several days but could last up to thirty days. In this phase, you would like to employ ten techniques that you believe will dislocate his

August 1, 2002 (B), Selection 1

expectations regarding the treatment he believes he will receive and encourage him to disclose the crucial information mentioned above. These ten techniques are: (1) attention grasp, (2) walling, (3) facial hold, (4) facial slap (insult slap), (5) cramped confinement, (6) wall standing, (7) stress positions, (8) sleep deprivation, (9) insects placed in a confinement box, and (10) the waterboard. You have informed us that the use of these techniques would be on an as-needed basis and that not all of these techniques will necessarily be used. The interrogation team would use these techniques in some combination to convince Zubaydah that the only way he can influence his surrounding environment is through cooperation. You have, however, informed us that you expect these techniques to be used in some sort of escalating fashion, culminating with the waterboard, though not necessarily ending with this technique. Moreover, you have also orally informed us that although some of these techniques may be used with more than once, that repetition will not be substantial because the techniques generally lose their effectiveness after several repetitions. You have also informed us that Zabaydah sustained a wound during his capture, which is being treated.

August 1, 2002 (B), Selection 2

Additionally, you received a memorandum from the [redacted] which you supplied to us. [redacted] has experience with the use of all of these procedures in a course of conduct, with the exception of the insect in the confinement box and the waterboard. This memorandum confirms that the use of these procedures has not resulted in any reported instances of prolonged mental harm, and very few instances of immediate and temporary adverse psychological responses to the training. [redacted] reported that a small minority of students have had temporary adverse psychological reactions during training. Of the 26,829 students trained from 1992 through 2001 in the Air Force SERE training, 4.3 percent of those students had contact with psychology services. Of those 4.3 percent, only 3.2 percent were pulled from the program for psychological reasons. Thus, out of the students trained overall, only 0.14 percent were pulled from the program for psychological reasons. Furthermore, although [redacted] indicated that surveys of students having completed this training are not done, he expressed confidence that the training did not cause any long-term psychological impact. He based his conclusion on the debriefing of

August 1, 2002 (B), Selection 3

consequences from the use of the waterboard. You have informed us that other services ceased use of the waterboard because it was so successful as an interrogation technique, but not because of any concerns over any harm, physical or mental, caused by it. It was also reported to be almost 100 percent effective in producing cooperation among the trainees. [redacted] also indicated that he had observed the use of the waterboard in Navy training some ten to twelve times. Each time it resulted in cooperation but it did not result in any physical harm to the student.

August 1, 2002 (B), Selection 4

pain accompanying serious physical injury. *See* Section 2340A Memorandum at 6. Drawing upon the TVPA precedent, we have noted that examples of acts inflicting severe pain that typify torture are, among other things, severe beatings with weapons such as clubs, and the burning of prisoners. *See id.* at 24. We conclude below that none of the proposed techniques inflicts such pain.

August 1, 2002 (B), Selection 5

Although the waterboard constitutes a threat of imminent death, prolonged mental harm must nonetheless result to violate the statutory prohibition on infliction of severe mental pain or suffering. *See* Section 2340A Memorandum at 7. We have previously concluded that prolonged mental harm is mental harm of some lasting duration, e.g., mental harm lasting months or years. *See id.* Prolonged mental harm is not simply the stress experienced in, for example, an interrogation by state police. *See id.* Based on your research into the use of these methods at the SERE school and consultation with others with expertise in the field of psychology and interrogation, you do not anticipate that any prolonged mental harm would result from the use of the waterboard. Indeed, you have advised us that the relief is almost immediate when the cloth is removed from the nose and mouth. In the absence of prolonged mental harm, no severe mental pain or suffering would have been inflicted, and the use of these procedures would not constitute torture within the meaning of the statute.

August 1, 2002 (B), Selection 6

<u>Specific Intent.</u> To violate the statute, an individual must have the specific intent to inflict severe pain or suffering. Because specific intent is an element of the offense, the absence of specific intent negates the charge of torture. As we previously opined, to have the required

August 1, 2002 (B), Selection 7

Based on the information you have provided us, we believe that those carrying out these procedures would not have the specific intent to inflict severe physical pain or suffering. The objective of these techniques is not to cause severe physical pain. First, the constant presence of personnel with medical training who have the authority to stop the interrogation should it appear it is medically necessary indicates that it is not your intent to cause severe physical pain. The personnel on site have extensive experience with these specific techniques as they are used in SERE school training. Second, you have informed us that you are taking steps to ensure that

August 1, 2002 (B), Selection 8

<u>August 1, 2002 (C)</u>

Letter to Alberto Gonzales from John Yoo

By John C. Yoo

Rome Statute establishing the International Criminal Court (ICC).[2] We believe that interrogation methods that comply with § 2340 would not violate our international obligations under the Torture Convention, because of a specific understanding attached by the United States to its instrument of ratification. We also conclude that actions taken as part of the interrogation of al Qaeda operatives cannot fall within the jurisdiction of the ICC, although it would be impossible to control the actions of a rogue prosecutor or judge. This letter summarizes our views; a

August 1, 2002 (C), Selection 1

expressed in § 2340. When it acceded to the Convention, the United States attached to its instrument of ratification a clear understanding that defined torture in the exact terms used by §

expressed in § 2340. When it acceded to the Convention, the United States attached to its instrument of ratification a clear understanding that defined torture in the exact terms used by § 2340. The first Bush administration submitted the following understanding of the treaty:

> The United States understands that, in order to constitute torture, an act must be *specifically intended* to inflict severe physical or mental pain or suffering and that mental pain or suffering refers to prolonged mental pain caused by or resulting from (1) the intentional infliction or threatened infliction of severe physical pain or suffering; (2) administration or application, or threatened administration or application, of mind altering substances or other procedures calculated to disrupt profoundly the senses or the personality; (3) the threat of imminent death; or (4) the threat that another person will imminently be subjected to death, severe physical pain or suffering, or the administration or application of mind-altering substances or other procedures calculated to disrupt profoundly the senses or personality.

S. Exec. Rep. No. 101-30, at 36. The Senate approved the Convention based on this understanding, and the United States included the understanding in its instrument of ratification.[4]

August 1, 2002 (C), Selection 2

make reservations, none of them apply here.[7] First, a reservation is valid and effective unless it purports to defeat the object and purpose of the treaty. Vienna Convention, art. 19. Our initial

August 1, 2002 (C), Selection 3

Second, a treaty reservation will not be valid if the treaty itself prohibits states from taking reservations. The Torture Convention nowhere prohibits state parties from entering

August 1, 2002 (C), Selection 4

Thus, we conclude that the Bush administration's understanding created a valid and effective reservation to the Torture Convention. Even if it were otherwise, there is no

August 1, 2002 (C), Selection 5

You have also asked whether interrogations of al Qaeda operatives could be subject to criminal investigation and prosecution by the ICC. We believe that the ICC cannot take action based on such interrogations.

August 1, 2002 (C), Selection 6

al Qaeda operatives is not occurring as part of such an attack. The United States' campaign against al Qaeda is an attack on a non-state terrorist organization, not a civilian population. If anything, the interrogations are taking place to elicit information that could prevent attacks on civilian populations.

August 1, 2002 (C), Selection 7

entitled to the protections of any of the Geneva Conventions. Interrogation of al Qaeda members, therefore, cannot constitute a war crime because article 8 of the Rome Statute applies only to those protected by the Geneva Conventions.

We cannot guarantee, however, that the ICC would decline to investigate and prosecute interrogations of al Qaeda members. By the terms of the Rome Statute, the ICC is not checked by any other international body, not to mention any democratically-elected or accountable one. Indeed, recent events indicate that some nations even believe that the ICC is not subject to the authority of the United Nations Security Council. It is possible that an ICC official would ignore the clear limitations imposed by the Rome Statute, or at least disagree with the President's interpretation of GPW. Of course, the problem of the "rogue prosecutor" is not limited to questions about the interrogation of al Qaeda operatives, but is a potential risk for any number of actions that have been undertaken during the Afghanistan campaign, such as the collateral loss of

August 1, 2002 (C), Selection 8

March 14, 2003

Re: Military Interrogation of Alien Unlawful Combatants
Held Outside the United States
By John C. Yoo

thought to extend to interrogations—the Fifth and Eighth Amendments—do not apply here. The Fifth Amendment provides in relevant part that "[n]o person . . . shall be deprived of life, liberty, or property, without due process of law." U.S. Const., amend V.[2] The Eighth Amendment bars the "inflict[ion]" of "cruel and unusual punishments." U.S. Const., amend. VIII. These provisions, however, do not regulate the interrogation of alien enemy combatants outside the United States during an international armed conflict. This is clear as a matter of the text and purpose of the Amendments, as they have been interpreted by the federal courts.[3]

March 14, 2003, Selection 1

The situation in which these issues arise is unprecedented in recent American history. Four coordinated terrorist attacks, using hijacked commercial airliners as guided missiles, took place in rapid succession on the morning of September 11, 2001. These attacks were aimed at

March 14, 2003, Selection 2

Given the ongoing threat of al Qaeda attacks, the capture and interrogation of al Qaeda operatives is imperative to our national security and defense. Because of the asymmetric nature of terrorist operations, information is perhaps the most critical weapon for defeating al Qaeda. Al Qaeda is not a nation-state, and has no single country or geographic area as its base of operations. It has no fixed, large-scale military or civilian infrastructure. It deploys personnel, material, and finances covertly and attacks without warning using unconventional weapons and methods. As the September 11, 2001 attacks and subsequent events demonstrate, it seeks to launch terror attacks against purely civilian targets within the United States, and seeks to acquire weapons of mass destruction for such attacks. Because of the secret nature of al Qaeda's operations, obtaining advance information about the identity of al Qaeda operatives and their plans may prove to be the only way to prevent direct attacks on the United States. Interrogation of captured al Qaeda operatives could provide that information; indeed, in many cases interrogation may be the only method to obtain it. Given the massive destruction and loss of life caused by the September 11 attacks, it is reasonable to believe that information gained from al Qaeda personnel could prevent attacks of a similar (if not greater) magnitude from occurring in the United States.

March 14, 2003, Selection 3

Johnson v. Eisentrager, 339 U.S. 763, 788 (1950). In wartime, it is for the President alone to decide what methods to use to best prevail against the enemy. *See, e.g., Flanigan Memorandum*

March 14, 2003, Selection 4

Power: South Vietnam and the Cambodian Sanctuaries (May 22, 1970).[8] The President's complete discretion in exercising the Commander-in-Chief power has been recognized by the courts. In the *Prize Cases*, 67 U.S. (2 Black) 635, 670 (1862), for example, the Court explained

March 14, 2003, Selection 5

conflicts"). It is well settled that the President may seize and detain enemy combatants, at least for the duration of the conflict, and the laws of war make clear that prisoners may be interrogated for information concerning the enemy, its strength, and its plans.[9] Numerous Presidents have

March 14, 2003, Selection 6

We conclude below that the Fifth Amendment Due Process Clause is inapplicable to the conduct of interrogations of alien enemy combatants held outside the United States for two independent reasons. First, the Fifth Amendment Due Process Clause does not apply to the President's conduct of a war. Second, even if the Fifth Amendment applied to the conduct of war, the Fifth Amendment does not apply extraterritorially to aliens who have no connection to the United States. We address each of these reasons in turn.

March 14, 2003, Selection 7

Id. at 273–74 (citations omitted).[10] If each time the President captured and detained enemy aliens outside the United States, those aliens could bring suit challenging the deprivation of their liberty, such a result would interfere with and undermine the President's capacity to protect the Nation and to respond to the exigencies of war.[11]

March 14, 2003, Selection 8

Nation's history. Chief Justice Marshall concluded for the Court in 1814 that "war gives to the sovereign full right to take the persons and confiscate the property of the enemy wherever found." *Brown v. United States*, 12 U.S. (8 Cranch) 110, 122 (1814). *See also Eisentrager*, 339

March 14, 2003, Selection 9

Second, even if the Fifth Amendment applied to enemy combatants in wartime, it is clear that that the Fifth Amendment does not operate outside the United States to regulate the Executive's conduct toward aliens. The Supreme Court has squarely held that the Fifth Amendment provides no rights to non-citizens who have no established connection to the country and who are held outside sovereign United States territory. *See Verdugo-Urquidez*, 494

March 14, 2003, Selection 10

55, 72 n.16 (D.D.C. 2002) ("The Supreme Court in *Eisentrager*, *Verdugo-Urquidez*, and *Zadvydas*, and the District of Columbia Circuit in *Harbury*, have all held that there is no extraterritorial application of the Fifth Amendment to aliens."). Indeed, in *Harbury v. Deutch*,

March 14, 2003, Selection 11

authority." *The Federalist No. 74*, at 415. Thus, earlier in this current armed conflict against the al Qaeda terrorist network, we concluded that "[t]he power of the President is at its zenith under the Constitution when the President is directing military operations of the armed forces." *Flanigan Memorandum* at 3. Correspondingly, during war Congress plays a reduced role in the

March 14, 2003, Selection 12

In order to respect the President's inherent constitutional authority to direct a military campaign against al Qaeda and its allies, general criminal laws must be construed as not applying to interrogations undertaken pursuant to his Commander-in-Chief authority. Congress cannot

March 14, 2003, Selection 13

on the President's constitutional authority. Moreover, we do not believe that Congress enacted general criminal provisions such as the prohibitions against assault, maiming, interstate stalking, and torture pursuant to any express authority that would allow it to infringe on the President's constitutional control over the operation of the Armed Forces in wartime. In our view, Congress may no more regulate the President's ability to detain and interrogate enemy combatants than it may regulate his ability to direct troop movements on the battlefield. In fact, the general applicability of these statutes belies any argument that these statutes apply to persons under the direction of the President in the conduct of war.[13]

To avoid this constitutional difficulty, therefore, we will construe potentially applicable criminal laws, reviewed in more detail below, not to apply to the President's detention and interrogation of enemy combatants pursuant to his Commander-in-Chief authority. We believe that this approach fully respects Congress's authority. First, we will not read a statute to create constitutional problems because we assume that Congress fully respects the limits of its own constitutional authority and would not knowingly seek to upset the separation of powers. Second, we will not infer a congressional attempt to spark a constitutional confrontation with the executive branch in wartime unless Congress clearly and specifically seeks to do so.

March 14, 2003, Selection 14

combatants would deprive the sovereign of a recognized prerogative. Historically, nations have been free to treat unlawful combatants as they wish, and in the United States this power has been vested in the President through the Commander-in-Chief Clause. As one commentator has

March 14, 2003, Selection 15

International Law, the right to treat such individuals as war criminals.").[14] The United States Supreme Court has recognized the important distinction between lawful and unlawful combatants. As the Supreme Court unanimously stated 60 years ago, "[b]y universal agreement and practice the law of war draws a distinction between the armed forces and the peaceful populations of belligerent nations *and also between those who are lawful and unlawful combatants.*" *Ex parte Quirin*, 317 U.S. 1, 30–31 (1942) (emphasis added).

Under traditional practice as expressed in the customary laws of war, the treatment of unlawful belligerents is left to the sovereign's discretion. As one commentator has stated, the treatment of "unprivileged belligerents . . . [is] left to the discretion of the belligerent threatened by their activities." Julius Stone, *Legal Controls of International Conflict* 549 (1954). Under our Constitution, the sovereign right of the United States on the treatment of enemy combatants is reserved to the President as Commander-in-Chief. In light of the long history of discretion given to each nation to determine its treatment of unlawful combatants, to construe these statutes to regulate the conduct of the United States toward such combatants would interfere with a well-established prerogative of the sovereign. While the Geneva Convention (III) Relative to the Treatment of Prisoners of War, Aug. 12, 1949, 6 U.S.T. 3316, T.I.A.S. 3364 ("GPW"), imposes restrictions on the interrogations of prisoners of war, it does not provide prisoner of war status to those who are unlawful combatants. *See Treaties and Laws Memorandum* at 8–9. Those restrictions therefore would not apply to the interrogations of unlawful belligerents such as al Qaeda or Taliban members.

March 14, 2003, Selection 16

With respect to assault, maiming, or interstate stalking, no such history or obvious legislative policy indicates an intention to regulate lawful military activities in an armed conflict. Although the torture statute, as we explain below, applies to persons acting under color of law, the legislative history indicates no intent to apply this to the conduct of military personnel. Indeed, as we explained in discussing the prerogative of the sovereign, it is well established that the sovereign retains the discretion to treat unlawful combatants as it sees fit.

March 14, 2003, Selection 17

ability to prosecute a war. As a general matter, we do not construe generally applicable criminal statutes to reach the conduct of the military during a war. Moreover, the application of these statutes to the conduct of the military during war would touch upon a prerogative of the sovereign, namely its discretion regarding the treatment of unlawful belligerents.[16] Congress has not provided a clear statement with respect to any of these statutes that would suggest that these canons of construction do not apply. Additionally, as we explained above, the UCMJ provides a specific statutory scheme that governs the conduct of the military and as the more specific enactment it governs here.

March 14, 2003, Selection 18

6. **Commander-in-Chief Authority**

Even if these statutes were misconstrued to apply to persons acting at the direction of the President during the conduct of war, the Department of Justice could not enforce this law or any of the other criminal statutes applicable to the special maritime and territorial jurisdiction against federal officials acting pursuant to the President's constitutional authority to direct a war. Even if an interrogation method arguably were to violate a criminal statute, the Justice Department could not bring a prosecution because the statute would be unconstitutional as applied in this context. This approach is consistent with previous decisions of our Office involving the application of federal criminal law. For example, we have previously construed the congressional contempt statute not to apply to executive branch officials who refuse to comply with congressional subpoenas because of an assertion of executive privilege. In a published 1984 opinion, we concluded:

March 14, 2003, Selection 19

163–64. And should the statute not be construed in this manner, our Office concluded that the Department of Justice could not enforce the statute against federal officials who properly execute the President's constitutional authority. "The President, through a United States Attorney, need not, indeed may not, prosecute criminally a subordinate for asserting on his behalf a claim of executive privilege. Nor could the Legislative Branch or the courts require or implement the prosecution of such an individual." 8 Op. O.L.C. at 141. We opined that "courts . . . would

March 14, 2003, Selection 20

information necessary to prevent future attacks upon the United States and its citizens. Congress can no more interfere with the President's conduct of the interrogation of enemy combatants than it can dictate strategic or tactical decisions on the battlefield. Just as statutes that order the President to conduct warfare in a certain manner or for specific goals would be unconstitutional, so too are laws that would prevent the President from gaining the intelligence he believes necessary to prevent attacks upon the United States.

March 14, 2003, Selection 21

of interrogations, we must examine whether these statutes apply. Federal criminal statutes generally do not apply within the special maritime and territorial jurisdiction of the United States. *See United States v. Bowman*, 260 U.S. 94, 98 (1922). As noted above, this opinion

March 14, 2003, Selection 22

(2001). Section 7 defines the term "special maritime and territorial jurisdiction," which we conclude includes permanent U.S. military bases outside the United States, like the U.S. Naval Station, Guantanamo Bay ("GTMO"). Section 3261 defines military extraterritorial jurisdiction. We conclude that all persons who are neither members of the Armed Forces nor persons accompanying or employed by the Armed Forces are subject to the special maritime and territorial jurisdiction of the United States when they are in locations that Section 7 defines as part of that jurisdiction. Members of the Armed Forces and persons accompanying or employed by them, however, are subject to a slightly different rule. Members of the Armed Forces are subject to military discipline under the UCMJ anyplace outside the United States for conduct that would constitute a felony if committed within the special maritime and territorial jurisdiction of the United States. Those accompanying or employed by the Armed Forces can be prosecuted in an Article III court for their conduct outside the United States that would constitute a felony offense if committed within the special maritime and territorial jurisdiction of the United States. Finally, members of the Armed Forces and those accompanying or employed by the military are punishable for misdemeanor offenses in an Article III court when they commit such offenses within the special maritime and territorial jurisdiction of the United States.

As a general matter, GTMO and other U.S. military bases outside the United States fall within the special maritime and territorial jurisdiction of the United States.[17] Section 7(9) of Title 18 of the U.S. Code provides, in relevant part, that the special maritime and territorial jurisdiction of the United States includes:

> offenses committed by or against a national of the United States ... on the premises of United States ... military ... missions or entities in foreign States, including the buildings, parts of buildings, and land appurtenant or ancillary thereto or used for purposes of those missions or entities, irrespective of ownership.

18 U.S.C.A. § 7(9)(A).[18] By its terms, this section applies to GTMO and other U.S. military bases in foreign states, although no court has interpreted the scope of section 7(9)'s reach.[19]

March 14, 2003, Selection 23

2. Criminal Statutes Applicable in the Special Maritime and Territorial Jurisdiction of the United States

Because the interaction of 18 U.S.C. § 7 and 18 U.S.C. § 3261(a) renders the criminal statutes that apply in special maritime and territorial jurisdiction applicable to the conduct of members of the Armed Forces, and those accompanying or employed by the Armed Forces, we have examined below the criminal statutes that could conceivably cover interrogation conduct. Specifically, we have addressed: assault, 18 U.S.C. § 113; maiming, 18 U.S.C. § 114; and interstate stalking, 18 U.S.C. § 2261A. Of course, as we explained above, various canons of construction preclude the application of these laws to authorized military interrogations of alien enemy combatants during wartime.

March 14, 2003, Selection 24

No court has definitively addressed the minimum thresholds of injury necessary to rise to the level of "substantial bodily injury" or "serious bodily injury," respectively. Nonetheless,

March 14, 2003, Selection 25

Finally, section 113 prohibits assault with intent to commit murder and assault with the intent to commit any other felony except murder or sexual abuse crimes.[33] 18 U.S.C. §

March 14, 2003, Selection 26

may be more difficult to establish absent such contact. Here, as long as the interrogators do not section 113(a)(2), the intent to torture appears to be the most relevant. As we will explain *infra* Part II.C.2, to satisfy this intent element, the interrogator would have to intend to cause other severe physical pain or suffering or to cause prolonged mental harm. Absent such intent, the interrogator would not have committed assault with intent to torture. We caution, however, that specific intent, as will be discussed in more detail in Part II.C.2., can be inferred from the factual circumstances. *See also United States v. Hinton*, 31 F.3d 817, 822 (9th Cir. 1994).[34]

b. **Maiming**

Another criminal statute applicable in the special maritime and territorial jurisdiction is 18 U.S.C. § 114. Section 114 makes it a crime for an individual (1) "with the intent to torture (as defined in section 2340), maim, or disfigure" to (2) "cut[], bite[], or slit[] the nose, ear, or lip, or cut[] out or disable[] the tongue, or put[] out or destroy[] an eye, or cut[] off or disable[] a limb or any member of another person." 18 U.S.C. § 114. It further prohibits individuals from "throw[ing] or pour[ing] upon another person any scalding water, corrosive acid, or caustic substance" with like intent. *Id.*[35]

March 14, 2003, Selection 27

had been established.). Moreover, the defendant's method of maiming must be one of the types the statute specifies—i.e., cutting, biting, slitting, cutting out, disabling, or putting out—and the injury must be to a body part the statute specifies—i.e., the nose, ear, lip, tongue, eye, or limb. *See United States v. Stone*, 472 F.2d 909, 915 (5th Cir. 1973). Similarly, the second set of acts applies to a very narrow band of conduct. It applies only to the throwing or pouring of some sort of scalding, corrosive, or caustic substance. *See id.*

Here, so long as the interrogation methods under contemplation do not involve the acts enumerated in section 114, the conduct of those interrogations will not fall within the purview of this statute. Because the statute requires specific intent, i.e., the intent to maim, disfigure or torture, the absence of such intent is a complete defense to a charge of maiming.

c. **Interstate Stalking**

Section 2261A of Title 18 prohibits "[w]hoever . . . travels in interstate or foreign commerce or within the special maritime and territorial jurisdiction of the United States . . . with the intent to kill, injure, harass, or intimidate another person, and in the course of, or as a result of, such travel places that person in reasonable fear of the death of, or serious bodily injury to that person."[36] Thus, there are three elements to a violation of section 2261A: (1) the defendant

March 14, 2003, Selection 28

To establish the first element, the prosecution need only show that the defendant engaged in interstate travel. Section 2261A also applies to "travel[] . . . *within* the special maritime and

March 14, 2003, Selection 29

To establish the requisite intent, the prosecution must demonstrate that the defendant undertook the travel with the specific intent to harass, or intimidate another. *See Al-Zubaidy*, 283 F.3d at 809 (the defendant "must have intended to harass or injure [the victim] at the time he crossed the state line"). Thus, for example, a member of the Armed Forces who traveled to a base solely pursuant to his orders to be stationed there, and subsequently came to be involved in the interrogation of operatives, would lack the requisite intent. He would have traveled for the

March 14, 2003, Selection 30

There are two criminal prohibitions that apply to the conduct of U.S. persons outside the United States: the War Crimes Act, 18 U.S.C. § 2441, and the prohibition against torture, 18 U.S.C. §§ 2340–2340A. We conclude that the War Crimes Act does not apply to the interrogation of al Qaeda and Taliban detainees because, as illegal belligerents, they do not qualify for the legal protections under the Geneva or Hague Conventions that section 2441 enforces. In regard to section 2340, we conclude that the statute, by its terms, does not apply to

March 14, 2003, Selection 31

1. **War Crimes**

Article 3 of the Geneva Conventions. We have previously concluded that this statute does not apply to conduct toward the members of al Qaeda and the Taliban. *See Treaties and Laws*

Memorandum at 8–9. We reached this conclusion because we found al Qaeda to be a non-governmental terrorist organization whose members are not legally entitled to the protections of GPW. Since its members cannot be considered to be POWs under the Convention, conduct toward members of al Qaeda could not constitute a grave breach of the Geneva Conventions.

March 14, 2003, Selection 32

2. **18 U.S.C. §§ 2340–2340A**

Section 2340A of Title 18 makes it a criminal offense for any person "outside the United States [to] commit[] or attempt[] to commit torture."[41] The statute defines "the United States" as "all areas under the jurisdiction of the United States including any of the places described in" 18 U.S.C. § 5,[42] and 18 U.S.C.A. § 7.[43] 18 U.S.C. § 2340(3).[44] Therefore, to the extent that interrogations take place within the special maritime and territorial jurisdiction, such as at a U.S. military base in a foreign state, the interrogations are not subject to sections 2340–2340A. If, however, the interrogations take place outside the special maritime and territorial jurisdiction and are otherwise outside the United States, the torture statute applies. Thus, for example, interrogations conducted at GTMO would not be subject to this prohibition, but interrogations conducted at a non-U.S. base in Afghanistan would be subject to section 2340A.[45]

March 14, 2003, Selection 33

Conclusion

For the foregoing reasons, we conclude that the Fifth and Eighth Amendments do not extend to alien enemy combatants held abroad. Moreover, we conclude that different canons of construction indicate that generally applicable criminal laws do not apply to the military interrogation of alien unlawful combatants held abroad. Were it otherwise, the application of these statutes to the interrogation of enemy combatants undertaken by military personnel would conflict with the President's Commander-in-Chief power.

We further conclude that CAT defines U.S. international law obligations with respect to torture and other cruel, inhuman, or degrading treatment or punishment. The standard of conduct regarding torture is the same as that which is found in the torture statute, 18 U.S.C. §§ 2340–2340A. Moreover, the scope of U.S. obligations under CAT regarding cruel, inhuman, or degrading treatment or punishment is limited to conduct prohibited by the Eighth, Fifth and Fourteenth Amendments. Customary international law does not supply any additional standards.

Finally, even if the criminal prohibitions outlined above applied, and an interrogation method might violate those prohibitions, necessity or self-defense could provide justifications for any criminal liability.

Please let us know if we can be of further assistance

John C. Yoo
Deputy Assistant Attorney General

March 14, 2003, Selection 34

April 4, 2003

Working Group Report on Detainee Interrogations in the Global War on Terrorism: Assessment of Legal, Historical, Policy, and Operational Considerations
Classified by the Department of Defense

(U) Our review is limited to the legal and policy considerations applicable to interrogation techniques applied to unlawful combatants in the Global War on Terrorism interrogated outside the sovereign territory of the United States by DOD personnel in DOD interrogation facilities. Interrogations can be broadly divided into two categories, strategic and tactical. This document addresses only strategic interrogations that are those conducted: (i) at a fixed location created for that purpose; (ii) by a task force or higher level component; and (iii) other than in direct and immediate support of on-going military operations. All tactical interrogations, including battlefield interrogations, remain governed by existing doctrine and procedures and are not directly affected by this review.

April 4, 2003, Selection 1

2. u ~~(S/NF)~~ **Incentive/Removal of Incentive**: Providing a reward or removing a privilege, above and beyond those that are required by the Geneva Convention, from detainees, (Privileges above and beyond POW-required privileges).

3. u ~~(S/NF)~~ **Emotional Love**: Playing on the love a detainee has for an individual or group.

4. u ~~(S/NF)~~ **Emotional Hate**: Playing on the hatred a detainee has for an individual or group.

5. u ~~(S/NF)~~ **Fear Up Harsh**: Significantly increasing the fear level in a detainee.

6. u ~~(S/NF)~~ **Fear Up Mild**: Moderately increasing the fear level in a detainee.

7. u ~~(S/NF)~~ **Reduced Fear**: Reducing the fear level in a detainee.

8. u ~~(S/NF)~~ **Pride and Ego Up**: Boosting the ego of a detainee.

9. u ~~(S/NF)~~ **Pride and Ego Down**: Attacking or insulting the ego of a detainee, not beyond the limits that would apply to a POW.

10. u ~~(S/NF)~~ **Futility**: Invoking the feeling of futility of a detainee.

11. u ~~(S/NF)~~ **We Know All**: Convincing the detainee that the interrogator knows the answer to questions he asks the detainee.

12. u ~~(S/NF)~~ **Establish Your Identity**: Convincing the detainee that the interrogator has mistaken the detainee for someone else.

13. u ~~(S/NF)~~ **Repetition Approach**: Continuously repeating the same question to the detainee within interrogation periods of normal duration.

14. U ~~(S/NF)~~ **File and Dossier:** Convincing detainee that the interrogator has a damning and inaccurate file, which must be fixed.

15. U ~~(S/NF)~~ **Mutt and Jeff:** A team consisting of a friendly and harsh interrogator. The harsh interrogator might employ the Pride and Ego Down technique.

16. U ~~(S/NF)~~ **Rapid Fire:** Questioning in rapid succession without allowing detainee to answer.

17. U ~~(S/NF)~~ **Silence:** Staring at the detainee to encourage discomfort.

18. U ~~(S/NF)~~ **Change of Scenery Up:** Removing the detainee from the standard interrogation setting (generally to a location more pleasant, but no worse).

19. U ~~(S/NF)~~ **Change of Scenery Down:** Removing the detainee from the standard interrogation setting and placing him in a setting that may be less comfortable; would not constitute a substantial change in environmental quality.

20. U ~~(S/NF)~~ **Hooding:** This technique is questioning the detainee with a blindfold in place. For interrogation purposes, the blindfold is not on other than during interrogation.

21. U ~~(S/NF)~~ **Mild Physical Contact:** Lightly touching a detainee or lightly poking the detainee in a completely non-injurious manner. This also includes softly grabbing of shoulders to get the detainee's attention or to comfort the detainee.

22. U ~~(S/NF)~~ **Dietary Manipulation:** Changing the diet of a detainee; no intended deprivation of food or water; no adverse medical or cultural effect and without intent to deprive subject of food or water, e.g., hot rations to MREs.

23. U ~~(S/NF)~~ **Environmental Manipulation:** Altering the environment to create moderate discomfort (e.g., adjusting temperature or introducing an unpleasant smell). Conditions would not be such that they would injure the detainee. Detainee would be accompanied by interrogator at all times.

24. U ~~(S/NF)~~ **Sleep Adjustment:** Adjusting the sleeping times of the detainee (e.g., reversing sleep cycles from night to day.) This technique is NOT sleep deprivation.

25. U ~~(S/NF)~~ **False Flag:** Convincing the detainee that individuals from a country other than the United States are interrogating him.

26. U ~~(S/NF)~~ **Threat of Transfer:** Threatening to transfer the subject to a 3rd country that subject is likely to fear would subject him to torture or death. (The threat would not be acted upon nor would the threat include any information beyond the naming of the receiving country.)

U ~~(S/NF)~~ The following list includes additional techniques that are considered effective by interrogators, some of which have been requested by USCENTCOM and USSOUTHCOM. They are more aggressive counter-resistance techniques that may be appropriate for detainees who are extremely resistant to the above techniques, and who the interrogators strongly believe have vital information. All of the following techniques indicate the need for technique-specialized training and written procedures to insure the safety of all persons, along with appropriate, specified levels of approval and notification for each technique.

27. U ~~(S/NF)~~ **Isolation**: Isolating the detainee from other detainees while still complying with basic standards of treatment.

28. U ~~(S/NF)~~ **Use of Prolonged Interrogations**: The continued use of a series of approaches that extend over a long period of time (e.g., 20 hours per day per interrogation).

29. U ~~(S/NF)~~ **Forced Grooming**: Forcing a detainee to shave hair or beard. (Force applied with intention to avoid injury. Would not use force that would cause serious injury.)

30. U ~~(S/NF)~~ **Prolonged Standing:** Lengthy standing in a "normal" position (non-stress). This has been successful, but should never make the detainee exhausted to the point of weakness or collapse. Not enforced by physical restraints. Not to exceed four hours in a 24-hour period.

31. U ~~(S/NF)~~ **Sleep Deprivation**: Keeping the detainee awake for an extended period of time. (Allowing individual to rest briefly and then awakening him, repeatedly.) Not to exceed 4 days in succession.

32. U ~~(S/NF)~~ **Physical Training:** Requiring detainees to exercise (perform ordinary physical exercises actions) (e.g., running, jumping jacks); not to exceed 15 minutes in a two-hour period; not more than two cycles, per 24-hour periods) Assists in generating compliance and fatiguing the detainees. No enforced compliance.

33. U ~~(S/NF)~~ **Face slap/ Stomach slap:** A quick glancing slap to the fleshy part of the cheek or stomach. These techniques are used strictly as shock measures and do not cause pain or injury. They are only effective if used once or twice together. After the second time on a detainee, it will lose the shock effect. Limited to two slaps per application; no more than two applications per interrogation.

34. U ~~(S/NF)~~ **Removal of Clothing**: Potential removal of all clothing; removal to be done by military police if not agreed to by the subject. Creating a feeling of helplessness and dependence. This technique must be monitored to ensure the environmental conditions are such that this technique does not injure the detainee.

35. U ~~(S/NF)~~ **Increasing Anxiety by Use of Aversions:** Introducing factors that of themselves create anxiety but do not create terror or mental trauma (e.g., simple presence of dog without directly threatening action). This technique requires the commander to develop specific and detailed safeguards to insure detainee's safety.

April 4, 2003, Selection 2

(U) We recommend:

U ~~(S/NF)~~ 1. The working group recommends that techniques 1-26 on the attached chart be approved for use with unlawful combatants outside the United States, subject to the general limitations set forth in this Legal and Policy Analysis; and that techniques 27-35 be approved for use with unlawful combatants outside the United States subject to the general limitations as well as the specific limitations regarding "exceptional" techniques as follows: conducted at strategic interrogation facilities; where there is a good basis to believe that the detainee possesses critical intelligence; the detainee is medically and operationally evaluated as suitable (considering all techniques to be used in combination); interrogators are specifically trained for the technique(s); a specific interrogation plan (including reasonable safeguards, limits on duration, intervals between applications, termination criteria and the presence or availability of qualified medical personnel) is developed; appropriate supervision is provided; and, appropriate specified senior level approval is given for use with any specific detainee (after considering the foregoing and receiving legal advice).

U
(~~S/NF~~) 2. SECDEF approve the strategic interrogation facilities that are authorized to use the "exceptional techniques" (such facilities at this time include Guantanamo, Cuba; additional strategic interrogation facilities will be approved on a case-by-case basis).

April 4, 2003, Selection 3

● Red
○ Yellow
○ Green

UNCLASSIFIED

1A
of 11

War on Terrorism
Detainee Interrogation Working Group
Summary of Analysis and Recommendations
Pertaining to Unlawful Combatants Outside of the U.S.[1]

	Utility	Law IAW U.S. Interpretation		
Proposed Interrogation Techniques [2] (see attached description/limitations)	Contribution to Intelligence Collection (Useful)	Torture Convention [Torture]	Torture Convention [Cruel, Inhuman Degrading]	U.S. Domestic Law
1. Direct	High	●	●	●
2. Incentive or Removal	High	●	●	●
3. Emotional Love	High	●	●	●
4. Emotional Hate	High	●	●	●
5. Fear Up Harsh	High	●	●	●
6. Fear Up Mild	High	●	●	●
7. Reduced Fear	High	●	●	●
8. Pride and ego up	High	●	●	●
9. Pride and ego down	High	●	●	●
10. Futility	High	●	●	●
11. We Know All	High	●	●	●
12. Establish Your Identity	High	●	●	●

Note: Green denotes no significant constraint on use raised by the respective area of consideration listed at top of each column, assuming adequate procedural safeguards. Yellow indicates area of consideration does not preclude use but there are problematic aspects that cannot be eliminated by procedural safeguards (see footnote). Red indicates major issue in area of consideration that cannot be eliminated.

UNCLASSIFIED

April 4, 2003, Selection 4

● Red
○ Yellow
◍ Green

UNCLASSIFIED

War on Terrorism
Detainee Interrogation Working Group
Summary of Analysis and Recommendations
Pertaining to Unlawful Combatants Outside of the U.S.[1]

1B
of 11

Proposed Interrogation Techniques [2] (see attached description/limitations)	Policy: Consistency with Historical U.S. Forces Interrogation Role	Consistency with Prior U.S. Public Statements	Consistency with Major Partner Nation Views	Effect on Captured U.S. Forces	Potential Adverse Effect for Participants/ Supervisors/COC	Potential Effect on Detainee Prosecutions	Other	Recommendation: Re Unlawful Combatants
1. Direct	◍	◍	◍	◍	◍	◍	○	◍
2. Incentive or Removal	◍	◍	○ 3	◍	◍	◍ 4	○	◍
3. Emotional Love	◍	◍	◍	◍	◍	◍	○	◍
4. Emotional Hate	◍	◍	◍	◍	◍	◍	○	◍
5. Fear Up Harsh	◍	◍	◍	◍	◍	◍	○	◍
6. Fear Up Mild	◍	◍	◍	◍	◍	◍	○	◍
7. Reduced Fear	◍	◍	◍	◍	◍	◍	○	◍
8. Pride and ego up	◍	◍	◍	◍	◍	◍	○	◍
9. Pride and ego down	◍	◍	○ 5	◍	◍	◍	○	◍
10. Futility	◍	◍	◍	◍	◍	◍	○	◍
11. We Know All	◍	◍	◍	◍	◍	◍	○	◍
12. Establish Your Identity	◍	◍	◍	◍	◍	◍	○	◍

Note: Green denotes no significant constraint on use raised by the respective area of consideration listed at top of each column, assuming adequate procedural safeguards.
Yellow indicates area of consideration does not preclude use but there are problematic aspects that cannot be eliminated by procedural safeguards (see footnote).
Red indicates major issue in area of consideration that cannot be eliminated.

UNCLASSIFIED

April 4, 2003, Selection 5

● Red
○ Yellow
○ Green

UNCLASSIFIED

2A
of 11

Proposed Interrogation Techniques [2] (see attached description/limitations)	Utility: Contribution to Intelligence Collection (Useful)	Law IAW U.S. Interpretation: Torture Convention [Torture]	Torture Convention [Cruel, Inhuman Degrading]	U.S. Domestic Law
13. Repetition Approach	Low	◍	◍	◍
14. File and Dossier	High	◍	◍	◍
15. Mutt and Jeff	High	◍	◍	◍
16. Rapid Fire	High	◍	◍	◍
17. Silence	Medium	◍	◍	◍
18. Change of Scenery Up	High	◍	◍	◍
19. Change of Scenery Down	High	◍	◍	◍
20. Hooding	High	◍	◍	◍
21. Mild Physical Contact	High	◍	◍	◍
22. Dietary Manipulation	High	◍	◍	◍
23. Environmental manipulation	High	◍	◍	◍
24. Sleep Adjustment	High	◍	◍	◍
25. False Flag	High	◍	◍	◍

Note: Green denotes no significant constraint on use raised by the respective area of consideration listed at top of each column, assuming adequate procedural safeguards.
Yellow indicates area of consideration does not preclude use but there are problematic aspects that cannot be eliminated by procedural safeguards (see footnote).
Red indicates major issue in area of consideration that cannot be eliminated.

UNCLASSIFIED

April 4, 2003, Selection 6

UNCLASSIFIED

2B of 11

Legend: Red (●) / Yellow (○) / Green (hatched)

Proposed Interrogation Techniques [2] (see attached description/limitations)	Policy: Consistency with Historical U.S. Forces Interrogation Role	Policy: Consistency with Prior U.S. Public Statements	Policy: Consistency with Major Partner Nation Views	Policy: Effect on Captured U.S. Forces	Policy: Potential Adverse Effect for Participants/ Supervisors/COC	Policy: Potential Effect on Detainee Prosecutions	Policy: Other	Recommendation: Re Unlawful Combatants
13. Repetition Approach	Green	Green	Green	Green	Green	Green	Yellow	Green
14. File and Dossier	Green	Green	Green	Green	Green	Green	Yellow	Green
15. Mutt and Jeff	Green	Green	Yellow [6]	Green	Green	Green	Yellow	Green
16. Rapid Fire	Green	Green	Green	Green	Green	Green	Yellow	Green
17. Silence	Green	Green	Green	Green	Green	Green	Yellow	Green
18. Change of Scenery Up	Green	Green	Green	Green	Green	Green	Yellow	Green
19. Change of Scenery Down	Green	Green	Green	Green	Green	Green	Yellow	Green
20. Hooding	Green	Green	Green	Green	Green	Green	Yellow	Green
21. Mild Physical Contact	Green	Green	Green	Green [7]	Green	Green	Yellow	Green
22. Dietary Manipulation	Green	Green	Green	Green	Green	Green	Yellow	Green
23. Environmental Manipulation	Green	Green	Green [8]	Green	Green	Green	Yellow	Green
24. Sleep Adjustment	Green	Green	Green	Green	Green	Green [9]	Yellow	Green
25. False Flag	Green	Green	Green	Green	Green	Green	Yellow	Green

Note: Green denotes no significant constraint on use raised by the respective area of consideration listed at top of each column, assuming adequate procedural safeguards.
Yellow indicates area of consideration does not preclude use but there are problematic aspects that cannot be eliminated by procedural safeguards (see footnote).
Red indicates major issue in area of consideration that cannot be eliminated.

UNCLASSIFIED

April 4, 2003, Selection 7

UNCLASSIFIED

3A of 11

Legend: Red (●) / Yellow (○) / Green (○)

Proposed Interrogation Techniques [2] (see attached description/limitations)	Utility: Contribution to Intelligence Collection (Useful)	Law IAW U.S. Interpretation: Torture Convention [Torture]	Law IAW U.S. Interpretation: Torture Convention [Cruel, Inhuman Degrading]	Law IAW U.S. Interpretation: U.S. Domestic Law
26. Threaten to transfer to a 3rd country	Medium	Green	Green	Green
27. Isolation	High	Green [11]	Green [12]	Green [13]
28. Use of Prolonged interrogations	High [17]	Green	Green	Green
29. Forced Grooming	High	Green	Green [19]	Yellow [20]
30. Prolonged Standing	High	Green	Green	Green
31. Sleep Deprivation	High	Green	Green	Green
32. Physical Training	High	Green	Green	Green
33. Face or Stomach Slap	High	Green	Green	Green
34. Removal of Clothing	High	Green	Yellow [34]	Yellow [35]
35. Increasing Anxiety by Use of Aversions	High	Green	Yellow [38]	Yellow [39]

Note: Green denotes no significant constraint on use raised by the respective area of consideration listed at top of each column, assuming adequate procedural safeguards.
Yellow indicates area of consideration does not preclude use but there are problematic aspects that cannot be eliminated by procedural safeguards (see footnote).
Red indicates major issue in area of consideration that cannot be eliminated.

UNCLASSIFIED

April 4, 2003, Selection 8

- ● Red
- ○ Yellow
- ◍ Green

Proposed Interrogation Techniques [2] (see attached description/limitations)	Policy: Consistency with Historical U.S. Forces Interrogation Role	Consistency with Prior U.S. Public Statements	Consistency with Major Partner Nation Views	Effect on Captured U.S. Forces	Potential Adverse Effect for Participants/ Supervisors/COC	Potential Effect on Detainee Prosecutions	Other	Recommendation: Re Unlawful Combatants
26. Threaten to transfer to a 3rd country	Green	Green	Green	Green	Green	Green [10]	Yellow	Green
27. Isolation	Green [14]	Green	Yellow [15]	Green	Green	Green [16]	Yellow	Green E (Cbt.C)
28. Use of Prolonged Interrogations	Green	Green	Green	Green	Green	Yellow [18]	Yellow	Green E (GO/FO)
29. Forced Grooming	Yellow [21]	Green	Yellow [22]	Green	Green	Yellow	Yellow	Green E (GO/FO)
30. Prolonged Standing	Green	Green	Green	Green	Green	Green [23]	Yellow	Green E (GO/FO)
31. Sleep Deprivation	Green	Green	Yellow [24]	Yellow	Yellow	Yellow [25]	Yellow [26]	Green E (Cbt.C)
32. Physical Training	Green	Green	Green	Green	Green	Yellow [27]	Yellow	Green E (GO/FO)
33. Face or Stomach Slap	Yellow [28]	Green	Green [29]	Yellow [30]	Yellow [31]	Yellow [32]	Yellow [33]	Green E (GO/FO)
34. Removal of Clothing	Green	Green	Yellow	Green [36]	Green	Yellow	Yellow [37]	Yellow E (Cbt.C)
35. Increasing Anxiety by Use of Aversions	Green	Green	Yellow	Green [40]	Green	Yellow [41]	Yellow	Yellow E (Cbt.C)

Note: Green denotes no significant constraint on use raised by the respective area of consideration listed at top of each column, assuming adequate procedural safeguards.
Yellow indicates area of consideration does not preclude use but there are problematic aspects that cannot be eliminated by procedural safeguards (see footnote).
Red indicates major issue in area of consideration that cannot be eliminated.

UNCLASSIFIED

April 4, 2003, Selection 9

Description of Interrogation Techniques

1. **Direct**: Asking straightforward questions.
2. **Incentive/Removal of Incentive**: Providing a reward or removing a privilege, above and beyond those that are required by the Geneva Convention, from detainees.
3. **Emotional Love**: Playing on the love a detainee has for an individual or group.
4. **Emotional Hate**: Playing on the hatred a detainee has for an individual or group.
5. **Fear Up Harsh**: Significantly increasing the fear level in a detainee.
6. **Fear Up Mild**: Moderately increasing the fear level in a detainee.
7. **Reduced Fear**: Reducing the fear level in a detainee.
8. **Pride and Ego Up**: Boosting the ego of a detainee.
9. **Pride and Ego Down**: Attacking or insulting the ego of a detainee, not beyond the limits that would apply to a POW.
10. **Futility**: Invoking the feeling of futility of a detainee.
11. **We Know All**: Convincing the detainee that the interrogator knows the answer to questions he asks the detainee.
12. **Establish Your Identity**: Convincing the detainee that the interrogator has mistaken the detainee for someone else.
13. **Repetition Approach**: Continuously repeating the same question to the detainee within interrogation periods of normal duration.
14. **File and Dossier**: Convincing detainee that the interrogator has a damning and inaccurate file, which must be fixed.
15. **Mutt and Jeff**: A team consisting of a friendly and harsh interrogator. The harsh interrogator might employ the Pride and Ego Down technique.

UNCLASSIFIED

April 4, 2003, Selection 10

UNCLASSIFIED

Description of Interrogation Techniques (cont'd)

16. **Rapid Fire**: Questioning in rapid succession without allowing detainee to answer.

17. **Silence**: Staring at the detainee to encourage discomfort.

18. **Change of Scenery Up**: Removing the detainee from the standard interrogation setting (generally to a location more pleasant, but no worse).

19. **Change of Scenery Down**: Removing the detainee from the standard interrogation setting and placing him in a setting that may be less comfortable; would not constitute a substantial change in environmental quality.

20. **Hooding**: This technique is questioning the detainee with a blindfold in place. For interrogation purposes, the blindfold is not on other than during interrogation.

21. **Mild Physical Contact:** Lightly touching a detainee or lightly poking the detainee in a completely non-injurious manner. This also includes softly grabbing of shoulders to get the detainee's attention or to comfort the detainee.

22. **Dietary Manipulation:** Changing the diet of a detainee; no intended deprivation of food or water; no adverse medical or cultural effect and without intent to deprive subject of food or water, e.g., hot rations to MREs.

23. **Environmental Manipulation**: Altering the environment to create moderate discomfort (e.g., adjusting temperature or introducing an unpleasant smell). Conditions would not be such that they would injure the detainee. Detainee would be accompanied by interrogator at all times.

24. **Sleep Adjustment:** Adjusting the sleeping times of the detainee (e.g., reversing sleep cycles from night to day.) This technique is NOT sleep deprivation.

25. **False Flag**: Convincing the detainee that individuals from a country other than the United States are interrogating him.

26. **Threat of Transfer**: Threatening to transfer the subject to a 3rd country that subject is likely to fear would subject him to torture or death. (The threat would not be acted upon, nor would the threat include any information beyond the naming of the receiving country.)

UNCLASSIFIED

April 4, 2003, Selection 11

UNCLASSIFIED

Description of Interrogation Techniques (cont'd)

27. **Isolation**: Isolating the detainee from other detainees while still complying with basic standards of treatment.

28. **Use of Prolonged Interrogations**: The continued use of a series of approaches that extend over a long period of time (e.g., 20 hours per day per interrogation).

29. **Forced Grooming**: Forcing a detainee to shave hair or beard. (Force applied with intention to avoid injury. Would not use force that would cause serious injury.)

30. **Prolonged Standing:** Lengthy standing in a "normal" position (non-stress). This has been successful, but should never make the detainee exhausted to the point of weakness or collapse. Not enforced by physical restraints. Not to exceed four hours in a 24-hour period.

31. **Sleep Deprivation**: Keeping the detainee awake for an extended period of time. (Allowing individual to rest briefly and then awakening him, repeatedly.) Not to exceed 4 days in succession.

32. **Physical Training**: Requiring detainees to exercise (perform ordinary physical exercises actions) (e.g., running, jumping jacks); not to exceed 15 minutes in a two hour period; not more than two cycles per 24 hour period. Assists in generating compliance and fatiguing the detainees. No enforced compliance.

33. **Face slap/ Stomach slap**: A quick glancing slap to the fleshy part of the cheek or stomach. These techniques are used strictly as shock measures and do not cause pain or injury. They are only effective if used once or twice together. After the second time on a detainee, it will lose the shock effect. Limited to two slaps per application; no more than two applications per interrogation.

34. **Removal of Clothing**: Potential removal of all clothing; removal to be done by military police if not agreed to by the subject. Creating a feeling of helplessness and dependence. This technique must be monitored to ensure the environmental conditions are such that this technique does not injure the detainee.

35. **Increasing Anxiety by Use of Aversions**: Introducing factors that of themselves create anxiety but do not create terror or mental trauma (e.g., simple presence of dog without directly threatening action). This technique requires the commander to develop specific and detailed safeguards to insure detainee's safety.

UNCLASSIFIED

April 4, 2003, Selection 12

April 16, 2003
Counter-Resistance Techniques in the War on Terrorism
By Donald H. Rumsfeld

MEMORANDUM FOR THE COMMANDER, US SOUTHERN COMMAND

SUBJECT: Counter-Resistance Techniques in the War on Terrorism (S)

(U) ~~(S/NF)~~ I have considered the report of the Working Group that I directed be established on January 15, 2003.

(U) ~~(S/NF)~~ I approve the use of specified counter-resistance techniques, subject to the following:

(U) a. The techniques I authorize are those lettered A-X, set out at Tab A.

(U) b. These techniques must be used with all the safeguards described at Tab B.

(U) ~~(S)~~ c. Use of these techniques is limited to interrogations of unlawful combatants held at Guantanamo Bay, Cuba.

April 16, 2003, Selection 1

(U) ~~(S/NF)~~ If, in your view, you require additional interrogation techniques for a particular detainee, you should provide me, via the Chairman of the Joint Chiefs of Staff, a written request describing the proposed technique, recommended safeguards, and the rationale for applying it with an identified detainee.

April 16, 2003, Selection 2

TAB A

INTERROGATION TECHNIQUES

(U) ~~(S//NF)~~ The use of techniques A - X is subject to the general safeguards as provided below as well as specific implementation guidelines to be provided by the appropriate authority. Specific implementation guidance with respect to techniques A - Q is provided in Army Field Manual 34-52. Further implementation guidance with respect to techniques R - X will need to be developed by the appropriate authority.

(U) ~~(S//NF)~~ Of the techniques set forth below, the policy aspects of certain techniques should be considered to the extent those policy aspects reflect the views of other major U.S. partner nations. Where applicable, the description of the technique is annotated to include a summary of the policy issues that should be considered before application of the technique.

A. (U) ~~(S//NF)~~ Direct: Asking straightforward questions.

B. (U) ~~(S//NF)~~ Incentive/Removal of Incentive: Providing a reward or removing a privilege, above and beyond those that are required by the Geneva Convention, from detainees. [Caution: Other nations that believe that detainees are entitled to POW protections may consider that provision and retention of religious items (e.g., the Koran) are protected under international law (see, Geneva III, Article 34). Although the provisions of the Geneva Convention are not applicable to the interrogation of unlawful combatants. consideration should be given to these views prior to application of the technique.]

C. (u) ~~(S//NF)~~ Emotional Love: Playing on the love a detainee has for an individual or group.

D. (u) ~~(S//NF)~~ Emotional Hate: Playing on the hatred a detainee has for an individual or group.

E. (u) ~~(S//NF)~~ Fear Up Harsh: Significantly increasing the fear level in a detainee.

F. (u) ~~(S//NF)~~ Fear Up Mild: Moderately increasing the fear level in a detainee.

G. (u) ~~(S//NF)~~ Reduced Fear: Reducing the fear level in a detainee.

H. (u) ~~(S//NF)~~ Pride and Ego Up: Boosting the ego of a detainee.

I. (u) ~~(S//NF)~~ Pride and Ego Down: Attacking or insulting the ego of a detainee, not beyond the limits that would apply to a POW. [Caution: Article 17 of Geneva III provides, "Prisoners of war who refuse to answer may not be threatened, insulted, or exposed to any unpleasant or disadvantageous *treatment of any kind." Other nations that believe that detainees are entitled to* POW protections may consider this technique inconsistent with the provisions of Geneva. Although the provisions of Geneva are not applicable to the interrogation of unlawful combatants, consideration should be given to these views prior to application of the technique.]

J. (u) ~~(S//NF)~~ Futility: Invoking the feeling of futility of a detainee.

K. (u) ~~(S//NF)~~ We Know All: Convincing the detainee that the interrogator knows the answer to questions he asks the detainee.

L. (u) ~~(S//NF)~~ Establish Your Identity: Convincing the detainee that the interrogator has mistaken the detainee for someone else.

M. (u) ~~(S//NF)~~ Repetition Approach: Continuously repeating the same question to the detainee within interrogation periods of normal duration.

N. (u) ~~(S//NF)~~ File and Dossier: Convincing detainee that the interrogator has a damning and inaccurate file, which must be fixed.

O. (u) ~~(S//NF)~~ *Mutt and Jeff: A team consisting of a friendly and harsh* interrogator. The harsh interrogator might employ the Pride and Ego Down technique. [Caution: Other nations that believe that POW protections apply to detainees may view this technique as inconsistent with Geneva III, Article 13 which provides that POWs must be protected against acts of intimidation. Although the provisions of Geneva are not applicable to the interrogation of unlawful combatants, consideration should be given to these views prior to application of the technique.]

P. (u) ~~(S//NF)~~ Rapid Fire: Questioning in rapid succession without allowing detainee to answer.

Q. (u) ~~(S//NF)~~ Silence: Staring at the detainee to encourage discomfort.

R. (u) ~~(S//NF)~~ Change of Scenery Up: Removing the detainee from the standard interrogation setting (generally to a location more pleasant, but no worse).

S. (u) ~~(S//NF)~~ Change of Scenery Down: Removing the detainee from the standard interrogation setting and placing him in a setting that may be less comfortable;

interrogation setting and placing him in a setting that may be less comfortable, would not constitute a substantial change in environmental quality.

T. (u) ~~(S//NF)~~ Dietary Manipulation: Changing the diet of a detainee; no intended deprivation of food or water; no adverse medical or cultural effect and without intent to deprive subject of food or water, e.g., hot rations to MREs.

U. ~~(S//NF)~~ Environmental Manipulation: Altering the environment to create moderate discomfort (e.g., adjusting temperature or introducing an unpleasant smell). Conditions would not be such that they would injure the detainee. Detainee would be accompanied by interrogator at all times. [Caution: Based on court cases in other countries, some nations may view application of this technique in certain circumstances to be inhumane. Consideration of these views should be given prior to use of this technique.]

V. (u) ~~(S//NF)~~ Sleep Adjustment: Adjusting the sleeping times of the detainee (e.g., reversing sleep cycles from night to day.) This technique is NOT sleep deprivation.

W. (u) ~~(S//NF)~~ False Flag: Convincing the detainee that individuals from a country other than the United States are interrogating him.

X. (u) ~~(S//NF)~~ Isolation: Isolating the detainee from other detainees while still complying with basic standards of treatment. [Caution: The use of isolation as an interrogation technique requires detailed implementation instructions, including specific guidelines regarding the length of isolation, medical and psychological review, and approval for extensions of the length of isolation by the appropriate level in the chain of command. This technique is not known to have been generally used for interrogation purposes for longer than 30 days. Those nations that believe detainees are subject to POW protections may view use of this technique as inconsistent with the requirements of Geneva III, Article 13 which provides that POWs must be protected against acts of intimidation; Article 14 which provides that POWs are entitled to respect for their person; Article 34 which prohibits coercion and Article 126 which ensures access and basic standards of treatment. Although the provisions of Geneva are not applicable to the interrogation of unlawful combatants, consideration should be given to these views prior to application of the technique.]

April 16, 2003, Selection 3

TAB B
GENERAL SAFEGUARDS

(u) ~~(S//NF)~~ Application of these interrogation techniques is subject to the following general safeguards: (i) limited to use only at strategic interrogation facilities; (ii) there is a good basis to believe that the detainee possesses critical intelligence; (iii) the detainee is medically and operationally evaluated as suitable (considering all techniques to be used in combination); (iv) interrogators are specifically trained for the technique(s); (v) a specific interrogation plan (including reasonable safeguards, limits on duration, intervals between applications, termination criteria and the presence or availability of qualified medical personnel) has been developed; (vi) there is appropriate supervision; and, (vii) there is appropriate specified senior approval for use with any specific detainee (after considering the foregoing and receiving legal advice).

(U) The purpose of all interviews and interrogations is to get the most information from a detainee with the least intrusive method, always applied in a humane and lawful manner with sufficient oversight by trained investigators or interrogators. Operating instructions must be developed based on command policies to insure uniform, careful, and safe application of any interrogations of detainees.

(U) ~~(S//NF)~~ Interrogations must always be planned, deliberate actions that take into account numerous, often interlocking factors such as a detainee's current and past performance in both detention and interrogation, a detainee's emotional and physical strengths and weaknesses, an assessment of possible approaches that may work on a certain detainee in an effort to gain the trust of the detainee, strengths and weaknesses of interrogators, and augmentation by other personnel for a certain detainee based on other factors.

(U) ~~(S//NF)~~ Interrogation approaches are designed to manipulate the detainee's emotions and weaknesses to gain his willing cooperation. Interrogation operations are never conducted in a vacuum; they are conducted in close cooperation with the units detaining the individuals. The policies established by the detaining units that pertain to searching, silencing, and segregating also play a role in the interrogation of a detainee. Detainee interrogation involves developing a plan tailored to an individual and approved by senior interrogators. Strict adherence to policies/standard operating procedures governing the administration of interrogation techniques and oversight is essential.

(U) ~~(S//NF)~~ It is important that interrogators be provided reasonable latitude to vary techniques depending on the detainee's culture, strengths, weaknesses, environment, extent of training in resistance techniques as well as the urgency of obtaining information that the detainee is known to have.

(U) ~~(S//NF)~~ While techniques are considered individually within this analysis, it must be understood that in practice, techniques are usually used in combination; the cumulative effect of all techniques to be employed must be considered before any decisions are made regarding approval for particular situations. The title of a particular technique is not always fully descriptive of a particular technique. With respect to the employment of any techniques involving physical contact, stress or that could produce physical pain or harm, a detailed explanation of that technique must be provided to the decision authority prior to any decision.

April 16, 2003, Selection 4

August 14, 2003
RE: FW: Taskers ("Interrogation Wish List")
Author Unknown

> The gloves are coming off gentleman regarding these detainees, [redacted] b1
> [redacted] has
> made it clear that we want these individuals broken. Casualties
> are mounting
> and we need to start gathering info to help protect our fellow
> soldiers from
> any further attacks. I thank you for your hard work and your
> dedication.
> MI ALWAYS OUT FRONT!
>

August 14, 2003, Selection 1

IMAGE CREDITS

PART 1:
POLITICS, SOVEREIGNTY, AND SECRECY

Fig. 1.1
Photo: C-SPAN.

Fig. 1.2
Photo: General Records of the United States Government, National Archives.

Fig. 1.3
Image: *New York Times.*

Fig. 1.4
Image: US Department of the Treasury.

Fig. 1.5
Publicly held government document.

Fig. 1.6
Publicly held government document.

Fig 1.7
Photo: Shane T. McCoy, US Navy.

Fig 1.8
Drawing: Courtesy SteelCell of North America.

Fig 1.9
Drawing: Courtesy SteelCell of North America.

Fig. 1.10
Photo: C-SPAN.

Fig 1.11
Publicly held government document.

Fig 1.12
Publicly held government document.

PART 2:
AN ATLAS OF EXTRAORDINARY RENDITION

Fig. 2.1
Photo: Google, DigitalGlobe.

Fig. 2.2
Photo: Google, DigitalGlobe, Maoabc.com.

Fig. 2.3
Photo: Google, DigitalGlobe.

Fig. 2.4
Photo: Google, DigitalGlobe, Tele Atlas.

Fig. 2.5
Photo: Google, Cnes/Spot Image.

Fig. 2.6
Photo: Google, GeoEye, Basarsoft.

Page 111
Photo: Shane T. McCoy, US Navy.

Fig. 2.7–2.10
Drawings: Center for Human Rights and Global Justice, New York University School of Law.

Fig. 2.11
Photo: Google, DigitalGlobe.

Figs. 2.12–2.15
Drawings: Human Rights Watch, © Mohammed Shoroeiya

Fig. 2.16
Photo: Google, DigitalGlobe.

Fig. 2.17
Photo: Google, DigitalGlobe.

2.18–2.19
Photos: Google, Panoramio, © Jasmine Picôt-Chapman.

2.20
Photo: Google, Panoramio, © Pygor.

Figs. 2.21–2.25
Drawings: Center for Human Rights and Global Justice, New York University School of Law.

Fig. 2.26
Photo: The Center for Public Integrity, photographer unknown.

Fig. 2.27
Drawing: Associated Press.

Figs. 2.38–2.30
Photos: Associated Press.

Fig. 2.31
Photo: Photographer unknown.

APPENDICES

Figs. A.1–A.4
Image: US Senate.

Fig. A.5
Photo: Google, DigitalGlobe.

Fig. A.6
Drawing: *Palestine Youth* message board, shabab.ps, artist unknown.

Fig. A.7
Photo: Google, DigitalGlobe, Tele Atlas.

Fig. A.8
Photo: Google, GeoEye.

Fig. A.9
Photo: *The Public Record*, photographer unknown.
Fig. A.10
Photo: *Daily News Egypt*, photographer unknown.

Fig. A.11
Photo: Google, Panoramio, © khamis.

Fig. A.12
Photo: Google, DigitalGlobe, ORION-ME.

Fig. A.13
Photo: Yola Monakhov, Panos Pictures.

Fig. A.15
Photo: Google, DigitalGlobe, GeoEye.

Fig. A.16
Photo: Google, GeoEye.

Appendix C: The Memos
Images: Publicly held government documents.

BIBLIOGRAPHY

60 Minutes. "Hard Measures: Ex-CIA Head Defends Post-9/11 Tactics." April 29, 2012. http://www.cbsnews.com/news/hard-measures-ex-cia-head-defends-post-9-11-tactics/.

Ackerman, Spencer. "Senate Torture Report to Be Kept from Public for 12 Years after Obama Decision." *Guardian,* December 12, 2016. https://www.theguardian.com/us-news/2016/dec/12/obama-senate-cia-torture-report-september-11-classified.

Ackerman, Spencer, Dominic Rushe, and Julian Borger. "Senate Report on CIA Torture Claims Spy Agency Lied about 'Ineffective' Program." Guardian, December 9, 2014. https://www.theguardian.com/us-news/2014/dec/09/cia-torture-report-released.

ACLU. "Biography of Plaintiff Abou Elkassim Britel." https://www.aclu.org/other/biography-plaintiff-abou-elkassim-britel.

Agamben, Giorgio. *State of Exception.* Translated by Kevin Attell. Chicago: The University of Chicago Press, 2005.

———. *Homo Sacer: Sovereign Power and Bare Life.* Translated by Daniel Heller-Roazen. Stanford: Stanford University Press, 1998.

Amnesty International. *"Rendition" and Secret Detention: A Global System of Human Rights Violations.* New York: Amnesty International, 2006.

Arendt, Hannah. *The Human Condition.* Chicago: University of Chicago Press, 1958.

Associated Press. "Halliburton Gets Gitmo Contract." *Fox News,* June 21, 2005. http://www.foxnews.com/story/0,2933,159930,00.html.

Authorization for Use of Military Force Against Terrorists. Public Law 107-40—Sept. 18, 2001. http://www.gpo.gov/fdsys/pkg/PLAW-107publ40/pdf/PLAW-107publ40.pdf.

BBC News. "Bush Admits to CIA Secret Prisons." September 7, 2006. http://news.bbc.co.uk/2/hi/americas/5321606.stm.

Baird, George. *The Space of Appearance.* Cambridge, MA: MIT Press, 2003.

Benjamin, Mark. "Inside the CIA's Notorious 'Black Sites.'" *Salon,* December 15, 2007. http://www.salon.com/2007/12/15/bashmilah/.

Black, Crofton and Edmund Clark. *Negative Publicity: Artefacts of Extraordinary Rendition.* New York: Aperture Foundation, 2015.

Bush, George W. *Decision Points.* New York: Crown Publishers, 2010.

———. "Remarks in Greeley, Colorado." George W. Bush White House Archives, October 25, 2004. http://georgewbush-whitehouse.archives.gov/news/releases/2004/10/20041025-4.html.

Butler, Judith. *Precarious Life: The Powers of Mourning and Violence.* New York: Verso, 2006.

Cageprisoners. *Citizens No More 'War on Terror' Abuses in Bosnia and Herzegovina.* July 2007. https://www.therenditionproject.org.uk/documents/RDI/070701-CAGE-Citizens-No-More.pdf.

Carter, Claire C. *Covert Operations: Investigating the Known Unknowns.* Santa Fe, NM: Radius Books, 2014.

Center for Human Rights and Global Justice. *Surviving the Darkness: Testimony from U.S. "Black Sites."* New York: New York University School of Law, 2007.

Central Intelligence Agency. *Death Investigation—Gul RAHMAN.* Memorandum for James L. Pavitt, Deputy Director of Operations of the Central Intelligence Agency, from unknown author. January 28, 2003.

Cheney, Dick. *In My Time: A Personal and Political Memoir.* New York: Threshold Editions, 2011.

Cole, David. *The Torture Memos: Rationalizing the Unthinkable.* New York: The New Press, 2009.

Cole, Matthew, and Brian Ross. "EXCLUSIVE: CIA Secret 'Torture' Prison Found at Fancy Horseback Riding Academy." *ABC News,* November 18, 2009. http://abcnews.go.com/Blotter/cia-secret-prison-found/story?id=9115978.

Council on Foreign Relations. "Democratic Debate Transcript, New Hampshire." June 3, 2007, http://www.cfr.org/elections/democratic-debate-transcript-new-hampshire/p13520.

Crispin, Shawn W. "US and Thailand: Allies in Torture." *Asia Times,* January 25, 2008. http://atimes.com/atimes/Southeast_Asia/JA25Ae01.html.

Cryptome. "CIA Torture Pseudonyms Update." December 15, 2014. http://cryptome.org/2014/12/cia-torture-nyms.htm.

Day, Matthew. "CIA 'Ordered Cage to Hold Prisoners in Poland'." *The Telegraph.* June 20, 2012. http://www.telegraph.co.uk/news/worldnews/europe/poland/9344520/CIA-ordered-cage-to-hold-prisoners-in-Poland.html.

Deleuze, Gilles, and Félix Guattari. *A Thousand Plateaus: Capitalism and Schizophrenia.* Minneapolis: University of Minnesota Press, 1987.

Deutsche Welle. "Questions Arise Over US Base in Kosovo." December 10, 2005. http://www.dw.de/dw/article/0,,1810615,00.html

Dunlap, Charles J. "Lawfare: A Decisive Element of 21st-Century Conflicts?" *Joint Force Quarterly* 54, no. 3 (2009): 34–39.

Dyer, Candice. "Made in Georgia: Prefab Jail Cells." *Atlanta Journal Constitution,* August 16, 2009.

Easterling, Keller. *Enduring Innocence: Global Architecture and Its Political Masquerades.* Cambridge, MA: MIT Press, 2005.

______. "The Zone." In *Visionary Power: Producing the Contemporary City.* Edited by Christine de Baan, Joachim Declerck, and Veronique Patteeuw, 75–86. Rotterdam: NAi Publishers, 2007.

______. "Zone: The Spatial Softwares of Extrastatecraft." *Places,* June 2012. https://placesjournal.org/article/zone-the-spatial-softwares-of-extrastatecraft/.

Edelson, Chris. "Exploring the Limits of Presidential Power." American Constitution Society Blog. December 2, 2013. https://www.acslaw.org/acsblog/exploring-the-limits-of-presidential-power.

Elden, Stuart. *Terror and Territory: The Spatial Extent of Sovereignty.* Minneapolis: University of Minnesota Press, 2009.

Elliott, Michael. "Welcome to Camp X-Ray." *Time,* January 20, 2002. http://www.time.com/time/magazine/article/0,9171,195299,00.html.

Executive Order 13491. Ensuring Lawful Interrogations. January 22, 2011. https://www.archives.gov/federal-register/executive-orders/2009-obama.html.

Feinstein, Dianne. "Feinstein, Bond Announce Intelligence Committee Review of CIA Detention and Interrogation Program." US Senate, March 5, 2009. http://www.feinstein.senate.gov/public/index.cfm/press-releases?ID=d882ff87-5056-8059-763f-e15d555d5f89.

______. "Senate Intelligence Committee Chairman Dianne Feinstein Remarks on Committee Report on CIA Detention, Interrogation Program." US Senate, December 9, 2014. http://www.feinstein.senate.gov/public/index.cfm/files/serve/?File_id=c0710e63-f518-40f5-a90d-7e788c9c91a3.

______. "Statement on Intel Committee's CIA Detention, Interrogation Report." US Senate, March 11, 2014. http://www.feinstein.senate.gov/public/index.cfm/press-releases?ID=db84e844-01bb-4eb6-b318-31486374a895.

Fisher, Max. "Photos from Guantanamo's force-feeding facilities." *Washington Post.* May 10, 2013. https://www.washingtonpost.com/news/worldviews/wp/2013/05/10/photos-from-guantanamos-force-feeding-facilities/?utm_term=.fe9671b06c46.

Foer, Franklin. "The Source of the Trouble." *New York Magazine,* June 7, 2004. http://nymag.com/nymetro/news/media/features/9226/.

Foucault, Michel. "Governmentality." In *The Essential Foucault.* Edited by Paul Rabinow and Nikolas Rose, 229–245. New York: New Press, 2003.

Frampton, Kenneth. *Labor, Work and Architecture: Critical Essays 1968-1982* (Cambridge, MA: MIT Press, 1985).

______. "Towards a Critical Regionalism: Six Points for an Architecture of Resistance," in *The Anti-Aesthetic: Essays on Postmodern Culture* ed. Hal Foster (New York: The New Press, 2002)

Friedersdorf, Conor. "Dick Cheney Defends the Torture of Innocents." *Atlantic,* December 15, 2014. http://www.theatlantic.com/politics/archive/2014/12/dick-cheney-defends-the-torture-innocents/383741/.

Funk, McKenzie. "A Detainee's Story: The Man Who Has Been to America." *Mother Jones.* September/October 2006. http://www.motherjones.com/politics/2006/09/detainees-story-man-who-has-been-america/.

Galison, Peter. "Removing Knowledge." *Critical Inquiry* 31, no. 1 (Autumn 2004): 229–43.

German Foreign Policy. "Examined and Interrogated" June 20, 2008. http://www.german-foreign-policy.com/en/fulltext/56167.

Gilmore, Gerry J. "High-Value Detainees Moved to Gitmo; Bush Proposes Detainee Legislation." US Department of Defense, September 6, 2006. http://archive.defense.gov/news/newsarticle.aspx?id=721.

Globalsecurity.org. "Guantánamo Bay – Camp Delta." January 2012.

Goldman, Adam, and Matt Apuzzo. "Romania CIA Prison: Central Intelligence Agency Used Secret Makeshift Prison for its Most Valuable Detainees." *Associated Press,* December 18, 2011.

Goldman, Adam and Kathy Gannon. "Death Shed Light on CIA 'Salt Pit' Near Kabul." Associated Press. March 28, 2010. http://www.nbcnews.com/id/36071994/ns/us_news-security/t/death-shed-light-cia-salt-pit-near-kabul/#.Wc7p0NOGNE4.

Greenberg, Karen J. "When Gitmo Was (Relatively) Good." *Washington Post,* January 25, 2009. http://www.washingtonpost.com/wp-dyn/content/article/2009/01/23/AR2009012302313.html.

Greenberg, Karen J., and Joshua L. Dratel, eds. *The Torture Papers: The Road to Abu Ghraib.* Cambridge, UK: Cambridge University Press, 2005.

Grey, Stephen. *Ghost Plane: The True Story of the CIA Torture Program.* New York: St. Martin's Press, 2006.

Harris, Shane, and Tim Mak. "What the Torture Report Kept Hidden." *Daily Beast,* December 10, 2014. http://www.thedailybeast.com/articles/2014/12/10/what-the-torture-report-kept-hidden.html.

Hayden, Michael V. "A Conversation with Michael Hayden [Rush Transcript; Federal News Service]." Council on Foreign Relations, September 7, 2007. https://www.cfr.org/event/conversation-michael-v-hayden-0 .

Herridge, Catherine. "Inside Guantánamo Bay, a Study in Contrasts." *Fox News,* January 31, 2009. http://www.foxnews.com/story/2009/01/31/inside-guantanamo-bay-study-in-contrasts.html.

Hersh, Seymour M. "The Killing of Osama bin Laden." *London Review of Books* 37, no. 10 (May 21, 2015): 3–10. http://www.lrb.co.uk/v37/n10/seymour-m-hersh/the-killing-of-osama-bin-laden.

Horton, Scott. "The Guantánamo 'Suicides': A Camp Delta Sergeant Blows the Whistle." *Harper's Magazine,* March 2010. http://harpers.org/archive/2010/03/the-guantanamo-suicides/.

———. "Inside the CIA's Black Site in Bucharest." *Harper's.* Dec. 8, 2011

Human Rights First. "Guantánamo by the Numbers." October 21, 2016. http://www.humanrightsfirst.org/sites/default/files/gtmo-by-the-numbers.pdf.

Human Rights Watch. "Delivered Into Enemy Hands: US-Led Abuse and Rendition of Opponents to Gaddafi's Libya." Sept. 5, 2012. https://www.hrw.org/report/2012/09/05/delivered-enemy-hands/us-led-abuse-and-rendition-opponents-gaddafis-libya.

———. "Double Jeopardy: CIA Renditions to Jordan." April 7, 2008. https://www.hrw.org/report/2008/04/07/double-jeopardy/cia-renditions-jordan.

———. "Guantanamo: Detainee Accounts." October 26, 2004. https://www.hrw.org/legacy/backgrounder/usa/gitmo1004/gitmo1004.pdf.

———. Locked Up Alone: Detention Conditions and Mental Health at Guantánamo. New York: Human Rights Watch, 2008. https://www.hrw.org/report/2008/06/09/locked-alone/detentio

———. "US: Ex-Detainees Describe Unreported CIA Torture." October 3, 2016. https://www.hrw.org/news/2016/10/03/us-ex-detainees-describe-unreported-cia-torture.

———. "U.S. Operated Secret 'Dark Prison' in Kabul." December 19, 2005. http://www.hrw.org/news/2005/12/18/us-operated-secret-dark-prison-kabul.

International Committee of the Red Cross. *ICRC Report on the Treatment of Fourteen "High Value Detainees" in CIA Custody.* Washington, DC: ICRC, 2007.

Jackson, Robert. "Introduction: Sovereignty at the Millennium." In *Sovereignty at the Millennium,* edited by Robert Jackson, 1–8. Oxford: Blackwell Publishers, 1999.

Jacobs, Ben. "Donald Trump Renews Support for Waterboarding at Ohio Rally: 'I Like It a Lot.'" *Guardian,* June 28, 2016. https://www.theguardian.com/us-news/2016/jun/28/donald-trump-ohio-rally-isis-torture-tpp-rape.

Jaffer, Jameel, ed. *The Drone Memos: Targeted Killing, Secrecy, and the Law.* New York: New Press, 2016.

Johnston, David. "At a Secret Interrogation, Dispute Flared Over Tactics." *New York Times,* September 10, 2006. http://www.nytimes.com/2006/09/10/washington/10detain.html.

Johnston, David, and Mark Mazzetti. "A Window Into C.I.A.'s Embrace of Secret Jails." *New York Times,* August 12, 2009. http://www.nytimes.com/2009/08/13/world/13foggo.html.

"Joint Resolution to Authorize the Use of United States Armed Forces against Those Responsible for the Recent Attacks Launched against the United States." (PL 107-40, September 18, 2001).

Kalmo, Hent and Quentin Skinner, eds. *Sovereignty in Fragments: The Past, Present and Future of a Contested Concept.* Cambridge: Cambridge University Press, 2013.

Khalili, Laleh. *Time in the Shadows: Confinement in Counterinsurgencies.* Stanford: Stanford University Press, 2013.

Khan, Azmat. "John Rizzo: CIA's Enhanced Interrogation 'Necessary and Effective.'" *Frontline,* September 13, 2011. http://www.pbs.org/wgbh/frontline/article/john-rizzo-cias-enhanced-interrogation-necessary-and-effective/.

Khanna, Satyam. "Obama on Appointing Special Prosecutor to Investigate Bush's Crimes: 'We Need to Look Forward.'" *Think Progress,* January 11, 2009. http://thinkprogress.org/security/2009/01/11/34654/obama-special-prosecutor-torture/.

Krasner, Stephen D. *Problematic Sovereignty: Contested Rules and Political Possibilities.* New York: Columbia University Press, 2001.

Lefebvre, Henri. *The Production of Space.* Translated by Donald Nicholson-Smith. Malden: Blackwell Publishing, 1991.

Leopold, Jason. "Gitmo Spent $300,000 on Liquid Supplements While Denying a 'Mass Hunger Strike'." *Vice News.* August 18, 2014. https://news.vice.com/article/gitmo-spent-300000-on-liquid-supplements-while-denying-a-mass-hunger-strike.

Lewis, Paul. "The Documents That Disappeared: How a Furious CIA-Senate Row Erupted." *Guardian,* March 12, 2014. http://www.theguardian.com/world/2014/mar/12/cia-senate-row-documents-feinstein-brennan.

Lind, Maria, ed. *Abstraction.* Cambridge, MA: MIT Press, 2013.

______. "Introduction." In Lind, *Abstraction,* 10–20.

Losurdo, Domenico. *Liberalism: A Counter History.* New York: Verso, 2011.

Low, Lisa. *The Intimacies of Four Continents.* Durham: Duke University Press, 2015.

Martin, Reinhold. "Public and Common(s)," *Places Journal,* January 2013, https://doi.org/10.22269/130124.

Mayer, Jane. *The Dark Side: The Inside Story of How the War on Terror Turned into a War on American Ideals.* New York: Doubleday, 2008.

Mazzetti, Mark. "C.I.A. Destroyed Tapes of Interrogations." *New York Times,* December 6, 2007. http://www.nytimes.com/2007/12/06/washington/06cnd-intel.html.

______. "C.I.A. Report Found Value of Brutal Interrogation Was Inflated." *New York Times,* January 20, 2015. http://www.nytimes.com/2015/01/21/world/cia-report-found-value-of-brutal-interrogation-was-inflated.html.

Mertins, Detlef. *Mies.* London: Phaidon Press, 2014.

Metahaven. *Black Transparency: The Right to Know in the Age of Mass Surveillance.* Berlin: Sternberg Press, 2015.

Miami Herald. "'Platinum' Captives Held at Off-Limits Gitmo Camp." February 7, 2008. http://www.miamiherald.com/news/nation-world/world/americas/guantanamo/article1932471.html.

Mies van der Rohe, Ludwig. "Industrial Building." In *G: An Avant-Garde Journal of Art, Architecture, Design and Film 1923–1926,* edited by Detlef Mertins and Michael W. Jennings. Los Angeles: Getty, 2010.

Military Order of November 13, 2001, Detention, Treatment, and Trial of Certain Non-Citizens in the War Against Terrorism, 66 Fed. Reg. 57833 (November 16, 2001).

Morris, Errol. "The Certainty of Donald Rumsfeld (Part 2)." *New York Times,* March 26, 2014. https://opinionator.blogs.nytimes.com/2014/03/26/the-certainty-of-donald-rumsfeld-part-2/.

Moore, Rob. "SteelCell Caters to Nation's Detention Industry." *AccessNorthGa.com,* November 27, 2011.

Moynihan, Daniel Patrick. *Secrecy: The American Experience.* New Haven: Yale University Press, 1998.

New York Times. "2005: In a Word," December 25, 2005. http://www.nytimes.com/2005/12/25/weekinreview/2005-in-a-word.html.

______. "The Guantánamo Docket," November 2008. http://projects.nytimes.com/guantanamo.

______. "The Guantánamo Docket: High Value," November 2008. http://projects.nytimes.com/guantanamo/detainees/high-value.

______. "Quotation of the Day." August 19, 2006. http://query.nytimes.com/gst/fullpage.html?res=9905E7DE143FF93 AA25757C0A9609 C8B63&scp= 2&sq=The+Decider&st=nyt.

Nougayrede, Natalie. "NATO Base in Kosovo Home to 'Secret' American Prison." *Le Monde,* November 25, 2005. http://www.watchingamerica.com/lemonde000065.shtml.

Office of the Director of National Security. "Summary of the High Value Detainee Program." http://archive.defense.gov/pdf/thehighvaluedetaineeprogram2.pdf.

On the Media. "Seymour Hersh, NYC Nail Salons, and Ebola-Free Liberia." May 15, 2015. http://www.wnyc.org/story/on-the-media-2015-05-15.

Paglen, Trevor, and A. C. Thompson. *Torture Taxi: On the Trail of the CIA's Rendition Flights.* Hoboken: Melville House, 2006.

______. "Selected CIA Aircraft Routes, 2001–2006." In An *Atlas of Radical Cartography.* Edited by Lize Mogel and Alexis Bhagat. Los Angeles: Journal of Aesthetics and Protest Press, 2007.

Palan, Ronen. *The Offshore World: Sovereign Markets, Virtual Places, and Nomad Millionaires.* Ithaca, NY: Cornell University Press, 2003.

Perlez, Jane, Raymond Bonner, and Salman Masood. "An Ex-Detainee of the U.S. Describes a 6-Year Ordeal." *New York Times.* January 5, 2009. http://www.nytimes.com/2009/01/06/world/asia/06iqbal.html?mcubz=3.

Poitras, Laura. *Astro Noise: A Survival Guide for Living Under Total Surveillance.* New York: Whitney Museum of American Art, 2016.

Priest, Dana. "CIA Avoids Scrutiny of Detainee Treatment." *Washington Post,* March 3, 2005.

———. "CIA Holds Terror Suspects in Secret Prisons." *Washington Post,* November 2, 2005. http://www.washingtonpost.com/wp-dyn/content/article/2005/11/01/AR2005110101644.html.

———. "Wrongful Imprisonment: Anatomy of a CIA Mistake." *Washington Post,* December 4, 2005. http://www.washingtonpost.com/wp-dyn/content/article/2005/12/03/AR2005120301476.html.

Priest, Dana and Barton Gellman. "U.S. Decries Abuse but Defends Interrogations." *Washington Post,* December 26, 2002. http://www.washingtonpost.com/wp-dyn/content/article/2006/06/09/AR2006060901356.html.

———. "Former CIA Spy Boss Made an Unhesitating Call to Destroy Interrogation Tapes." *Washington Post,* April 24, 2012. https://www.washingtonpost.com/lifestyle/style/former-cia-spy-boss-made-an-unhesitating-call-to-destroy-interrogation-tapes/2012/04/24/gIQAkdTXfT_print.html.

Presidential Proclamation No. 2525, Alien Enemies—Japanese (December 07, 1941).

Presidential Proclamation No. 2526, Alien Enemies—German (December 07, 1941).

Presidential Proclamation No. 2527, Alien Enemies—Italians (December 07, 1941).

Presidential Proclamation No. 7463, 66 Fed. Reg. 48199 (Sept. 18, 2001).

Rabat, Tom Walker and Sarah Baxter. "Revealed: the terror prison US is helping build in Morocco," *The Times.* February 2, 2006.

Rancière, Jacques. *The Politics of Aesthetics: The Distribution of the Sensible.* London: Continuum, 2004.

Rizzo, John. *Company Man: Thirty Years of Controversy and Crisis in the CIA.* New York: Scribner, 2014.

Rodriguez, Jose A. *Hard Measures: How Aggressive CIA Actions After 9/11 Saved American Lives.* New York: Threshold Editions, 2012.

Rose, David. "Why Bagram is Guantanamo's Evil Twin and Britain's Dirty Secret." *Daily Mail,* December 9, 2009. http://www.dailymail.co.uk/home/moslive/article-1232665/Why-Bagram-Guantanamos-evil-twin-Britains-dirty-secret.html.

Rosenberg, Carol. "Parole Board Declares Never-Charged Abu Zubaydah a Forever Prisoner." *Miami Herald,* October 26, 2016. http://www.miamiherald.com/news/nation-world/world/americas/guantanamo/article110891862.html.

Ross, Sherwood. "Rendition and the 'Global War on Terrorism': 28 Nations Have Supported the US in the Detention and Torture of 'Suspects'." *Global Research,* April 1, 2010. https://www.globalresearch.ca/rendition-and-the-global-war-on-terrorism-28-nations-have-supported-the-us-in-the-detention-and-torture-of-suspects/18419.

Rumsfeld, Donald. *Known and Unknown: A Memoir.* New York: Sentinel, 2011.

———. *Pieces of Intelligence: The Existential Poetry of Donald H. Rumsfeld.* Edited by Hart Seely. New York: Free Press, 2003.

Sassen, Saskia. *Losing Control? Sovereignty in the Age of Globalization.* New York: Columbia University Press, 1996.

Schmitt, Carl. *Political Theology: Four Chapters on the Concept of Sovereignty.* Chicago: University of Chicago Press, 2005.

Schwartz, Alexandra. "Turning the Torture Report into a Book." *New Yorker,* December 19, 2014. http://www.newyorker.com/books/page-turner/melville-house-publishes-torture-report.

Spiegel Online. "'Everyone Knew What Was Going On in Bondsteel,'" December 5, 2005. http://www.spiegel.de/international/0,1518,388556,00.html.

Strauss, Michael J. *The Leasing of Guantánamo Bay.* Westport, CT: Praeger Security International, 2009.

Tenet, George. *At the Center of the Storm: My Years at the CIA.* New York: Harper Collins Publishers, 2007.

Thürer, Daniel. "The 'Failed State' and International Law." International Committee of the Red Cross, December 31, 1999. https://www.icrc.org/eng/resources/documents/article/other/57jq6u.htm.

Toobin, Jeffrey. "Camp Justice." *New Yorker,* April 14, 2008. http://www.newyorker.com/reporting/2008/04/14/080414fa_fact_toobin.

Torturing Democracy. "Read the Key Documents," accessed November 7, 2016. http://nsarchive.gwu.edu/torturingdemocracy/documents/.

United Nations Human Rights Council. A/HRC/13/42. JOINT STUDY ON GLOBAL PRACTICES IN RELATION TO SECRET DETENTION IN THE CONTEXT OF COUNTERING TERRORISM OF THE SPECIAL RAPPORTEUR ON THE PROMOTION AND PROTECTION OF HUMAN RIGHTS AND FUNDAMENTAL FREEDOMS WHILE COUNTERING TERRORISM. New York: United Nations. February 19, 2010.

United States. "Agreement Between the United States and Cuba for the Lease of Lands for Coaling and Naval stations; February 23, 1903." Avalon Project, Yale Law, October 30, 2011. http://avalon.law.yale.edu/20th_century/dip_cuba002.asp.

———. "Lease to the United States by the Government of Cuba of Certain Areas of Land and Water for Naval or Coaling Stations in Guantánamo and Bahia Honda; July 2, 1903." Avalon Project, Yale Law School, accessed October 30, 2011. http://avalon.law.yale.edu/20th_century/dip_cuba003.asp.

———. "Transcript of Platt Amendment (1903)." Our Documents. Washington: The National Archives and Records Administration. Accessed October, 30 2011. http://www.ourdocuments.gov/doc.php?flash=true&doc=55&page=transcript.

———. "Treaty Between the United States of America and Cuba; May 29, 1934." Avalon Project, Yale Law, October 30, 2011. http://avalon.law.yale.edu/20th_century/dip_cuba001.asp.

US Department of Defense. Contract N62470- 04-D-4017. February 2, 2004. HaliburtonWatch.org. http://www.halliburtonwatch.org/reports/concap04.pdf.

———. "DoD News Briefing—Secretary Rumsfeld and Gen. Myers." February 12, 2002. http://archive.defense.gov/transcripts/transcript.aspx?transcriptid=2636.

———. *Status of Taliban and Al Qaida.* Memorandum for Richard B. Myers, Chairman of the Joint Chiefs of Staff, from Donald R. Rumsfeld, Secretary of Defense. January 19, 2002.

———. *Working Group Report on Detainee Interrogations in the Global War on Terrorism: Assessment of Legal, Historical, Policy, and Operational Considerations.* April 4, 2003.

US Department of Justice. *Interrogation of al Qaeda Operative.* Memorandum for John Rizzo, Acting General Counsel of the Central Intelligence Agency, from Jay S. Bybee, Assistant Attorney General. August 1, 2002.

———. *Legality of the Use of Military Commissions to Try Terrorists.* Memorandum for the Counsel to the President, from Patrick F. Philbin, Deputy Assistant Attorney General. November 6, 2001.

———. *Re: Application of Treaties and Laws to al Qaeda and Taliban Detainees.* Memorandum for Alberto R. Gonzales, Counsel to the President and William J. Haynes II, General Counsel to the Department of Defense, from Jay S. Bybee, Assistant Attorney General. January 22, 2002.

———. *Re: Military Interrogation of Alien Unlawful Combatants Held Outside the United States.* Memorandum for William J. Haynes II, General Counsel of the Department of Defense, from John C. Yoo, Deputy Assistant Attorney General. March 14, 2003.

———. *Re: Potential Legal Constraints Applicable to Interrogations of Persons Captured by U.S. Armed Forces in Afghanistan.* Memorandum for William J. Haynes II, General Counsel of the Department of Defense, from Jay S. Bybee, Assistant Attorney General. February 26, 2002.

———. *RE: Possible Habeas Jurisdiction of Aliens Held in Guantánamo Bay, Cuba.* Memorandum for William J. Haynes II, General Counsel, Department of Defense, from Patrick F. Filbin, Deputy Assistant Attorney General and John C. Yoo, Deputy Assistant Attorney General. December 28, 2001.

———. *RE: Treaties and Laws Applicable to the Conflict in Afghanistan and to the Treatment of Persons Captured by U.S. Armed Forces in That Conflict.* Memorandum for Alberto R. Gonzales, Counsel to the President, from John C. Yoo, Deputy Assistant Attorney General. November 31, 2001.

US News & World Report. "Al Qaeda's Desert Inn." May 25, 2003.

US Senate. *Committee Study of the Central Intelligence Agency's Detention and Interrogation Program.* Senate Select Committee on Intelligence, December 9, 2014. http://purl.fdlp.gov/GPO/gpo53907.

———. *Committee Study of the Central Intelligence Agency's Detention and Interrogation Program, Additional Minority Views.* 2014. http://www.intelligence.senate.gov/sites/default/files/press/additional-minority.pdf.

———. *The Senate Intelligence Committee Report on Torture.* Brooklyn: Melville House, 2014.

US White House. "Address to a Joint Session of Congress and the American People." September 20, 2001. https://georgewbush-whitehouse.archives.gov/news/releases/2001/09/20010920-8.html.

———. *Decision Re: Application of the Geneva Convention on Prisoners of War to the Conflict with Al Qaeda and the Taliban.* Memorandum for President George W. Bush, from Alberto R. Gonzales, Counsel to the President. January 25, 2002.

———. *Humane Treatment of al Qaeda and Taliban Detainees.* Memorandum to Richard B. Cheney, Vice President et al. from President George W. Bush. February 7, 2002.

———. "President Discusses Creation of Military Commissions to Try Suspected Terrorists." September 6, 2006. https://georgewbush-whitehouse.archives.gov/news/releases/2006/09/20060906-3.html.

———. "Remarks by the President Upon Arrival." September 16, 2001. https://georgewbush-whitehouse.archives.gov/news/releases/2001/09/20010916-2.html.

Varnedoe, Kirk. "Why Abstract Art." In Lind, *Abstraction,* 48–64.

Vicens, AJ. "Here Are Some of the Worst Conservative Reactions to the CIA Torture Report." *Mother Jones,* December 9, 2014. http://www.motherjones.com/politics/2014/12/senate-torture-report-dick-cheney-conservative-responses.

Walker, Tom, and Sarah Baxter. "Revealed: The Terror Prison U.S. is Helping Build in Morocco." *Sunday Times,* February 12, 2006. http://www.informationclearinghouse.info/article11883.htm.

Wall Street Journal. "Ex-CIA Directors: Interrogations Saved Lives." December 10, 2014. http://www.wsj.com/articles/cia-interrogations-saved-lives-1418142644.

Weiner, Tim. *Legacy of Ashes: The History of the CIA.* New York: Anchor Books, 2008.

Welna, David. "New Gitmo Plan Would Relocate Some Detainees to U.S." *National Public Radio,* July 29, 2015. http://www.npr.org/sections/parallels/2015/07/29/427318480/new-gitmo-plan-would-relocate-some-detainees-to-u-s.

———. "Trump Has Vowed to Fill Guantánamo with 'Some Bad Dudes'—But Who?" *National Public Radio,* November 14, 2016. http://www.npr.org/sections/parallels/2016/11/14/502007304/trump-has-vowed-to-fill-Guantanamo-with-some-bad-dudes-but-who.

Whitlock, Craig. "Jordan's Spy Agency: Holding Cell for the CIA." *Washington Post,* December 1, 2007. http://www.washingtonpost.com/wp-dyn/content/article/2007/11/30/AR2007113002484.html?sid=ST2007120100473.

WikiLeaks. "GITMO FILES." September 14, 2011. http://wikileaks.org/gitmo/.

Worthington, Andy. "UN Secret Detention Report (Part One): The CIA's "High-Value Detainee" Program and Secret Prisons." June 15, 2010. http://www.andyworthington.co.uk/2010/06/15/un-secret-detention-report-part-one-the-cias-high-value-detainee-program-and-secret-prisons/.

Wyatt, Edward. "Publisher Names 9/11 Charities." *New York Times,* July 21, 2005. http://www.nytimes.com/2005/07/21/books/publisher-names-911-charities.html.

Yoo, John. *War by Other Means: An Insider's Account of the War on Terror.* New York: Atlantic Monthly Press, 2006.

ACKNOWLEDGEMENTS

Thank you to Mabel O. Wilson, for everything. Thank you to Felicity D. Scott, Mark Wasiuta, and Craig Buckley. To Michael Sorkin and Cecilia Fagel at Urban Research. And to Isaac Gertman for his extreme patience and design acumen. To Mark Wigley and David Hinkle at Columbia University GSAPP. And to my colleagues in the Critical, Curatorial, and Conceptual Practices in Architecture program. Thank you to Jake Matatyaou and Jacob Moore for their insight, comments, and sharp edits. To Lindsey Wikstrom Lee for her enthusiasm and skill in developing the drawings of black site facilities. And to Stephen Hoban and Caitlin Blanchfield for their close reading and careful copy edits. To Meg Satterthwaite, Nikki Reisch, Sarah Robinson, and Sidra Mahfooz at the Center for Human Rights and Global Justice NYU School of Law. To Ruth Blakeley and the Rendition Project for giving me access to their prisoner rendition data. To Keller Easterling and Laura Kurgan. And to Glen Cummings, Eric Crowe, Andy Vann, Leigha Dennis, Brad Stell, Kevin Conway, and Ian Fuller. Thank you to Andrew Ross, Nikhil Pal Singh, Cristina Beltrán, Tom Sugrue, and Thuy Linh Tu at NYU. To Omar Khan, Jordan Geiger, Miriam Paeslack, Miguel Guitart, Hadas Steiner and my students at the University at Buffalo. Thank you to Mary Casper and *PLAT* who published, in a different form, "Technologies of Dislocation." To everyone at the MacDowell Colony, especially David Macy, Michelle Fornabai, Nikole Brouchard, Yengeniya Baras, and Gyan Shrosbree. And of course, thank you to Rita Carver, Mark Carver, Roger Fertig, and especially Jess Ngan.

TERREFORM

Terreform is a nonprofit 501(c)3, urban research and advocacy group founded in 2005 by Michael Sorkin. Its mission is to investigate the forms, policies, technologies, and practices that will yield equitable, sustainable and beautiful cities for our urbanizing planet.

Terreform works in close affiliation with Michael Sorkin Studio whose members donate their time and skills to its projects: Makoto Okazaki, Ying Liu,Jie Gu, Qiuyun Chen, Jose Vargas Hidalgo, Pablo Ibero, Zhen Quan, Joseph Sevene.

Sponsors

Terreform depends on and thanks generous donors of the past and present, and looks forward to a league of future supporters, a network of like-minded people and organizations.

ELYSIUM

Holcim Foundation for Sustainable Construction, George Sorkin, Michael Sorkin Studio, and an anonymous donor.

MEGALOPOLIS

Elise Jaffe+Jeffrey Brown, Frank and Berta Gehry, Graham Foundation for Advanced Studies in the Fine Arts, Institute for Transportation and Development Policy, Jean Louis Bourgeois, Southern California Institute of Architecture, Turenscape, The Venice Biennale–2010 American Pavilion.

METROPOLE

Furthermore–A Program of the J.M.Kaplan Fund, Safdie Architects, Rockwell Group, The City College of New York–Bernard and Anne Spitzer School of Architecture.

CITY

Elisabeth Block, Diller Scofidio + Renfro, Roberta Brandes Gratz, Richard Menaker, TEN Arquitectos.

UR BOOKS

UR 01

Gowntown: A 197-X Plan for Upper Manhattan
Terreform

UR 02

Waterproofing New York
Denise Hoffman Brandt and Catherine Seavitt Nordenson, Editors

Contributors: Lance Jay Brown; Nette Compton; Deborah Gans; Jeffrey Hou; Lydia Kallipoliti; Signe Nielsen; Kate Orff; Thaddeus Pawlowski; Sandra Richter; Janette Sadik-Khan; Hilary Sample; Judd Schechtman; Gullivar Shepard; Michael Sorkin; Byron Stigge; Erika Svendsen, Lindsay Campbell, Nancy F. Sonti and Gillian Baine; Georgeen Theodore

UR 03

2100: A Dystopian Utopia
The City After Climate Change
Vanessa Keith / StudioTEKA
Introduction by Saskia Sassen

UR 04

Adventures in Modernism:
Thinking with Marshall Berman
Jennifer Corby, Editor

Contributors: Jamie Aroosi; Marshall Berman; Todd Gitlin; Marta Gutman; Owen Hatherley; Esther Leslie; Andy Merrifield; Ali Mirsepassi; Joan Ockman; Kirsteen Paton; Robert Snyder

UR 05

Beyond the Square:
Urbanism and the Arab Uprisings
Deen Sharp and Claire Panetta, Editors

Contributors: Khaled Adham; Susana Galán; Azam Khatam; Ed McAllister; Julie Mehretu; Duygu Parmaksizoglu; Aseel Sawalha; Helga Tawil-Souri

UR 06

Mahometan & Celestial's
Encyclopaedic Guide to Modernity
Comprising a Manual of Useful Instruction
Essential to Attainment of the Urbane
by the Savage, the Barbarous, and the
Half-Civilized Alike
Steven Flusty with Pauline C. Yu

UR 07

Zoned Out!
Race, Displacement, and City Planning
in New York City
Editors: Tom Angotti and Sylvia Morse

Contributors: Tom Angotti; Philip DePaolo; Peter Marcuse; Sylvia Morse; Samuel Stein

UR 08

Letters to the Mayors of China: Kongjian Yu and the Future of the Chinese City
Terreform, Editor

Contributors: Ai Weiwei; Thomas J. Campanella; Zhongjie Lin; Xuefei Ren; Peter G. Rowe; Michael Sorkin; Daniel Sui; Julie Sze

UR 09

Occupy All Streets: Olympic Urbanism and Contested Futures in Rio de Janeiro
Bruno Carvalho, Mariana Cavalcanti and
Vyjayanthi Rao Venuturupalli, Editors

Contributors: Bruno Carvalho; Mariana Cavalcanti with Julia O'Donnell and Lilian Sampaio; Gabriel Duarte with Renata Bertol; Beatriz Jaguaribe with Scott Salmon; Guilherme Lassance; Bryan McCann; Theresa Williamson; Vyjayanthi Rao Venuturupalli

UR10

The Helsinki Effect
Public Alternatives to the Guggenheim Model of Culture-Driven Development
Terike Haapoja, Andrew Ross, and Michael Sorkin, Editors

Contributors: Miguel Robles Duran; Terike Haapoja; Juhani Pallasmaa; Andrew Ross; Michael Sorkin; Kaarin Taipale; Mabel Wilson; Sharon Zukin

UR11

Spaces of Disappearance
The Architecture of Extraordinary Rendition
Jordan H. Carver

UR12

Downward Spiral:
El Helicoide's Descent from Mall to Prison
Celeste Olalquiaga and Lisa Blackmore, Editors

Contributors: Pedro Alonso, Carola Barrios, Ángela Bonadies, Bonadies & Olavarría, Rodrigo Blanco Calderón, René Davids, Liliana De Simone, Luis Duno-Gottberg, Diego Larrique, Vicente Lecuna, Engel Leonardo, Albinson Linares, Sandra Pinardi, Iris Rosas, Alberto Sato, Elisa Silva, Federico Vegas, Jorge Villota. Designed by Álvaro Sotillo and Gabriella Fontanillas (VACA).

UR13:

New York City (Steady) State: Home Grown
Terreform

UR14

Gregory Ain and the Social Landscape:
From the Single-Family House to Cooperative Housing
Anthony Fontenot, Editor

Contributors: Anthony Denzer; Anthony Fontenot; Anali Gharakhani; Nicholas Olsberg

Forthcoming Books

Open Gaza
Michael Sorkin, Vyjayanthi Rao, and Deen Sharp, Editors
Contributors: Salem Al Qudwa; Hadeel Assali; Tareq Baconi; M. Christine Boyer; Damiano Cerrone; Alberto Foyo; Nasser Golzari; Nassos Hadjipapas; Mahdi Sabbagh with Meghan McAllister; Denise Hoffman Brandt; Jon Houston; Rim Kalsoum; Romi Khosla; Craig Konyk; Omar Jabary Salamanca; Rafi Segal with Chris Mackey; Yara Sharif; Terreform; Omar Youssef

Why Yachay?
Cities, Knowledge, and Development
Terreform, Editor
Contributors: Tom Angotti; Nicholas Anastasopoulos; Xabier E.Barandiaran and David Vila-Viñas; Felipe Correa; Ana María Durán; María Cristina Gomezjurado Jaramillo; Mauricio Moreno; Jorge Ponce Arteta; Thomas Purcell, Maribel Cadenas Álvarez and Miquel Fernández-González; Miguel Robles-Duran; Michael Sorkin; Achva Benzinberg Stein; Japhy Wilson and Manuel Bayón

New York City (Steady) State: Waste Not
Terreform

The Nanjing Charter
Eric Owen Moss Architects

Between Catastrophe and Revolution:
Essays in Honor of Mike Davis
Daniel Bertrand Monk and Michael Sorkin, Editors
Contributors: Mauro Caraccioli; Bruno Carvalho; William Connolly; Mustafa Dikec; Anthony Fontenot; Jairus Victor Grove; David Harvey; Susanna Hecht; Andrew Herscher; Jonathan Lethem; China Miéville; Daniel Bertrand Monk; Jason Moore; Jacob Mundy; Ana Muñiz; Christian Parenti; Andrew Ross; Rebecca Solnit; Michael Sorkin; Rob Wallace; Mabel O. Wilson

50 Ways to Game a City
Loophole Planning in Contemporary Mumbai
Vyjayanthi Rao Venuturupalli with Vineet Diwadkar

02.05.2005
28.04.2005
08.05.2005
28.04.2005
30.04.2005
30.04.2005
30.04.2005
05.05.2005
01.05.2005
07.05.2005
01.05.2005
01.05.2005
28.04.2005
28.04.2005
30.04.2005
28.04.2005
30.04.2005
29.04.2005
30.04.2005
19.08.2005

12.05.2005
AUG 2005
28.04.2005
03.05.2005
29.04.2005
30.04.2005
01.05.2005

D

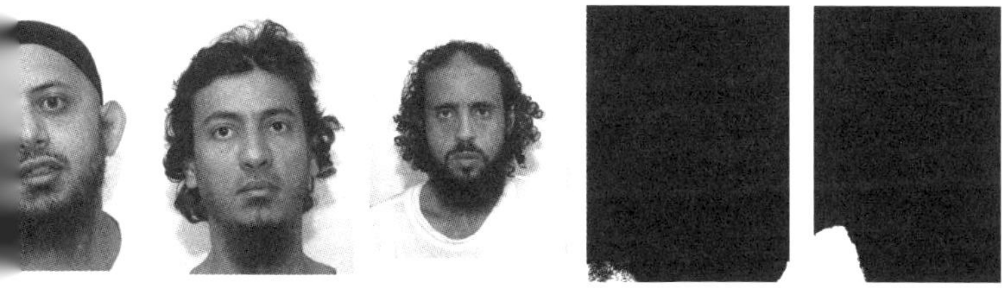

In 2011 Wikileaks released thousands of pages of documents concerning Guantánamo Bay prisoners including 765 Detainee Assessment Briefs (DABs). Over half of the briefs included individual prisoner photos, each one shown here.